Educating Students With Autism

Educating Students With Autism

A Quick Start Manual

Jo Webber
Brenda Scheuermann

pro·ed
An International Publisher

8700 Shoal Creek Boulevard
Austin, Texas 78757-6897
800/897-3202   Fax 800/397-7633
www.proedinc.com

© 2008 by PRO-ED, Inc.
8700 Shoal Creek Boulevard
Austin, Texas 78757-6897
800/897-3202   Fax 800/397-7633
www.proedinc.com

Library of Congress Cataloging-in-Publication Data

Webber, Jo.
    Educating students with autism: a quick start manual / Jo Webber,
Brenda Scheuermann.
       p. cm.
    Includes bibliographical references and index.
    ISBN-13: 978-1-4164-0255-8
    1. Autistic children—Education—Handbooks, manuals, etc.   2. Autism
in children—Handbooks, manuals, etc.   I. Scheuermann, Brenda.   II. Title.
    LC4717.W43   2007
    371.94—dc22

                                                               2007007569

Art Director: Jason Crosier
Designer: Vicki DePountis
This book is designed in FairfieldLH and Agenda.

Printed in the United States of America

6   7   8   9   10   11   12   13   14   15   27   26   25   24   23   22   21   20   19   18

Contents

Introduction   xi

Chapter 1. Introduction to Autism   1
What Is Autism?   1
Characteristics   3
    Communication and Language Deficits   3
    Cognitive Deficits   4
    Social Deficits   6
    Sensory Processing Deficits   7
    Stereotypic Behavior   7
Theories About Autism   9
Diagnosis   11
Autism Resources   11
Summary   12
References   16

Chapter 2. Applied Behavior Analysis   17
The A–B–C Model   17
    Antecedents   19
    Behaviors   21
    Consequences   22
Data Collection   31
    Data Collection Systems   32
    Graphing   36
Summary   39
References   41

Chapter 3. Instructional Strategies: Discrete Trial   43
Discrete Trial Teaching   43
    How to Conduct DTT   44
    Planning   64
    Things to Avoid   64
    Advantages and Disadvantages   64
Summary   69
References   69

Chapter 4. Instructional Strategies: Naturalistic/Milieu Teaching and Grouping   71
Naturalistic/Milieu Teaching   71
    Procedures   72
    Planning   78
    Advantages and Disadvantages   80
    Interaction of DTT and Naturalistic/Milieu Teaching   82
Grouping   83
    Sequential Group Instruction   86
    Concurrent Group Instruction   86
    Tandem Group Instruction   87

Summary   87
References   88

Chapter 5. Providing Structure in the Classroom   89

Structuring Through Procedures and Routines   90
    Teach a First–Then Procedure   93
    Teach Left–Right Orientation and Top–Down Orientation   93
    Teach Waiting   93
    Teach Finishing   94
    Refrain From Changing Routines and Procedures   94
Structuring Through Visual Schedules   94
    Whole-Class Schedules   94
    Individual Schedules   97
Structuring With Visual Supports   101
    Visual Support Through Physical Organization   102
    Visual Support Through Materials   103
    Visual Support Through Video and Computers   108
    Additional Visual Supports   108
    TEACCH   110
Summary   112
References   114

Chapter 6. Supervision of Teaching Adults   115

Roles and Responsibilities   115
    Paraprofessional   116
    Shadow   116
    Speech–Language Pathologist   116
    Occupational Therapist   117
    Physical Therapist   118
    Adaptive Physical Education Teacher   118
    School Nurse   118
    School Psychologist   119
    Behavior Specialist   119
    Job Coach   119
Creating an Educational Team   120
    Team Building   120
    Consistency   120
    Communication   121
Coordination, Consultation, and Problem Solving   122
    Coordination   122
    Consultation and Training   124
    Problem Solving   125
Summary   126
References   127

Chapter 7. Curriculum Development   129

Curricular Considerations   131
Curriculum Development Process   133
    Setting Long-Term Goals   133
    Developing an Individualized Curricular Inventory   133
    Refining the Curriculum   135

Determining What to Teach This Year   139
Choosing Academic Goals   139
Determining Current Functioning Level Within a Curriculum   140
Units of Instruction   140
Writing Goals and Objectives   142
Learning Levels   143
A Word About Generalization   144
Summary   145
References   145

Chapter 8. Collecting Progress Data   147

Progress Data Collection Techniques   147
Developing Recording Forms   152
When to Collect Progress Data   160
Notebook Files   163
Summary   163
Appendix: Progress Data Collection Forms   167
Event Recording With Prompt Notations for a Task Analysis,
With Graphing Option   168
Event Recording With Numbered Prompt Notations,
With Graphing Option   169
Duration Recording Form   170
Rate Data Form   171
Task Analytic Data Form With Prompt Levels and Graphing Option   172
Trial-by-Trial Data Sheet   173
Trial-by-Trial Data Sheet With Preprinted Codes   174
Data Collection Sheet for Use With Controlled Presentations   175
Naturalistic/Milieu Teaching Progress Data Form   176
Naturalistic/Milieu Progress Data Form With Preprinted Codes   177

Chapter 9. Teaching Language and Communication Skills   179

Language Characteristics   179
Components of Language   180
Verbal Operants   181
Assessing Language and Communication   182
Assessment of Basic Language and Learning Skills   183
Additional Assessment Strategies   184
Choosing the Best Form of Communication   185
Augmentative and Alternative Communication Systems   186
Choosing an AAC System   190
Teaching Strategies   191
Manding   192
Motor Imitation   193
Verbal Imitation   193
Receptive Language   193
Tacting   193
Intraverbals   194
Additional Teaching Strategies   194
Summary   195
References   196
Appendix: Assessment of Language Function and Form   199

Chapter 10. Socialization and Inclusion 201

Socialization Characteristics of Students With Autism 201

Socialization and Inclusion 201

Strategies for Teaching Socialization Skills 204

    Teacher-Mediated Interventions 205

    Peer-Mediated Interventions 209

Facilitating Generalization of Social Skills 211

Summary 212

References 212

Chapter 11. Functional Behavioral Assessment 215

How to Conduct a Functional Assessment 217

    Step 1. Gather Indirect Data About the Behavior and the Context(s) in Which It Occurs 217

    Step 2. Conduct Observations in Contexts Associated With the Challenging Behaviors 219

    Step 3. Analyze Data 226

    Step 4. Develop Hypotheses 229

    Step 5. Develop an Intervention Plan 232

    Step 6. Monitor the Interventions 234

Summary 234

References 236

Appendix: Functional Behavioral Assessment Forms 237

    Brief Functional Assessment Interview Form 238

    Functional Behavioral Assessment Inventory 239

    Functional Analysis Screening Tool (FAST) 243

    Antecedent–Behavior–Consequence (A–B–C) Report Form 246

    Structured A–B–C (Antecedent–Behavior–Consequence) Analysis Form 248

    Hypothesis Development Form 250

    Behavior Management Analysis Chart 251

Chapter 12. Reducing Challenging Behaviors 253

Positive Behavioral Supports 253

Behavior Intervention Plans 253

Antecedent Strategies for Preventing Challenging Behaviors 254

Consequence Strategies for Reducing Challenging Behaviors 258

    Differential Reinforcement 258

    Extinction 262

    Response Cost 262

    Time-Out 264

    Aversives 264

    Overcorrection 267

Other Interventions for Reducing Challenging Behaviors 268

Summary 268

References 270

Appendix: Behavior Intervention Plan 271

Chapter 13. Collecting Data for Monitoring Behaviors Targeted for Reduction 273

Forms for Event Recording 273

Forms for Duration Recording 275

Forms for Recording Multiple Behaviors or Monitoring Behaviors
in Multiple Students   276
Developing and Using Data Collection Forms   279
Summary   280
Appendix: Data Collection Forms for Behaviors Targeted for Reduction   289
Restricted Event Recording Form (With Calculations)   290
Restricted Event Recording Form (Without Calculations)   291
Multiple Restricted Event Recording Form   292
Unrestricted Event Recording Form (Rate of Occurrences)   293
Unrestricted Event Recording Form (Total Occurrences)   294
Self-Graphing Data Collection Chart for Unrestricted Event Recording   295
Form for Recording Multiple Unrestricted Event Behaviors
Over Multiple Activities   296
Duration Recording Form   297
Self-Graphing Data Collection Form for Duration Recording   298
Form for Recording Total Time Accumulated When Monitoring
Duration of Behavior   299
Form for Monitoring Multiple Target Behaviors   300
Form for Monitoring Multiple Target Behaviors (Self-Graphing)   301
Form for Simultaneously Monitoring One Restricted Event Behavior
for More Than One Student   302
Form for Simultaneously Monitoring Different Target Behaviors
for Multiple Students   303

Chapter 14. Interventions for Specific Challenging Behaviors   305
Noncompliance   306
Aggression   307
Stereotypic Behaviors   308
Self-Injurious Behavior   311
Summary   311
References   313

Chapter 15. Understanding and Working With Families   315
Challenges for Families of Children With Autism   315
The Struggle to Figure Out What Is Wrong   315
Learning to Live With Autism   316
A Child With Autism May Affect All Aspects of Family Life   318
Essential Practices in Effective Home–School Collaboration   318
Know Yourself   321
Know Your Families   321
Maintain Regular and Frequent Communication   322
Types of Support Needed by Families   327
Summary   328
References   328

Chapter 16. Epilogue   331
References   338

Appendix A: Resources Pertaining to Autism   343

Appendix B: Handouts for Professional Team Training   347

Appendix C: Commercially Available Curricula   379

Appendix D: A Typical School Day at Valdez Intermediate School
for Jamie and His Classmates   383

Glossary   389

Subject Index   401

About the Authors   415

Contents

x

Introduction

This is a book for teachers, administrators, related service personnel, parents, and other individuals who have the responsibility of teaching children and youth with autism. It is especially intended for educators and other individuals who need immediate guidance about how to plan, organize, implement, and monitor an educational program. Teaching students with autism is arguably one of the most difficult teaching assignments because such students typically are unmotivated to cooperate and learn, may be lacking skills in several developmental areas, and may be manifesting an array of challenging behaviors. To complicate matters, long-term outcomes for individuals with autism relate to the intensity and quality of the educational programs provided. Thus, school personnel find themselves under great pressure to provide the best possible instruction to these students.

Unfortunately, in the field of autism there is much debate concerning what constitutes the best educational strategies. We are convinced that those strategies based in applied behavior analysis (ABA) result most reliably in positive learning outcomes for most students with autism, particularly young children and individuals with low cognitive functioning. ABA encompasses many methodologies, as will be shown in this book, and relies on consistent assessment, persistent and frequent instruction, and data-based evaluation. We also recognize that other approaches not specifically based in ABA include techniques, such as visually cued instruction, that effectively meet the needs of students with autism, so we discussed them as well.

Rather than targeting all students with autism, we designed this book for adults who work with students who have autism and also have significant cognitive delays. We also developed the book with the public schools in mind. However, many of the strategies recommended in this book can be used in other educational situations and may be adapted for individuals with Asperger syndrome or high-functioning autism (HFA). Furthermore, we attempted to construct this book and write it in such a way that any adult with some type of teaching responsibility will be able to apply the major teaching approaches easily and successfully.

We drew upon empirical research and what are currently considered best practices for the education of students with autism. It appears that teachers of students with autism are more likely to be effective if they:

- understand the nature of the syndrome of autism, including characteristic deficits and excesses, and the relationship of these characteristics to educational programming;
- are able to use highly specialized instructional techniques to instruct a wide range of skills and knowledge;
- are able to assess challenging behavior, develop effective interventions to reduce such behavior, and teach new, functional replacement behaviors;
- are able to systematically and objectively monitor students' progress and use these data to make instructional decisions and adjust programs;
- are aware of which practices have a substantial evidence base concerning effectiveness for students with autism and, conversely, which interventions are unproven or controversial and thus should not be a part of a child's educational program;
- are able to effectively organize, supervise, and coordinate teams of individuals (multiple teachers, paraprofessionals, therapists, trainers) who provide services to students; and

- are able to be a partner to parents and others in order to augment the educational outcomes for all their students.

We understand that too often, teachers are unprepared or underprepared for the considerable challenges of effectively instructing one or more students with autism. There are many reasons for this, including poor preservice preparation. As a result, many teachers and other school personnel must quickly learn these specialized techniques "on the job." If that is the case, this book will help. Our intention was not to provide an in-depth study of autism or educational approaches to autism but, rather, to offer immediate, practical assistance to teachers and other professionals to enable them to plan for instruction, organize their classroom, manage behavior, coordinate the teaching team, and monitor progress. To that end, the book's text is succinct and is accompanied by many examples, forms, and sample materials.

We organized this book in a way that roughly corresponds with what teachers need to know to plan and implement instruction. In addition, we designed particular features to provide teachers with the tools they need to do so. Chapter 1 is a brief overview of autism, its characteristics, major theories explaining autism, and implications for educational programming. Chapter 2 describes fundamental concepts of ABA and offers examples of educational applications for students with autism. Chapter 3 explains discrete trial teaching (DTT), a well-documented teaching method rooted in ABA, and the teaching method of choice for instruction in most new skills. Chapter 4 extends preferred teaching strategies to naturalistic, or milieu, teaching, another strategy based in ABA that is primarily aimed at the maintenance and generalization of functional skills. This strategy is used in natural environments where specific skills are most needed. Discrete trial teaching and naturalistic/milieu teaching together form the basis of a very strong educational program. Chapter 4 also explains how to use group instruction to teach students with autism, an important consideration given the vast number of skills these students need to learn and the limited personnel and time resources of most classrooms. Because children and youth with autism do best when the environment is clear and predictable, Chapter 5 describes how to achieve clarity and predictability by providing structure in the form of procedures and routines, schedules, and visual supports.

Teaching students with autism requires the involvement of many adults with teaching responsibilities, whom we call *teaching adults,* and includes teachers, paraprofessionals, and related service personnel, among others. Furthermore, because program intensity and consistency is important for students with autism, coordination and collaboration among all teaching adults is necessary for success and may require a great deal of teacher time. Chapter 6 provides recommendations for collaborating, coordinating, and communicating with members of the teaching team and other adults who will have an impact on students' learning. Chapter 7 describes strategies for the all-important task of curriculum development (e.g., determining what skills each student needs to learn). This is a critical element of educational programming for children with autism, and one that too often is left to chance or approached in a haphazard, unsystematic way. Closely related to curriculum development is progress monitoring. Determining if a student has learned what was taught requires thoughtful planning and implementation. Chapter 8 presents an explanation of progress data collection strategies and a variety of forms for monitoring students' progress on target objectives. Reproducible forms are provided in the chapter appendix for your use.

Chapter 9 contains a comprehensive discussion of and recommendations for teaching language and communication skills, including language and communication characteristics of children with autism, essential components of language, how to choose a communication system, and instructional strategies for each element of language. Chapter 10 describes strategies for teaching social skills and improving students' social interactions. Because socialization is most effectively addressed using typically developing peers, we also discuss inclusion and how to address socialization goals in inclusion settings in this chapter.

In Chapter 11, we turn our attention to managing the challenging behaviors that are often characteristic of children and youth with autism. We describe how to use functional behavior assessment (FBA) to assess challenging behavior and to identify patterns associated with, and functions served by, those behaviors. We show how this information can be used to develop effective interventions for reducing challenging behaviors and increasing alternative appropriate, functional behaviors. Reproducible copies of the FBA forms we discuss in this chapter are provided in the chapter appendix.

In Chapter 12, we explain strategies for reducing challenging behaviors through antecedent interventions and consequence interventions. Consequence interventions include a hierarchy of behavior reduction strategies. Because challenging behaviors are often targeted on Individualized Education Programs (IEPs) or behavior intervention plans (BIPs), progress in reducing/eliminating these behaviors should be documented. In Chapter 13, we provide sample forms for monitoring behaviors targeted for reduction and explanations regarding how to use each form. Chapter 14 presents specific strategies for reducing the challenging behaviors associated with autism, including noncompliance, aggression, self-stimulatory behavior, and self-injurious behavior.

Chapter 15 provides information relevant to working with families. Families need to be partners with teachers in managing their child's education program. To facilitate this partnership, teachers need to have (a) some understanding of the demands of parenting a child with autism and (b) strategies for communicating and collaborating with family members. Recently, autism has received much attention in the media, without much quality control as to supporting evidence for various proposed programs. For this reason, teachers and other educators must be informed consumers: They need to be able to distinguish legitimate interventions and treatments from questionable ones and should be able to respond appropriately when they are asked to use a program or technique that is not supported by evidence. In Chapter 16 we present an overview of popular autism intervention programs. For each program, we provide an explanation of the program and its theoretical underpinnings, and summarize the research supporting and/or refuting the program.

The appendices present additional material to help teachers design and implement educational programs. Appendix A provides a list of resources for further information about autism and about teaching students with autism. Appendix B consists of handouts of information from each chapter that may be used to train other adults in how to use the techniques we recommend in this book. Appendix C is a list of commercially available curricula for teaching functional skills, including self-care skills, social skills, basic academic skills, and communication skills. Appendix D presents a description of a "typical day" at school for students with autism. Readers will recognize the strategies presented throughout the book as they are applied in the context of a busy classroom. Finally, we provide a glossary of terms used throughout the book for your reference.

Our book is designed to be immediately useful for teachers, that is, as a "quick-start" guide for assessing, teaching, and documenting progress. Special features of the book that readers will find helpful include the following:

- At-a-Glance: concise lists, brief descriptions, examples, or other material to illustrate concepts and skills described in the text

- Focus Here: in-depth coverage of concepts introduced in the text, including detailed instructions or guidelines for using various techniques presented in the text, explanations of concepts, and descriptions of programs or other material that provide readers with more specific information about the skills and concepts discussed

- Figures: many examples of the forms used for teaching students with autism, including the areas of assessment and progress monitoring
- Resources: lists of materials, programs, support services, organizations, and other information that teachers and other adults who are responsible for educational planning for students with autism will find helpful

This is a book that we wish had been available to us when we first taught students with autism. The book addresses many of the questions that we encounter in our work with teachers, administrators, and parents. Although it does not address everything that experienced teachers and other professionals will eventually want to know about autism and best educational practices, it will provide sufficient guidance for a teacher to use research-based strategies to begin developing effective educational programs for students with autism. Good luck, and enjoy this unique teaching experience!

Introduction to Autism

If you've been assigned to teach one or more students with autism and/or related disorders and wonder what to do next, this book is for you. These students, more so than most other special education students, will not progress academically without good teaching. A dedicated teacher is important, but dedication alone is not sufficient for success. You must have technical knowledge of various practices and the persistence to teach students who may struggle to learn even basic skills, who typically prefer to be left alone, and who often regress once skills are mastered. In many instances, you will face tantrums, aggression, and various bizarre behaviors, especially when you attempt to teach the student. Do not despair. In this book, we will provide ample information to help you be successful. You stand to gain not only instructional expertise but also the reward of witnessing hard-earned progress.

We will begin by discussing the characteristics of students with autism so that the practices we recommend make sense. We will also present a few theoretical explanations for this perplexing disorder. The theory that underlies most of our recommended treatments for autism is behavioral theory, or *applied behavior analysis* (ABA), which we will describe in Chapter 2. Subsequent chapters pertain to effective teaching strategies, pointers for structuring a classroom and supervising other professionals, and a process for curriculum development. Other chapters focus on progress monitoring, communication, and socialization. Finally, we will teach you how to manage difficult behaviors and establish teacher–parent partnerships. We feel certain you will find this book easy to understand and quite informative, a veritable "bible" for those new to the field of autism.

What Is Autism?

Interestingly, the first account of an individual with autism is thought to be that of a boy found wandering in the wilderness of France in 1799. It was believed that the boy had been raised by wolves, because he could not talk; seemed oblivious to heat, cold, and people; and spent hours rocking back and forth. Jean-Marc-Gaspard Itard, a physician, accepted the challenge of educating Victor, as the boy came to be known, by teaching him social, self-help, cognitive, and communication skills. Itard's (1801/1972) detailed account of Victor's education is both fascinating and informative. It was not until 140 years later, however, that this set of particular characteristics was presented as a syndrome called *autism*.

In 1943, Leo Kanner, a psychiatrist, wrote a case study of 11 children "whose condition differs so markedly and uniquely from anything reported so far, that each case merits ... a detailed consideration of its fascinating peculiarities" (Kanner, 1943/1985, p. 11). What Kanner then called *infantile autism* was marked by cognitive, communication, and affective deficits, with the overriding symptom being apparent withdrawal from the world. The term *autism,* derived from "auto," meaning self, described what Kanner observed as an absorption with alternate realities.

For many years, children who displayed the symptoms described by Kanner were thought to have a form of psychosis or schizophrenia. In 1980, however, the diagnostic system used by psychiatrists and psychologists, the third edition of the *Diagnostic and Statistical Manual of Mental Disorders* (*DSM–III;* American Psychiatric Association, 1980), broke with traditional thinking and included infantile autism under a category called *Pervasive Developmental Disorder* (PDD). The major characteristics of PDD included (a) absence of or odd social interactive behaviors, (b) verbal and nonverbal communication deficits, and (c) repetitive, often odd, behavior. At-a-Glance 1.1 lists disorders currently included as PDD in the revised fourth edition of the manual (American Psychiatric Association, 2000). Individuals with the most severe symptoms are diagnosed as having an *autistic disorder.*

Since 1980, much has been written about whether there is a difference between autism and other forms of PDD. Consequently, you will often hear people talk about *autism spectrum disorders* (ASD), or refer to a child as "autistic-like." This means that although symptoms across the disorders are similar, individuals will differ in the number of symptoms they exhibit, the severity of their symptoms, and, sometimes, age of onset. Some researchers believe that differentiating categories of PDD is problematic because of the great overlap of characteristics and the failure to designate a specific cause for each PDD subtype. Other researchers believe that we must try to identify subclassifications of PDD because of the wide variance of characteristics in individuals who have diagnoses that fall into this category.

For teachers, however, the specific type of PDD is not as important as the manifested characteristics. What matters most in terms of educational planning and implementation are the following:

1. the degree to which a child responds to his or her environment, especially people;
2. the intellectual level, typically measured as an intelligence quotient (IQ); and
3. the quality and quantity of communicative behaviors.

At-a-Glance 1.1 Autism Spectrum Disorders

A. **Asperger Syndrome (AS):** Average or above-average intelligence and well-developed language; show deficits in social interaction and some motor problems; typically show restricted patterns of interests and activities.
B. **Autistic Disorder:** Marked impairments in social interaction, verbal communication, and nonverbal communication and a lack of symbolic or imaginative play. Includes stereotypic behaviors.
C. **Childhood Disintegrative Disorder:** Social, motor, and/or communication skills decline after a few years of normal development.
D. **Pervasive Developmental Disorder–Not Otherwise Specified (PDD-NOS):** Shows milder forms of some of the symptoms for autistic disorder and may have a later age of onset.
E. **Rett's Disorder:** Show some symptoms of autistic disorder with physical and motor differences; diagnosed only in females.

Note. From the *Diagnostic and Statistical Manual of Mental Disorders* (4th ed., text rev.), 2000, Washington, DC: American Psychiatric Association.

Children with mild forms of PDD, referred to as *high-functioning autism* (HFA) or with *Asperger's syndrome* (AS), may have typical speech and IQs but display odd interpersonal interaction and other social skills. At the other end of the spectrum, children with more severe symptoms, often diagnosed as an autistic disorder, typically have mental retardation, often have no language at all, and seldom initiate social interactions. They are also said to have *low-functioning autism* (LFA). These two populations require teachers to make different curricular decisions and use several different instructional techniques. In this book, we focus on teaching students with LFA, which we will refer to as *autism*. For information on teaching students with mild forms of PDD, HFA, or Asperger syndrome, we refer the reader to *Asperger Syndrome: A Guide for Educators and Parents* (Myles & Simpson, 2003).

Characteristics

The characteristics of individuals with an autism spectrum disorder or PDD are unique and fascinating. In severe forms of the disorder, characteristics are exhibited in all of the following categories: communication and language deficits, cognitive disorders, social deficits, sensory processing deficits, and stereotyped behavior. Symptoms appear before the age of 3 years and are sometimes obvious as early as ages 12 to 18 months. It is currently thought that autism may affect as many as 1 in 150 children (Centers for Disease Control, 2006) and four to five times more boys than girls. In 2005, 193,637 students diagnosed with autism were served in special education, up from 22,664 in 1994.

Communication and Language Deficits

One of the most common characteristics of individuals with autism relates to language and communication. Many children with autism—an estimated 50%—never develop speech, remaining mute, and typically master only rudimentary forms of communication (e.g., crying, whining). On the other hand, children who do develop speech may display very odd communicative behaviors that render their language nonfunctional. The inability to effectively communicate may negatively affect cognitive and social development, and it often results in prolonged dependent relationships. Without language, people cannot ask for what they want, cannot protest situations they dislike, cannot participate in conversations or ask questions, and will not easily obtain knowledge through language avenues (i.e., talking, reading, and writing). Thus, one of the most important tasks for teachers of students with autism involves teaching communication and language skills.

The most problematic language characteristic for individuals with LFA is a *general lack of motivation to communicate*. They just do not seem interested in interacting with people. This means that teachers will have to work hard at devising ways to motivate their students to master communication skills that seemingly have no intrinsic value for them. Those with LFA who do communicate readily seem to be limited to rote responses to other persons' queries, requests for things they want, and refusal of or protests against things they do not want. They seldom choose to converse, declare, or explore ideas. Furthermore, students who do master speech may display perseveration and echolalia.

Perseveration means that the child repeats words or phrases over and over, almost in a hyperactive fashion. For example, a child may repeat, "Want a cookie, want a cookie, want a cookie, want a cookie, want a cookie," in response to a request to perform a task. *Echolalia* refers to the behavior of repeating, or echoing, words or phrases said by others, with no regard for the meaning. For example, a child may repeat a TV commercial for Kmart when he wants to go outside. When they first learn to talk, typically developing children usually demonstrate echo responses as a way to practice speech behaviors; children with autism, however, might continue excessive echoing behavior into adulthood. Interestingly, perseveration and echolalia are thought to have communicative intent, for example, as a way of expressing anxiety or desires. We *always* want to look for communicative intent in every behavior of a student with autism, even if the behavior at first appears bizarre or nonfunctional to us.

Individuals with autism who are verbal also tend to use restricted language with little variation in vocabulary or meanings. They are usually extremely literal in their language use, ascribing one meaning to one word. For example, *high* may be literally interpreted as "above people's heads." So, when the physical education teacher says, "Jump high," the student with autism climbs up on the bleachers and jumps up and down. While this type of example may seem humorous, the functional implications of such literal interpretation are devastating.

Individuals with autism are often described as robotic, perhaps because they tend to speak in a monotone or wooden voice with little inflection and display stilted, nonverbal communication. For example, a student may stand very straight, arms at side, no smile, and no eye contact and say in a flat tone, "Help me. John pulled my hair." The inappropriate *prosody* (use of cadence, rhythm, and pitch) and lack of motor behavior to supplement interaction causes the listener to miss much in terms of meaning. In fact, as listeners, we may miss the point entirely. Verbal students with autism will also tend to talk *at* the listener rather than *with* another, firing facts at you with no expectation of reciprocity.

Immature grammar also characterizes autism. There is a propensity to use only short sentences in noun–verb format and to overuse questions in place of declarations. Another peculiarity is a tendency to reverse pronouns. Instead of using the pronoun "I," individuals with autism will often use "you," for example, "You want a cookie?" to mean "I want a cookie." Although students with autism seem to understand language better than they can produce it, they may still have trouble understanding subtle meanings or words and phrases that they have not heard before. They may even have trouble understanding familiar vocabulary delivered in a different tone of voice. We will discuss language problems in more depth in Chapter 9.

Cognitive Deficits

One reason individuals with autism have such a difficult time with language acquisition may be due to the nature of their cognitive deficits. Language and cognition are so closely interrelated that we are not sure which one comes first. If cognition is impaired, language acquisition is adversely affected. If language is impaired, cognitive development is adversely affected, because language is the primary method for acquiring and transmitting knowledge.

Several cognitive characteristics typically define individuals with autism. One of these characteristics is what we call *here-and-now thinking*. Typically developing children ages 2 to 5 years see the world only from their own viewpoint and their own experiences. Logic escapes them. If they see five Santas on the street, there are five Santas. What they see is what they believe. They also tend to be very *literal thinkers*, failing to understand a variety of interpretations or perceptions. Most individuals with autism do not progress from this stage of cognitive development. They usually are not able to take another person's perspective or understand something from another person's point of view. This symptom is discussed in the literature as "theory of mind" or "mindblindness" (Baron-Cohen, 1995). Individuals with ASD typically think only in terms of what they have experienced, and they usually lack the ability to empathize or to "read" subtle social cues. For example, if you tell a student with autism that today is your birthday, rather than replying "Happy Birthday," the student will probably recite that her birthday is on August 22nd, at which time she will be 15 years old. This will probably be stated without much enthusiasm or any expectation of a subsequent conversation, and certainly with no interest about the fact that it is your birthday.

Another characteristic of individuals with autism that is present in typically developing young children is a propensity to focus on irrelevant stimuli in the environment. For example, a young child may call a cat a dog because they both have fur and walk on all fours, failing to notice the differences in tail, shape, size, and so forth. Individuals with autism also have this propensity to *overselect stimuli*: focusing on one aspect to the exclusion of others. For example, in trying to teach a student the color *red*, the teacher may present a green card and a red card, asking the student to point to the red card. Unbeknownst to the teacher, the corner of the red card is torn. Thus, the student may learn to point to the red card when given the cue to "point to red" not because of its redness but because of the torn corner. In this case, the student did not learn that color was the salient discriminator. Many researchers believe that individuals with autism learn everything (language, interaction skills, academic tasks) through a rote memory process (Grandin, 1995). This tendency to memorize responses based on overselected stimuli severely hampers learning, particularly in terms of discrimination and concept development.

Overreliance on rote memory also leads to *restricted or rigid thinking patterns*. Individuals with autism do not seem open to new and different events, ideas, or people. In fact, they often actively avoid new situations and become very upset at changes in their surroundings, routines, or activities. As young children, they often fail to explore their environment or appear curious about various toys, people, or items. Instead, they may sit for hours in one spot manipulating one toy, usually for self-stimulation purposes, failing to play appropriately or experiment with it. Imaginary and cooperative play is usually absent. Lack of curiosity and motivation to explore the environment in turn restricts opportunities to learn vocabulary and to interact with people.

This restricted, literal, and overfocused thinking also makes it difficult for students with autism to *generalize learning*. They do not seem able to easily associate events across time and settings. If they learn a task under one set of conditions, we cannot assume they can perform the task in different settings, later in the day, with different people, or with different requirements. Imagine how difficult it must be to have to memorize everything you learn with little ability to draw from prior learning or to make connections between similar experiences. How overwhelming and confusing life would be. No wonder children with autism just want to be left alone.

A final cognitive problem common to individuals with autism is *mental retardation*. Most children with LFA also have mental retardation, which is characterized by low intelligence as compared to that of other same-age individuals and by adaptive behavior deficits (deficits in self-help skills, social skills, and communication skills). The more severe the retardation, the more all other developmental areas will be delayed. Interestingly, some individuals with autism, although appearing mentally retarded, show *islands of precocity*, also known as *splinter skills*. An individual who cannot take care of his basic needs may at the same time be a gifted artist, a math whiz, or a talented musician, or have impressive calendar abilities, such as the ability to correctly match the day of the week to any date (e.g., knowing that March 18, 1850, was a Tuesday). Unfortunately, these types of abilities have caused adults to overestimate the general cognitive abilities of individuals with autism and to ascribe to myths claiming that the child is really a genius just waiting to be "freed." This unique *savant* characteristic may be the one that makes this disorder so fascinating. If an individual can memorize sets of cards, why can he or she not easily learn skills needed to live and work independently?

Social Deficits

According to Kanner (1943/1985), the most defining characteristic of autism is an aloof, affective quality. From early ages, these children seem to prefer interaction with objects rather than with people. Some parents have reported that their child with autism does not cuddle or anticipate being picked up. Others parents report a lack of eye contact or social smiling in response to parental interactions. On the other hand, there may be laughing or smiling for no apparent reason. Some caretakers have noted that their child screams when held and seems oblivious to their proximity. Others have stated that their infant is "the best kid ever" because she will sit for hours by herself, seldom demanding adult attention and never "getting into anything."

Not only do children with autism seem disinterested in others, they seem *unable to attend to social cues*. This symptom is manifested very early when, as toddlers, children with autism fail to engage in *joint attention* with adults. Joint attention is a shared social experience. For example, a typically developing child may see a bird and turn to his mother while pointing to the bird until the mother also looks and says something. Or a toddler may bring a toy over to the mother, hand it to her, and wait for a verbal response before taking it back to resume playing. Joint attention is a precursor to language acquisition and social development. In addition to lack of joint attention, children with autism also fail to attend to the facial expressions of other persons or to other nonverbal cues. Typically, a mother's facial expression is a sufficient cue for a child to cease an inappropriate activity. Children with autism, however, seem oblivious to what is happening with others unless they are specifically cued to attend.

Because of their lack of attention to the environment in general, particularly the social context, and their social language deficits, individuals with autism rarely attain *social competence*, which pertains to other persons' perceptions of one's social abilities. Socially competent individuals make friends easily, maintain important relationships, and know when and where to say things so other persons will not be offended. As a result, they are positively regarded by others. Socially competent individuals exhibit tact and manners. Almost all individuals diagnosed with a PDD display deficits in the skills needed for social competence, which is referred to as *social skills deficits*. Social skills are specific skills necessary for appropriate interactions, such as maintaining an appropriate body distance, using eye contact, initiating conversations, asking for help, accepting criticism, handling teasing, and using appropriate greetings. Remember, though, that students with autism will probably just memorize these skills under specific conditions; therefore, we cannot assume that mastery of a repertoire of social skills will lead to social competence. We will discuss ways to teach and facilitate social competence in detail in Chapter 10.

Interacting with parents and playing with other children are the primary methods for early language and social development, behaviors that unfortunately are not characteristic of children with autism. Because language, cognition, and social development are interrelated, researchers now think that the symptom of autistic aloneness may be a function of cognitive and communication deficits rather than an emotional condition. However, failure to interact with others in turn negatively affects communication and cognitive development. This presents a triple challenge for teachers. How do we impart knowledge to someone who doesn't talk and won't attend to us? How do we teach someone to talk who actively limits his or her life experiences and does not want to interact with others? How do we socialize someone who has to memorize everything, hates change, and can't talk?

Sensory Processing Deficits

One fascinating trait that characterizes autism has to do with how auditory, visual, and tactile stimuli are perceived. For example, children with autism may act as though they are deaf and/or blind. They may fail to respond to their name being called or may ignore the fact that someone has asked them a question. On the other hand, they may show extreme reactions to sudden loud noises or, even more puzzling, to innocuous noises, such as the sound of someone chewing. They may not appear to notice people or playground equipment in a park, instead focusing only on a small string on the ground. In addition, many individuals with autism appear to be *tactilely defensive*; that is, they do not like to be touched. Interestingly, it seems that soft touching is most repellent to them, while harder pats or deep pressure may be more appealing.

Individuals with autism may show distinct preferences for certain textures of clothing, food, or toys. For example, some children may prefer soft foods, such as puddings. Other children may prefer only cotton clothing with short sleeves. Many children will limit their diet to three or four foods or their wardrobes to only a few outfits that meet their criteria for texture. Many of these children will react negatively to fluorescent lighting (perhaps because of the hum); others will flick lights on and off as a form of visual self-stimulation. Many children with autism are attracted to furry toys, while others shun anything not smooth and cold. Parents have reported, for example, that some children with autism spend time pressing their cheeks to a cold tile floor as a preferred activity. Other children will display definite preferences for rooms of a certain size and particular furniture arrangements. This may relate to the reliance on rote memory that we described earlier. The good news is that individuals with autism make their preferences well known. It does not take long before most adults in the child's life are accommodating the child's idiosyncrasies to avoid excessive protesting behavior.

Stereotypic Behavior

Related to the concept that individuals with autism perceive the world in very different ways is a propensity to demonstrate *stereotypic* (habitual and repetitive) behaviors. Stereotypic behavior is typically a characteristic of an individual who has had a history of sensory deprivation, for example, someone who has long resided in nonstimulating institutions. Individuals with autism, however, characteristically exhibit this type of behavior despite rich, stimulating environments. They may display one or more of the following behaviors: rocking repetitively, flicking fingers and flapping hands, pacing, scratching, twirling self and objects, thrusting the arms, walking on the toes, hyperventilating, contorting the face, humming, clicking, and staring. Even without obvious sensory deprivation, these individuals seem to crave certain types of sensory input. We can only speculate as to whether this is because (a) they are not receiving enough environmental input (perhaps due to impaired receptive neurological capabilities), thus providing their own, or (b) they are receiving too much stimulation (perhaps due to impaired neurological screening functions) and engage in repetitive behaviors to escape it. We call behaviors that function as sensory input *self-stimulatory behaviors*. Almost all children with LFA—and many with HFA—engage in excessive self-stimulatory behavior.

Sometimes individuals with autism display repetitive behaviors that cause themselves injury, which are called *self-injurious behavior* (SIB). Examples of SIB include head banging, head hitting, eye picking, shoulder biting, severe tantrums, scratching and picking, or hand or arm biting. When an individual with autism engages in such behaviors, they do not seem to cause the person any pain. On the other hand, being hit or scratched by another person does seem to cause pain. Perhaps we could assume that SIB is a form of self-stimulation, but most researchers (e.g., Carr et al., 1994) now think that SIB more often is a way to communicate desires or a way to express frustration or fear.

Although individuals with autism are known to demonstrate aggressive behavior toward others, these behaviors, which usually are not stereotypical in nature, are also thought to be an attempt to communicate feelings and desires. Aggressive behaviors such as screaming, pulling hair, biting, destroying property, running away, hitting and kicking, pinching, banging head to head, tearing others' clothes, and spitting have been reported by parents and teachers. These behaviors most often occur when the individual with autism is being forced to do something he or she does not want to do, cannot do, or is afraid to do. They also may occur when the person is frustrated; frightened by too much noise, light, or verbal or tactile input; or has been introduced to a new situation. We will discuss ways to manage unwanted behavior, including stereotypic behavior, SIB, and aggression, in Chapters 11 through 14. At-a-Glance 1.2 summarizes the common characteristics of autism.

At-a-Glance 1.2 Common Characteristics of Autism

Speech and Language Difficulties

Deficits in language, including mutism, perseveration, and echolalia

Lack of communicative intent

Lack of communicative reciprocity (e.g., does not appear to be listening)

Idiosyncratic speech (e.g., favorite words or phrases that do not pertain to what was said)

Literal, rigid use of speech, usually with immature grammar

Lack of appropriate use of prosody (intonation) and nonverbal communication

Problems with language comprehension

Cognitive and Perceptual Impairments

Here-and-now thinking (literal, restricted, and rigid patterns)

Lack of curiosity and motivation to explore the environment

Tendency to overselect irrelevant environmental stimuli and not attend to important phenomena (e.g., social cues)

Lack of appropriate play, especially imaginary play

Obsessive desire for sameness and repetition

Good rote memory in some instances

Occasionally, extraordinary skills (memory, math, art)

Mental retardation often may be present

Social Interaction Deficits

Resistance to being touched, cuddled, or held

Lack of joint attention in infancy

Lack of response to name

May appear oblivious to parental presence

Inability to relate to other persons in an ordinary manner (e.g., tends to ignore or avoid people)

Isolation from the outside world (autistic aloneness)

Little or no eye contact or social smiling

Prefers objects to people and often treats people as objects (e.g., uses another person's hands to reach something up high)

No true friendships

Lack of social reciprocity or empathy (e.g., does not understand how other people feel or view the world)

Social skill and social competency deficits

Sensory Processing Deficits

Extreme fear reactions to loud noises, strangers, new situations, changes, surprises

Underresponsive to physical pain and interaction of other individuals

May appear as deaf and blind

Distinct food and clothing preferences often related to texture

Tactile defensiveness

Stereotypic Behaviors

Stereotypic (habitual and repetitive) movements, such as rocking or spinning objects

Stereotypic activities and interests (e.g., putting objects in a certain order)

Compulsive adherence to a few routines and/or activities (e.g., watching dishwashers, drawing trains)

Preoccupation with a few objects (e.g., favorite stim toys)

Self-injurious behaviors (SIB)

Tantrums and aggressive behaviors may be present

Theories About Autism

There are few disorders that are more perplexing than autism. What could possibly cause such a unique combination of problems that are so debilitating in nature? In 1801, Itard speculated that Victor had acquired his peculiar pattern of behavior because he had been abandoned by his parents and virtually raised in the wild. Without parents, Victor failed to learn language and social skills and resorted to acting like an animal. Assuming that Victor's problems were caused by a deprived environment, Itard reasoned that Victor could be habilitated through a stimulating environment that included intensive instruction. He set about to prove the powerful influence of environmental stimulation. Although after several years Victor acquired some speech and many social skills, he remained functionally retarded, unable to live without supervision. Itard concluded his case study by admitting that his experiment had failed because the effects of early environmental deprivation were not totally reversed. He actually apologized to the French government for his failure.

Itard ascribed the cause of Victor's problems to a failure to learn basic skills. Today, we call that a *behavioral explanation* for the phenomenon. If children fail to learn to walk, talk, and interact appropriately at a young age, the remedy is to teach them basic skills so they can catch up with their peers. This explanation assumes that people are, for the most part, what they learn as a function of life's experiences. *Behavioral theory* holds that changing life experiences can result in changes in individual responses. This is probably the basis for special education in general. Not unlike Itard, special educators believe that intensive skills instruction will offset faulty learning and prevent further problems. In fact, this is probably true for most special education students, including students with autism. However, as in Itard's experiment, no instructional interventions have been shown to "cure" autism. We might therefore assume that faulty learning alone cannot explain such a handicapping condition.

As a result of Kanner's work in 1943, several professionals (e.g., Bettleheim, 1967) ascribed the cause of autism to *psychogenic pathology*. For many years, children with autism were thought to be withdrawing from the world because of cold, unresponsive, punitive parents, particularly mothers. This assumption was based on relatively few case studies, beginning with Kanner's comments that "there were few really warmhearted fathers and mothers" (Kanner, 1985, p. 50) of the children in the autistic group. The mothers became known as "refrigerator mothers," and psychodynamic treatments, such as ego enhancement and play therapy, were prescribed. It took many years and much research before parents of children with autism were able to overcome the blame, guilt, and professional bullying associated with this widely accepted explanation. Fortunately, as more and more cases of autism were identified, the idea that parents could cause the syndrome was generally discarded.

One statement in Kanner's case study, overlooked for many years, is now the prevalent explanation of autism. Kanner (1985) wrote that the children he was describing seemed to come into the world biologically unable to form "affective contact" (p. 50). A *biological explanation* for the disorder, such as genetic predisposition or abnormal brain structure and chemistry, prevails today (Centers for Disease Control, 2005; National Research Council, 2001). Many studies continue to be conducted to (a) identify specific gene patterns unique to individuals with autism, (b) study parts of the brain, particularly the cerebellum and the cortex, that may be structurally different, and (c) pinpoint aberrant neurochemical (dopamine, seratonin, norepinephrine) activity. Although a definitive cause for autism has not been discovered (and there could be many), researchers in the field commonly accept that the brains of individuals with autism work differently than typical brains.

As researchers learn more about how the human brain functions, particularly in regard to social cognition, more precise explanations of autistic behavior may be forthcoming. Biological explanations imply medical interventions, such as psychopharmacology. Many students with autism may be taking prescribed medications to enhance attention, decrease anxiety and hyperactivity, and control seizure disorders, which are common among many adolescents with autism. However, because the exact neurobiological basis of autism is not known, medications that specifically target autism have not been developed. In fact, empirically based educational treatments are most often prescribed, not for the purpose of curing the disorder but rather to alleviate as many symptoms as possible. Thus, pending more definitive research findings, teachers continue to have the primary responsibility for treating this perplexing disorder.

Diagnosis

A diagnosis of autism or a related disorder is usually accomplished through the use of behavioral assessment measures by experienced assessment personnel. There are several such measures, which consist of a list of characteristics that are rated by parents or other adults who know the child. If children show a certain quantity or quality of the listed characteristics, they likely have autism, as opposed to other types of disorders, such as mental retardation or emotional disturbance without autism. A differential diagnosis can also be obtained by trained professionals using the *DSM–IV–TR*, which contains specific behavioral descriptions of all disorders in the autism spectrum. Some school personnel and many researchers use the *Autism Diagnostic Observation Schedule* (ADOS; Lord, Rutter, DiLavore, & Risi, 1999) and the *Autism Diagnostic Interview–Revised* (ADI-R; Lord, Rutter, & Le Couteur, 1994) to classify ASDs, although the lengthy administration time and training requirements may be a deterrent to their use. Usually children are first diagnosed around the age of 2 to 3 years, when language and social delays become apparent. However, some researchers have claimed to be able to diagnose probable autism in children as young as 18 months of age by using indicators such as absence of joint attention and not responding to name (Filipek et al., 1999).

Medical tests, such as blood tests, electroencephalography (EEG), and magnetic resonance imaging (MRI), are sometimes recommended, although no definitive medical test for autism exists (Wang, 1997). Biological tests are usually recommended to ascertain the existence of other disorders that might be treatable, such as metabolic disorders, allergies, thyroid dysfunctions, seizure disorders, sleep dysfunctions, and chromosomal disorders (e.g., microcephaly). Perhaps in the near future, the exact etiology of autism will become obvious, making it easier to diagnose and treat. Until that time, multiple forms of assessment information should be used, not only for the purpose of diagnosing the disorder but also to facilitate educational planning.

In any case, teachers should not be diagnosing autism, but they may be asked to participate in the process. Furthermore, teachers may be asked to help parents interpret diagnostic reports and discuss the implications of different diagnoses. We recommend that teachers become familiar with some of the more common assessment instruments (see Resources 1.1). Furthermore, it might be helpful to read through the diagnostic indicators of all PDDs as described in the *DSM–IV–TR*. Ask the educational diagnostician or the school psychologist to share a copy of this manual with you.

Autism Resources

One very important function for teachers of students with autism is to act as a resource for parents and family members, particularly individuals with a young child with autism or another PDD. Once a child is diagnosed with autism or a related disorder, the parents seek information, often quite desperately, about the disorder and the best treatments. We know that early intervention produces the best results for these children, particularly when language delays are involved. Parents (and teachers) therefore must find out as much as possible about the disorder as soon as possible. This book will not provide extensive information, just enough to get you started and help you to know where to look further. Resources 1.2 provides a list of organizations that might be helpful to parents and professionals. Appendix A contains lists of journals, periodicals, and books pertaining to autism. Teachers should share information in a responsible way—not by disseminating information about

Resources 1.1 Instruments for Diagnosis of Autism

Autism Diagnostic Interview–Revised (ADI)
  (Lord, C., Rutter, M., & Le Couteur, A., 1994) and the
Autism Diagnostic Observation Schedule (ADOS)
  (Lord, C., Rutter, M., DiLavore, P. C., & Risi, S., 1999)
  Western Psychological Services (WPS)
  12031 Wilshire Blvd.
  Los Angeles, CA 90025
  www.wpspublish.com

Autism Screening Instrument for Educational Planning, 3rd ed. (ASIEP-3)
  (Krug, D. A., Arick, J. R., & Almond, P. J., 2008)
  PRO-ED
  8700 Shoal Creek Blvd.
  Austin, TX 78757-6897
  www.proedinc.com

Childhood Autism Rating Scale (CARS)
  (Shopler, E., Reichler, R. J., & Renner, B. R., 1988)
  Western Psychological Services
  12031 Wilshire Blvd.
  Los Angeles, CA 90025
  www.wpspublish.com

Gilliam Autism Rating Scale, 2nd ed. (GARS-2)
  (Gilliam, J. E., 2006)
  PRO-ED
  8700 Shoal Creek Blvd.
  Austin, TX 78757-6897
  www.proedinc.com

Psychoeducational Profile, 3rd ed. (PEP-3)
  (Schopler, E., Lansing, M. D., Reichler, R. J., & Marcus, L. M., 2005)
  PRO-ED
  8700 Shoal Creek Blvd.
  Austin, TX 78757-6897
  www.proedinc.com

treatments or causes that are suspect or not proven, but by engaging in a continual effort to acquire information about best practices and research. Recommendations for effective ways of collaborating with parents and families will be presented in Chapter 15.

Summary

Autism is an intriguing disorder primarily characterized by (a) extensive communication and social deficits and (b) restricted patterns of thinking and behaving. To date, we do not know what causes autism or how to cure it. However, we do know that good teachers can make a huge difference in terms of positive outcomes for individuals with autism. Most research supports treatment based on behavioral

(text continues on p. 16)

Resources 1.2 Parent and Professional Organizations and Information Sources

American Association on Intellectual and Developmental Disabilities (AAIDD)
444 N. Capitol St., NW
Suite 846
Washington, DC 20001-1512

American Speech-Language-Hearing Association (ASHA)
10801 Rockville Pike
Rockville, MD 20852
800-638-8255
Fax: 240-333-4705
http://www.asha.org

APSE (formerly Association for Persons in Supported Employment)
1627 Monument Ave., Rm. 301
Richmond, VA 23220
804-278-9187
Fax: 804-278-9377
http://www.apse.org

Association for Behavior Analysis International (ABA)
1219 South Park St.
Kalamazoo, MI 49001-5052
269-492-9310
Fax: 269-492-9316
e-mail: mail@abainternational.org
http://www.abainternational.org/

Association for Retarded Citizens (ARC)
1010 Wayne Ave., Suite 650
Silver Spring, MD 20910
301-565-3842/800-433-5255
Fax: 301-565-3843
http://www.TheArc.org

Autism Society of America (ASA)
7910 Woodmont Ave., Suite 300
Bethesda, MD 20814-3067
301-657-0881
Fax on-demand: 800-329-0899
http://www.autism-society.org
(*Note.* Often there are state and local chapters)

Autism Speaks
2 Park Ave., 11th Floor
New York, NY 10016
212-252-8676
Fax: 212-252-8676
http://www.autismspeaks.org

Autism Research Institute
4182 Adams Ave.
San Diego, CA 92116
Fax: 619-563-6840
http://www.autismwebsite.com/ari/index.htm

The Cambridge Center for Behavioral Studies
336 Baker Ave.
Concord, MA 01742-2107
978-369-2227
Fax: 978-369-8584
http://www.behavior.org/

The Center for Autism and Related Disorders (CARD)
19019 Ventura Blvd., 3rd Floor
Tarzana, CA 91356
818-345-2345
Fax: 818-758-8015

Council for Exceptional Children (CEC)
1110 N. Glebe Rd., Suite 300
Arlington, VA 22201
888-232-7733
Fax: 703-264-9494
http://www.cec.sped.org
(*Note.* Subdivisions: Division on Developmental Disabilities [DDD; http://www.dddcec.org/] and the Council for Children with Behavioral Disorders [CCBD; http://www.ccbd.net/])

Cure Autism Now Foundation (CAN) (merged with Autism Speaks)
5455 Wilshire Blvd., Suite 2250
Los Angeles, CA 90036-4272
888-828-8476
Fax: 323-549-0547
http://www.cureautismnow.org

Division TEACCH
The University of North Carolina at Chapel Hill
CB #6305
Chapel Hill, NC 27599
919-966-2174
Fax: 919-966-4127
http://www.teacch.com

Education Resources Information Center (ERIC)
http://www.eric.ed.gov/

Families for Early Autism Treatment (FEAT)
PO Box 255722
Sacramento, CA 95865-5722
916-843-1536
http://www.feat.org

Federation for Children with Special Needs
1135 Tremont St., Suite 420
Boston, MA 02120
617-236-7210 or 800-331-0688 (in Massachusetts)
Fax: 617-572-2094
http://www.fcsn.org

MAAP Services for Autism and Asperger Spectrum
PO Box 524
Crown Point, IN 46308
219-662-1311
Fax: 219-662-0638
http://www.maapservices.org

National Dissemination Center for Children with Disabilities (NICHCY)
> PO Box 1492
> Washington, DC 20013-1492
> 800-695-0285
> Fax: 202-884-8441
> http://www.nichcy.org

National Institute of Child Health and Human Development
> PO Box 3006
> Rockville, MD 20847
> 800-370-2943
> Fax: 301-984-1473
> e-mail: NICHDInformationResourceCenter@mail.nih.gov
> http://www.nichd.nih.gov

National Institutes of Health (NIH) *Autism Research Network*
> http://www.autismresearchnetwork.org/AN/

The Organization for Autism Research
> 2000 North 14th St., Suite 480
> Arlington, VA 22201
> 703-243-9710
> http://www.researchautism.org/

RESNA Technical Assistance Partnership
> 1700 Moore St., Suite 1540
> Arlington, VA 22209-1903
> 703-524-6686
> Fax: 703-524-6630
> http://www.resna.org/taproject

The Schafer Autism Report
> 9629 Old Plaeerville Rd.
> Sacramento, CA 95827
> http://www.sarnet.org/

TASH
> 1025 Vermont Ave., Floor 7
> Washington, DC 20005
> 202-263-5600
> Fax: 202-637-0138
> http://www.tash.org

Wright's Law
> Information about special education law
> http://www.wrightslaw.com/

Yale University Child Study Center
> Developmental Disabilities Clinic
> 230 S. Frontage Rd.
> New Haven, CT 06520
> 203-785-5759
> Fax: 203-785-7402
> http://info.med.yale.edu/chldstdy/autism

theory, even though the disorder has a biological etiology. In the next chapter, we will present several behavioral teaching strategies related to the unique characteristics covered in this chapter. You will probably be able to apply these strategies effectively after reading this manual. If you feel you need more intensive training, we recommend that you attend conferences or in-service presentations to acquire additional expertise.

References

American Psychiatric Association. (1980). *Diagnostic and statistical manual of mental disorders* (3rd ed.). Washington, DC: Author.

American Psychiatric Association. (2000). *Diagnostic and statistical manual of mental disorders–Text revision* (4th ed., text rev.). Washington, DC: Author.

Baron-Cohen, S. (1995). *Mindblindness: An essay on autism and theory of mind.* Cambridge, MA: The MIT Press.

Bettleheim, B. (1967). *The empty fortress.* Chicago: Free Press.

Carr, E. G., Levin, L., McConnachie, G., Carlson, J. I., Kemp, D. C., & Smith C. E. (1994). *Communication-based intervention for problem behavior.* Baltimore: Brookes.

Centers for Disease Control. (2005). *What causes ASDs and is there a treatment?* Retrieved August 12, 2005, from http://www.cdd.gov/ncbddd/autism/asd_treatments.htm

Centers for Disease Control. (2006, February 3). *Autism information center: Frequently asked questions—prevalence.* Retrieved April 15, 2007, from http://www.cdc.gov/ncbddd/autism/faq _prevalence.htm#whatisprevalence

Filipek, P. A., Accardo, P. J., Baranek, G. T., Cook, E. H., Dawson, G., Gordon, B., et al. (1999). The screening and diagnosis of autistic spectrum disorders. *Journal of Autism and Developmental Disorders, 29*(6), 439–484.

Grandin, T. (1995). The learning style of people with autism: An autobiography. In K. A. Quill (Ed.), *Teaching children with autism: Strategies to enhance communication and socialization.* New York: Delmar.

Itard, J. (1972). *The wild boy of Aveyron* (E. Fawcett, P. Ayrton, & J. White, Trans.). London: NLB. (Original work published 1801)

Kanner, L. (1985). Autistic disturbances of affective contact. In A. M. Donnellan (Ed.), *Classic readings in autism.* (pp. 11–53). New York: Teachers College Press. (Original work published 1943)

Lord, C., Rutter, M., DiLavore, P. C., & Risi, S. (1999). *Autism diagnostic observation schedule (ADOS).* Los Angeles: Western Psychological Services.

Lord, C., Rutter, M., & Le Couteur, A. (1994). *Autism diagnostic interview–Revised (ADI-R).* Los Angeles: Western Psychological Services.

Myles, B. S., & Simpson, R. L. (2003). *Asperger syndrome: A guide for educators and parents* (2nd ed.). Austin, TX: PRO-ED.

National Research Council. (2001). *Educating children with autism.* Washington, DC: National Academy Press.

Wang, C. H. (1997). Medical indications for diagnostic tests in children with autism. *Advocate, 29*(6), 11–14.

Applied Behavior Analysis

As you learned in Chapter 1, individuals with autism present an array of unique characteristics that pose special challenges for teachers. Traditional methods of instruction commonly used in general education (e.g., large-group instruction, lecture, worksheets, cooperative group activities) or even special education (e.g., one-to-one instruction to explain skills and concepts) are usually ineffective with these students. Because of their unique characteristics, students with autism require specialized teaching and management strategies if they are to learn.

Fortunately, a specialized technology of instruction and behavior-change procedures exists. This technology is formally known as *applied behavior analysis* (ABA) and consists of principles and procedures that have been carefully and systematically researched for more than 50 years. The instructional and management strategies that have emerged from this research effectively address the educational needs of a wide range of learners, including children and youth with autism. ABA involves (a) applying these behavioral principles for instructional and behavior management purposes and (b) evaluating whether your interventions resulted in desired outcomes. Teachers who use these methods correctly increase the likelihood of achieving desired outcomes in their students with autism (Bristol et al., 1996; Maurice, 1996; National Research Council, 2001).

We wish to point out that many practitioners and parents adhere to a very narrow and erroneous view of ABA. ABA *is not* a curriculum or a single instructional strategy, nor was it "invented" for exclusive use with children with autism. ABA includes an array of assessment, intervention, and evaluation procedures. Practitioners can develop individualized programs by selecting those procedures that are likely to be effective for a given student and can monitor those procedures to ensure that they are producing the desired outcomes. If one procedure is not effective, other ABA procedures are available.

ABA is based upon several basic assumptions, described in Focus Here 2.1. Teachers should learn these principles well, because they will be invaluable in assessing behavioral and instructional needs, planning interventions, and problem solving if interventions fail to produce desired results.

The A–B–C Model

All of the instructional and behavior management principles of ABA can be categorized in an easy-to-understand format called the A–B–C model. We illustrate this model as:

Antecedents ⟶ **Behavior** ⟵ **Consequences**

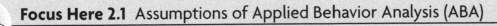

Focus Here 2.1 Assumptions of Applied Behavior Analysis (ABA)

1. **A person's learning history and biological makeup influence his or her current behavior.** Individuals' learning histories influence what they presently do to get needs met. For example, a student may have learned that screaming and hitting his head is an effective way to avoid disliked tasks. Another child may have learned that she gets to eat her favorite foods at snack time if she cries when other foods are given to her. The term *biological makeup* means that some students have biological conditions that make certain behaviors more likely to occur. For example, as you learned in Chapter 1, abnormal brain chemistry or structure and/or genetic conditions may increase the likelihood that students will exhibit stereotypic or self-injurious behavior or will be highly distractible, inattentive, or anxious. Despite the influence of past learning and biological makeup, it is possible to teach new behaviors, strengthen appropriate behaviors, and reduce inappropriate behaviors using the ABA principles and procedures described throughout this book.

2. **All voluntary behavior is governed by basic principles.** Both appropriate and inappropriate behaviors can be explained by one or more of the basic principles of ABA: positive reinforcement, negative reinforcement, extinction, punishment, stimulus control, modeling, and shaping. These seven principles serve as the basis for this book and will be explained in later chapters. Because *all* voluntary behavior can be explained by these principles, it is important for educators to be able to assess inappropriate behavior to determine which principle(s) are at work. Educators and other practitioners who are able to identify the principle that explains an inappropriate behavior (or that explains the absence of appropriate behavior) are better able to design effective interventions. For example, a teacher who understands negative reinforcement might determine that a student's tantrum behavior is being negatively reinforced when he is allowed to avoid compliance because of the tantrum. Knowing this, the teacher will probably develop an intervention that will teach the student more appropriate ways of expressing refusal, and he or she may also modify how commands are given to increase the likelihood of compliance. This intervention is more likely to be effective than if the teacher had simply tried to punish the student for the tantrums.

3. **Behavior is functional and enables students to get needs met.** This means that even an inappropriate behavior serves a purpose. Although most children learn socially acceptable ways of getting needs met, students with autism often do not. For example, most children learn to use words, gestures, or other appropriate forms of communication to express wants and needs. Because children with autism characteristically have significant deficits in communication skills, they must use whatever behaviors they know to get things that they want, to communicate hunger or discomfort, to communicate that they dislike something, and so forth. The behaviors they know (e.g., stereotypic behaviors, self-injurious behaviors, screaming, crying, grabbing) are largely inappropriate. Of course, as we noted in the discussion of the first principle, children learn at a young age that these behaviors often successfully result in desired outcomes; that is, they work well for the child. Effective teachers and other practitioners will assess the function, or purpose, that an inappropriate behavior serves for a student and then develop interventions to teach appropriate behaviors that will serve the same function. The process of identifying functions of challenging behavior is called *functional behavioral assessment;* we explain how to conduct such an assessment in Chapter 11.

4. **Behavior is influenced by external and internal antecedent events.** External events that may set the stage for a behavior include environmental conditions (e.g., noise level, crowds, distracting stimuli such as a flickering lightbulb), certain tasks (e.g., disliked or difficult tasks, social initiations by adults or other students), or schedule (e.g., early or late in the day, just before lunch). Internal antecedent events include emotional states (e.g., anger, anxiety) or physical states (e.g., hunger, illness, fatigue). For example, the cafeteria may be associated with increases in inappropriate behavior for some students with autism who dislike the noise levels, the echoing sounds, or the crowded tables. Likewise, a child

who has a stuffy nose may be less compliant because of the discomfort associated with that condition and his or her inability to communicate that discomfort. Teachers who understand the influence of environmental events are better able to plan how those events might be modified or to identify skills the student needs to learn to better respond to those events.

In this model, *antecedents* (A) are events that occur before behaviors and that are related to particular behaviors. *Behavior* (B) refers to either behavioral excesses or deficits. *Consequences* (C) are events that follow a behavior and that influence whether that behavior will be repeated. The arrows indicate that both antecedents and consequences affect behavior. This is an important concept; it means we should assess how both antecedents and consequences may be contributing to behavior, and, as a result, should consider modifying antecedents, just as we attempt to modify consequences, to increase desired behavior and reduce inappropriate behavior. The following sections describe each of the components of the A–B–C model and how they apply in teaching students with autism.

Antecedents

As stated previously, antecedents are events that occur prior to a targeted behavior and are associated with the occurrence or nonoccurrence of target behaviors. Antecedents should be assessed to determine their influence on inappropriate behaviors, as will be discussed in Chapter 11. In addition, teachers should plan specific antecedents that will serve the purpose of eliciting the desired behaviors. For example, using picture schedules to cue students what they are to do during the day is an antecedent intervention. Providing a mid-morning snack for a student who becomes less compliant when she is hungry is another example of a planned antecedent intervention.

A more precise use of antecedents for teaching and behavior management is known as *stimulus control*. According to Scheuermann and Hall (2008), stimulus control refers to a condition in which a specific behavior or class of behaviors predictably occurs in response to a specific stimulus or class of stimuli. When used for stimulus control, an antecedent is called a *discriminative stimulus*, or S^D. S^Ds are specific antecedents that predictably cue specific behaviors. These behaviors tend to occur somewhat "automatically" in the presence of these S^Ds. Our lives are filled with examples of stimulus control; for example, the telephone rings (S^D), and you pick up the receiver and say, "Hello" (behavior). The ring serves as an S^D for you to pick up the receiver—you typically don't pick up the receiver and say, "Hello," unless you hear the ring. Or when a new acquaintance extends his hand and says, "Hi, my name is John" (S^D), you grasp his hand and reply, "Hi, John. I'm glad to meet you" (behavior). Again, this particular behavior predictably occurs in the presence of that S^D.

Stimulus control is a valuable teaching tool for students with autism because it makes the learning environment much clearer and more predictable. These students tend to rely on rote memory, so once they are taught how to respond to specific environmental cues, they understand what is expected and tend to respond appropriately. When cues are unclear or when students do not understand what is expected, they are likely to try to avoid or escape the situation. Students can be cued to act

At-a-Glance 2.1 Examples of Stimulus Control

Discriminative Stimulus (S^D)	Behavior
Verbal S^D	
Adult says:	
"Ready to work!"	Student puts hands in lap and looks at teacher.
"Time for group."	Each student sits on his or her carpet square in the group area.
"Quiet hands!"	Student stops self-stimulatory behavior and puts hands in lap.
Nonverbal S^D	
Teacher claps her hands twice.	Student looks at teacher.
Teacher signs "wait."	Student sits in assigned "wait" chair.
Mechanical S^D	
Timer rings.	Student returns toy to shelf and goes to his or her desk.
Teacher uses "cricket" clicker.	Student who is running away from teacher stops immediately.
Schedule as an S^D	
Student enters classroom in the morning.	Student removes coat, hangs coat on a hook, and places backpack in cubby.
Student finishes toileting.	Student washes hands and returns to classroom.
Student finishes task.	Student places task in "finished box" and retrieves next task.
Routine as an S^D	
Student approaches the lunchroom. Worker is waiting at the end of the lunch line.	Student hands the worker his or her lunch card.
Student gets in car.	Student fastens seat belt.
Bus pulls up to bus stop, and door opens.	Student enters bus.
Student approaches fast-food counter.	Student places order.
Student enters checkout lane at grocery store.	Student unloads cart.

in certain ways through use of a variety of S^{D}s: verbal signals, nonverbal signals, mechanical signals, schedules, or routines. At-a-Glance 2.1 lists sample S^{D}s that could be used to elicit specific behaviors.

While students with autism may learn to respond to some S^{D}s without special instruction (e.g., they typically learn that the end of one activity within the daily schedule signals the beginning of another familiar activity), most students will need to be taught S^{D}s and the expected responses. Focus Here 2.2 describes the steps in establishing stimulus control; Chapter 3 will provide more in-depth information about using stimulus control for instructional purposes.

Focus Here 2.2 How to Establish Stimulus Control

1. Determine the desired response: what you want the student to do or stop doing. For example, you may wish for the student to begin work, respond to a greeting, look at you, stop self-stimulatory or self-injurious behavior, stop an activity, or move to another activity.

2. Choose a word, phrase, sound, gesture, or other specific signal as the discriminative stimulus (S^D). The S^D that you select should be (a) easy to use; (b) related to the behavior—that is, not something that the student sees or hears except when the target behavior is called for; and (c) something that will get the student's attention—that is, it must be noticeable by the student even when there are many distractions.

3. Present the S^D and immediately prompt the desired response (see Chapter 3 for help in using prompts).

4. Reinforce the student for the desired response.

5. After the student begins responding consistently to the S^D, gradually fade the prompting.

6. Once the desired response is established (i.e., the student consistently exhibits the response, with no prompts, when the S^D is presented), gradually begin to fade the reinforcement (reinforce the student once in a while but not after every response, eventually eliminating reinforcement).

7. When prompts and reinforcement are eliminated and the behavior regularly occurs in the presence of the S^D, you have achieved stimulus control.

Behaviors

The second part of the A–B–C model, *behavior,* refers to behavior(s) that are the target of an intervention. These can be language behaviors, such as answering yes/no questions, initiating social greetings, or using sign language to make requests; motor behaviors, such as hitting a ball, hopping on one foot, climbing stairs, or riding a bike; play or leisure behaviors, such as stacking blocks, playing a video game, or operating a DVD player; work/daily living behaviors, such as folding towels, stocking shelves, or wiping tables; and self-help behaviors, such as combing hair, tying shoes, or toileting. Some behaviors need to be taught using the methods we describe in Chapters 3 and 4. Some behaviors need to be increased, strengthened, or improved using reinforcement procedures that will be described later in this chapter. And some behaviors need to be reduced or eliminated using behavior reduction procedures, which we will introduce later in this chapter and deal with more extensively in Chapters 12 and 14.

It is important to be able to specifically describe target behaviors so you will know to apply behavior change or teaching interventions and discern whether those interventions worked. Such descriptions are called *operational definitions* of behavior. A good rule of thumb for determining if a definition of a behavior is adequately operationalized is that two people should be able to look at the student and agree on whether the behavior as defined is occurring (Scheuermann & Webber, 2002). Operational definitions of target behaviors will enable teachers and staff members to be consistent in prompting, measuring, and providing consequences for particular behaviors. Vague descriptions of behavior will result in ineffective interventions and inaccurate measures of progress. For example, if "good sitting" is selected as a target behavior for a student, the teachers and paraprofessionals who work with that student may all have different ideas about what constitutes "good sitting." Because each person has a different opinion, each one is likely to expect and reinforce different behaviors, making it very difficult for the student to learn the behavior. If, on the other hand, that target behavior is described in operational terms, such as "sits with feet on floor, hands down, facing forward, eyes open," everyone is more likely to be consistent in identifying and reinforcing occurrences of that behavior. The student will more quickly acquire the expected behavior, and data will reflect reliable information about it. At-a-Glance 2.2 lists examples and nonexamples of operational definitions of behavior.

Consequences

The last part of the A–B–C model, *consequences*, determines whether the behavior will be repeated. If the consequence is something the student likes, the behavior will probably be repeated. We call this *reinforcement*.

In the following sections, we explain reinforcement: its forms, types of reinforcing consequences, and how to use reinforcement effectively. We expand upon the use of reinforcement in Chapter 11, in which we explain how to use behavioral assessment to identify effective reinforcing consequences for students with autism.

Of course, sometimes consequences are used to reduce or eliminate behaviors. If an individual dislikes a consequence, chances are that the behavior will not be repeated. Using consequences to reduce or eliminate undesired behaviors is known as *punishment*. Because children with autism characteristically exhibit many behavioral excesses that interfere with learning and socialization, we devote two later chapters to describing processes and techniques to reduce challenging behaviors.

Positive Reinforcement

Reinforcement is defined as any consequence that increases the likelihood that a behavior will be repeated. *Positive reinforcement* is the process in which a consequence (a *positive reinforcer,* or *reinforcer*) is presented following a response and, as a result, that same response is likely to be exhibited again in the future. For example, each

At-a-Glance 2.2 Examples and Nonexamples of Operational Definitions of Behaviors

Examples

- Looks at teacher: student looks at teacher's face.
- Sharing: student uses toys or materials with one or more other students without grabbing objects or hitting other students.
- Tantrums: student screams and hits head with fists.
- Waits quietly: student sits in "wait chair" with hands in lap and with no vocalizations.
- Self-injures: student bites his or her own arm or hand.
- Aggressive: student grabs teacher's hair or clothing.

Nonexamples

- Acts silly
- Self-injures
- Is noncompliant
- Plays nicely
- Works hard

time a student responds correctly during individual teaching time, you give her a piece of cereal and praise her. If she continues responding correctly, you could assume that you have positively reinforced her. In another example, as a student plays appropriately without self-stimulation, you praise him and place a sticker on his chart that he can exchange later for his special stim toy. If the behavior of playing appropriately continues to occur, you can assume that the praise, sticker, and subsequent stim toy are positive reinforcers for this child.

Positive reinforcement is a powerful tool that will help teachers increase students' appropriate behaviors. However, remember that one of the principles of ABA is that all voluntary behaviors are governed by the same principles. This means that inappropriate behavior may also be maintained by positive reinforcement. For example, Tim cries when he must wait for his milk at lunchtime. The teacher notices that he is crying and says, "Don't cry, Tim. Here's your milk." What does Tim learn? He learns that if he cries, he gets his milk! In other words, he is positively reinforced for crying. If a student frequently exhibits one or more inappropriate behaviors, you must ask yourself how those behaviors are being reinforced: Does the student get something he or she wants or likes as a result of the inappropriate behavior? Does the student avoid something unpleasant? This information will help you design an effective intervention. One way to identify potential reinforcing consequences of inappropriate behaviors is through functional behavioral assessment, which we will discuss in Chapter 11.

Types of reinforcers. Reinforcers are classified as either primary or secondary. *Primary reinforcers* are those things that we intrinsically like or need for survival, such as food and drink. Primary reinforcers are usually highly effective. In fact, some very young children or individuals with low cognition may respond best to primary reinforcers.

Secondary reinforcers are those consequences that individuals have learned to like or value. These reinforcers are classified as *social* (e.g., praise), *material* (e.g., objects), *activity* (e.g., playing a game), or *token* (e.g., chips, stickers, money). Token reinforcers are usually exchanged at a later time for a more powerful backup reinforcer. For example, a student might earn a sticker for every 3 minutes of on-task behavior. After 15 minutes, if he has at least four stickers, he earns a few minutes to engage in his favorite activity. Because of the more abstract nature of token reinforcement, this may not be the most effective reinforcement system for some students. However, if possible, you should work toward establishing a token system. Token systems are widely used, and students may be able to achieve greater independence if they learn to understand and value such a system.

To help you select potential reinforcers, At-a-Glance 2.3 lists a variety of primary and secondary reinforcers that were evaluated in a study by Atkinson et al. (1984). These researchers used the *Autism Reinforcer Checklist* (Atkinson et al., 1984) with preschoolers, elementary-age children, and adolescents with autism to determine their most- and least-preferred reinforcers. Students seemed to like "junk" foods (e.g., crackers, chips, cookies), reinforcers that reflected light or that involved movement (e.g., bubbles, mirrors, climbing, wagon rides), and social reinforcers that involved social interactions (e.g., tickling, hugging, patting). Least-preferred reinforcers were "healthy" foods (e.g., cereal, raisins, fruits, vegetables), activities involving special materials (e.g., Play-Doh, painting), and aggressive social activities (e.g., pinching cheeks, whistling).

Another category of secondary reinforcers that often are effective for students with autism is *idiosyncratic reinforcers*. These are activities, materials, and so forth that would be either neutral or unappealing for most students but which may function as a reinforcer for a student with autism. By definition, idiosyncratic reinforcers

At-a-Glance 2.3 Most and Least Preferred Reinforcers as Identified by the *Autism Reinforcer Checklist*

Reinforcer Category	Most	Least
Edible reinforcers	Crackers	Licorice
	Cookies	Raisins
	Marshmallows	Cheerios
	Cupcakes	Apples
	Ice cream	Jell-O
	Juice	Raw vegetables
	Soda pop	Candy canes
	Doughnuts	Oranges
	Popcorn	Milk
	Corn chips	Frosting
Material reinforcers	Toy instruments	Paper and crayons
	Bubbles	Play-Doh
	Balloons	Hats
	Mirrors	Coloring books
	Blocks	Beads
Social reinforcers	Tickling	Blowing
	Smiling	Pinching cheeks
	Praising	Twitching noses
	Hugging	Back scratching
	Patting	Whistling
Activity reinforcers	Going for walks	Having mom leave class
	Watching popcorn pop	Cutting pictures from magazines
	Rocking	Making pictures with popcorn, noodles, or string
	Musical instruments	
	Time alone	Stringing beads
	Water play	Taping and tearing paper
	Clapping hands	Playing with paper
	Playing in front of mirror	Crayons
	Field trips	Drawing pictures
	Running outside	Stories in teacher's lap
	Drinking out of pop bottles	Finger painting with paint, pudding, or whipping cream
	Climbing	Wagon rides
	Flushing toilet	

Note. From "Brief Report: Validation of the Autism Reinforcer Checklist for Children," by R. P. Atkinson, W. R. Jenson, L. Rovner, S. Cameron, L. Van Wagenen, and B. P. Petersen, 1984, *Journal of Autism and Developmental Disorders, 14*(4), p. 432. Copyright 1984 by Springer. Reprinted with permission.

are unique to the child. Idiosyncratic reinforcers may be self-stimulatory behaviors (e.g., flicking the fingers, flapping the hands, rocking), rituals (e.g., lining up objects, performing certain movements in a particular order), or simply unusual foods or activities. For example, we discovered that one former student would be highly compliant during instructional activities to obtain the reinforcer of sitting in the teacher's car for a few minutes. An effective reinforcer for another student was using a spray bottle of water to clean the counters in the classroom. Still another student's preferred reinforcer was a bite of lemon.

As you learned in Chapter 1, most students with autism characteristically engage in one or more self-stimulatory behaviors. The desire to engage in these behaviors may be so strong that it interferes with attempts to teach or interact with the student. The good news is that this means those behaviors are highly reinforcing to the student. For this reason, we believe it is sometimes appropriate to allow students to earn time to engage in these stereotypic behaviors as reinforcement for compliance, task completion, good verbal behaviors, or other desired behaviors. Although some professionals disagree with allowing students to earn self-stimulatory time as reinforcement, we believe that teachers should take advantage of the motivating power of these behaviors to encourage the student to engage in behaviors that the student would otherwise be unlikely to exhibit. In fact, for some students, self-stimulation time may be the only effective reinforcer. If you decide to use self-stimulation as a reinforcer, you should observe the following cautions:

1. The self-stimulatory behavior should *only* be allowed after the student has completed a task directed by the teacher (that is, ensure that the self-stimulation time is contingent upon desired behavior).
2. The amount of self-stimulation time should gradually be reduced while concurrently increasing the amount of required work time.
3. You should introduce other, more socially acceptable forms of reinforcers.

Consider using the types of toys or materials listed in At-a-Glance 2.4; these potential reinforcers may function as effective substitutes for self-stimulatory behavior by providing sensory input similar to that offered by various self-stimulatory behaviors. These reinforcers will allow the student to access highly desired sensory stimulation without the social stigma attached to behaviors such as flicking the fingers. In any case, teachers must learn to carefully observe students to identify potential idiosyncratic reinforcers that might not be discovered through more traditional channels.

How to choose reinforcers. Teachers who are astute observers and who understand the concept of reinforcement should have little trouble identifying reinforcers for their students. For example, does a child with autism prefer particular activities, foods, materials, and/or self-stimulatory or idiosyncratic behaviors? The answer to this question will suggest potential reinforcers for that child. Does the child prefer to be left alone? If the answer is yes, allowing the child "alone time" contingent upon correct completion of a task or request could be used as a reinforcer.

Of course, asking other persons who know the child, including the child's parents, may reveal helpful information about possible reinforcers. Another way to identify reinforcers is *reinforcer sampling*. To do this, simply place several potential reinforcers (e.g., food items, toys, materials) on a table and allow the child access to the items. The items that he or she picks up may be reinforcers for him or her.

Use reinforcement correctly. Correct use of reinforcement means employing effective reinforcers and making access to them contingent upon desired behaviors. One of the challenges in teaching students with autism is finding effective reinforcers. These students characteristically do not like consequences that other children

At-a-Glance 2.4 Potential Substitutes for Self-Stimulatory Behaviors

Sensory System Stimulated by Self-Stimulatory Behavior	Potential Replacement Toys or Materials
Visual	Toys that use light or movement in some way, such as a prism, pinwheel, kaleidoscope, ViewMaster, or Lite-Brite; toys that have interesting visual features, such as a Slinky, a lava lamp, wind-up toys, perpetual motion balls, string puppets, yo-yos
Auditory	Toys that make music or noise, such as talking figures; music boxes; iPod; noise-makers; clickers; seashells; karaoke machines; audiotapes or compact discs of students' favorite noises, such as electronic beeps, water running, people talking or singing, animal noises, or white noise
Tactile	Toys or other items that have interesting textures, such as Silly Putty, Slime, Koosh balls, finger paints, beanbags, Beanie Babies, plastic bubble wrap, hand exercise balls, "worry" beads or rocks, or pieces of cloth with a variety of textures (velvet, burlap, chenille, suede, satin, fur)
Vestibular	Toys or activities that provide rocking, swinging, or twirling movement, such as a rocking horse or rocking chair, hammock, swing, tire swing, trampoline, pogo stick, Sit-and-Spin, Ring-Around-the-Rosy, large exercise balls or barrels, somersaults
Proprioceptive[a]	Toys or activities that involve movement of or sensation to the joints, such as wearing wrist or ankle weights; performing isometric exercises; hanging on monkey bars or chin-up bars; using hand weights, weight machines, grip-strengthening exercise tools; performing gymnastic exercises, cartwheels, somersaults, etc.
Olfactory	Items that offer pleasant odors, such as cologne or aftershave, either worn on the student's body or placed on a handkerchief; scratch-and-sniff stickers, scented markers, unlit scented candles or pieces of candle wax, lotions, scented air fresheners
Gustatory	Food items that offer interesting tastes or textures, such as gum, mints, hard candies, chewy foods, crunchy foods, airy foods, or fizzy drinks (e.g., sparkling water, sparkling juice)

[a]Most of the activities listed as substitutes for proprioceptive self-stimulatory behaviors should be used with parent permission and with guidance from an occupational therapist, physical therapist, or physical education teacher.

find reinforcing (e.g., movie time, attention from the teacher, hugs, stickers, games). On the contrary, characteristic atypical behaviors of students with autism, such as isolation or self-stimulatory behaviors, are usually highly self-reinforcing. This does not mean that secondary reinforcement cannot be used with students with autism. It simply means that teachers must be creative in identifying reinforcers or that students must be taught to value more traditional types of reinforcers. Secondary reinforcers can be taught through a process called *pairing,* which means presenting a primary reinforcer simultaneously with the second reinforcer. The primary reinforcer is then gradually faded.

Another important rule for using reinforcement correctly is that reinforcement must be *contingent* upon desired target behaviors; that is, the student only gains access to the reinforcer when he or she exhibits the target behavior. If the target behavior is not displayed or not displayed to desired criterion levels, the reinforcer is withheld. It is very important that the rules for earning reinforcement be clear and unambiguous for students with autism. This is accomplished by being highly consistent in delivering reinforcers: Giving them only after desired behaviors are exhibited. Focus Here 2.3 offers guidelines for using positive reinforcement correctly.

Reinforcement schedules. One of the questions that practitioners often pose regarding how to use reinforcement concerns its frequency: How often should I reinforce? Should I reinforce every behavior? How can I teach a student to work for longer periods of time before reinforcement is given? These questions pertain to *reinforcement schedules,* or determining when reinforcement will be given. Technically, there are many different schedules of reinforcement; for our purposes, however, we will describe four general approaches to scheduling reinforcement. These four approaches should be sufficient for most reinforcement intervention programs used in classroom or home teaching situations.

The first type is a *continuous schedule of reinforcement* (CRF), in which every correct response is reinforced. Continuous schedules are helpful for initial teaching of new skills; reinforcing each correct response while withholding reinforcement for incorrect responses helps the student quickly learn what is expected. For example, to teach Jacob a classroom entry procedure, Ms. Price uses a continuous schedule of reinforcement. She holds a cup where Jacob can see it and places small pieces of dry cereal in the cup as soon as Jacob completes each step of the process: hangs up his jacket in the correct spot, places his bookbag and lunch in his cubby, retrieves his daily picture schedule from its spot on the bulletin board, and sits in his chair. As soon as he sits in his chair correctly, she praises him and gives him the cup to eat the cereal. In another example of continuous reinforcement, Mr. Collins allows Hodari to play with his kaleidoscope for a minute each time he writes his name and address correctly during handwriting practice.

Continuous schedules of reinforcement are effective for establishing new skills. Most of the time, however, teachers and other practitioners should move from a continuous schedule to a schedule in which some, but not all, target behaviors are reinforced. Using a continuous schedule after the new behavior is established may result in *satiation,* a condition in which the student tires of the reinforcer, thus making it ineffective for motivating the student to produce the desired behavior. For example, a child who receives a sip of juice every time he signs "juice" may eventually tire of the juice and therefore no longer be motivated to use that sign.

Moving from a CRF schedule to an *intermittent schedule of reinforcement,* in which some, but not all, instances of the target behavior are reinforced, involves a process known as *thinning* the reinforcement schedule. *Thinning* refers to the process of gradually reducing the frequency of reinforcement, usually in a systematic, planned fashion using one of the reinforcement schedules described next.

We will explain three types of intermittent reinforcement schedules: *ratio schedules, response duration schedules,* and *interval schedules.* In *ratio schedules,* reinforcement is given after a predetermined *number of behaviors.* For example, once Tarique learned to use his picture communication cards to request a break or desired object (using a CRF schedule), his teacher began reinforcing him on a ratio schedule, first after every two requests, eventually after every four requests, then after an average of five requests. Ratio schedules are appropriate for discrete behaviors that can be easily counted (see the section on data collection later in this chapter). Ratio schedules would be appropriate for behaviors such as making requests, following

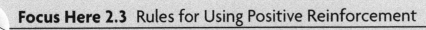

Focus Here 2.3 Rules for Using Positive Reinforcement

1. **Reinforce immediately after the desired behavior occurs.** This is how students learn that certain behaviors result in reinforcement. A delay between the behavior and getting the reinforcer decreases the likelihood that the student will learn what behavior is expected.

2. **Allow access to reinforcers only *after* the target behavior occurs.** This means that reinforcers must be *contingent* upon the behavior: The student doesn't get the reinforcer until the behavior is displayed. Controlling access to desirable reinforcers is a way to motivate students to exhibit appropriate behaviors.

3. **Use social reinforcers in addition to primary, material, token, or idiosyncratic reinforcers.** Although social reinforcers typically are not natural reinforcers for students with autism, you may be able to teach students to like them. This is done through a process called *pairing:* simultaneously presenting the social reinforcer with whatever other reinforcer you are using. For example, you might clap and enthusiastically say, "Good talking!" as you give a student a toy he or she has correctly requested. Gradually reduce the use of other reinforcers while maintaining the social reinforcers.

4. **Use primary reinforcers if needed to establish control, but pair them with other types of reinforcers.** Primary reinforcers are important for teaching a new behavior or to teach students to value secondary reinforcers. For students to attain any degree of independence, however, they must learn to like secondary reinforcers, including token reinforcers. Remember to choose secondary reinforcers by considering the nature of students' likes, dislikes, and preferred self-stimulatory activities.

5. **Gradually reduce the use of primary reinforcers.** The process of gradually reducing reliance on primary reinforcers in favor of other, more naturally occurring types of reinforcers is called *fading.* Once desired new behaviors are being exhibited regularly and frequently, gradually stop using the primary reinforcers while keeping secondary reinforcers in place.

6. **Rely on natural reinforcers as much as possible.** A natural consequence for saying, "Drink, please," is that the student gets a drink. A natural consequence for correctly operating the CD player without self-stimulation is allowing the student to listen to a CD. Rely on natural reinforcers as much as possible because they will maintain desired behaviors even in the absence of other reinforcers. For example, although you may initially use primary reinforcers to teach a student to initiate greetings, the goal is for the natural consequence of other individuals' responses to the greetings to eventually maintain the behavior.

7. **Use small amounts of reinforcers each time.** For example, if you are using food reinforcers, give the student only small amounts, such as one piece of popcorn or a small sip of milk, after each response. If you are using activity or material reinforcers, allow the student access to the activity or material for a few minutes or less. There are two reasons for this rule. First, providing large amounts of food or long periods of time to use other reinforcers may result in *satiation,* which is the condition that occurs when the reinforcer loses its value because the child has tired of it. The second reason for using small amounts of reinforcers is that time spent engaged in reinforcement activity is time taken away from instruction.

8. **Reduce the frequency of reinforcement.** When you are teaching a new behavior, you should reinforce the student for each correct response (*continuous reinforcement*). Once the student is exhibiting the behavior regularly, you should gradually move to *intermittent reinforcement,* which is giving reinforcement only after several behaviors (for event-type behaviors) or several minutes of the behavior (for duration-type behaviors). Do not move too abruptly from continuous reinforcement to intermittent reinforcement, or the student may not maintain the skill through the transition. For example, if you have been giving a student a piece of cereal for every few seconds of sitting quietly during group, you should gradually increase the time that he or she is required to sit to earn a piece of cereal (e.g., 10 seconds, 20 seconds, 30 seconds, 1 minute).

directions, solving math problems, placing silverware in the correct place in the dishwasher, completing assembly tasks, and so forth.

Response duration schedules are used when the goal is to increase the amount of time that a behavior occurs by reinforcing the individual for increasingly longer periods during which the behavior is continually exhibited. For example, Ms. Hunter set a goal for Marcus to work on his vocational task for 15 consecutive minutes without stopping to engage in self-stimulatory behavior. He can currently work only up to 2 minutes. Ms. Hunter begins intervention by setting a timer for 2 minutes. If Marcus is on task the entire 2 minutes, she praises him and gives him a plastic chip that he places in a container. She then resets the timer for another 2 minutes. At the end of the 15-minute worktime, Marcus counts his chips and exchanges them for a reinforcer that he chooses from a reinforcer menu. Once Marcus is working consistently for 2-minute periods, Ms. Hunter increases the work intervals to 3 minutes. She continues increasing the time Marcus is required to work before being reinforced until he can work for the target goal of 15 minutes. Response duration schedules are appropriate for sustained behaviors such as working on assigned tasks, engaging in play or leisure activities, remaining in seat, quiet-hands, or sitting appropriately next to a peer.

The last type of intermittent reinforcement schedule is an *interval schedule of reinforcement,* which can be used for either discrete behaviors or ongoing behaviors. In this schedule, reinforcement is given for the first instance of the target behavior following a predetermined period. For example, during playtime, Ms. Carver sets a timer for 3 minutes. When the timer rings, she observes each of her five students. Each student who is engaging in appropriate play behavior (an ongoing behavior) at that moment is praised and given a small piece of cracker or cookie. She then resets the timer for another 3-minute period. Eventually, she will increase the length of the reinforcement intervals. In another example, Ms. McCall, a speech–language pathologist, uses an interval schedule of reinforcement with her small language group. During language sessions, she sets a timer; as soon as the timer rings, each student is reinforced for his or her first appropriate use of language (a discrete behavior): Chase is reinforced as soon as he correctly answers a yes/no question, Madison is reinforced when she makes a request using her communication device, Harry is reinforced for appropriately responding to a conversational stimulus, and so forth. Once each student has been reinforced, Ms. McCall once again sets the timer.

As you can see, interval schedules allow the adult to simultaneously monitor and reinforce several students at once without having to count behaviors or time the duration of behavior exhibited by each student. Of course, interval schedules could also be used with a single student, making them a useful tool for monitoring one student's behavior while working with another student. For example, while Mr. Flores works individually with Samantha (using a CRF schedule), Tomas is working independently on a task. Mr. Flores uses a timer to mark a brief interval. When the timer rings, he reinforces Tomas as soon as Mr. Flores observes him working correctly. Beginning with 1-minute intervals, Mr. Flores has gradually increased the interval in 15-second increments as Tomas' on-task behavior has improved; the intervals are now 2 minutes long.

Negative Reinforcement

Negative reinforcement means that an aversive condition is avoided or ended by exhibiting a particular behavior. For example, a child cries for a toy in the store, and the parent gives the child the toy to stop the crying. The parent has been negatively reinforced because the aversive condition (crying) ends when the child gets what he or she wants. This type of reinforcement is negative because of the aversive condition that is removed or avoided and is reinforcement because it results in a behavior being repeated under similar circumstances. The parent in the previous example is likely to exhibit the same behavior (giving the child what he wants) under similar conditions in the future.

Negative reinforcement is often effective for students with autism because there are many things they do not like or want to avoid. Remember that children with autism often do not like social interaction. Allowing students to earn "alone time" contingent upon task completion or compliance with a teacher request may be highly effective. For example, Tony does not like anyone in close physical proximity. Tony's teachers use negative reinforcement to increase Tony's compliance. They sit next to Tony until he completes a task (or portion of a task) and then move away. During vocational time, Tony is required to place a certain number of labels on envelopes as the teacher sits next to him. When he finishes, the teacher moves away from him for a brief time. Tony gradually is required to complete a greater amount of work before the teacher moves away.

Despite the potential effectiveness of negative reinforcement, we recommend that it be used only if you are unable to identify positive reinforcers. If you use negative reinforcement, the negative condition should not appear aversive to anyone except the child with autism, and the negative condition should be something that you would not hesitate to use with any other student (Scheuermann & Webber, 2002). For example, sitting next to a student is not aversive to most students but may be an aversive situation for students with autism. You should *not* place a student in physical pain or discomfort, nor should you create any extremely negative conditions, such as by yelling or speaking to him or her in a harsh tone of voice.

Negative reinforcement sometimes explains students' inappropriate behavior: Remember the ABA rule that all behavior is governed by the same principles. Some students have learned that aggressive or self-abusive behavior allows them to escape disliked tasks or situations. Thus, the aversive condition—the disliked task or situation—is avoided or escaped from by tantrums or other challenging behavior. This increases the likelihood that the child will exhibit the same behavior under similar conditions in the future. For example, Steven dislikes operating appliances; each time he is expected to do so, he attempts to attack the teacher. Allowing him to avoid the task when he grabs the teacher's hair would negatively reinforce his aggression. Another example is Erica, who bites her arm when she is required to sit in group. The teacher says, "No biting, Erica!" and moves her chair away from the group. Erica now sits quietly. Erica will undoubtedly quickly learn that if she bites her arm, she gets to escape the unpleasant situation of sitting in group. A better strategy for these students would be to use (a) positive reinforcement for each step in operating an appliance for Steven and for sitting quietly in group for Erica and/or (b) one of the behavior reduction techniques described next for the unacceptable behaviors.

Behavior Reduction Procedures

The behavioral excesses characteristic of children and youth with autism usually interfere with compliance, task completion, responsiveness to social situations, and the potential for successful integration in mainstream environments. These excesses must be reduced or eliminated to allow students the opportunity to be more fully integrated into mainstream environments. The ABA procedures we have described so far will help reduce or eliminate self-stimulatory behaviors, aggressive behaviors, self-injurious behaviors, or other undesirable excesses. In addition, the instructional methods, curricular considerations, and communication and socialization interventions described in Chapters 3 through 10 are critical elements of preventive programs (i.e., programs designed to prevent challenging behaviors through teaching and strengthening new behaviors). Because challenging behaviors are often well established and resistant to intervention, however, direct behavior reduction procedures may be needed in addition to quality instruction and attention to antecedents. Because behavior reduction procedures are easily misused, particularly with students who exhibit high levels of challenging behaviors, we devote two chapters to these and other strategies for reducing or eliminating challenging behaviors. These strategies are explained in Chapters 12 and 14.

Data Collection

An important component of ABA involves collecting data to monitor students' performance on target skills. All teachers use various forms of data to monitor students' learning (e.g., end-of-chapter tests, projects, quizzes). For teachers of students with autism, however, monitoring student progress through the use of objective performance measures is essential. These students have such significant excesses and deficits that without objective data that allow them to monitor small increments of progress, teachers may not be able to detect behavioral changes. Informal observation of students' progress will be insufficient to determine whether an intervention is working. Monitoring student behaviors with objective data measures allows us to know definitively if our teaching strategies are working so that we can either continue to use effective strategies or change ineffective ones.

For students with autism, we use data collection for two general purposes: to monitor progress in learning new skills and to monitor behaviors targeted for reduction. For example, Ms. Price teaches students with autism. Her students are learning manding, tacting, and intraverbals, as well as many different functional skills. In addition, Ms. Price has targeted various behaviors for reduction, including self-injurious behaviors, self-stimulatory behaviors, and noncompliance. Ms. Price uses a variety of data systems to objectively monitor each student's progress on his or her target behaviors in these areas. She monitors the behaviors that each student is learning as well as the particular behaviors targeted for reduction.

In this section, we describe several ways to collect data to objectively monitor students' performance. All of the data collection systems described in the following sections may be used for monitoring progress in learning new skills (e.g., language skills, functional skills) and reductions in undesirable behaviors.

Data collection for either progress monitoring or behavior reduction requires four steps:

1. You must determine the correct data collection system for the target behavior you wish to monitor. The data collection system must match the target behavior.

2. You will need data forms to record data as you observe a student's behavior. Choosing an easy-to-use, appropriate form may mean the difference between collecting meaningful, accurate data and either not collecting data at all or gathering data that do not accurately reflect the target behavior. Because data forms are important, we provide multiple examples of forms and how to use them in Chapter 8, which offers forms for monitoring progress on newly learned skills, and Chapter 13, which includes forms for monitoring behaviors targeted for reduction.

3. You need to graph the raw data that has been recorded on your data forms. We explain how to graph data in this chapter.

4. You must regularly and frequently examine graphed data to determine if sufficient progress is being made on behaviors targeted for increase or reduction. If the data indicate sufficient progress, you can continue the interventions and data collection procedures. If, however, they indicate lack of progress or that the behavior is not changing quickly enough, you may need to modify or change the interventions while continuing to monitor the behaviors using objective data systems.

Data Collection Systems

It isn't difficult to measure behavior. The steps in measuring behavior are listed in At-a-Glance 2.5.

You will be able to monitor all types of target behaviors through two types of approaches to data collection: *permanent product recording* and *observational recording.* In the first type of system, data are collected from a tangible product resulting from the behavior. For example, you might count the number of puzzle pieces correctly placed during a leisure activity, the number of letters written on a paper during writing time, or the number of dishes washed or pieces of mail placed in the correct mailboxes during work time. The advantage of permanent product recording is that data can be collected after the behaviors occur, which means that you do not need to directly watch the student to measure behavior.

Many behaviors that are instructional targets do not result in permanent products. For example, there are no tangible results of using signs to request items, hitting oneself or others, or playing with a toy. These behaviors must be measured using observational recording. Observational recording systems include *event recording, duration recording,* and *latency recording.* Event recording is used when the goal is to increase or decrease the *number of times* a student exhibits a target behavior. Event recording is used for behaviors that have the following characteristics:

- have a clearly observable beginning and end (e.g., pointing to named objects, following directions, saying words);

- do not occur over long periods of time (because behaviors such as sleeping, staring out the window, and vacuuming likely occur for extended periods of time, they are not appropriate for event recording); and

- do not occur at extremely high frequencies (because they occur too quickly to count, flapping the hands or flicking the fingers would not be appropriately counted with event recording).

Event recording is easy to use: Simply record a tally mark each time the target behavior occurs during the observation period. Other methods for event recording include golf stroke counters, hand-held digital counters, or placement of a small object (e.g., marble, block, paper clip) into a container each time the target behavior occurs.

At-a-Glance 2.5 How to Measure Target Behaviors

1. Write an operational description of the target behavior.

2. Determine which measurement system you will use.

3. Decide when and for how long you will measure the behavior.

4. Measure the behavior for three to five observation periods (baseline) before you begin the intervention.

5. Continue to measure the behavior frequently and regularly.

6. Convert raw data, if necessary.

7. Graph the data using a simple line graph.

8. Frequently review the graphed data to make decisions about the intervention: continue the intervention, modify the intervention, or change to a new intervention.

Once you determine that event recording is the appropriate data collection method for a particular behavior, you must next decide which type of event recording to use: *restricted event* or *unrestricted event*. In restricted event recording, the target behavior is expected to occur only in response to a specific stimulus (e.g., number of times that a student follows a verbal direction, number of sight words read correctly, or number of puzzle pieces correctly placed). For example, Jason is a student who screams and bites his hand when he doesn't want to do something, a behavioral excess (self-injurious behavior) that reflects a behavioral deficit in communication skills (he lacks the skills to communicate that he does not want to do something). In Jason's case, screaming and biting his hand are restricted events because they occur only in response to a direction or when a task is presented. To use restricted event–type behaviors, you must record the number of stimuli (that is, the number of opportunities to respond, such as the number of directions given) as well as the number of times the target behavior occurred (see Chapters 8 and 13 for samples of recording forms for restricted events), and then convert the data to a percentage to be graphed; we describe how to convert and graph data later in this chapter.

Unrestricted event recording (Scheuermann & Webber, 2002, refer to this as *nonrestricted event*) is used if the target behavior can occur at any time; that is, it does not occur in response to a specific external stimulus (see Chapters 8 and 13 for sample forms for unrestricted event recording). Examples of unrestricted events include screaming, initiating a greeting, asking for a drink, and biting. To graph unrestricted event data, simply graph the number of times the target behavior occurs during the designated observation period.

In certain cases, unrestricted event data will need to be graphed as *rate data*. *Rate* refers to how frequently a behavior occurs within a specified time. Sometimes our goal is to increase or decrease how many times a behavior is exhibited within a particular period of time. For example, we may want to reduce the number of times Isabella says, "No," during a work time or increase the number of times Joshua initiates a play interaction during recess. Data reflecting these behaviors are most accurately reported as rate, which is often the data collection method of choice when the goal is to increase or decrease a student's response fluency. For example, before intervention, Harry is able to complete picnic packets at a rate of only 4 packets during each day's work time, or an average rate of .2 packets per minute. Harry's teacher sets a goal of 3 packets per minute. After intervention begins, his fluency of work completion increases; Harry is now able to complete 1 packet per minute. We discuss response fluency further in Chapter 7.

For target behaviors that occur over a long period of time and have a clear beginning and end (e.g., how long it takes a student to use the rest room, how long it takes a student to complete an assigned task, or how long a student sits next to a peer without grabbing), *duration recording* is the data collection system to use. A stopwatch is a convenient way to measure the duration of behaviors, or you may simply record start and stop times of the target behavior, as shown in the sample forms provided in Chapters 8 and 13. Duration data should be graphed as minutes and/or seconds. At-a-Glance 2.6 lists a variety of target behaviors and the appropriate measurement system for each behavior.

Finally, *latency recording* is used to measure how long it takes a target behavior to begin once a cue for the behavior is given. For example, latency recording would be the appropriate measurement system for monitoring how long it takes a student to begin working once her work is placed in front of him or her, how long it takes a student to begin following a direction, how long it takes a student to begin to eat once lunch is given, or how long it takes a student to select a toy when he is taken to the play area. Latency recording is done simply by timing the lapse between the cue and the onset of the target behavior; a stopwatch is a convenient tool for this purpose. Latency data are graphed as minutes and/or seconds.

At-a-Glance 2.6 Data Collection Systems for Specific Target Behaviors

Sometimes, more than one data collection system could be used. In these cases, the most appropriate system is listed first.

Behaviors Targeted for Increase	Data Collection System
Responding to greetings	Restricted event recording
Number of coins counted correctly	Restricted event recording
Number of directions followed	Restricted event recording
Number of tasks completed without assistance	Restricted event recording
Initiating a request	Unrestricted event recording
Initiating verbal greetings	Unrestricted event recording
Number of packets collated	Unrestricted event recording
Number of menus wiped clean	Unrestricted event recording
How long it takes to put on socks and shoes	Duration recording
How long it takes to complete assigned task	Duration recording
Sitting next to peers without hitting	Duration recording
Keeping glasses on face	Duration recording
Amount of time spent engaged in a social activity	Duration recording
Amount of time it takes to brush teeth	Duration recording
Amount of time spent in cafeteria during lunch before beginning self-stimulatory behavior	Latency recording
Beginning work once task is given	Latency recording
Time it takes a student to begin following a direction	Latency recording

Behaviors Targeted for Reduction	Data Collection System
Biting	Unrestricted event recording
Hitting self	Unrestricted event recording (however, if the hits occur at a high rate, use duration recording)
Grabbing teacher's clothing	Unrestricted event recording
Screaming	Unrestricted event recording or duration recording
Hitting peers	Unrestricted event recording
Hitting teacher in response to a direction	Restricted event recording
Flapping hands	Unrestricted event recording or duration recording
Rocking	Unrestricted event recording or duration recording
Making noise	Unrestricted event recording or duration recording
Having a tantrum	Event recording (restricted or unrestricted, depending upon the situation) or duration recording

Sometimes teachers object to data collection because they believe they do not have the time. A popular misconception about data collection is that you must collect data on every student, every response, and all day long, which, of course, would be unmanageable. You should collect *samples* of student performance. When a student is learning a new skill or when you first begin interventions to reduce a challenging behavior, those behaviors should be monitored more frequently. Once the student is responding consistently with the new skill or the challenging behavior is exhibited less frequently or the student reaches criterion on the target behavior, you may reduce how often you formally monitor the behavior. For example, Justin exhibits severe self-injurious behaviors (self-hitting, self-biting). Because of the severity of these behaviors and because they tend to occur throughout the day, his teacher uses tally marks on a data form to count every instance of self-injury. Before intervention, Justin was hitting or biting himself approximately 40 times per day. Once the intervention works (Justin's instances of self-injury drop dramatically to less than 10 instances per day), the teacher is able to monitor Justin's behavior less frequently. Justin's teacher continues to monitor Justin's behavior by taking brief samples of self-injury data during three 15-minute periods each day until Justin reaches a criterion of zero instances of self-injury per day for 5 consecutive days.

Another example is Leah, who is learning to point to picture communication cards to request items during snack time. At first, Leah's teacher counts how many requests Leah makes by using her picture cards during each snack time. As Leah's skills in requesting snack items improve, the teacher counts only twice per week. However, when the teacher begins teaching Leah to use her picture communication cards to request desired lunch items in the cafeteria, she again measures that behavior daily. Once Leah consistently requests lunch items without assistance, the teacher moves to periodic probes of this behavior. We further discuss when to collect data, including how to collect data on multiple students simultaneously, in Chapters 8 and 13.

How long you measure each behavior depends upon the target behavior. Some behaviors that occur infrequently might be counted over the entire day. For example, Austin screams infrequently, so each time he screams, his teacher records that instance. This may be anywhere from a few minutes to the entire day. In the previously described case of Justin, he exhibited a high number of self-injurious behaviors spread over the course of the day rather than a high number during any particular time period. Because these behaviors occur throughout the day, Justin's teacher chooses to count each instance of the behavior. As another option, for a behavior that occurs frequently throughout the day, you may measure the behavior during the time when it is most likely to occur or is most problematic. For example, if Sasha's crying predictably increases just before lunch, that would be the time to collect data on the crying behavior; if Kenedy's pinching and hitting occurs most frequently during group time, data collection on those behaviors should be done during that time.

To determine whether a specific intervention is effective, you should measure a behavior before you begin intervention. The data you collect before intervention are called *baseline data*. Baselines should be established whether you are trying to decrease or increase a target behavior. For example, Abigail engages in high rates of self-stimulatory behavior, a behavioral excess that needs to be reduced. Prior to intervention, the teacher collects five data samples of Abigail's self-stimulatory behavior. Then, because the data collected during intervention do not indicate a reduction in the amount of time spent in the target behavior, the teacher modifies the intervention. Subsequently, the data indicate a decrease in the behavior. A different example would be Jason, the student we described earlier who screams and bites his hand to tell his teacher he doesn't want to do something. As we noted, this behavior reflects a behavioral deficit in communication skills. Before teaching Jason to sign "No" and reinforcing him for using the sign, his teacher collects baseline data by counting how many times Jason currently signs "No" to express that he does not want to do something. Jason displays no instances of appropriate negation (e.g., signing "No") during each of the three 30-minute periods over the 3 days that the teacher counts this behavior. During intervention, Jason's teacher continues to count his instances of signing "No." Because the data show a steady increase in the number of times Jason signs "No," she can assume the intervention was successful. There is one exception to the rule about collecting baseline data: If the target behavior is dangerous to the child or others, you should *not* collect baseline data. Skip this, begin intervention immediately, and continue to measure to determine that the behavior is decreasing.

As we noted previously, one important step in data collection is finding or designing a data collection form. Possibilities for data-collection forms abound on the Internet and in commercially produced curricula and books. Whatever forms you choose, make sure that they are appropriate for the target behavior, the purpose for monitoring that behavior (e.g., to increase or decrease the behavior), and the data collection system you are using. We provide many examples of data collection forms in Chapters 8 and 13. If you are clear on your purpose for collecting data, and the measurement system that is appropriate for the target behavior, choosing or designing data forms is easy.

Graphing

Once you have gathered your data, you are now ready to create a graph. Line graphs are very versatile for this purpose, although you could also use bar graphs. A few of the data collection forms that we provide in this chapter and in Chapters 8 and 13 provide a way for you to graph raw numbers or percentage of correct responses right on the form. If your data form does not have such an option, you will need to develop a separate graph. You can use software (e.g., Excel) to develop graphs, or you can graph by hand.

Converting Data for Graphs

Graphing is an essential step in the data collection process. Raw data recorded on data forms are usually not very useful by themselves because it is difficult to determine from tally marks or time notations whether behaviors are changing in the desired direction or how quickly they are changing. Also, the raw data sometimes will need to be converted into a percentage or other format for accurate interpretation. For these reasons, the next steps after collecting raw data are to convert the data, if necessary, and record them on a graph. This visual representation makes interpretation of data much easier and also makes it easier to communicate with other persons about a student's progress.

How you set up your graph is important. Before doing so, you must decide if you should construct a raw number graph or a percentage graph. In other words, you need to determine whether you should convert your raw data. For example, knowing that Taneisha followed 10 directions on Monday and 6 directions on Tuesday appears to show that she was less compliant on Tuesday. If we also know, however, that Taneisha was given 15 directions on Monday and 7 directions on Tuesday, a different picture emerges. If we convert these raw data into percentages, we see that Taneisha was compliant for 67% of the directions on Monday and 86% on Tuesday, a definite improvement.

Knowing when to convert data is essential to reporting data that are meaningful and accurate. At-a-Glance 2.7 provides an overview of the rules for converting data. For unrestricted event recording, you may graph the number of behaviors that occur *if* your observation periods are the same length of time each time you collect data. For this reason, we recommend that when collecting unrestricted event data, you choose a predetermined amount of time for collection so that the time factor will not vary. For example, you may decide to collect data on the number of packets a student completes each day during a 20-minute work period. Or, if you are trying to teach a student to initiate requests, you could graph the number of times he initiates requests in a 1-hour period, during lunch and playtime daily.

In the case of restricted events, you may graph the number of behaviors if you provide the same number of opportunities to respond each session or day. For example, let's say you are interested in teaching a student to point to a picture of an object or animal when you provide a description of it (e.g., for a lion, "Point to the one that roars," or "Point to the one that lives in the jungle"). If you give one of those cues 10 times each teaching session, you could graph the number of times the student correctly points to the lion in 10 trial sessions. In another example, if you were trying to teach a student to complete all 9 steps (opportunities) of going through the lunch line, you could graph the number of steps completed correctly in the 9-step lunch-line procedure each lunch period. In the case of a student who puts materials in her mouth each time anything is placed in front of her, you might graph the number of times she mouths a material during the first 20 materials she is given each day.

It may be difficult to provide a consistent number of opportunities to respond each day when monitoring restricted event behaviors. If the number of opportunities to respond varies from one observation period to the next, you will need to convert your data to a percentage (e.g., the percentage of cues to which the student correctly points to the lion picture, the percentage of directions followed each day, the percentage of peer questions answered, the percentage of steps completed correctly). Reporting only the number of correct responses for a restricted event behavior would produce data that are not meaningful. For example, Ms. Gonzalez reports that

At-a-Glance 2.7 Rules for Converting Data

The following chart will help guide your decision making about data conversion

Data Collection System	Condition	What to Graph
Unrestricted event data	If observation time remains constant	Number of behaviors
Unrestricted event data	If observation time varies	Rate
Restricted event data	Number of opportunities to respond is always the same	Number of behaviors
Restricted event data	Number of opportunities to respond varies	Percentage
Duration		Number of minutes and/or seconds that behavior occurred
Latency		Number of minutes and/or seconds it takes for target behavior to begin

Anthony answered 10 questions correctly on Monday and 15 questions correctly on Tuesday. At first glance, it appears that Anthony did better on Tuesday. However, on Monday, Anthony answered 10 out of 10 questions correctly (100%), but on Tuesday he answered only 15 out of 18 questions correctly (83%). Reporting this behavior (answering questions correctly) as a percentage is the best way to provide accurate information about Anthony's performance. To calculate a percentage, use the following equation:

$$\text{Percentage of responses that are correct} = \frac{\text{Number of correct responses}}{\text{Number of opportunities to respond}} \times 100$$

As we noted previously, sometimes it is appropriate to convert unrestricted event data to a rate. For rate data, figure the rate per time unit (minutes, seconds, etc.) per day by counting the number of responses and dividing by the total amount of time observed, as shown in the following equation:

$$\text{Rate of behavior per minute, hour, day} = \frac{\text{Number of responses}}{\text{Total time observed}}$$

For duration recording, you can graph either the amount of time a behavior occurred (e.g., the number of minutes it takes a student to toilet after lunch) or the percentage of available time a behavior occurred (e.g., the percentage of circle time the student remains in his place). In the latter case, you must record data pertaining to both the total time of the circle activity each day *and* the amount of time the student stayed seated because circle time may vary in length from day to day. If you measure the amount of time a behavior occurs several times during a day (such as toileting, which usually occurs two to three times a day) you may want to convert the data to the average number of minutes spent toileting per day. Calculate the percentage of an allotted time that a behavior occurs with this equation:

$$\text{Percentage of time that student responds} = \frac{\text{Total response time}}{\text{Total observed or allotted time}} \times 100$$

Compute the average duration of a behavior with the following equation:

$$\text{Average duration} = \frac{\text{Total response time for all sessions (in seconds)}}{\text{Number of sessions, opportunities, or observation times}} \div 60$$

For latency data, record the number of seconds or minutes it takes a student to begin a behavior (e.g., going to his calendar after entering the room each morning). You can also graph the average amount of latency time if there are multiple times during the day that you count. For example, you may want to graph the average latency for Cindy to begin work after being given a task. In this case, you would need to count the number of tasks (opportunities) given to Cindy each day and the amount of latency time each time she is given a task. The equation for figuring average latency is as follows:

$$\text{Average latency} = \frac{\text{Total latency for all sessions (in seconds)}}{\text{Number of sessions, opportunities, or observation times}} \div 60$$

Graph Construction

The vertical axis on a graph depicts the response or target behavior. This axis should be labeled to clearly indicate what you were counting, which is typically the target behavior specified in your objective. The horizontal axis, a little longer in proportion, is labeled to reflect the time element (e.g., days, sessions, weeks). Divide each axis into equal increments. You will decide the vertical increment size based on whether you are graphing a percentage or raw number and on what you anticipate to be the final performance numbers. The horizontal increments should be based on how much time you think it might take the student to master the objective.

It is usually desirable to graph the baseline data—the original level of student performance of the target behavior before intervention. Baseline data are plotted on the graph with a dotted vertical line between the baseline and teaching conditions. Do not connect data points across this line. Draw in the mastery criterion as a horizontal line that starts at the vertical axis to clearly depict the target criterion (low for reductive purposes, high for progress purposes). Figures 2.1 through 2.4 provide sample line graphs showing data graphed for unrestricted event behaviors, rate, percentage, and duration.

We provide more information about how to efficiently maintain up-to-date graphs in Chapter 8. Graphing is typically the most rewarding part of data collection: It provides visual evidence of your teaching successes and can facilitate communication about a student's progress.

Summary

Students with autism have unique needs that require specialized instructional strategies. The types of instructional and behavior management approaches that are traditionally used with typical students or students with other types of disabilities will

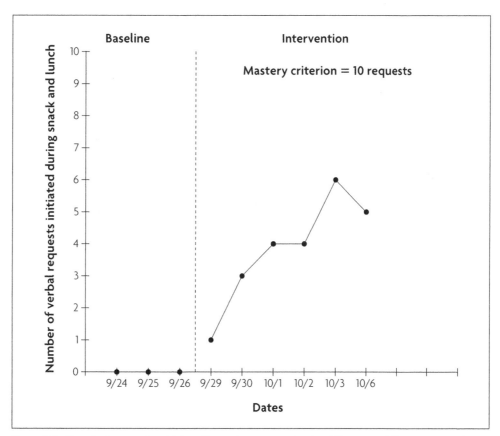

Figure 2.1. Sample line graph with baseline and mastery criterion (10 requests) for unrestricted event data.

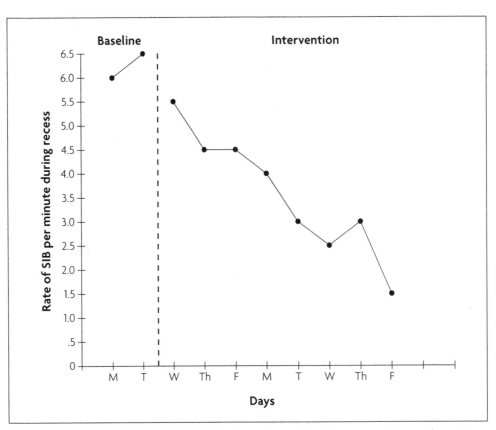

Figure 2.2. Sample line graph with baseline and mastery criterion (0 instances) for rate data. SIB = self-injurious behavior.

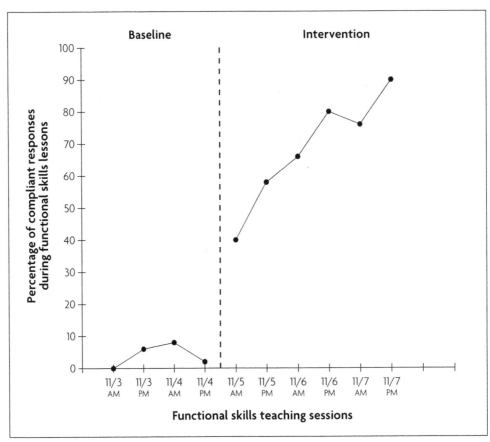

Figure 2.3. Sample line graph with baseline and mastery criterion (90%) for percentage data.

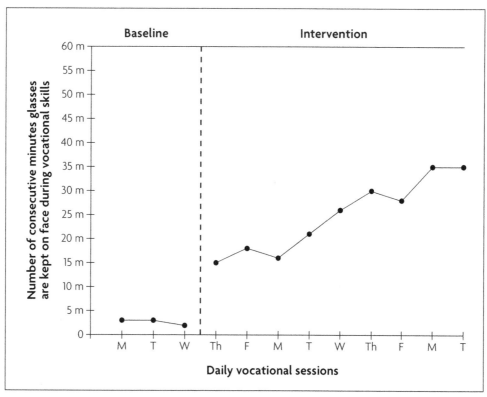

Figure 2.4. Sample line graph with baseline and mastery criterion (60 consecutive minutes) for duration data.

usually be ineffective for students with autism. The instructional model that has proven to be the most effective for this population is called applied behavior analysis, or ABA.

ABA procedures are based on the concept that a behavior is inexorably tied to the antecedents that precede it and the consequences that follow it. These antecedents and consequences can be manipulated to increase the likelihood that desired behaviors will occur and undesired behaviors will be reduced or eliminated.

ABA-based interventions include antecedent manipulation, stimulus control, data collection, positive and negative reinforcement, and certain behavior reduction techniques. These interventions provide a wide array of tools for teaching students with autism and for managing the behavioral excesses characteristic of this population.

References

Atkinson, R. P., Jenson, W. R., Rovner, L., Cameron, S., Van Wagenen, L., & Petersen, B. P. (1984). Brief report: Validation of the Autism Reinforcer Checklist for Children. *Journal of Autism and Developmental Disorders, 14,* 429–433.

Bristol, M. M., Cohen, D. J., Costell, M., Denckla, T. J., Eckberg, R., Kallen, R., et al. (1996). State of science in autism: Report to the National Institutes of Health. *Journal of Autism and Developmental Disorders, 26,* 121–154.

Maurice, C. (Ed.). (1996). *Behavioral intervention for young children with autism.* Austin, TX: PRO-ED.

National Research Council, Division of Behavioral and Social Sciences and Education, Committee on Educational Interventions for Children with Autism. (2001). *Educating children with autism* (C. Lord & J. P. McGee, Eds.). Washington, DC: National Academy Press.

Scheuermann, B., & Hall, J. (2008). *Positive behavioral supports for the classroom.* Columbus, OH: Merrill/Pearson Educational.

Scheuermann, B., & Webber, J. (2002). *Autism: Teaching DOES make a difference.* Belmont, CA: Wadsworth.

Instructional Strategies: Discrete Trial

It is very important for teachers of students with autism to learn to use applied behavior analysis (ABA) principles in the classroom. As you learned in Chapter 2, ABA principles are based on the **A**ntecedent–**B**ehavior–**C**onsequence paradigm: Teachers must manipulate antecedents and consequences such that they elicit targeted student behavior and prevent or reduce undesirable student behavior. Using ABA implies that instruction is teacher-directed, objectives are expressed in behavioral terms, student progress is monitored, and student well-being guides all instructional decisions (Alberto & Troutman, 2006).

You also learned in Chapter 2 that ABA is not one particular teaching strategy but multiple applications of a theory set forth to explain human behaviors and responses. Several teaching strategies commonly used for students with autism are derived from ABA theory. In fact, any procedure involving clear classroom structure, copious teacher directives and prompts, predetermined target behaviors, regular feedback on performance, and consistent monitoring is probably based in ABA. We want to recommend two well-researched ABA teaching strategies that we think you should master to teach your students with autism the responses, skills, routines, and activities they need to learn. One strategy, known as *discrete trial teaching* (DTT), is often directly associated with, and sometimes referred to as, ABA. The second strategy, *naturalistic, or milieu, teaching,* also uses ABA principles explained in Chapter 2. We will present DTT in this chapter and discuss naturalistic/milieu teaching in Chapter 4, where we will also discuss ways to instruct students in groups to approximate how students (a) learn in general education classrooms and (b) work in integrated employment settings.

Discrete Trial Teaching

In Chapter 1, we noted that individuals with autism have a difficult time making sense of their world because of their cognitive, communicative, and sensory-processing deficits. Individuals with these types of deficits need teachers and other adults to provide clarity in the form of cues, instructions, expectations, and feedback to facilitate their ability to learn. Fortunately, using teaching strategies based on ABA principles adds much-needed clarity for students with neurological impairments.

One of the most popular ABA teaching strategies for students with autism is a lesson-presentation format, DTT, also known as *trial-by-trial training* or *discrete trial format* (DTF). In fact, many parents request that their children receive intensive DTT in schools because positive outcomes from the use of it have been widely documented (Choutka, Doloughty, & Zirkle, 2004; Lovaas, 1987; Maurice, 1993). DTT has many advantages—but also some disadvantages—so it should not be the only teaching strategy used and should not comprise an entire educational program.

It is a method primarily for teaching and drilling new responses and skills such that the child knows exactly what response is expected, receives assistance in performing, gets immediate feedback on the performance, and is given something desirable when his or her performance is correct. DTT is a relatively simple process for both teachers and students, and its use allows for the drill-and-practice that students who do not attend well will need so they can learn. DTT has the added advantage of monitored performance through data collection, a very desirable aspect of teaching, and incorporates enough structure such that the teaching adults stay consistent in their presentation and students relax into the teaching activity. DTT can and should be applied frequently and intensely by paraprofessionals, related service personnel, and family members for direct skill training. Usually DTT is applied in a one-on-one format, although it can be used in small-group situations as well.

DTT is directly based on the A–B–C paradigm, specifically, on the principle of stimulus control. In Chapter 2, we noted that stimulus control means that particular behaviors occur in the presence of specific antecedents but do *not* occur in the presence of other antecedents. For example, when we tell a student to get her coat, we want her to walk to the closet and get a coat. When we tell a student to "sit down," we do not want her to walk to the closet to get a coat. We want the response of walking to the closet and getting a coat to come under the control of the instruction "Get your coat." We obtain stimulus control through *discrimination training,* in which students learn to match their behavior to certain external stimuli rather than behaving randomly. The ability to discriminate both visually and auditorally among various stimuli is the basis for learning how to read, write, compute math problems, talk, perform self-help skills, follow directions, and so forth. It therefore is one of the first cognitive skills we should teach children.

Discrimination training involves giving clear cues or antecedents (e.g., "Get your coat"); prompting the student, if necessary, to behave a certain way (e.g., take her hand, walk her to the closet, point to the coat); and consequating her actions (i.e., "Good getting your coat!" when she grasps the coat and pulls it out of the closet, but no reinforcement [silence] if she does something else). The prompt and reinforcers should eventually be faded so that the cue ("Get your coat") by itself occasions or elicits the correct response (going to the closet and pulling out the coat). When the cue alone produces correct behavior, we say the behavior has come *under stimulus control.*

DTT is an intensive method for bringing discrete behaviors or responses under stimulus control. Again, it is best used for new learning or when a student needs drill-and-practice to master behaviors or skills. Children with autism who have many new skills to learn usually benefit from DTT. A drill-and-practice format is a good one for students with autism because these children do not easily discriminate stimuli, acquire new skills, or generalize their learning. It would be rare for you to present a new behavior, skill, or activity and have your student with autism learn it after one teaching session.

How to Conduct DTT

DTT refers to a series of learning opportunities, each with a clear onset and end, that are called *trials.* Several trials are presented in each learning session. Trials are teacher-directed, brief, and clear. Each trial consists of five components (discussed next as steps and listed in At-a-Glance 3.1). A trial consists of the presentation of the five components just one time. *Massed trials* occur when the same series of steps with the same antecedent is presented several times in a row. Once the learner has acquired a skill and we present a single trial every once in a while just to check for skill retention, we refer to these trials as *distributed trials.*

Step 1: Discriminative Stimulus

Step 1 is a presentation of the antecedent stimulus, usually the teacher's instruction, to which you want the student to respond. Remember that an antecedent stimulus is any external variable, such as a person, place, event, verbal instruction, time of day, temperature, or object, that cues someone to behave. In this case, the antecedent

At-a-Glance 3.1 Five Components of Discrete Trial Training

1. **Discriminative Stimulus (S^D)**
   a. Get attention first.
   b. Make it clear and simple.
   c. Make it prominent.
   d. Make it relevant.
   e. Give S^{D}s consistently at first.
   f. Give only one S^D per trial.

2. **Prompt**
   a. Administer as part of the antecedent.
   b. Should be the least-intrusive prompt that is effective.
   c. Plan to fade the prompt systematically.
   d. Probe occasionally to see if prompts have become unnecessary.

3. **Response**
   a. Ensure it is something the student needs to learn.
   b. Define it operationally.
   c. Ensure that you are able to observe it and measure it.

4. **Consequence**
   a. Reinforce correct responses; DO NOT reinforce incorrect responses.
   b. Ensure that the reinforcers are effective.
   c. Manipulate the power of the reinforcers.
   d. Use frequent reinforcement for new learning, then fade to intermittent reinforcement.
   e. Reinforce prompted trials in most cases.
   f. Make consequences immediate and consistent.
   g. Make consequences contingent on specified student behavior.
   h. Be sure punishing and reinforcing consequences are distinctly different; use only the mild punisher, "No," for incorrect responding or give no response at all.

5. **Intertrial Interval**
   a. Record data.
   b. Make instructional decisions (e.g., change prompt).
   c. Reinforce other behaviors, but keep student on task.
   d. Move to quicker intervals as the student becomes more fluent in responses.
   e. Manipulate nature of intertrial interval according to individual reactions.

stimulus is very specific to what is being taught. In Chapter 2, we explained that this type of antecedent stimulus is known as a *discriminative stimulus* (S^D) and is delivered by the teaching adult. We say a stimulus is discriminative (S^D) when we choose it specifically to cue certain behavior that other stimuli should not cue. For example, the printed word *man* is an S^D for reading or saying *man,* while the printed word *dog* is an S^D for reading *dog.* We do not want people reading *dog* when other stimuli are present (e.g., the word *cat*). Once students learn that they will receive reinforcement for doing what we say or responding in ways that we want (discriminative learning), further learning is facilitated, and we are on the way to obtaining stimulus control.

Choosing and delivering S^Ds requires some thought and consideration. Because students with autism perceive external variables differently from the way that most people do, we need to be careful about the S^Ds we choose and how we present them in a DTT lesson.

Recommendations for Choosing and Delivering S^Ds

1. **Elicit attention before delivering an S^D.** Obviously, there would be no point in presenting an S^D if the student is not attending to the teacher. Thus, teachers should first teach the student to sit down with his or her face forward, feet on floor, hands quiet, and eyes preferably on the teacher or task. A teacher may want attending behavior when he says, "Get ready," "Look," "Ready," or "Quiet" or says the student's name (what we call a pre-S^D). However, it is important to fade these pre-S^Ds as the child learns to attend to the teacher's presence or the learning situation (e.g., sitting in the chair means attending to task). Teach attending by prompting and praising it, but do not use multiple trials just to obtain it. The actual reinforcer for attending becomes the privilege of moving quickly to a learning trial that concludes with powerful reinforcement for correct responding. In other words, we do not want you to just use drill-and-practice attending, getting ready to work, or eye contact. This preattending training should be combined with relatively easy subsequent learning trials followed by strong reinforcement. The following dialogue is an example:

TEACHER:	"Look" (pre-S^D).
STUDENT:	Sitting, glances at teacher and does not exhibit any self-stimulatory behaviors (correct behavior).
TEACHER:	"Good" (reinforcement). "Point to shirt" (S^D).
STUDENT:	Touches shirt (correct behavior).
TEACHER:	"Good pointing to shirt!" Rubs student's chest (reinforcement).
TEACHER:	"Look" (pre-S^D).
STUDENT:	Attending (correct behavior).
TEACHER:	"Point to button" (S^D).
STUDENT:	Points to button (correct behavior).
TEACHER:	"Good pointing to button!" Gives a sip of juice (reinforcement).

2. **The S^D should be clear and simple.** Remember that we are attempting to make external variables clearer for students with autism and make it easier for them to tell the differences among stimuli (discrimination). You must pick a simple S^D, one that has a clear beginning and ending. If the S^D is a verbal instruction (which it usually is), use few words and say the complete S^D every time. Avoid run-on commands such as "Get the ball, throw it to Jeff, and don't forget to grasp the ball correctly." Instead, use S^Ds such as "Point to _____," an S^D for receptive understanding of vocabulary, or "Put in," as an S^D for fol-

lowing one-stage commands to place one object inside another. "Tell me more about that" might be an S^D for expanded language or explanations. If the S^D is not verbal, consider visual clarity. For example, a picture of a toothbrush is an S^D for brushing teeth, the use of green stickers on toys is an S^D for playing with the toy, and the international sign for "No" is an S^D for *not* doing something.

3. **Make the S^D prominent.** When teachers are beginning discrimination training, we recommend making the S^D more prominent than other stimuli so that the student has an easier time attending to it. For example, when giving verbal S^Ds, say them a little louder than other things you say and only use the most important words (e.g., "Go to swing," rather than "Mike, go swing if you want to"). If you are beginning to train pictures as S^Ds, make the pictures big or the color bold. Once the student begins to match the appropriate behavior to the S^D easily, fade the decibel levels or picture size to better approximate natural S^Ds.

4. **Make the S^D relevant to the task.** Choose the S^D that precisely reflects what you want students to do. Certainly, pictures of items, as in the toothbrush example, are very relevant S^Ds. Try to do the same with verbal S^Ds. For example, if you want a student to line up with his or her peers, say "Line up," not "Get ready for lunch" or "Time to go now." At some point you will need to loosen stimulus control, which we will discuss later, but when teaching new skills, choose a clear, concise, and relevant S^D, and use the same one each time until correct responding is fairly reliable. It will then be important to bring the behavior under the control of other related S^Ds (e.g., "Get ready for lunch").

5. **Be consistent until you obtain stimulus control.** Because you are trying to develop stimulus control and teach a student who has difficulty in discriminating how to do just that, we recommend initially using the same S^D every time a certain response is required until the student responds reliably to the original S^D with less prompting. We then recommend "loosening" stimulus control by varying the commands and who gives them.

Initially, this means that everyone (e.g., other teachers, paraprofessionals, related service personnel) should use the same command or instruction, picture, or any other cue to elicit specific responses. This will require careful communication among everyone who works with the student, as well as all family members. It will not be helpful, for example, to have the teacher cueing dressing with the S^D "Put on," while the parents are telling the child to "Get dressed." This may only serve to confuse the student and prolong the time needed to acquire the skill. Once the skill is produced several times with little prompting, however, you should vary the S^D to avoid having the student fall rigidly under the control of just one S^D.

6. **Use only one S^D followed by a short pause per trial.** Do not repeat an S^D multiple times when the student does not respond. This may be difficult for the teaching adults to learn because we think that giving multiple commands helps understanding. In the case of students with autism, however, this is usually not so. Excessive verbiage tends to inhibit understanding. Refrain from scenarios such as the following: "John, give me the ball. Give me the ball. John. Look. Give me the ball." If the student does not respond to the first S^D within about 5 to 7 seconds, we recommend that the teacher provide a consequence by stating, "No," or turning the head, and then begin a new trial immediately, this time using a prompt to ensure correct responding and reinforcement on the second trial if correct responding occurs.

Photo 3.1 illustrates a classroom example of an S^D.

Step 2: Prompt

Prompting is probably one of the most important components of effective instruction in general and DTT in particular. A *prompt* is extra assistance given to individuals to help them learn to respond correctly. An example of a prompt would be forms that the Internal Revenue Service provides to make it more likely that people will complete them correctly. A teacher who whispers "Sssss" when a child is stuck on

Photo 3.1. Discriminative stimulus (S^D): Four coins are placed on a paper. The teacher asks, "What is it?"

the word *snake* is giving a prompt. A mother who puts a spoon into the toddler's hand the correct way is providing a prompt. Road signs are a prompt for correct driving behavior. The world is full of prompts.

Types of Prompts. Prompting is especially important in new learning for preventing errors and enhancing motivation to participate. For most things we learn, the prompts are soon eliminated as we learn to perform without them. Some of us, however, remain dependent on prompts forever (e.g., reminders for remembering anniversaries and birthdays or of what to buy at the store, kitchen timers, e-mail reminders). Notice that there are various types of prompts:

1. *verbal prompts,* such as verbal instructions (e.g., a teacher saying, "Remember to keep your hands to yourself while walking down the hall") or hints ("This word is a scary animal");
2. *visual prompts,* such as road signs, colored lights, a picture schedule, a taped outline signaling where to sit or stand, or someone pointing to the correct answer (also known as a *gestural prompt*). *Models* (e.g., watching someone else perform the behavior or a video model of one's own behavior) are another example of a visual prompt;
3. *physical* or *manual prompts,* such as a physical education teacher placing a student's hand on the bat correctly or a teacher putting a child's hand on his head in response to the S^D, "Touch your head."

Another type of prompt that can be embedded in an S^D is called a *within-stimulus prompt.* In this prompt, the assistance is built into the S^D to increase the likelihood of a correct response. For example, while teaching a student to discriminate his written name, you might place two cards in front of him—one card with his name and one card with another student's name. The card with the correct name could be twice as large as the other card. Size, a within-stimulus prompt that is part of the S^D, makes it more likely that the student will pick the correct card when asked to point to his name. Many of us are familiar with the within-stimulus prompt for printing a letter. Dotted lines depicting the letter are provided so students can trace the letter. The dotted lines are gradually faded until the student has to produce the letter without a prompt. Other examples are printed arrows to indicate which picture to circle on a worksheet or a loud voice to indicate the correct answer to a question (e.g., "Who's buried in GRANT's tomb?").

An additional type of within-stimulus prompt is a *positional prompt,* in which the S^D is placed in close proximity to the student, thus making it more likely to be chosen. For example, while teaching a student to identify dimes and nickels, you move the nickel close to the student and keep the dime further away. You then give the S^D, "Point to nickel." In this case, close proximity is a prompt. You would gradually move the dime closer to the nickel to achieve true discrimination. Gestural, model, physical, and within-stimulus prompts are shown in Photos 3.2 through 3.5.

Photo 3.2. Gestural prompt: The teacher says, "Put with same," and points to the correct answer.

Photo 3.3. Model prompt: The teacher says, "Point to nose," as she models the action.

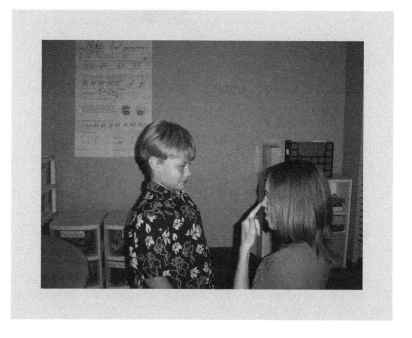

Photo 3.4. Physical prompt: The teacher says, "Point to nickel," as she takes child's hand and points to the correct coin.

Photo 3.5. Within-stimulus prompt: The teacher says, "Put word with object." (The correct object is much larger than the other objects.)

How to Prompt. A prompt should be administered simultaneously with the S^D if it is a within-stimulus prompt or shortly (1–3 seconds) after the S^D. You should use prompts when students need assistance to perform the correct response so you can provide them with reinforcement. We want students to receive frequent reinforcement and to perform correctly many times without any incorrect responses. This is called *errorless learning* and is very important as a strategy for keeping your students motivated to work with you. If they do not receive reinforcers at a fairly high rate, they may become frustrated and begin displaying inappropriate behaviors. However, we also must prevent students from learning to view the prompt as the target S^D. The prompt *must* be eliminated so that the student's behavior comes under the control of the intended S^D. In other words, we do not want students to respond only when a prompt is given.

The point is that prompted responses should be a temporary step toward independently producing target behaviors. You thus will need to get rid of, or *fade,* the prompts as soon as you can while still maintaining high-frequency correct responding. We do not want to create *prompt dependence* (i.e., the child comes to rely on the prompt as a "crutch" in order to respond correctly). Remember also that individuals with autism tend to overselect and focus on irrelevant stimuli; that is, it is possible for the student to come under the control of the prompt but not the S^D. In the previously used example of the dime and nickel, prompt dependence would occur if the student learns to pick whatever coin is closest to him rather than attending to and discriminating the verbal label (dime, nickel, penny, quarter). Even though many of us require prompts throughout our lives for some things, the vast majority of human behaviors are performed without such assistance. If we want students to live and work independently, we must prevent excessive dependence on prompts, particularly ones that require the presence of other people.

Since students with autism easily become dependent on prompts, you need to use the most inconspicuous and nonintrusive—but effective—prompts and fade them as quickly as possible. When teaching a new response, we recommend that you initially use the most intrusive prompt necessary to obtain the correct response (this may be a physical or partially physical prompt). For example, you might want to teach a student to imitate a motor movement (touch head). The first time you present the S^D, "Do this," and touch your head, pause about 5 to 7 seconds. If the student does not attempt to imitate you, take her hand and put it on her head (full physical prompt). Reinforce correct prompted trials at this point. After a few correct and reinforced trials, only push her elbow up (partial physical prompt), point to her head in the next trial, and then present only the S^D ("Do this" plus modeling hand on head). The quicker you can eliminate the prompts and still elicit regular correct responding, the better. See Photo 3.6 for an illustration of a partial physical prompt.

A key component of prompt fading pertains to manipulating the *power* of your reinforcers so that your student receives the better reinforcers for correct responses, requiring ever less intrusive prompts. Avoid powerful reinforcers if you have to revert to intrusive prompts after you have begun fading and the child has correctly

Photo 3.6. Partial physical prompt faded from full physical prompt: The teacher says, "Roll a snake," and pushes child's elbow.

responded with less prompting. (Reverting to intrusive prompts after incorrect responding from the student is called *error correction;* we will discuss this later in this chapter.) For example, if the student has responded correctly when you just point to her head but then does not respond correctly on the next trial, revert to pushing her elbow for one trial, praise a correct response, but save the stim toy access, a more powerful reinforcer, for the next trial in which she responds correctly with only the pointing (less-intrusive prompt).

As we noted previously, students with autism tend to become dependent on a prompt; therefore, we recommend using prompts thoughtfully. Depending on what you are teaching, you will need to carefully plan the prompting and prompt-fading strategies. As soon as possible, we want the child to learn target responses, skills, routines, or activities such that assistance is no longer required and the child can perform independently. This is when we know the student has mastered the target skill. Focus Here 3.1 lists a few techniques for fading prompts. Effective prompting is an extremely important teaching strategy. At-a-Glance 3.2 offers a list of tips for effective prompting during DTT.

Focus Here 3.1 Techniques for Systematically Fading Prompts

1. **Decreasing assistance or most-to-least prompting.** With this technique, you start with the most intrusive prompt required, gradually moving to the use of weaker prompts. This works well when teaching new skills because it helps avoid confusion and increases the chances that your student will receive frequent reinforcement (because you don't allow incorrect responses). You can start fading prompts after one correct trial but should return to the intrusive prompt if the student begins responding incorrectly (see Focus Here 3.3: Tips for Error Correction). Adjust your reinforcement so that the more powerful reinforcers are given for correct responses with each prompt-fading step. For example, a teacher gives the discriminative stimulus (S^D), "What's your name?" and the prompt "Jim." If the student says, "Jim," the teacher reinforces heavily and then gives the S^D, "What's your name?" and the prompt, "J—." If the student says, "Jim," the teacher reinforces heavily. If the student does not respond correctly, the teacher goes back to "Jim" as a prompt for the next trial, provides praise, and then tries the prompt "J—" for yet another trial. If the student responds correctly, the teacher reinforces heavily. The next fading step may be that the teacher makes a "J" silently and then just moves her or his mouth as though she or he is going to say "J." Finally, no prompt should be required. As correct responses are obtained for each fading step, the teacher should praise correct responding if more intrusive prompts are necessary but give more desirable reinforcers (e.g., food, toys) for correct responding with less prompting.

2. **Increasing assistance or least-to-most prompting.** Increasing assistance begins with a probe for independent responding followed by the addition of prompts a little at a time, as needed. For example, a teacher might give the S^D, "Put the pencil in the drawer," and wait to see what the student does. If the student responds incorrectly or not at all, the teacher would use a verbal prompt (the least intrusive prompt) on the next trial: The S^D, "Put the pencil in the drawer," would be followed by the prompt, "The drawer by the lamp." If the student does not perform correctly, the teacher would next try adding a more intrusive visual prompt, perhaps pointing at the pencil and indicating the drawer. Only after incorrect responding to the less intrusive prompts would the teacher try a physical prompt, such as taking the student's hand, picking up the pencil, walking the student to drawer, assisting the student in opening the drawer, then hand-over-hand dropping of the pencil into the drawer. Least-to-most prompting may result in several incorrect trials and thus less reinforcement and lower motivation. On the other hand, it avoids the risk of prompt dependence because prompts will be easier to fade.

3. **Time Delay.** Time delay is a procedure in which—assuming that the student is motivated to respond to obtain a reinforcer—the teacher delays prompting for predetermined amounts of time to obtain nonprompted, correct responses. A prompt is added after the designated amount of time, but prompted trials are not generally reinforced. This technique is best for skills that have been acquired and are being practiced. For example, the teacher gives an S^D, "What do you wear on your head?" and waits up to 7 seconds for the student to respond. If the student does not respond, the teacher says, "Hat" (prompt). The student says, "Hat." The teacher quickly repeats, "What do you wear on your head?" Hopefully, the student will respond "Hat," in which case the teacher should deliver reinforcement (e.g., "Yes, good").

At-a-Glance 3.2 Tips for Effective Prompting

1. **Choose the least intrusive but most effective prompts.** Make sure that you give enough assistance so that the student can emit a correct response but not so much help that the student learns to wait for your help.

2. **Wait long enough after an S^D (2–3 seconds) before prompting for the student to respond.** Avoid prompting so quickly that the student does not have time to respond without a prompt.

3. **Only prompt if the student is attending.** If the student is not attending, begin another trial by getting his or her attention and presenting the S^D.

4. **Begin a new trial (present the S^D again) and add a more intrusive prompt if the child responds incorrectly, rather than correcting the child within the same trial.** We do not want to teach a behavior chain in which the child learns to behave incorrectly and wait to be corrected. See Focus Here 3.3 for tips for error correction.

5. **Provide a variety of prompts that can be progressively withdrawn.** Physical prompts may be the most difficult to fade.

6. **Use within-stimulus prompts whenever possible.** Using prompts that directly relate to the S^D reduces the risk of the student attending to the prompt instead of the S^D.

7. **Plan to fade the prompt systematically as soon as possible.** The plan for prompt fading should be specified such that everyone who is working with the student knows how much prompting to administer at any given time.

8. **Give more desirable reinforcers for correct responses that need less prompting** after the student acquires the response at that prompt level.

9. **Probe occasionally to assess whether the response has been mastered independently.** A *probe* is a trial or set of trials given without prompts. Usually, such a set is given when first beginning to teach a desired behavior or skill. As you learned in Chapter 2, we call this type of assessment a *baseline* (what the student can do without any instruction or assistance). You also want to conduct a few unprompted trials during instruction while systematically fading the prompt. You may find that the student can perform independently and does not need further prompting. This type of probe is a return to baseline conditions. We further discuss baseline and other graphing terminology in Chapters 2, 7, and 8.

Step 3: Response

The *response* is the targeted student behavior. Simply put, the teacher must know precisely what he or she wants the student to do so that the teacher will know the best way to prompt it and whether to reinforce a response. Because we never want to reinforce incorrect responding, the response must be *operationally defined,* which means the desired behavior(s) should be specified in measurable and observable terms. Operationally defining a behavior was covered in Chapter 2, and we will talk about writing goals and objectives in Chapter 7. In the case of DTT, it is best to choose discrete, precisely defined student responses that can be communicated to all teaching adults and can be easily counted for accountability purposes.

After being given the S^D and an optional prompt, the student may do one of the following: not respond at all, give an incorrect or incomplete response, or respond correctly. Researchers usually recommend that the teacher wait about 5 to 7 seconds for a response, although some teachers may find that waiting a bit longer facilitates correct responding (Behavior Analysts, Inc., 2001). Some students just need a little more time to comprehend the S^D. What we want to avoid is noncompliance; that is, the student does not want to respond, so he or she waits out the teacher. If this occurs, the teacher should treat the nonresponse as an incorrect response. It is absolutely imperative that only correct responses receive reinforcement.

Operationally defining correct responses will take practice. For example, if we ask a student to imitate our behavior of head-touching (right palm on top of head), will it be correct if the student places her right hand on the side of her head or on the back of her head, or only uses one finger to touch her head? We do not want teachers attempting to decide what to reinforce in the middle of an instructional trial. The decision should be made before the trial begins and should be written down for further reference. Imitating head-touching may be specified as placing the palm of either hand flat on top of head within 5 seconds of the S^D, "Do this," with the teacher placing her or his palm on top of her or his head. At-a-Glance 3.3 provides some examples of well-specified target responses and of poorly defined responses. Photo 3.7 illustrates a correct response.

Photo 3.7. Correct response: Child places an object with a like object in a matching activity.

S^D	Operational Definition	Ambiguous Definition
"Touch red."	Student places hand on the red card or points to it.	Student indicates red card.
"Count the blocks."	Student will pick up one block at a time, placing it in the teacher's hand and counting each one sequentially.	Student will count blocks appropriately.
"Say *cookie.*"	Student will verbalize *cookie* loud enough for the teacher to hear it and will use correct articulation.	Student will say *cookie.*
"Do this" (touches head).	Student will imitate teacher behavior with either hand (touch head—palm on top of head, touch nose—index finger or whole hand only on nose, stick out tongue—tongue protrudes at least ⅛ inch) within 5 seconds of the S^D.	Student copies teacher's behaviors.
"What do you want?"	Student will sign a full sentence, "I want _____" (sandwich, milk, chips) within 5 seconds of the S^D during lunch time.	Student indicates what he or she wants when eating.
"Brush your teeth."	Student will retrieve toothbrush and toothpaste, put toothpaste on toothbrush, turn on cold water, wet toothbrush, turn off water, brush top and bottom teeth, turn on water, rinse off toothbrush, rinse out mouth, turn off water, dry hands and mouth, replace toothpaste cap, put toothpaste and toothbrush in holder.	Student brushes teeth appropriately.

Step 4: Consequence

The reaction of the teacher—or any other adult—to the student's response is called a *consequence.* As noted in Chapter 2, consequences can result in increased student responding, maintenance of the same rate of responding, or decreased student responding. Consequences that maintain or increase future rates of responding are called *reinforcers,* and consequences that result in decreased student responding are called *punishers.* DTT is a strategy for teaching new behaviors or practicing appropriate behavior, so we are most interested in the application of reinforcers as consequences. See Photo 3.8 for an illustration of the use of reinforcement.

The only time you would consider using punishment in DTT is following incorrect responses for the purpose of reducing them. However, if you are conscientious about effective prompting, there should be few trials in which the student responds inappropriately. We also want students to enjoy working with teaching adults and be motivated to do this, so we want to avoid punitive consequences; instead, we should ensure that the students receive frequent reinforcement. If, however, a student emits an incorrect response, you will need to let her or him know that you don't want that response again. We recommend either a mild punisher in the form of a "No," with little voice inflection or expression and little eye contact, or no response at all (i.e., absence of reinforcement). In this way, the student will learn that certain behaviors are followed by desirable consequences while others are followed by not much of

Photo 3.8. Reinforcer: The teacher smiles and says, "Good writing!" as she gives child a treat.

anything. Theoretically, the target responses should increase in frequency and the incorrect responses should decrease.

It is important that you give much thought and consideration to your reinforcement strategies. Remember that students with autism must learn many behaviors, skills, and activities but typically are not motivated to do so. Effective reinforcement (see Chapter 2) will provide the missing motivation. Focus Here 3.2 provides a list of pointers for using reinforcement in DTT.

Focus Here 3.2 Pointers for Effective Reinforcement During Discrete Trial Training (DTT)

1. **Make sure the reinforcers are something that the student desires.** Conduct a reinforcer survey and have a variety of possible reinforcers available. Deliver reinforcers in very small portions to avoid *satiation* (student gets too much of something and will no longer work for it). You can use a carpenter's apron with multiple pockets to keep various reinforcers handy. You will know if a reinforcer is effective by observing how it affects the student's behavior. Does the student readily accept the reinforcer? Does the student seem to want to emit more responses to get additional reinforcement? Does the student try to grab the reinforcer without working? Does correct responding increase or maintain with certain reinforcers? Remember that what works for one student may not work for another student. Sensory input may be the most powerful reinforcer for individuals with autism. Students may work for long periods of time to earn self-stimulation time (i.e., flapping, twirling, rocking). They may also enjoy vibration, favorite music, blowing bubbles, furry toys, and/or a favorite place in the room. For example, we know a teacher who has a remote control for her boombox. After a successful student response, she turns on a favorite song for 3 to 5 seconds and then turns it off in preparation for the next trial.

2. **Manipulate the power of a reinforcer** by depriving students of those things that will be used to reward correct learning responses so they will be more motivated to obtain them. When you are trying

to get a student to do something difficult, which may include *most* new learning in the case of students with autism, the rule of thumb is to use powerful, frequent reinforcement. Usually the most powerful are the primary reinforcers (e.g., food, drink). For student(s) with autism, food preferences are often limited, causing a greater danger of satiation. If you use food as reinforcement, we recommend that you use very small bits (e.g., raisins, Cheerios, Fruit Loops, pieces of cookies, small spoonfuls of pudding) for each trial and not use chewy or long-lasting foods (e.g., hard candy). You should also vary the types of food if the student likes a variety of foods and intersperse with trials that are reinforced by swallows of a favorite drink. Reinforcers will generally be more powerful if the student does not have access to them *except* through appropriate responding. This means that food is not readily available to students, except during mealtimes, unless they earn it, and favorite food may only be available for certain "work." Similarly, self-stimulation is not allowed unless the student has earned the privilege. The good news is that self-stimulation always seems to be a powerful reinforcer for which there is no danger of satiation. The bad news is that many types of self-stimulation are not in the teacher's control (e.g., regurgitation), may be harmful to the student (e.g., holding breath or hyperventilating), and/or may interfere with, rather than facilitate, learning (e.g., staring off into space). Teachers must be able to control giving and removing the reinforcer to obtain instructional control.

3. **Be sure the student can discriminate the consequence.** Positive consequences should be exaggerated and clearly different from the consequences for incorrect responses. We want the student to realize that he or she has been reinforced. Remember that subtlety is wasted on students with autism. Be dynamic, smiling, and demonstrative when administering reinforcement. Be bland and unsmiling after incorrect responses. Teachers will need to make a clear distinction between consequences for correct and incorrect responses to teach students to discriminate between what is expected and what is not.

4. **Make the consequence contingent on the best student response.** We need to teach the student that his or her behavior dictates what the teacher will do next. If the student does what we want, something positive will follow. If the student does something we do not want, nothing or a slight punisher ("No") will follow. Teachers therefore will need to refrain from giving students things just to make them feel good. It is difficult to gain instructional control of and motivate students with autism, so we must take advantage of the influence of reinforcement. Only give reinforcers after the student has given a correct response, preferably the best response. Also, when first beginning training, tell the student why the reinforcer was given (e.g., stating, "Good pointing to red!" while giving the student a raisin).

5. **Deliver the consequence immediately after the target response.** Do not hesitate or make the student wait for reinforcement because he or she may forget which behavior resulted in reinforcement and will be less likely to learn the contingency and to respond correctly during the next trial. Waiting also may allow the student to emit an inappropriate behavior after the correct one. If this happens, no reinforcement should be given. For example, a student is given the S^D, "Say *cookie*." She or he may say, "Cookie," and while the teacher is reaching for the cookie, slap her or his head. The teacher's hesitation allowed self-abusive behavior to intervene. A reinforcer should *never* follow self-abusive behavior, so the teacher lost an opportunity to reinforce the correct response of "Cookie." During the next trial, the teacher should have the cookie readily available to place in the student's mouth immediately after he or she says, "Cookie."

6. **Deliver consequences consistently.** When you are first beginning to teach a behavior, use a *continuous schedule* of reinforcement (reinforce *every* correct response, even prompted ones). As the student acquires a behavior, a reinforcer may be given for every other or every few behaviors (intermittent reinforcement) and given unpredictably, which is called a *variable schedule of reinforcement* (i.e., on an average of 5 correct responses). In either case, be consistent in reinforcing correct responses at regular intervals and clearly *not* reinforcing incorrect responding.

7. **Make sure that the student is able to obtain reinforcers fairly easily.** This means not requiring responses that are too difficult. We want students to remain motivated; we do not want them to get frustrated or discouraged. If a response is difficult for the student to produce, use a more desirable reinforcer. If the response is an easy one, requires prompting, or has been mastered, use less desirable reinforcers. In other words, save the most powerful reinforcers for the most difficult responses.

8. **Use frequent social reinforcement.** We recommend pairing social reinforcement, such as praise ("Good," "Right") and smiles, with any other types of reinforcers that might be used. As reinforcers such as food and sensory input are faded, which they need to be, we want social reinforcers to continue to motivate the behavior. If students with autism learn to like social reinforcement, the teacher will no longer have to use other types of reinforcers. Social reinforcement has the advantage of easy and quick administration under various conditions. In addition, social reinforcement is a more appropriate motivator than food in school and at work. At some point even frequent social reinforcement should be faded if the teacher is to gain stimulus control. For example, no one praises you for stopping at red lights because you are just under the control of the colored light. Another example would be that no one is telling you that you are reading each of these words correctly. You have come under control of the printed letters.

Step 5: Intertrial Interval

The *intertrial interval* is a period of time after the consequence has been given and before a new trial begins. When you are teaching new skills to students unfamiliar with DTT, the intertrial interval may be as long as 3 to 5 seconds. As you become more fluent with DTT, obtain instructional control, and see the student respond consistently to your S^Ds, you should reduce the interval to 1 second or less. This will ensure more responses per minute and serve to motivate the student to keep working for longer periods of time (Fovel, 2002).

The intertrial interval (a) allows distinction among trials, (b) gives the teacher time to record student responses and decide about the next trial's prompts, and (c) provides time to reinforce attending behaviors and establish rapport. In DTT, each trial should be perceived as a separate learning situation. This may seem a bit stilted, but it is easier for individuals with autism if they can easily determine when the teacher is expecting certain behaviors. This distinction also helps teachers stay focused and consistent with the instructional components.

In Chapter 8 you will learn about data-collection techniques that you can use during the intertrial interval. To make various instructional decisions, you will want to know the number of correct responses and the amount of prompting needed. Although you will not need to record every response, you should decide how much and what kind of data to gather for various purposes. Teachers may also use the intertrial interval to decide if the next trial should be prompted and what type of prompt to use.

The intertrial interval also allows time to relate to your student while not requiring difficult responding. If you are using primary reinforcers, the intertrial interval provides time for the student to eat or drink the reward. Photo 3.9 shows the teacher recording data during the intertrial interval. Teachers may want to be playful with the student or reinforce general good behavior. Gradually lessen the time between trials until you are delivering trials at a fluent and fairly rapid pace. For some students, fast-paced trials work best to keep them attending and responding, for example, taking a 3- to 5-second break after every 5 to 10 trials (Carnine, 1976). For

Photo 3.9. Recording response to "tracing name" while student consumes treat.

other students, time between trials allows them to recover from their hard work and get ready for some more. Try to be flexible with the intertrial interval, allowing student reactions and experience to dictate exactly how long or if it will occur.

Error Correction

We have encouraged you to use effective prompting techniques to prevent your students from making errors; however, as you begin to fade your prompts, errors may occur. Sometimes your students will respond either incorrectly or not at all. In these cases, you will need to know what to do to elicit correct responding and prevent further incorrect responding or lack of response. The purpose of a correction procedure is to clearly indicate that the incorrect response will not be reinforced and to begin another trial right away, usually with more-intrusive prompting, to ensure a correct response and some reinforcement as soon as possible.

When you are correcting an error, be sure to present the S^D again (start another trial) before prompting the student. We want to avoid teaching an incorrect response–prompt–correct response chain, which might occur if, for example, a student responds incorrectly to an S^D, waits for the teacher to correct him, and then gets a reinforcer—all in the same trial. Make it clear that (a) incorrect responses do not get reinforced and (b) there will be another trial to obtain the correct response. The error-correction trial may require a prompt, but use the least intrusive, most effective prompt necessary, and try to fade it after one trial. You also do not want to give the most powerful reinforcers during error-correction trials. Save the most desirable reinforcers for unprompted or less prompted correct responses. Focus Here 3.3 provides some tips for error correction.

The following are some examples of DTT scenarios.

Scenario 1

Teacher and student are sitting next to a table, facing each other. A shoe, a sock, and a shirt are on the table.

TEACHER: "Dana, ready?" (pre-S^D).

STUDENT: Looks at teacher.

Focus Here 3.3 Tips for Error Corrections

1. For new learning: As you are fading prompts and the student makes an error, use more intrusive prompts the next trial, praise a correct response, and then fade the prompt to your original level on the next trial. If the response is correct at this point, reinforce heavily. If the student again makes an incorrect response, revert to more intrusive prompting for two trials and consider fading the prompt at a slower pace.

2. Once students can respond appropriately and you are working on more fluent responses: When a student makes an error, the teacher should say, "No," present the discriminative stimulus (S^D) again with no prompt, and—if the student responds correctly—reinforce heavily. If the student makes another error, the teacher should say, "No," again and use a prompt on the next trial. Praise a correct response, move to some other S^D (a different, perhaps easier command), and come back to the original S^D in a few trials with no prompt. If the response is correct, reinforce heavily.

3. Once students have mastered a response and you are probing for maintenance: If a student responds incorrectly, the teacher should say, "No," present the S^D again, and wait up to 7 seconds (time delay). If the student responds correctly, reinforce heavily. If the student again makes an error, use a subtle prompt on the next trial and then present an unprompted trial. More desirable reinforcers should be used for unprompted trials.

4. If students make an error during generalization (different conditions): Go immediately to a prompted trial and then present the unprompted trial again. Use only as much prompting as is believed to be necessary. Correct responding with no prompts should be heavily reinforced.

5. Once students have responded correctly a few times, vary the trials: In other words, mix demands from several skill areas to avoid too many trials in a row on one skill. We want to avoid boredom and promote motivation to participate and learn. After an error, always return to at least one trial in which a response had been incorrect to practice correct responding one more time before the session ends. Teaching sessions should be ended—if at all possible—with success and powerful reinforcement.

TEACHER: "Point to shoe" (S^D).

STUDENT: Points to shoe.

TEACHER: "Good, Dana. You pointed to shoe." Gives a raisin (reinforcer). Records on data sheet and changes position of items on the table (intertrial interval).

TEACHER: Looks at student.

STUDENT: Looks at teacher.

TEACHER: "Point to shirt" (S^D). Points to shirt (visual prompt).

STUDENT: Points to shirt.

TEACHER: "Good pointing to shirt." Gives a raisin (reinforcer). Records on data sheet. Rotates position of items on the table (intertrial interval).

Scenario 2

Teacher and student are sitting next to each other with a book in front of them.

TEACHER: "Michael, ready."

STUDENT: Looks at teacher and then at book.

TEACHER: "What is this?"

STUDENT: Looking at picture, replies, "Boat."

TEACHER: "Good. It's a boat. What is this?" (points to a second picture [S^D]). "Tell me in a complete sentence" (prompt).

STUDENT: "It's a horse."

TEACHER: "Good talking, Michael." Pats Michael's knee (reinforcer). Records on data sheet (intertrial interval).

Scenario 3

Teacher is sitting across a table from student. Teacher has picture cards and real objects (candy bar, lemon, cookie).

TEACHER: "Delise, look" (pre-S^D).

STUDENT: Stares off into space.

TEACHER: "Delise, look." Moves head to front position (prompt).

STUDENT: Faces teacher.

TEACHER: "Good. Match this." Places a picture of a cookie in front of student (S^D) and points to cookie (visual prompt).

STUDENT: Places cookie on picture.

TEACHER: "Good matching!" Pats student's arm and gives a bite of cookie (reinforcer). Records data (intertrial interval).

TEACHER: "Look" (pre-S^D).

STUDENT: Looks at teacher.

TEACHER: "Match this." Places a picture of a lemon in front of student.

STUDENT: Places cookie on lemon picture.

TEACHER: "No" (mild punisher).

TEACHER: "Match this." Places picture of lemon on table (S^D) and points to lemon (prompt–error correction).

STUDENT: Places lemon on correct picture.

TEACHER: "Good matching lemon. Match this." Again places lemon picture on table.

STUDENT: Places lemon on picture.

TEACHER: "Good matching." Gives a pat on the arm and a tickle (reinforcer). Records data (intertrial interval).

TEACHER: "Match this." Places cookie picture on table.

STUDENT: Places cookie on correct picture.

TEACHER: "Good." Gives a bite of cookie. "Match this." Places lemon picture on table.

STUDENT: Places lemon on picture.

TEACHER: "Good." Tickles and pats arm.

Photos 3.10 through 3.14 illustrate another discrete trial sequence.

Photo 3.10. Discriminative stimulus (S^D): The teacher performs an action and says, "Do this."

Photo 3.11. Response: Child imitates the teacher's action.

Photo 3.12. Consequence: The teacher says, "Good job!" and smiles (reinforcement).

Photo 3.13. Primary reinforcer: Child receives a treat.

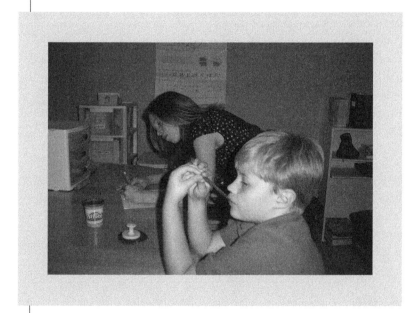

Photo 3.14. Intertrial interval: The teacher records the response while child eats the treat.

Motivating Students to Work

Typically, participation in DTT is not aversive to students with autism. At first, you may encounter resistance to doing the work, but after receiving multiple reinforcers, students will probably learn to enjoy engaging in DTT with their teacher. To keep students motivated to participate and learn, keep some of these suggestions in mind:

1. Initially establish yourself as a reinforcer by giving very desirable reinforcers for easy tasks.
2. At first, do not take the student away from desired activities to engage in DTT. Begin DTT when other, more desirable activities—such as use of a computer or TV—are not occurring. Have a favorite item (e.g., a music box) on the table with you. Once students learn that reinforcement is available in DTT, enticing them to the table will not be necessary.

3. Use effective prompts so that students do not make many errors.
4. Use effective reinforcers and reinforce all correct responses, even those that are prompted. Reinforce unprompted correct responses with more powerful reinforcers.
5. Avoid punishment and criticism.
6. Use a rapid pace of presentation. Eventually reduce the intertrial interval to about 1 second.
7. Have all your materials ready and at the table so down time is kept to a minimum.
8. Vary trials to avoid boredom.
9. Intersperse easy and difficult tasks to take advantage of behavioral momentum.
10. Begin with short teaching sessions (a few trials) and gradually work up to longer sessions (up to 30 to 50 minutes).
11. Make the work fun and ensure that the student is successful.

Planning

To administer DTT effectively, the teacher should develop lesson plans that specify all the major components of a trial for a given behavior, skill, or activity. A good DTT lesson plan will include a targeted behavior, a specified S^D, prompting and prompt-fading procedures, and a well-specified data-collection technique. Figure 3.1 provides a sample lesson plan form. Teachers will also need to develop or adopt data-collection forms that match specific objectives and are conducive to use of DTT. Sample data collection forms are discussed in Chapter 8, and reproducible data-collection forms are located in the chapter appendix. Finally, teachers need to train all adults who might be working with their students with autism. Consistency is an important component of DTT; therefore, everyone needs to become proficient in the training technique and familiar with the completed lesson plans. They also need to recognize the importance of student progress and data collection. We will discuss more about training other teaching adults in Chapter 6.

Things to Avoid

DTT is a highly effective and efficient teaching technique. Like any technique, however, caution must be used to avoid mistakes. New users of DTT often make the types of errors described in Focus Here 3.4. We recommend that you frequently monitor your own use of DTT—and others who use DTT with your students—to make sure these errors are avoided. If a student is not progressing under a DTT program, one or more of the errors listed in Focus Here 3.4 might be the reason.

Advantages and Disadvantages

Unfortunately, much controversy has surrounded the use of DTT (Choutka et al., 2004; Green, 1996; Gresham & MacMillan, 1997; Scott, Clark, & Brady, 2000). This controversy is partly the result of some claims by Lovaas, Koegel, Simmons, and Long (1973) concerning extreme positive effects from use of the procedure with typical children and youth with autism, which have been challenged by other researchers (e.g., Gresham & MacMillan, 1997). However, DTT *has* been shown to be an effective instructional technique for many students with autism for whom other

Student Name: Sam

Goal: Sam will identify common food items.

Objective: Given an apple, cereal, a banana, chips, and the verbal cue, "Show me _____," Sam will point to the correct item 9 out of 10 times for three consecutive sessions.

Reinforcement Schedule: Reinforce on average of 3 correct responses (music box, bites of food)

S^D	Prompt & Fade	Response	Data Collection	Comments
1. Four food items on table in front of student and teacher cue, "Show me _____" (apple, cereal, banana, chips)	Most-to-least prompting technique: 1.1. Take his hand and point to item 1.2. Touch his hand 1.3. Teacher points to item 1.4. Move correct item closer 1.5. No prompt	**Correct:** Sam points to correct items with index finger within 5 seconds of the S^D **Incorrect:** 1. No response 2. Points to incorrect item 3. Picks up or hands item to teacher	**Codes:** + = correct response – = incorrect response FP = full physical prompt PP = partial physical prompt G = gestural prompt V = verbal prompt TD = time delay **Recording Technique:** Frequency counts of correct, incorrect, and prompted responses, and notations of types of prompts	

Figure 3.1. Sample DTT lesson plan.

Focus Here 3.4 Things to Avoid in DTT

1. Allowing student to become too dependent on the pretrial discriminative stimulus (S^D). Fade the verbal request for attention so that the student will learn that when working with teaching adults, attention is required for every trial.

2. Rigidly requiring eye contact when it probably is not necessary. Do not necessarily wait for eye contact or demand eye contact before giving an S^D if the student seems to be attending. Sometimes, however, eye contact is appropriate, and you should prompt it.

3. Using nonassertive verbal S^Ds. Make sure to use enough voice volume and a body stance that elicits attention to your verbal cue. Wimpy S^Ds may not be salient!

4. Repeating the S^D without starting a new trial. Avoid confusion by providing distinct trials.

5. Using ineffective prompts. Make sure your prompts result in appropriate responding.

6. Fading prompts too quickly. Try for errorless learning.

7. Creating prompt dependence. Don't forget to use the least intrusive but most effective prompts and fade them as soon as possible. Use probes to monitor the need for prompts.

8. Using a prompt to correct a behavior within the same trial rather than starting a new trial. Avoid creating a passive learner.

9. Allowing too many incorrect trials to occur. Two unprompted incorrect trials in a row are a cue to add a prompt on the next trial. In new learning situations, add a prompt in the next trial after an error.

10. Punishing incorrect responding without providing guidance for correct responses. With few exceptions, responses should be correct and reinforced.

11. Failing to reinforce correct behavior, including attending and unsolicited appropriate behaviors. Make the entire session a reinforcing activity.

12. Giving the reinforcer without labeling the contingent behavior. Be sure to tell the student which behavior earned the reinforcer ("Good answering!").

13. Pacing the trials too slow or too fast. Avoid boredom and distraction. Avoid confusion.

14. Failing to plan for generalization. You want to obtain stimulus control in natural environments.

15. Becoming distracted. Be consistent. Complete all components of each trial.

16. Adhering rigidly to any format. Be creative and flexible, based on each student's responding.

approaches have failed (Heflin & Simpson, 1998; Lovaas & Smith, 1989; Maurice, 1993; Smith & Lovaas, 1997). Further controversy has erupted because some professionals have promoted DTT as (a) the only way to teach children with autism, therefore recommending exclusive use of DTT in educational programs for children with autism; and (b) effective only with rigid adherence to a program of 40-hour per week one-on-one training sessions. Parents or professionals in the field of autism who promote this use of DTT have brought much pressure to bear on other parents and school personnel to provide this expensive, all-consuming regimen (Devlin & Harber, 2004). The main advantages of DTT are the following:

1. Intensive drill-and-practice opportunities are possible.
2. DTT is easy to train and to conduct, so all teaching adults can use the technique with little training.
3. DTT is easy to implement in a classroom situation.

4. Instruction is clearly scripted.
5. Data collection is facilitated.
6. DTT is an effective way to obtain instructional control of the learner (e.g., attending, sitting, working, regular responding).

We recommend the intensive use of DTT, especially for young children, for learning new skills, and for learning that requires teacher-directed, intensive drill-and-practice. This means that for students who have not learned many skills, who may not attend well, who display many inappropriate behaviors, or who have not learned how to learn, intensive DTT should be seriously considered. Certainly anyone would learn more with many hours of one-on-one training. If you had, for example, a tennis coach working with you that amount of time, you might become a very good tennis player. All children will probably learn better with lower student–teacher ratios and more intensive and frequent instruction. You should try to provide many sessions of DTT per day for those students who need them.

DTT does have some disadvantages, particularly in vast doses. The biggest disadvantage of DTT pertains to generalization. The real world is not made up of short, clear S^Ds with prompts and reinforcement for correct responding. We must aim for stimulus control and for appropriate behavior under a variety of conditions (S^Ds); therefore, the DTT format may need to be loosened as the student progresses, or—even better—another instructional technique, such as naturalistic or milieu teaching (see Chapter 4), might be incorporated. Other disadvantages include the following:

1. Instructions (S^Ds) and reinforcers may be contrived (i.e., do not relate to natural situations), and the teaching session may also need to compete with other, more powerful reinforcers (e.g., favorite activities).
2. The drill-and-practice nature of DTT may teach rote, rigid responding (Sundberg & Partington, 1998).
3. Skills are usually taught in isolation and may impede generalization.
4. The nonfunctional nature of DTT may motivate students to avoid DTT sessions.
5. DTT may not be the best format for teaching socialization skills, as we will demonstrate in Chapter 10.
6. DTT may not be the best method for teaching manding (requesting) and intra-verbal (conversational) skills, as will be shown in Chapter 9.
7. Most students need to learn to work in groups and function independently (that is, without teacher cues to respond). Extended periods of time in a one-on-one, intensive training format may preclude such learning.

Finally, it is often not feasible to provide 30 to 40 hours per week of one-on-one training programs. The child may not be up to that much work or may become overly dependent on one learning format and a few trainers. Parents may feel too much pressure to provide this kind of training every waking hour, at great personal and economic expense. School administrators often struggle to provide extremely low student–teacher ratios, and school personnel struggle to conduct so much intensive instruction.

We do not believe that the only advantage of DTT lies in a 40-hour-a-week program. Although many hours of tennis instruction would likely improve tennis skills, so might fewer hours of tennis instruction. We believe that progress can be documented with as many hours of DTT as it is possible to provide; however, more-intensive instruction is better than less-intensive instruction (Devlin & Harber, 2004). Inspect the formative assessment data and make decisions about what would

At-a-Glance 3.4 Teacher's Checklist for Discrete Trial Training

Planning

- ❑ Have you operationally defined obtainable and functional target behaviors?
- ❑ Have you determined a prompt fading procedure?
- ❑ Have you specified functional S^Ds?
- ❑ Have you trained all pertinent personnel?
- ❑ Did you have data collection forms?
- ❑ Did you have the required materials ready?

Conducting trials

- ❑ Did you have the student's attention?
- ❑ Was your S^D prominent?
- ❑ Were your S^Ds brief and consistent?
- ❑ Were your prompts effective?
- ❑ Did you reinforce appropriate responses and behavior?
- ❑ Were your reinforcers effective?
- ❑ Was the student motivated to work with you?
- ❑ Were your reinforcer and your "No" distinctly different?
- ❑ Did you use social reinforcement?
- ❑ Did you use error-correction techniques for an incorrect response or no response?
- ❑ Did you give the reinforcers often enough to keep the student working and trying?
- ❑ Were your trials distinct and complete?
- ❑ Did you record data after each trial?
- ❑ Did you switch tasks and reinforcers often?
- ❑ Did you end your training session on a positive note?

General

- ❑ Did you graph your data?
- ❑ Did you analyze your data?
- ❑ Did you adjust your lesson plan accordingly?

benefit your students. Refrain, however, from refusing to engage in DTT because you do not like the technique or feel disloyal to the author of another technique. Student needs—not teacher preferences—should guide all instructional decisions.

Furthermore, we do not believe in extremely rigid administration of DTT. We encourage teachers to become comfortable with the procedure and learn to enjoy it. Adhere to the major components, but be flexible enough to make adjustments as students need them. Finally, we believe that parents, paraprofessionals, and related service personnel *can* also learn how to use DTT. We encourage many people to learn how to conduct DTT sessions and to do so whenever new learning, drill-and-practice, or highly structured strategies are indicated. At-a-Glance 3.4 provides a teacher checklist for conducting DTT, and Resources 3.1 provides sources for additional information about DTT.

Resources 3.1 Information Sources for Discrete Trial Teaching

Behavior Analysts, Inc. (2001). *QuickTips: Behavioral teaching strategies.* Pleasant Hill, CA: Author.

DeBoer, S. R. (2007). *How to do discrete trial training.* Austin, TX: PRO-ED.

Chassman, M. (1999). *One-on-one: Working with lower-functioning children with autism and other developmental disabilities.* Verona, WI: IEP Resources.

Fovel, J. T. (2002). *The ABA program companion: Organizing quality programs for children with autism and PDD.* New York: DRL Books.

Leaf, R., & McEachin, J. (1999). *A work in progress: Behavioral management strategies and a curriculum for intensive behavioral treatment of autism.* New York: Different Roads to Learning.

Lovaas, O. I. (1983). *Teaching developmentally disabled children: The ME book.* Austin, TX: PRO-ED.

Lovaas, O. I. (2003). *Teaching individuals with developmental delays: Basic intervention techniques.* Austin, TX: PRO-ED.

Maurice, C., Green, G., & Luce, S. C. (1996). *Behavioral intervention for young children with autism.* Austin, TX: PRO-ED.

Scheuermann, B., & Webber, J. (2002). *Autism: Teaching DOES make a difference.* Belmont, CA: Wadsworth.

Summary

With the information in this chapter, you should be able to teach discrete skills and activities to most students with low-functioning autism and PDD. Of course, DTT is not the only procedure you must master, but if you use it, you are well on your way to success. DTT is known to be highly effective, and we recommend that you use this strategy as often as possible. We believe that DTT should be used more often than is currently done in public schools settings and that all teaching adults should be trained to use it. Because of the high probability of success, we predict that you will greatly enjoy using this technique. In the next chapter, we will offer information about naturalistic/milieu teaching as another strategy based in ABA that has been found to be effective with students with autism and has been recommended in combination with DTT.

References

Alberto, P. A., & Troutman, A. C. (2006). *Applied behavior analysis for teachers* (7th ed.). Upper Saddle River, NJ: Merrill/Prentice Hall.

Behavior Analysts, Inc. (2001). *QuickTips: Behavioral teaching strategies.* Pleasant Hill, CA: Author.

Carnine, D. W. (1976). Effects of two teacher presentation rates on off-task behavior, answering correctly, and participation. *Journal of Applied Behavior Analysis, 9,* 199–206.

Choutka, C. M., Doloughty, P. T., & Zirkel, P. A. (2004). The "discrete trials" of applied behavior analysis for children with autism: Outcome-related factors in the case law. *The Journal of Special Education, 38,* 95–103.

Devlin, S. D., & Harber, M. M. (2004). Collaboration among parents and professionals with discrete trial training in the treatment for autism. *Education and Training in Developmental Disabilities, 39*(4), 291–300.

Fovel, J. T. (2002). *The ABA program companion: Organizing quality programs for children with autism and PDD.* New York: DRL Books.

Green, G. (1996). Early behavioral intervention for autism: What does research tell us? In C. Maurice (Ed.), *Behavioral intervention for young children with autism: A manual for parents and professionals* (pp. 29–44). Austin, TX: PRO-ED.

Gresham, F. M., & MacMillan, D. L. (1997). Autistic recovery? An analysis and critique of the empirical evidence on the Early Intervention Project. *Behavioral Disorders, 22,* 185–201.

Heflin, L. J., & Simpson, R. L. (1998). Interventions for children and youth with autism: Prudent choices in a world of exaggerated claims and empty promises: Part I. Intervention and treatment option review. *Focus on Autism and Other Developmental Disabilities, 13,* 194–211.

Lovaas, O. I. (1987). Behavioral treatment of normal educational and intellectual functioning in young autistic children. *Journal of Consulting and Clinical Psychology, 57,* 165–167.

Lovaas, O. I., Koegel, R., Simmons, J., & Long, J. S. (1973). Some generalization and follow-up measures on autistic children in behavior therapy. *Journal of Applied Behavior Analysis, 6,* 131–166.

Lovaas, O. I., & Smith, T. (1989). A comprehensive behavioral theory of autistic children: Paradigm for research and treatment. *Journal of Behavior Therapy and Experimental Psychiatry, 20,* 17–29.

Maurice, C. (1993). *Let me hear your voice: A family's triumph over autism.* New York: Ballantine Books.

Scott, J., Clark, C., & Brady, M. (2000). *Students with autism: Characteristics and instructional programming.* San Diego, CA: Singular.

Smith, T., & Lovaas, O. I. (1997). The UCLA Young Autism Project: A reply to Gresham and MacMillan. *Behavioral Disorders, 22,* 202–218.

Sundburg, M. L., & Partington, J. W. (1998). *Teaching language to children with autism or other developmental disabilities.* Danville, CA: Behavior Analysts.

Instructional Strategies: Naturalistic/Milieu Teaching and Grouping

Naturalistic/Milieu Teaching

Naturalistic, or milieu, teaching procedures consist of a set of teaching strategies based on ABA principles that primarily are for the purpose of teaching communication and language (Westling & Fox, 2004). The word *milieu,* French for *environment* or *setting,* implies that instruction directly relates to the natural context. These strategies are also referred to as *natural environment training* (NET; Sundberg & Partington, 1998), *natural language paradigm* (NLP; Koegel, O'Dell, & Koegel, 1987), and *incidental teaching* (Hart & Risley, 1975). Naturalistic teaching basically differs from DTT in that the former occurs when students are naturally motivated to behave—usually because they want to obtain something in the environment. These strategies are not primarily used for drill-and-practice purposes because such natural situations do not occur frequently enough; instead, these techniques are very effective for maintenance and generalization training (Kaiser, Yoder, & Keetz, 1992).

Unlike DTT, the antecedent stimuli in naturalistic/milieu teaching situations often occur naturally (e.g., the child sees a water fountain or a favorite food item), and the reinforcing consequences are the desired item. As noted in the previous chapter, in DTT, the teacher presents the antecedent and consequences, which may be unrelated to the student's response. Naturalistic/milieu teaching originally evolved in an attempt to address the generalization problem inherent in trial training by including commonly accepted generalization strategies such as (a) teaching behaviors under various conditions, preferably in natural environments with naturally occurring stimuli; and (b) loosening stimulus control (e.g., Stokes & Baer, 1977). The incidental component implies that instruction (in most cases pertaining to language responses) is embedded in other, often naturally occurring, situations. For example, during lunch, which is the main context, the teacher embeds language instruction for requesting ("Pizza, please") and refusing ("No, thank you").

The underlying assumption of naturalistic/milieu teaching is that the teacher will take advantage of naturally occurring "teachable moments" to prompt and reinforce functional behavior, particularly communication responses. An example would be a student taking your hand and leading you to the cabinet that contains snacks. This is a perfect opportunity to teach requesting (*manding*) and labeling (*tacting*). For example, teach the student to say "Eat," or "I want cookie, please," or "Please open the door," and then ask him or her, "What is this?" before giving it to the student. If you ignore the student or just offer a cookie when the student takes you to the cabinet, you have squandered a teachable moment. For students with autism, such moments are relatively few and far between. Because students with autism may seldom initiate interactions, naturalistic/milieu teaching also allows the teacher to "set up" or contrive situations that are likely to elicit interest. For example, a teacher may hide a piece of the student's favorite puzzle. When the student becomes aware that the piece is missing and looks at the teacher, a teachable moment has occurred. The teacher can now teach language responses or a problem-solving strategy in a meaningful context.

Naturalistic/milieu teaching consists of several features:

1. The S^D is something that interests the student. In some instances, the S^D occurs naturally (e.g., someone turns on a favorite TV program while you are walking through a department store); in other occurrences, the S^D is deliberately constructed (e.g., the teacher purposefully puts a student's coat on the wrong hook). In either case, the student attends to the S^D without the teacher prompting him or her to attend.
2. Student responses result in reinforcement related to the S^D, which is not always the case in DTT. For example, in a naturalistic teaching procedure, a student who asks for the cookie will very likely get it. In DTT, completing a puzzle may earn the unrelated enforcer of a sip of juice.
3. In naturalistic teaching, the student will eventually receive a desired object or situation, even after some incorrect responses. We do not keep the student working until we get a correct response, as we do in DTT.
4. Naturalistic/milieu teaching differs in that instruction is brief and is not repeated until another such opportunity arises. Thus, students do not get massed practice trials, as they do in DTT.

Naturalistic/milieu teaching has been found to be effective for teaching spontaneous speech, sign language, one-word and multiword responses, and use of communication boards and vocal output devices (Kaiser et al., 1992). It has also been recommended for use in conjunction with DTT for students with autism (Fovel, 2002; Leaf & McEachin, 1999; Lovaas, 1982; Scheuermann & Webber, 2002; Scott, Clark, & Brady, 2000; Sundberg & Partington, 1998).

Procedures

Naturalistic/milieu teaching consists of four main procedures:

1. model,
2. mand–model,
3. time delay, and
4. environmental manipulation.

Model

Three things must occur before a naturalistic/milieu teaching procedure can be used:

1. the student must show interest in an S^D,
2. the teacher must control access to the S^D, and
3. the teacher must establish joint attention with the student after noting his or her interest.

The ability to observe students and know what they might be thinking, desiring, or protesting is an important teacher skill, especially when working with students who have low language abilities. Teachers should get to know their students well and should teach other adults about students' preferences and how to recognize them. Students can indicate interest in various ways; for example, they may look at an object, touch it, walk to it, pick it up, act agitated, point to it, look at you, register a different facial expression, show different body language, and/or verbalize. Teachers must *always* observe for interest indicators.

There will be relatively few opportunities to take advantage of such interest on the part of students with autism because they typically have a restricted range of interests, as was noted in Chapter 1. Of course, some S^Ds, such as favorite foods or stim toys, will always evoke interest; therefore, we recommend not making these items easily available. Instead, require students to use language or other functional behaviors to obtain them. Also make sure that the student cannot obtain too many desired objects, activities, and so forth, or create a desired situation without displaying the target behaviors. In other words, once you know what things pique a student's interest, make sure you can determine when the student can access them so you can take advantage of teaching opportunities. Use prompts to prevent grabbing, running, climbing, crying, and other inappropriate responses.

Once you note a student's interest, you should obtain *joint attention,* which means shared attention. This might be accomplished, for example, by also showing interest in the S^D, by prompting (e.g., stating, "Look"), by standing in front of the S^D, by holding the S^D in front of the student, or by physically moving the student's head to face you. Once joint attention is established, you can begin an instructional sequence. When using a model procedure, you will model (or demonstrate) a functional behavior related to the student's desire.

A modeling procedure typically is used for new learning when a student does not know how to perform the target behavior. For example, in the case of the missing puzzle piece, the teacher might have modeled looking on the floor or in the puzzle box to prompt the student to search for the puzzle piece. On the other hand, if the instructional objective was expressive language, the teacher might have verbally modeled, through statements such as, "Where is the puzzle piece?" or "Help me, please." If the student responds correctly, the teacher should immediately praise the student and present the puzzle piece as reinforcement. The teacher might say, "Good searching for the puzzle piece. You found it," and give the student the object. In the case of language development, the teacher might use expanded language with the reinforcement, for example, saying, "Good asking for help. You needed help finding the puzzle piece so you could finish your puzzle," while giving the student the missing piece.

If, however, the student does not respond or responds incorrectly (e.g., screams when she or he sees that the puzzle piece is gone), the teacher should once again gain joint attention and model the correct response (e.g., "Where is my puzzle piece?"). A correct response at this point should be followed by praise and the desired outcome. If the student fails to respond or responds incorrectly a second time, the teacher should provide the correct model one more time (three times total) and produce the puzzle piece (or other desired outcome) unless an inappropriate behavior is occurring. Even though the student failed to emit the correct response, the teacher will prevent frustration and encourage motivation for future interaction by allowing the desired natural consequence. The student observed three correct models while interacting with the teacher. Even if a correct response was not forthcoming, it was encouraged and can be shaped again during a future teaching opportunity.

The modeling procedure can include other types of prompting, although, as with DTT, we do not want to use additional prompts unless they are necessary. For example, a student may be staring at an unopened soft drink in a plastic bottle. The teacher might model by pretending to twist the cap off. If the student has difficulty comprehending the model or does not initially try to twist the cap, the teacher could use a hand-over-hand prompt to twist the cap off. At the next opportunity, however, it would be best to use the model without a physical prompt to see if the student learned the skill. At-a-Glance 4.1 lists modeling steps. The following are some modeling scenarios:

Scenario 1

STUDENT: Sitting on the bus; points to McDonald's across the parking lot and grunts.

TEACHER: Sits in front of student and makes the correct manual sign for McDonald's and says, "McDonald's."

STUDENT: Continues to point to McDonald's.

TEACHER: Again makes correct manual sign for McDonald's and says, "McDonald's."

STUDENT: Approximates the correct sign and again looks across the parking lot.

TEACHER: Manually prompts correct sign while saying, "Yes, that's McDonald's. I bet you would like to go to McDonald's."

Scenario 2

TEACHER: Announces that it is time to go to lunch while standing in front of the classroom door.

STUDENT: Tries to get past the teacher to the door to go to lunch.

TEACHER: Models "Please move."

STUDENT: Continues to try to push the teacher aside.

TEACHER: Stands his or her ground and prevents the student from getting to the door. Models "Please move."

STUDENT: Says, "Please move."

TEACHER: Responds, "Oh, you want me to move. Sure I will." Moves to allow access to the door and lunch.

Scenario 3

TEACHER: Holds up a box of the student's favorite crackers.

STUDENT: Attempts to grab the box.

At-a-Glance 4.1 Naturalistic/Milieu Teaching Procedure: Model

❑ Note student interest in objects or situations.
❑ Establish joint attention with the student.
❑ Give appropriate model for the student to achieve the desired effect.
❑ If response is correct, praise and allow the desired effect.
❑ If response is incorrect, present the correct model again.
❑ If response is correct, praise and allow the desired effect.
❑ If response is incorrect, present the correct model a last time and allow the desired effect unless inappropriate behavior is occurring.

TEACHER:	Says, "Crackers, please."
STUDENT:	Says, "Crackers."
TEACHER:	Says, "Crackers, please."
STUDENT:	Responds, "Crackers, please."
TEACHER:	Says, "Good asking for crackers. These are your favorite kind," and gives one cracker.

Mand–Model

When students have *acquired* (can produce responses at least a few times) various functional behaviors, perhaps through DTT, the mand–model technique can be implemented to encourage use of these behaviors in generalized contexts. In this case, a mand is a verbal instruction or request, such as those used as S^Ds in DTT. For example, a teacher might mand, "Tell me what you want," or "Use your words," when the student tries to push his or her way to the door. With naturalistic/milieu teaching, teachers are encouraged to provide ample opportunities—through the use of interesting materials and situations—for students to use their learned behaviors in various settings during the day. Once the student shows interest, the teacher first gains joint attention and then instructs (mands) the student to produce language or another functional behavior to obtain the desired effect. If the student responds correctly, the teacher praises the student for the response and produces the desired result (e.g., gives the student a desired object when he or she asks for it).

If the student does not produce the desired behavior after the mand, the teacher produces a model for the student to imitate. The modeling procedure may include prompts, if needed. For example, a teacher might notice a student pulling at the back of her pants. The teacher might mand, "What do you want?" If the student continues to pull at her pants, the teacher might mand, "What do you want?" and add a model, "I want potty." At that point, if the student gives the correct response, the teacher should praise the student by stating, "Good asking to go potty," and take the student to the toilet. If the student again fails to emit the correct response, the teacher should mand and model the appropriate response one more time and deliver the desired effect, unless inappropriate behavior is occurring. If manding does not result in many correct behaviors, the student may need more modeling and prompting to acquire the behavior before being expected to emit it in response to a mand. Manding works well in situations involving choices. For example, a teacher may hold up juice and milk (S^D) while using the mand, "Tell me what you want." The student will now need to make a choice with or without teacher models. At-a-Glance 4.2 lists the steps of the mand–model procedure. The following are some scenario examples:

Scenario 1

TEACHER:	Turns on tape of favorite music and quickly turns it off.
STUDENT:	Walks to tape deck and reaches for it.
TEACHER:	Says, "Tell me what you want" (mand).
STUDENT:	Says, "Music."
TEACHER:	Replies, "Please turn on the music" (model).
STUDENT:	Says, "Please turn on the music."
TEACHER:	Responds, "That was good asking. You really like this music. Let's dance." Turns on music.

At-a-Glance 4.2 Naturalistic/Milieu Teaching Procedure: Mand–Model

- ❑ Set up and/or look for situations that stimulate student interest to respond.
- ❑ Note when student becomes interested.
- ❑ Establish joint attention with the student.
- ❑ Present a verbal mand related to the situation of interest.
- ❑ If response is correct, praise and allow desired effect.
- ❑ If response is incorrect, repeat mand and model, if necessary.
- ❑ If response is correct, praise and allow desired effect.
- ❑ If response is incorrect, repeat mand, repeat model, and allow the desired effect.

Scenario 2

TEACHER: Puts money in her desk when it is time for lunch.

STUDENT: Stands at door, rocking.

TEACHER: Says, "Get your lunch money from my desk" (mand).

STUDENT: Continues to rock.

TEACHER: Says, "Leah, get your lunch money" (mand).

STUDENT: Goes to desk and stands.

TEACHER: Opens drawer and gets part of the money (model).

STUDENT: Removes the rest of the money from the drawer.

TEACHER: Says, "Good getting your money. Now, let's go to lunch." Allows the student to leave room and walk to cafeteria.

Scenario 3

Timer goes off in the classroom.

STUDENT: Looks at teacher.

TEACHER: Looks expectantly and says, "Tell me what time it is, Tommy" (mand).

STUDENT: Continues to look at teacher.

TEACHER: Says, "Tell me what time it is" (mand), and then says, "It's time to go outside" (model).

STUDENT: Responds, "Time to go outside."

TEACHER: Says, "It's time to go outside" (model).

STUDENT: Says, "It's time to go outside."

TEACHER: Replies, "Good talking, Tommy. Let's go outside." Allows student outside.

Time Delay

The time-delay procedure is used when students (a) know how to produce behaviors but do not readily do so or (b) need practice in producing responses in generalized contexts. Time delay requires the teacher, when noticing student interest or distress, to establish joint attention and then wait 5 to 15 seconds for an appropriate student response before resorting to prompting. Time delay is especially useful in situations where the student needs some object or some type of assistance. For example, in the situation in which the student finds the door blocked and wants to go to lunch, the teacher could stand his or her ground, look at the student expectantly, and wait. If the student asks appropriately for the teacher to move, the teacher should praise the student and move so he or she can go to lunch. If the student fails to give a correct response, the teacher could use either a mand–model procedure ("Tell me what you want," or "Say, move please") or—if motivation is waning—a model procedure ("Move, please"). A correct response at this point should be followed by praise and the desired effect.

Time delay does not offer as much antecedent support for correct responding as model or mand–model. However, this procedure prevents teachers from offering too much assistance when the student is able to respond independently. In fact, time delay is a prompt-fading procedure (see Chapter 3). Again, the teacher can either contrive stimulating situations or take advantage of naturally occurring teaching opportunities. At-a-Glance 4.3 lists the steps in a time-delay procedure. The following are some scenario examples.

Scenario 1

Teacher puts favorite CD high on shelf.

STUDENT: Reaches for CD. Gets teacher's hand and raises it toward shelf.

TEACHER: Waits passively for 5 to 15 seconds.

STUDENT: Says, "Help, please."

TEACHER: Responds, "Good talking, Patrick. You need help. I'll get your CD." Gets CD and hands it to the student.

Scenario 2

STUDENT: During lunch, begins to eat carrots with her hands.

TEACHER: Moves plate away from student (S^D). Looks at her and waits (time delay).

STUDENT: Tries to grab plate.

TEACHER: Says, "Use your fork" (mand).

STUDENT: Picks up knife.

TEACHER: Says, "Use your fork" (mand). Points to fork (prompt).

At-a-Glance 4.3 Milieu Teaching Procedure: Time Delay

❑ Identify situations in which the student might require assistance or want something.
❑ In these situations, establish joint attention.
❑ Wait 5 to 15 seconds for a correct behavior while looking at the student expectantly.
❑ If response is correct, praise and allow desired effect.
❑ If response is incorrect, implement either mand–model or model procedures.

STUDENT: Picks up fork.

TEACHER: Responds, "Good using your fork to eat your carrots." Moves plate close to student and lets her eat independently.

Scenario 3

Job coach tells student to clean the counters but fails to give him a cleaning cloth.

STUDENT: Sprays cleaner on counter and looks around.

TEACHER: Gains eye contact and waits (time delay).

STUDENT: Says, "I need the cloth."

TEACHER: Responds, "Good asking. Here is your cloth. It would be difficult to clean without it." Moves away and allows student to finish task and receive reinforcement.

Environmental Manipulation

Because naturalistic/milieu teaching is dependent on student interest, instructional opportunities will only occur when there are objects and situations that pique such interest. To utilize these procedures, teachers must provide multiple interesting contexts. Teachers should also refrain from readily meeting student needs. An uninteresting environment and a teacher who does everything for the student will do little to facilitate functional behaviors, particularly communication. The teacher will need to elicit student interest and maintain it long enough to motivate the student to perform. There are several ways to manipulate school, home, and community settings to establish valuable teachable moments. Focus Here 4.1 explains how to use these methods.

Teachers should assess each student to determine those things that are likely to result in appropriate functional behavior or an opportunity to teach functional behavior. For example, you may not want to use disrupted routines or compulsions (see Focus Here 4.1) with a potentially aggressive student until that student learns several language responses or functional behaviors. You may not want to use surprise with students who have very low cognition because they may not recognize the surprise. You may not want to use barriers if students are likely to become extremely frustrated in trying to overcome them. It is also important to remember to progressively use fewer contrived situations so that students ultimately respond spontaneously and appropriately to naturally occurring environmental events, people, and objects. Be creative and attentive and remember that instruction should be occurring *all day long,* not just at specified times in the classroom.

As stated before, naturalistic/milieu teaching is a set of distinct techniques that must be used correctly to be effective. Good teachers will self-monitor their own performance and that of other adults under their supervision to ensure that errors are avoided. At-a-Glance 4.4 contains a list of things to avoid when conducting naturalistic/milieu teaching.

Planning

Although naturalistic/milieu teaching depends on random naturally occurring situations, the procedures will still take a good deal of prior planning. This is especially true if you are going to include environmental manipulation as a way to stimulate in-

Focus Here 4.1 Ways to Manipulate the Environment to Stimulate Student Interest

1. **Disrupted routines.** First teach students simple routines for getting materials, entering and leaving the classroom, putting together materials, making classroom transitions, eating lunch, and using daily living skills. Because individuals with autism typically prefer to adhere to such routines, occasionally breaking a routine will usually generate interest in reestablishing it. For example, after teaching a student to wash his or her hands after toileting, take the student to the sink before he or she toilets to stimulate an appropriate protest, a request to go to the toilet first, or a self-correction.

2. **Disrupted compulsions.** You might stimulate language or problem-solving behavior by interrupting some aspect of a student's compulsive behavior. For example, for a student who likes to straighten coats or desks, you could drop a coat on the floor or move a desk from the line. Be careful when using disrupted routines and compulsions so that you do not cause aggressive behavior. The student must be able to emit a correct response fairly easily to get what he or she wants, or you should use a model procedure and appropriate prompts to prevent anxiety and frustration.

3. **Interesting materials.** Sometimes teachers remove favorite or preferred objects to prevent distraction. You might, however, want to use these objects to elicit communication and other functional behaviors. For example, a student who likes to flap objects on his or her hand may be required to keep favorite "flappers" in a bag on a hook. When the student earns free time, he or she must ask for the flapper bag and describe the chosen flapper before receiving it.

4. **Leave unfulfilled.** Give the student only a limited number of materials or food so that she or he will want more. An example would be to give a student only a fourth of a glass of milk and hold the milk carton near you until she or he asks for more.

5. **Out of reach.** Place desired objects out of reach but within view of the student, or let the student watch as you put them in the cabinet. Require requests and/or expanded language to obtain these objects.

6. **Choices.** Provide many opportunities for the student to make choices during the day through verbal requests, sign language, vocal output devices, or picture choice boards. For example, the student may pick from three computer games by pointing to, asking for, or walking to the shelf to obtain the CD containing the game.

7. **Construct barriers.** Manufacture situations in which the student must seek assistance or figure out how to obtain the desired effect. For example, have the student put mail in the teachers' mailboxes where one mailbox is full. The student will need to ask for assistance to figure out how to handle such a situation.

8. **Surprise.** Use the element of surprise to stimulate responses. For example, put on a student's sweater before going outside. Sit on the floor instead of your chair at the start of group. Hand a student his or her toothbrush and tell the student to brush his or her hair. These actions—and others like them—may prompt communicative or corrective responses.

terest. As with any type of instruction, the teacher should develop lesson plans that specify target behaviors, types of models, and mands that might be required and describe the time-delay procedure, if one is to be used. Furthermore, the teacher should describe various S^Ds that could be established or that regularly occur each day. This lesson plan should also specify a data collection technique so that spontaneous responding is noted, as well as the types of prompts that might be required. Figure 4.1 depicts a sample lesson plan for naturalistic/milieu teaching.

At-a-Glance 4.4 Naturalistic/Milieu Teaching: What to Avoid

1. **Failing to attend to students.** Be a good observer of student preferences and interests and antici-pate student needs. *Everyone* should be observing for teachable moments.

2. **Failing to teach at opportune moments.** Take advantage of every opportunity to teach a func-tional behavior and teach everyone else to do the same. Students with autism have much to learn, and we cannot waste any opportunities to teach them.

3. **Failing to establish a stimulating context.** Provide many reasons for students to communicate or behave in other functional ways. We have to be as creative as possible about motivators because indi-viduals with autism typically are undermotivated.

4. **Giving too much assistance.** Even though we want you to anticipate student needs, we do not want you to meet all of them. When students need something, they are usually more motivated to be-have. We should take advantage of this motivation and shape functional behavior.

5. **Failing to attend to communicative attempts.** Be able to spot behaviors that are communicative in nature. This is the perfect time to teach appropriate communicative and language responses.

6. **Failing to fade prompts.** Remember that mands, models, and other prompts are crutches that must ultimately be faded. We want students to respond correctly to natural S^{D}s without assistance.

7. **Failing to reinforce correct responses with the appropriate related reinforcer.** If the performed behavior results in desired outcomes, the student will be more likely to produce that behavior again in similar situations. This means that we need to teach those behaviors that are likely to (a) get students what they want and (b) get them out of what they dislike. We then need to make sure that their new behaviors work for them. With new learning, reinforcement should be frequent. For old behavior, we should ultimately fade reinforcement and let natural consequences maintain behavior patterns.

8. **Failing to make the teaching interaction short and positive.** Naturalistic/milieu teaching should be short and sweet, and should end on a positive note. The point is to use a naturally occurring teach-ing opportunity to model and shape functional behavior, not to drill the student to mastery. The stu-dent should not become frustrated or anxious. Stop the teaching interaction when the student is suc-cessful, or is still motivated to respond, and provide related reinforcement.

Naturalistic/milieu teaching will be most successful if *everyone* instructs the student at each teachable moment. Teachers therefore need to make all teaching adults aware of various instructional opportunities, target behaviors, and support procedures. Consistency is important to the extent that

- prompts (models and mands) are effective and eventually faded,
- the training procedure is brief and positive, and
- it occurs when the student is naturally motivated to respond, thus resulting in targeted functional behaviors.

Advantages and Disadvantages

Naturalistic/milieu teaching has several advantages:

1. The first obvious advantage of naturalistic/milieu teaching is that students are motivated to respond because they want something to happen. Given that students with

Student Name: Brady

Goal: Brady will spontaneously request food items during meals.

Objective: During lunch, Brady will spontaneously request three food items (pizza, ketchup, milk) by handing pictures of these items when he wants them each day of the week.

S^D	Procedural Steps	Response	Data Collection	Comments
Lunch time with food items (pizza, milk, ketchup) available and Mayer-Johnson picture cards of each item	1. Spontaneous 2. Time delay: Wait 5–10 seconds. 3. Mand: "What do you want?" 4. Verbal prompt: "Hand me the card." 5. Visual prompt: Teacher points to card. 6. Physical prompt: Teacher uses hand-over-hand to help Brady grab the correct card and hand it to the teacher.	Brady hands the correct food picture to the teacher when he wants the food item.	S = spontaneous TD = time delay MQ = mand or question VIP = verbal prompt VP = visual prompt PP = physical prompt	Only provide Brady with small portions of food items as he requests them. Keep all items visible but out of reach.

Figure 4.1. Sample naturalistic/milieu teaching lesson plan.

autism are very difficult to motivate in learning situations, this is a very important advantage because it also decreases the probability of negative behavior.

2. Students' behaviors are prompted and reinforced in natural settings under natural conditions, thus enhancing generalized responding, which is also very important.

3. These strategies target functional (useful) behaviors as opposed to some prescribed, possibly nonfunctional, curriculum. For students with low cognition, everything we teach them should be useful to them now and in the future. We will talk more about functional curriculum development in Chapter 7. Suffice it to say that by design, naturalistic/milieu teaching should always target functional behavior because the student response needs to produce a desired effect for the student.

4. Naturalistic/milieu teaching can be done anywhere and at any time when something captures a student's interest. This increases opportunities to provide instruction and practice.

5. It combines a behavioral model with an interaction model in terms of instruction, approximating teaching strategies typically used in early childhood settings. This is especially important for language and communication training. Naturalistic/milieu teaching uses the behavioral principles of stimulus control, modeling, prompting, and reinforcement while also encouraging mutual engagement, joint attention, and expanded language (Kaiser, 1993). These techniques are especially useful for teaching manding and *intraverbals* (conversational interactions), as we will discuss in Chapter 9.

6. Finally, the components of naturalistic/milieu teaching have been found to be effective instructional procedures for individuals with low cognition (Charlop-Christy & Carpenter, 2000; Koegel, O'Dell, & Koegel, 1987; Westling & Fox, 2004). Resources 4.1 provides additional sources for information regarding naturalistic/milieu teaching.

As with any procedure, naturalistic/milieu teaching has a few disadvantages.

1. There may be limited opportunities for practice of any given behavior if emitting the behavior is dependent on low-frequency situations. For example, if we want a student who is being teased to come get the teacher when teasing occurs, there may only be a few instances of teasing, and the teacher would have to be present at the time of the incident to instruct the student on how to act. Although teachers can manufacture such teaching opportunities, practice opportunities are still limited in comparison to DTT.

2. Even with a creative teacher, a student may show little interest in the environment; thus teaching opportunities may also be limited in these cases.

3. Because we want naturalistic/milieu teaching to occur at *every* opportunity, more people will need to be involved as "teachers." This will require more training, more coordination, and more monitoring. These techniques are more difficult to learn because the teaching is not scripted and the prompting strategies are more complicated and are dependent on the nature of the student's initiation.

4. It is a bit more difficult to gather formative evaluation data (ongoing progress data) during this type of teaching because, for example, you may be in the middle of a mall or on the bus and not have access to data sheets.

5. Finally, naturalistic/milieu teaching is ongoing. There is no end to the session, the semester, or the school day. Although this may be a disadvantage for the teaching adults in that more work is required, it is a definite advantage for the student.

At-a-Glance 4.5 contains a teacher checklist for naturalistic/milieu teaching.

Interaction of DTT and Naturalistic/Milieu Teaching

As we have recommended, DTT is best used for skill development for new skills (language, early cognitive and academics, motor) and skills that require drill-and-practice to master. Naturalistic/milieu teaching works best when (a) student mo-

Resources 4.1 Information Sources for Milieu Teaching

Fovel, J. T. (2002). *The ABA program companion: Organizing quality programs for children with autism and PDD.* New York: DRL Books.

Hancock, T. B., & Kaiser, A. P. (2005). Enhanced milieu teaching. In R. McCauley & M. Fey (Eds.), *Treatment of language disorders in children.* Baltimore: Brookes.

Hart, B. M., & Rogers-Warren, A. K. (1978). Milieu teaching approaches. In R. L. Schiefelbusch (Ed.), *Bases of language intervention* (Vol. 2, pp. 193–235). Baltimore: University Park Press.

Kaiser, A. P., & Grim, J. C. (2005). Teaching functional communication skills. In M. E. Snell & F. Brown (Eds.), *Instruction of students with severe disabilities.* Upper Saddle River, NJ: Pearson.

Kaiser, A. P., Yoder, P. J., & Keetz, A. (1992). Evaluating milieu teaching. In S. F. Warren & J. Reichle (Eds.), *Causes and effects in communication and language intervention* (pp. 9–47). Baltimore: Brookes.

Koegel, R., & Koegel, L. (1997). *Teaching children with autism: Strategies for initiating positive interactions and improving learning opportunities.* Baltimore: Brookes.

Leaf, R., & McEachin, J. (Eds.). (1999). *A work in progress: Behavioral management strategies and a curriculum for intensive behavioral treatment of autism.* New York: Different Roads to Learning.

Lovaas, O. I. (1982). *Teaching developmentally disabled children: The ME book.* Austin, TX: PRO-ED.

Scheuermann, B., & Webber, J. (2002). *Autism: Teaching DOES make a difference.* Belmont, CA: Wadsworth.

Scott, J., Clark, C., & Brady, M. (2000). *Students with autism: Characteristics and instructional programming.* San Diego: Singular.

Sundberg, M. L., & Partington, J. W. (1998). *Teaching language to children with autism or other developmental disabilities.* Pleasant Hill, CA: Behavior Analysts.

Westling, D. L., & Fox, L. (2004). *Teaching students with severe disabilities* (3rd ed.). Upper Saddle River, NJ: Prentice Hall.

tivation to work with the teacher is low, (b) teaching certain language skills (e.g., manding, intraverbals), (c) teaching social interaction skills, and (d) teaching to maintenance and generalization (see Chapters 7, 9, and 10). In other words there are places for both DTT and naturalistic/milieu teaching in your program. We recommend that teachers become comfortable with all of these teaching techniques, plan for them to be used, use them frequently, and train all other teaching adults to apply them effectively. Intensive use of ABA strategies should form the basis for the entire educational program. At-a-Glance 4.6 provides a comparison of instructional components for both DTT and naturalistic/milieu teaching.

Grouping

DTT and naturalistic/milieu teaching can also be accomplished in a group format, which has many advantages. Although children with low-functioning autism might

At-a-Glance 4.5 Teacher's Checklist for Naturalistic/Milieu Teaching

Planning

- ❑ Have you identified potential naturalistic/milieu teaching opportunities for each student?
- ❑ Have you created a stimulating teaching environment and many teachable moments for each student?
- ❑ Have you specified functional behaviors for the student to learn in these situations?
- ❑ Have you specified models, mands, and a time-delay procedure for each situation?
- ❑ Have you trained all teaching adults to conduct naturalistic/milieu teaching strategies?
- ❑ Did you have data collection forms?

Conducting Procedures

- ❑ Did you notice many instances of student interest and communicative behaviors?
- ❑ Did you gain joint attention while the student is still interested?
- ❑ Did you know whether the student could produce some or all of the target behavior(s)?
- ❑ Did you know how much support the student would need to produce a correct behavior?
- ❑ If utilized, were your models and/or other prompts effective?
- ❑ If utilized, were your mands related to the target behavior and were they clear and concise?
- ❑ Did you have a prompt-fading procedure, such as time delay?
- ❑ Did you keep the teaching session short and positive?
- ❑ Did you allow the student access to the desired outcome?
- ❑ Did the student seem to enjoy the teaching session?
- ❑ Did you enjoy the teaching session?

General

- ❑ Did you apply naturalistic/milieu teaching strategies for at least 80% of the instances that a student independently attended to environmental stimuli or attempted to communicate in a given day?
- ❑ Did you collect and graph your data?
- ❑ Did you analyze your data and adjust your teaching strategies accordingly?
- ❑ Did you communicate with all teaching adults about spontaneous student behavior?

learn many things best in a one-on-one situation because of their typical inability to attend and their low motivation to participate with others, at some point they must learn to work with other individuals in a group format. Seldom in integrated school or work settings will a one-on-one format be available, and individuals who need such a format will remain isolated. Group instructional situations better approximate real-world situations. Students who can work in groups will benefit because they learn to work with fewer prompts, thinner reinforcement schedules, and looser antecedent controls; thus, they are not as dependent on teacher assistance. Group formats also allow for peer interaction and more spontaneous language opportunities. Finally, group instruction is more economically feasible because fewer adults can teach more students. In typical classrooms, students who work in groups actually receive more instructional time than if they require a one-on-one format.

At-a-Glance 4.6 Comparison of DTT and Naturalistic/Milieu Procedures

Teaching Component	DTT	Naturalistic/Milieu Teaching
Gaining attention (pre–discriminative stimulus [S^D])	Teacher provides a command to attend.	Something naturally interests and engages child's attention. Teacher must observe or set the stage for that "teachable moment."
S^D	Teacher pre-plans and presents the S^D, usually a verbal cue.	Stimulus is naturally occurring or one that the teacher contrives to motivate the student, usually an object or situation.
Prompt	Teacher plans prompts and fading procedure, which is usually very well structured to motivate responding. This often is a most-to-least prompt procedure with verbal and physical prompting.	Teacher often spontaneously prompts, most often with a least-to-most prompt procedure, usually with mands and models. Prompt depends on nature of child's initiation and abilities.
Responses	Used to teach various responses in all curricular domains, mostly at the acquisition and fluency levels (see Chapter 7).	Mostly used to teach language responses, especially requests. Developed to promote maintenance and generalization of trial learning.
Reinforcement	Teacher pre-plans the types of reinforcers and the schedule of delivery. The reinforcer often is not related to the response (e.g., bubbles blown for correct counting). Only correct responses are reinforced.	Reinforcer is directly related to the response and to what engaged the child's attention in the first place (e.g., child is given a piece of pizza when he or she requests it). The natural reinforcer is given after, at most, three attempts to elicit a correct response.
Trials	Trials are conducted in a series, usually with a 1:1 teacher–student ratio. The teacher and student are most often working at a table. Teaching sessions may last as long as 45 minutes.	Up to three instruction trials are embedded in naturally occurring situations. The trials are more loosely structured. The teaching session should be short and successful.
Data collection	Data are collected after each trial or a set number of trials.	Data are collected after each teaching session or at a later time, depending on the context.
Learner motivation	Teacher manipulates prompts, instructional pace, and reinforcement to keep the student motivated to respond.	Student is naturally motivated to respond to the S^D.
Rate of learning	Massed trials typically result in more rapid acquisition due to intense drill-and-practice.	Although opportunities for teaching trials are less frequent, required responses result immediately in a critical effect, thus offering powerful reinforcement. Motivation to learn is enhanced, and responding in similar situations may occur rapidly.

If a student is under verbal stimulus control in terms of compliance (e.g., "Look," "Jack, your turn," "Do this"), is attentive (makes eye contact, attends to teacher S^Ds), and responds to social reinforcement, group instruction might be effective. You can use group instruction to teach things that might naturally be performed in a group, such as social interaction skills and leisure-time activities. You would not use a group format to teach private behaviors, such as toileting and dressing, nor individually performed behaviors, such as grocery shopping. Group instruction has three possible formats: *sequential, concurrent,* and *tandem* (Reid & Favell, 1984).

Sequential Group Instruction

In sequential group instruction, the teacher teaches each student individually while in a group. Students not being instructed either watch or work on independent tasks. For example, a teacher may be conducting DTT with three students who are sitting opposite her at a small table. The teacher may be working on imitation. She starts to her right, saying, "Paula, do this" (touch head). Paula complies and receives praise and a Cheerio. The teacher moves to the next student: "Alex, do this" (sticks tongue out). Alex complies and receives praise and a Cheerio. Teacher moves to Tommy: "Do this" (touch nose and then touch head), visually prompting some of the response. Tommy complies, receiving praise and a Cheerio. The teacher pauses, praises all three students for good sitting and gives each student another Cheerio. She records responses on the data sheet and moves to Paula for language production: "Paula, what's this?" (book), and so forth. This type of group instruction could also be arranged such that each student is working on a different curricular domain. For example, Paula may be producing language responses while Alex and Tommy engage in fine-motor activities. Students learn to wait their turn, work independently for short periods of time, and attend to S^Ds with more distracters. For more than three students, the teacher might want to invest in a chair on wheels to move quickly from one end of the table to the other. Teachers need to be close enough to each student to provide prompting, if necessary.

A sequential format can also be used in naturalistic/milieu teaching. For example, our three students are sitting at the lunch table. The teacher holds up a can of juice and a carton of milk (S^D). The three students look at the drinks. The teacher looks at Paula and says (models), "Juice, please." Paula says, "Juice, please." The teacher responds, "Good talking, Paula; here is your juice." The teacher obtains another can of juice, makes eye contact with Alex, and waits (time delay). Alex says, "May I have juice, please?" The teacher replies, "Good asking, Alex," and gives him the juice. Obtaining another can of juice, the teacher looks at Tommy. Tommy continues to look at the drinks. The teacher says (mands), "Tell me what you want, Tommy." Tommy signs "milk." The teacher signs and speaks, "Good signing, Tommy," hands Tommy his milk, and quickly records data on her data sheet. In sequential group instruction, S^Ds, prompts, target objectives, and reinforcers may differ for each student, but the students remain grouped for the duration of the instructional session. It is possible to conduct instruction in this format with two to six students, depending on students' skills and levels of compliance.

Concurrent Group Instruction

Concurrent group instruction occurs when a group of students all need to learn the same skill. The teacher gives the same S^D to the entire group and either waits for individual responses or for a unison group response. For example, our group of three may all need to work on imitation skills. The teacher may give the S^D, "Do this" (touch head, or touch nose, or hands up, or clap hands). All three students are to imitate the teacher's behavior. If one of the students needs a prompt, the teacher may provide it, or better, have one of the students provide it. The teacher praises the group and gives tokens or other reinforcers to each individual, if necessary. If a student needs individual instruction, the teacher could conduct one trial, for example, with Paula while Tommy and Alex are counting their tokens.

Naturalistic/milieu teaching also can be conducted in a concurrent format. For example, Tommy, Paula, and Alex are working on puzzles. The classroom timer goes off. The teacher looks up expectantly and moves to the students. The students look at her and she waits (time delay). Paula and Tommy begin to put their puzzles away. The teacher looks at Alex and mands, "Put your puzzle away, Alex." Alex complies. The teacher praises the students: "Good listening for the timer and putting your materials away. It's time to get ready for lunch," and lets them move to the door.

Tandem Group Instruction

Tandem instruction is a gradual move from a one-on-one format to a group format by adding additional students, one at a time. This format works well for students who may not be compliant or may have difficulty attending to S^Ds, thus requiring a great deal of prompting. For example, Michael gets anxious and whines when other students get too close to him. For a few weeks, the teacher works one-on-one with Michael in a quiet area until Michael becomes familiar with the DTT format and has learned some basic skills. The third week, the teacher brings Tommy to the quiet area for one training session with Michael. The time spent instructing both Tommy and Michael in a group is gradually lengthened. Next, the teacher brings Alex to work with the two boys for one teaching session. Once Michael is working well with Tommy and Alex, more students could be added, the length of time Michael spends in a group might be lengthened, and/or the group could be moved from the quiet area. Michael can gradually learn to work in both concurrent and sequential formats with various other students. The point is that grouping is gradually introduced to allow Michael time to increase his attending and compliance skills.

Snell and Brown (2000) have offered several suggestions for enhancing the benefits of group learning by encouraging observational learning and motivation to participate:

1. Encourage students to listen to each other and to take turns.
2. Keep turns short. Give everyone a turn.
3. Use interesting materials.
4. Require attending before a turn is given.
5. Use multilevel instruction at appropriate instructional levels.
6. Teach students to reinforce and prompt each other.
7. Limit wait time by providing a quick pace and limiting group size.
8. Ensure that all students experience success.

Summary

Using the information in this chapter, you should be able to conduct naturalistic/milieu teaching strategies for all your students. Naturalistic/milieu teaching is known to be effective, and we recommend that the strategies be applied frequently. We also recommend moving students to group-instruction formats to encourage social interaction and independent functioning. However, one-on-one formats may always be necessary for teaching new or difficult skills to students with low-functioning autism because intensive, repetitive instruction has been found to be very effective for this purpose.

References

Charlop-Christy, M. H., & Carpenter, H. M. (2000). Modified incidental teaching sessions: A procedure for parents to increase spontaneous speech in their children with autism. *Journal of Positive Behavior Interventions, 2*(2), 98–112.

Fovel, J. T. (2002). *The ABA program companion: Organizing quality programs for children with autism and PDD.* New York: DRL Books.

Hart, B. M., & Risley, T. R. (1968). Establishing the use of descriptive adjectives in the spontaneous speech of disadvantaged preschool children. *Journal of Applied Behavior Analysis, 1,* 109–120.

Hart, B. M., & Risley, T. R. (1975). Incidental teaching of language in the preschool. *Journal of Applied Behavior Analysis, 8,* 411–420.

Kaiser, A. P. (1993). Functional language. In M. E. Snell (Ed.), *Instruction of students with severe disabilities* (pp. 347–378). Upper Saddle River, NJ: Prentice Hall.

Kaiser, A. P., Yoder, P. J., & Keetz, A. (1992). Evaluating milieu teaching. In S. F. Warren & J. Reichle (Eds.), *Causes and effects in communication and language intervention* (pp. 9–47). Baltimore: Brookes.

Koegel, R. L., O'Dell, M. C., & Koegel, L. K. (1987). A natural language teaching paradigm for non-verbal autistic children. *Journal of Autism and Developmental Disorders, 17,* 187–200.

Leaf, R., & McEachin, J. (Eds.). (1999). *A work in progress.* New York: DRL Books.

Lovaas, O. I. (1982). *Teaching developmentally disabled children: The ME book.* Austin, TX: PRO-ED.

Reid, D. H., & Favell, J. E. (1984). Group instruction with persons who have severe disabilities. A critical review. *Journal of the Association for Persons with Severe Handicaps, 9*(3), 167–177.

Scheuermann, B., & Webber, J. (2002). *Autism: Teaching DOES make a difference.* Belmont, CA: Wadsworth.

Scott, J., Clark, C., & Brady, M. (2000). *Students with autism: Characteristics and instructional programming.* San Diego, CA: Singular.

Snell, M., & Brown, F. (2000). Development and implementation of educational programs. In M. E. Snell & F. Brown (Eds.), *Instruction of students with severe disabilities* (pp. 115–172). Upper Saddle River, NJ: Prentice Hall.

Stokes, T., & Baer, D. (1977). An implicit technology of generalization. *Journal of Applied Behavior Analysis, 10,* 349–367.

Sundberg, M. L., & Partington, J. W. (1998). *Teaching language to children with autism or other developmental disabilities.* Pleasant Hill, CA: Behavior Analysts.

Westling, D. L., & Fox, L. (2004). *Teaching students with severe disabilities* (3rd ed.). Columbus, OH: Merrill.

Providing Structure in the Classroom

Individuals with autism work and learn best when they can predict what will happen next, when they are supported as they learn, and when excessive noise, light, people, demands, and surprises do not overwhelm them. In other words, we want to create a predictable environment that provides clarity, order, and support for the students. Under these conditions, students with autism and other neurological impairments do not have to work as hard to understand what is expected of them, so they make fewer mistakes and more often get what they want. Subsequently, they tend to remain calmer, more attentive, more compliant, and more independent in structured situations than they do in chaotic ones. One of the biggest challenges in teaching individuals with low-functioning autism is to motivate them to interact and participate in learning activities. Providing structure may be one of our best motivational techniques.

Adding structure to a classroom means predetermining the type of organization that will facilitate desired responses. This type of organizational support can be developed in the physical arrangement of the classroom, classroom procedures and routines, and teaching materials. Think about environmental structures that help all of us complete tasks or activities. For example, imagine going to a public cafeteria for dinner and that there is neither a predetermined procedure about how to obtain your food and pay for it nor the physical structure to facilitate it. People might be confusedly wandering erratically to place orders, grab food, and pay their bill. Such conditions would not be conducive to a pleasant dining experience. In fact, if you saw such chaos in the cafeteria, you might be very reluctant to enter it at all.

Fortunately, most cafeterias are structured so that people must enter and proceed in single file. No one is told this; the physical organization communicates what is expected. Ropes are often placed to ensure that the line remains single file, even in open areas. Enough servers are provided and spaced such that no matter where you may be in the line, someone is there to wait on you. Food is displayed in an organized fashion, usually by food group (meats, vegetables, salads); glass hoods cover the food so we know that we should not serve ourselves. People must move from left to right down the display line, with only enough room for one person's tray at a time, which prevents more than one person from standing in one spot at the same time. The necessary tools (tray, plates, utensils) are placed at the beginning of the line, indicating that these items should be obtained first, then a salad, then meat, and so forth, in a left-to-right fashion. Payment is typically at another designated area, thus preventing a bottleneck and frustrated diners. People who need assistance with their trays are given it, often without asking. There are high chairs with wheels to facilitate the movement of young children and large-print menus that can be read while waiting in line. The entire environment cues an orderly, efficient procedure; guides appropriate behavior; and, hopefully, results in a pleasant experience. This is the type of structure we want in our classrooms.

Structuring Through Procedures and Routines

An initial strategy for providing structure in your classroom is to pinpoint the behaviors that students and other teaching adults need to use on a regular basis such that learning tasks are accomplished and people remain comfortable and safe. In our example of the cafeteria, the manager knows that the goal is to move many people comfortably through a food line, through a pay line, to tables, through their meal, and out the door. As a teacher, you probably want to move students into the classroom, to their work areas, through learning tasks, to restrooms and the cafeteria, and out of the school at the end of the day. Once you know what you want the students and teaching adults in your classroom to do each day, you will be ready to develop simple, consistent procedures and routines.

Individuals with autism appear to prefer established procedures and routines. In fact, they often develop their own (e.g., always smelling a food before eating it, touching a chair before sitting in it, straightening all the boxes on a shelf upon entering a room). Procedures and routines add consistency, communicate expectations, and provide an orderly process for attaining learning goals. Procedures and routines become S^Ds for desired behavior and responses. Teaching adults also benefit from and appreciate consistent procedures and routines because expectations are clear, more time can be spent on instructing new skills, and students can rapidly become more independent, thus requiring less assistance. We recommend developing classroom procedures and routines for

- entering and leaving the classroom,
- obtaining materials,
- following the daily schedule,
- choosing activities,
- completing activities,
- making transitions,
- waiting,
- toileting, and
- eating.

Once procedures and routines are developed for each of these activities, you will need to task analyze each one and teach it to your students through the use of prompts, practice, and reinforcement. Students with low-functioning autism probably will not learn procedures and routines by watching others or by attending to subtle environmental cues. However, because individuals with autism tend to prefer routines, once they are learned, your students will probably faithfully, and possibly rigidly, adhere to them. At-a-Glance 5.1 provides some sample procedures and routines that might be useful. These are only examples and should be adapted as needed for individual students in your particular classroom situations.

Teach procedures and routines using DTT or naturalistic/milieu teaching. Provide prompts, and fade as many of them as possible. However, some prompts, such as certain visual cues or physical arrangements, may not need to be faded because they appear naturally and may likely encourage generalized responses. Reinforce students for following procedures and routines until they come under stimulus control. The following are some general recommendations for teaching procedures and routines.

(text continues on p. 93)

At-a-Glance 5.1 Common Classroom Procedures and Routines

Entering the Classroom

1. Open door.
2. *Walk* straight into classroom *quietly.*
3. If carrying items, go to cubby, closet, or desk.
4. Place items in proper place.
5. Check schedule.

Leaving the Classroom

1. Put away materials.
2. Go to cubby, closet, or desk.
3. Obtain items to take (e.g., items to go home, lunch money, kickball).
4. Line up at door.
5. *Walk* out of the classroom after teacher gives cue.

Obtaining Materials

1. Walk to the cubby, closet, or desk.
2. Open door or drawer.
3. Remove necessary materials (e.g., pens, pencils, paper, markers, pots, pans).
4. Ask teacher, if you need help.
5. Close closet, drawer, and so forth.
6. Take materials to proper place.

Following the Daily Schedule

1. Go to schedule.
2. Look at picture or word card at top or left.
3. Pull picture or word card from schedule (or take schedule with you).
4. Complete designated activity.
5. Remove that picture or word card.
6. Look at the next item to the left or on top.
7. Repeat steps.

Choosing Activities

1. Walk to the choice board.
2. Choose a picture, description, or item.
3. Take the picture, description, or item with you.
4. Go to the activity of choice.
5. Replace the picture, description, or item after completing the activity.

Completing Activities

(This will require cues to indicate when something is finished, such as finished boxes, bells, timers, or jigs).

1. Keep working until
   - finished box is full.
   - card is filled with tokens.
   - timer is sounded.
   - bell sounds.
   - music stops.
   - teacher stands up.
2. Put materials away.
3. Go to schedule and check it.

Making Transitions

1. Listen/watch for cue.
2. Stop working, eating, or playing when cue is given.
3. Stand up.
4. Check schedule.
5. *Walk* to wait chair or area if
   - others are not ready.
   - the bell has not sounded.
   - teacher says to wait.
6. Line up if leaving room in a group.
7. *Walk* to next activity or place.

Waiting

1. Listen/watch for cue to wait (teacher command, hand signal, red light).
2. Go to wait place (bench, chair) and sit.
3. Choose a wait activity (e.g., comic book, hand-held computer, MP3 player with headphones) and *quietly* perform activity.
4. Stop activity when there is a cue to move to next activity.
5. Put material away and move to next place.

Toileting

1. Ask to use toilet (signs, pictures, speech).
2. Wait for teacher to open bathroom door.
3. Go into bathroom and close door.
4. Go to toilet.
5. Pull down pants (or unzip pants).
6. Sit on toilet (or stand facing toilet).
7. Eliminate.
8. Pull up pants (zipper).

9. Flush toilet.
10. Go to sink and wash hands.
11. Dry hands.
11. Walk out of door.

Eating

1. Wash hands before sitting at table.
2. Sit with feet on floor and face front. Scoot chair close to table.
3. Put napkin on lap (or in shirt collar).
4. Shake milk and open carton.
5. Cut meat, if necessary.
6. Using fork or spoon, take a bite.
7. Keep second hand on lap.
8. Chew quietly, with mouth closed.

Teach a First–Then Procedure

Teach students to engage in activities in some set order. Teaching them a first–then order facilitates their understanding of the relationships among the steps of a procedure, the actual routines, and the students' own behavior and consequences. For example, teach your students to *first* work, *then* play. Or *first* pay attention, *then* respond. Or *first* wash hands, *then* dry hands. Or *first* check the schedule, *then* go to next activity. Or *first* comply, *then* receive a cookie bit. Establish the words *first–then* and cards with *first* and *then* printed on them as cues. Once the students learn to trust that you are not telling them they cannot have what they want but just that they need to perform another behavior first, they will become more compliant.

Teach Left–Right Orientation and Top–Down Orientation

Teach students to approach tasks either from left to right or from top to bottom. For example, reading and writing are from left to right, as are many work tasks, such as sorting and assembling. Pictures depicting daily schedules are usually arranged top–down, as are many life-skills procedures (e.g., drying after a bath, loading a dishwasher). Once a student learns to approach tasks in this way, many unfamiliar activities and tasks may become easier.

Teach Waiting

Teach students how to wait, which they will need to do in many life activities (e.g., to get lunch in the cafeteria, to board the bus, to buy a theater ticket, to do banking). Individuals will also be required to wait a turn, wait for others to get ready, wait to use the rest room, or wait for a bus or airplane. Learning how to wait consists of several components that teachers should consider when developing waiting procedures. For example, students will need to learn

- various cues for waiting (e.g., someone says "wait," the bathroom door is locked, and others are standing in line);
- where to wait (e.g., in line, in a waiting chair, in a waiting area);
- a waiting activity, such as looking at a book, listening to an audio player, or playing with a hand-held computer; and
- cues for "finished" waiting, such as, "It's your turn in line," the bus comes, someone comes out of the bathroom.

Waiting requires a variety of behaviors under various conditions, so simple waiting routines should be introduced early in the educational program and taught to generalization as soon as possible.

Teach Finishing

The concept of *finishing something* is also complex. There are many cues for finishing (e.g., food is gone, timer sounds, time of day, someone says to finish, people move away or people gather around). The word *finish* also has various meanings. For example, "Finish your dinner" means to eat it whether you like it or not. "Finish your work" means to do it all or complete the current step. "Finish playing" means to put up the toys and go to bed. A book is finished when the last page is read. Individuals with autism will need help in determining when something is finished or how much more remains before it is finished. We will talk about ways to cue *finished* later in this chapter.

Refrain From Changing Routines and Procedures

Once you have established routines and procedures and your students follow them regularly, refrain from changing them unless there is a good reason, such as trying to stimulate language production or loosen stimulus control. Individuals with autism typically find great comfort in routines and often become distressed when they are broken. We should take advantage of their preference for order and teach behavioral sequences that will enhance their learning and serve them well into adulthood.

Structuring Through Visual Schedules

Once procedures and routines have been developed, the teacher should then schedule the various classroom activities and people to enhance learning and independent functioning. Classroom schedules, which should be displayed visually, come in two basic types: *whole-class schedules* to clarify teaching activities and *individual schedules* to clarify each student's tasks and activities.

Whole-Class Schedules

One of the most important tasks for teachers of students with autism involves organizing the school day so that students and the teaching adults know what is expected of them. Our goal should be to keep students productively engaged in learning activities for at least 80% of the school day because students with autism learn slowly and we cannot afford to waste any instructional time. Keeping students engaged means planning instructional activities for the entire day and organizing the teaching adults (e.g., teaching assistants, speech therapists, occupational therapists and physical therapists, peer tutors, shadows) to engage them. Teachers will need to carefully plan and clearly communicate a daily and/or weekly schedule.

The schedule should be posted prominently in the classroom so that everyone can see it and understand it. It should also be constructed such that changes are easily communicated when, for example, someone is absent or speech therapy is canceled. The schedule could be written on the board each week, written on a laminated poster board, or developed as an overhead transparency projected on the wall. We recommend that the whole-class schedule include all activities for all students for the entire school day. It should also specify which adult has primary responsibility for each student at any given time. Figure 5.1 provides a sample classroom schedule.

You might want to consider the following questions when constructing whole-class schedules:

1. *What regular routines must occur at certain times each day?* Examples include bus arrivals and departures, lunch periods, recess, and toilet times. You will need to schedule instructional activities to accommodate these pre-set activities.

2. *How many teaching adults (or peers) are involved throughout the week?* Obtain related service schedules and request that these schedules not be changed without notice. For example, the speech therapist may work with three of your students on Monday morning and one student on Thursday afternoon. You will need to factor such activities into each student's schedule, and in your whole-class schedule, you should take advantage of the lower student–teacher ratio during those times. We recommend that if you are teaching in a self-contained classroom with several low-functioning students, you might ask the related-service personnel to come into your classroom to work in tandem with you to provide services instead of having the students move to another room. For example, on Monday morning the speech therapist can work with her group of students in one section of the room while you and the teaching assistant work with other students on language and communication goals. Or, the speech therapist can work with you to instruct a group of students in social communication. Or, the speech therapist might join you and your class for lunch, assisting with speech production during a time when the students might be most motivated to communicate. Such a structure will reduce the number of physical transitions required for students, possibly lessening their anxiety, and will allow teachers and teaching assistants to benefit from the expertise of related-service personnel. We will further discuss managing the various teaching adults in Chapter 6.

3. *What does each student need to learn?* Examine each student's goals and objectives and decide which things need to be taught intensively and which things need distributed practice. Make sure that each student is receiving adequate amounts of instruction for each designated objective.

4. *What is the typical length of teaching sessions?* For young children, one teaching session may initially be as short as 2 to 3 minutes. For scheduling purposes, however, sessions might be arranged by curricular area in 30-minute blocks. This allows for transitions and for about 20 to 25 minutes of naturalistic/milieu teaching in other skill areas. Older students, on the other hand, may be expected to work on a given task for up to 45 minutes. Generally speaking, teaching sessions might be a bit shorter for one-on-one situations because instruction is more intense.

5. *Will students be grouped for instruction, or do they require one-on-one instruction?* For students requiring one-on-one instruction, determine how many teaching sessions could be tolerated in a given day. It would be best to schedule at least two teaching adults

Weekly Schedule

Teacher: Deb   **Teaching Assistants:** Mary Jo, Dan, Carol

Time	Deb	Mary Jo	Dan	Carol	Other
8:00–8:15	Morning prep Planning/charts	Morning prep	Bring students from bus	Morning prep	
8:15–8:30	Morning prep	Students 1, 2, 3, 4, 5, 6, 7, 8 Checking individual schedules			
8:30–9:00	Child 1: Expressive sign	Children 4, 7, 8: Discrimination tasks	Child 5: Self-help skills	Child 6: Receptive language	Child 2: Speech group
9:00–9:30	Children 4, 7, 8: Expressive language	Children 1, 5: Receptive language	Children 2, 3: Discrimination tasks	Child 6: Self-help skills	
9:30–10:00	Children 1, 4, 8: Self-help skills	Children 2, 4: Prevocational activities	Children 5, 7: Fine-motor skills	Child 3: Gen. ed. music	Child 6: Occupational therapy
10:00–10:30	All students toilet and snack				Speech therapist for snack time
10:30–11:00	Child 6: Expressive language	Children 2, 4, 5: Imitation	Break	Children 3, 7, 8: Independent/ cognitive	Child 1: Peer tutor
11:00–11:30	Children 2, 4, 5, 6, 7, 8: Group language and singing.			Children 1, 3: Prevocational tasks	General education peers for singing
11:30–11:45	Preparation for lunch break Toilet, wash hands, groom, lunches, and money				
11:45–12:30	Expressive language (all students during lunch)	Break	Lunch supervision (all students)		
12:30–12:45	Break	Return to class, wash hands, check schedules			
12:45–1:15	Child 1: Receptive language	Child 3: Computer work	Children 4, 6, 7, 8: Social skills	Child 5: Gen. ed. physical education	
1:15–1:45	Children 1, 3, 4, 6, 7, 8: Leisure activities			Child 2: Gen. ed. computer class	
1:45–2:15	Children 2, 3, 5: Social studies	Children 1, 6, 7: Cooking	Child 8: Functional reading	Child 4: Work & McDonald's	
2:15–2:45	Children 2, 3, 5: Conversations		Child 8: Functional math		Peers for conversation
2:45–3:00	Children 1, 2, 3, 5, 6, 7, 8: Preparation for departure—toilet, wash				

Figure 5.1. Sample classroom schedule.

to rotate sessions to prevent boredom and facilitate generalization. For students who will be grouped, decide when they will be grouped and with whom.

6. *Does your classroom arrangement match your scheduled activities?* Are there quiet areas for instructing students who are inattentive during noisy times? Do students need access to bathrooms, the kitchen, or the laundry in the afternoon to learn self-help, work, and/or domestic skills? Try not to schedule too many students in the same space at the same time. Make sure the place that is set up for teaching is the best place for the student to learn the target objective. Try to schedule teaching in natural contexts as much as possible (i.e., naturalistic/milieu teaching) to facilitate generalization.

7. *Do students have integrated experiences outside the classroom?* If students are receiving community-based instruction, are engaged in work experiences, or are spending time in general education classes, note these on the schedule and note the person assigned to monitor student participation in those settings.

Individual Schedules

In addition to a whole-class schedule, your students with autism will most likely benefit from individual schedules, which can provide the student with information such as the following:

What activities are happening that day and in what order

What new activities might be occurring

What regular activities may not be occurring that day

What activities may have been changed (Hodgdon, 1995b)

Providing such information for each student will enhance motivation, compliance, and independence. Individual schedules are usually displayed visually for easier understanding, but they could also be dictated (e.g., on an audiotape or iPod) if the student responds well to auditory commands. The visual individual schedule might consist of concrete objects representing an activity, a written list, a sequence of pictures (either placed left–right or top–bottom), line drawings, or some combination of these options.

One way of providing structure is by teaching students to use individual schedules. The following are recommendations for making and using these schedules.

1. *Begin by teaching matching and sequencing.* Because students will need to be able to match the schedule symbol or object to the designated activity, teachers should teach matching skills early in the educational program. Once matching in general has been mastered, teach each student to match specific symbols or objects to specific activities or locations (e.g., matching objects, matching colors, matching pictures, matching words). Students will also need to be able to pick symbols in a sequence (top–down or left–right). For students with severe mental retardation, these two skills may take some time to teach; however, individual schedules will not be functional without them.

2. *Begin with concrete objects to represent scheduled tasks and activities.* If students do not understand symbols (pictures, line drawings, or the printed word), use concrete objects. For example, a spoon signifies lunch, an audiotape signifies music time, a small ball signifies physical education, a bolt signifies vocational time, a small chair or a piece of leather signifies the beanbag chair (leisure time). Concrete objects can be placed in cubbies, put in boxes, or Velcroed onto some type of backing. Attempt to move to more abstract symbols as soon as possible because concrete objects are not as portable, versatile, or unobtrusive as pictures and symbols. This means you will need to teach matching

objects to abstract symbols. One popular source of various-size abstract symbols (photos, line drawings, printed words) is available from the Mayer-Johnson Company (1994).

3. *Work toward printed schedules.* Although printed schedules are certainly the most versatile and efficient, students who never learn to read can probably be taught to interpret line drawings as symbols for activities and tasks. Pictures (actual or symbolic) are also viable. Pairing pictures and drawings or words and drawings allows anyone who is unfamiliar with the symbols to understand the schedule. If students master one-word descriptors, work toward two- and three-word descriptions (e.g., computer math work).

4. *Make the symbols salient.* The schedule symbols should stand out from the background material. Use a bold and large font, highlighting, and colors to draw the student's attention to the symbols. Once the student begins to decipher the symbols consistently, match the symbols to words and then fade these types of within-stimulus prompts so that typical everyday symbols, such as written schedules, begin to cue behavior.

5. *Provide finished indicators.* Finishing a task or activity can be indicated in several ways. The student can place a symbol in a different spot that signifies *finished*. The finished spot may in a designated pocket or in a "finished" box. The student may be taught to cover up each completed activity symbol with a black card (these would also need Velcro) or with a card that says *finished*. The student may be taught to turn the activity symbol around so only the back is visible once the activity is completed. You may teach students who can read to cross through the activity description or check it off. Laminating the schedules allows the students to erase the marks at the end of each day and reuse the schedule the next day.

6. *Develop schedules that are flexible.* Schedules will inevitably change as school-wide activities change and as the student progresses through the curriculum. We therefore recommend using a format that allows for daily changes. Include a pocket with extra symbols or words so sudden changes can be depicted visually.

7. *Use Velcro to affix objects or pictures to the schedule card.* Velcro will have many uses in instructional materials for students with low-functioning autism. Decide which side of the Velcro will adhere to objects and which side will adhere to backings so that you will be able to interchange schedule symbols across students and formats.

8. *Match the type of schedule to individual student characteristics.* Consider student preferences and cognitive abilities when developing a schedule. Some students may always rely on concrete representations while others may move quickly through pictures to the printed word. Some students may not like the sound or feel of Velcro backing. For these students, you could paste pictures onto the schedule or place pictures in library-card pockets that are affixed to the schedule card.

9. *Work toward portable schedules.* Schedules that are portable will allow students to use them in a wider variety of situations, for example, at a work site so the student will see a sequence of activities in that setting or the mall so the student can proceed through various shopping activities. A portable schedule might be taken on a trip in the car to indicate appropriate behavior. A schedule attached to a wall may not be as useful across settings as one that travels with the student. Possible materials that can be used for schedules include small notebooks or laminated poster board or construction paper. Schedules can be developed to fit into fanny packs, pockets, backpacks, wallets, or purses. Because most students with autism are ambulatory, portability should be a major consideration.

10. *Teach a routine of checking the schedule as each activity is completed.* Teach students the routine of checking their schedules after each task or activity is completed or in response to other cues (e.g., entering the class in the morning, timer, bell). We want to have each student eventually be able to come into the classroom, determine what he or she is to do, obtain the necessary materials, and get to work without teacher prompting. Similarly, we want to teach students to complete assignments, put materials away, and begin the next assignment without teacher prompting. Having the individual schedules guide students through these routines frees teaching adults to instruct students in other areas.

Figure 5.2 depicts some sample individual schedules. The left-top quadrant shows a series of boxes or cubbies containing concrete objects that represent learning activities in order from left to right. The soap bar represents toileting activities, such as washing hands; the spoon represents snack time; the stapler represents prevocational activities, such as collating; the plastic toilet represents a bathroom break. Students learn to carry the object with them to the activity and return it to the schedule area. A finished box is provided underneath or to the right of the cubby boxes so that the student can place the object in the finished box at the completion of the designated activity, moving to the next box to the right of the empty box to determine what to do next.

The right-top quadrant shows a schedule that matches small plastic objects with picture symbols to assist students in learning that the picture—not the object—indicates activities. Both the objects and the pictures are Velcroed onto the wall or a bulletin board. Both the object and the picture can be removed to indicate the beginning of an activity and placed in the finished folder upon completion. Remove the concrete objects gradually until the pictures alone guide the student to the appropriate activity. The bottom-left quadrant depicts multiple picture schedules with a top–down orientation. The pictures are Velcroed onto wide ribbons or poster strips and attached to the wall. Pictures are removed and placed into the finished box at the bottom of each strip to indicate that the activity has been completed.

Two variations on the finished box are to have a "finished" poster strip directly to the right of each schedule. As students complete an activity or task, they place the picture on the Velcro on their finished strip. In this way, the teacher can exchange the strips at the end of the day and not have to reconstruct the schedules for the students. Some teachers may find it convenient to have the students simply turn the pictures around, with the picture facing inward, as a sign that the activity has been completed. This would require small Velcro strips on each side of the picture. The last quadrant shows a written schedule matched to pictures to help students learn to read and respond to words rather than pictures. The pictures should be Velcroed so that they can gradually be removed and the student can be guided by words alone, as most of us are.

To be able to utilize individual schedules, the students will need to learn the following procedures:

Obtain their schedule upon entering the classroom

Review the schedule for the day

Check the schedule during transition times

Perform each task or activity signified by the picture, word, descriptor, or object in the order designated by the schedule

Designate that the task or activity has been completed

The students are often able to remove the word, picture, object, or activity symbol because it is Velcroed to a ribbon, to a poster board, to a clipboard, in a notebook, or on other backing. They can then take the schedule symbol to the designated area and match it to an activity. This becomes an S^D for beginning work. Once the task or activity is complete, students should be taught to signify this by placing the descriptor into a finished box, crossing it off, turning it over, or placing a finished symbol over it. Indicating *finished* cues a student (an S^D) to move to the next item on the schedule. The point is that the schedule acts as a cognitive organizer that prepares the student for what comes next and provides a procedure for recognizing the end of an activity and the commencement of another. Many of us use similar

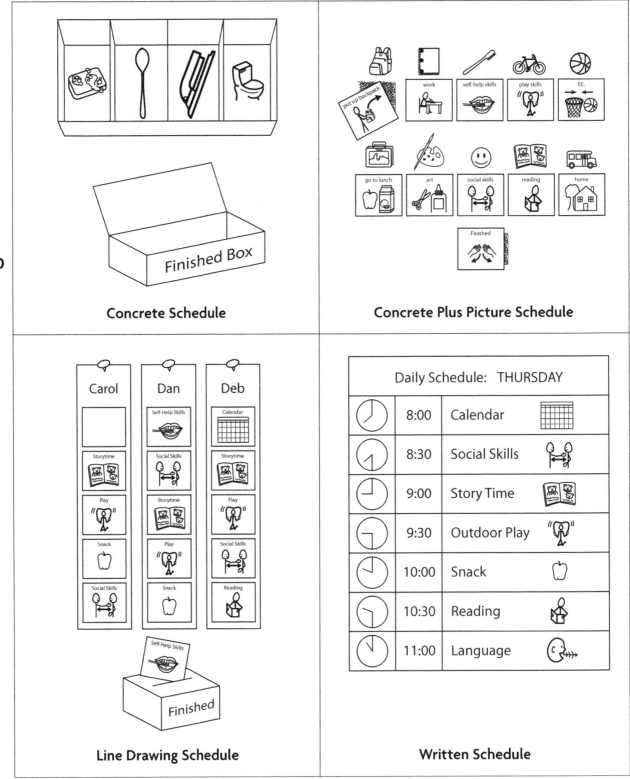

Figure 5.2. Sample individual schedules (concrete, pictures, line drawings, written).

visual supports in the form of lists or notations on a calendar that we check off or cross out throughout the day.

An individual schedule can also act to prevent inappropriate behavior or to redirect students who are engaging in inappropriate behavior. For example, if a student usually goes to lunch at 11:30 A.M., but today lunch will not occur until noon because of a school-wide assembly, a teacher could use the schedule to prevent the student from becoming upset about the change. The teacher could go over the schedule in the morning, pointing out the lunch change; have the student look at the schedule several times during the morning, reiterating the lunch change; and use the schedule to indicate that lunch will follow group time so the student will not think he or she has missed it. In addition, the schedule can be used to redirect students. For example, a student wanders to the corner and begins twirling a toy. The teacher could bring the schedule to the student (or the student to the schedule) and point to the next activity. If the schedule indicates that it is time for sorting tasks and toy time is later, compliance may very likely follow.

In Chapters 9 and 10 we will describe various ways to use schedules to enhance communication and socialization. For example, students can use a schedule to initiate discussion with parents or peers about what happened that day (Downing & Peckham-Hardin, 2001). If the schedule travels between home and school, it provides an opportunity for the teacher and parents to comment on activities, perhaps with sticky notes. An example would be schedules kept in a slide holder in a notebook so notes can be easily inserted. Schedules could also be used to enhance academic skills (Downing & Peckham-Hardin, 2001), such as including numbers to indicate how many tasks or activities are to be completed. A student may have to set five place settings for lunch (simple number recognition) or may be asked to match words on the schedule or place a card with the first letter of the word on the schedule symbol. Some students may be able to write their own schedules. At some point, schedules might become more than just a list of tasks or activities, incorporating information about what materials are needed for each activity, how long the activity should occur, and step-by-step instructions.

Structuring With Visual Supports

Individual schedules are one type of what we call *visual supports,* which are physical stimuli—such as body language, objects, physical structures, pictures, photographs, labels, printed materials, and organizational tools—that visually cue an individual to take action, not to take action, communicate, or just cognitively process something. Most people prefer visual cues because auditory cues are transient; they don't stay around for you to check at a later time and information told to you may be easily forgotten. If the information is provided in a visual form, however, you can repeatedly refer to it if needed. For example, you may attend a workshop about teaching students with autism. The presenter may lecture about the various strategies discussed in this book. How much would you remember without handouts, overhead transparencies, and perhaps the book itself? Reliance on visual aids is common. Visual aids may be imperative for individuals with autism because they have problems attending in general to environmental stimuli, particularly auditory stimuli. Transient stimuli make attending more difficult, while static stimuli (nontransient) assist attention and information processing (e.g., Dalrymple, 1995).

The cafeteria example we provided earlier in this chapter depicts the use of visual supports to facilitate the movement of large numbers of people through a fairly complex activity. Schools contain many types of visual supports: clocks, maps, signs, posters, and so forth. Your students with autism will need to learn to attend to and interpret these naturally occurring visual cues. They will also need additional cues to help them understand what to do or not do. We recommend that teachers think of various ways to use visual supports for instructional purposes, such as providing information, clarifying directions, locating destinations, making choices, and organizing the environment (Hodgdon, 1995a, 1995b).

Visual Support Through Physical Organization

One way to provide visual cues for students is through the physical arrangement of the classroom. You want students to perform in certain ways while preventing inappropriate behavior and lowering anxiety levels. You can use room dividers, bookshelves, window shades, tape on the floor, rugs, lockers, desks, plastic bins, labels, pictures, and partitions to indicate behavioral and curricular expectations. For example, you may have footprints on the floor that indicate where students are to walk, place tape on the floor in the shape of a chair to indicate where furniture should be placed, or put pictures and labels on shelves to indicate where materials are to be stored. The following are some general rules for classroom arrangement.

Communicate Curricular Expectations

Arrange your classroom such that specific areas designate particular activities. If you arrange your classroom to match your curriculum, students will learn quickly that being in certain areas indicates certain activities. For example, if the curriculum in an elementary classroom consists of language/communication training; self-help skills, such as toileting and eating; leisure skills, such as listening to music and art projects; and social skills, such as responding in a conversation, the classroom should be arranged to reflect this. There may be an area containing a few semicircle tables and chairs where language training and conversations are to occur. There may be an area with CD players, art supplies, and a round table for art and music activities. There may be a bathroom within the classroom and a long table for students to gather while having a snack. If independent work is required, there may need to be an area containing a few student desks arranged in a row and materials in nearby storage units. A free-time area might be on a carpet with the teacher's desk placed in a clearly separate location. Try to keep each area visually distinct. This can be accomplished by using partitions, carpets, or tape on the floor. It might also be accomplished through the use of color. Colors may be used to indicate each area of the room and the materials that match that area so that it is clear where students are to go and what they are to bring with them. For example, the communication table may have a yellow circle on it, yellow tubs with instructional materials may sit close by, yellow arrows lead to the communication area, and a yellow activity card cues each student to move to that area. All leisure activities might be marked with a blue label, blue tape outlines the area, and the shelves where leisure materials are stored are outlined in blue paper. We also recommend labeling everything (areas, materials, furniture) using print, pictures, and/or line drawings.

Eliminate Distracters

Try to eliminate visual distracters. Work areas, for example, should be free of mirrors, flickering lights, windows, and mobiles. You may want to cover windows if students are distracted by outside activities. As you get to know your students, you will learn the types of stimuli that elicit their attention. If possible, use such stimuli to focus attention on desired activities but mask or eliminate them if they draw attention away from instruction. For example, free-time areas should not be near work areas, as they may be distracting.

Manage Behavior

If students display inappropriate behavior, such as running away, lying on the floor, acting aggressively, screaming, or grabbing, arrange the environment to eliminate the antecedents for such behavior. For example, do not seat a student who runs near a door, and try blocking the door visually with a divider or locker. If students are "set off" by certain noises or lights, reduce or eliminate those things from your classroom. If a student destroys materials or grabs reinforcers, do not allow him or her independent access to such things until the student is taught to use them appropriately. Place valuable materials and foods up high or lock them in cabinets. If students are aggressive, seat them against a wall with a table in front of them so they cannot leave the table without teacher assistance. If a student requires physical management, make sure you can reach him or her within 2 to 3 seconds, no matter where you are in the room.

Enhance Transitions

Transitions are often confusing times for students with autism. You may want to facilitate transitions by, for example, placing arrows on the floor to indicate the path you want them to use to enter and/or exit the classroom. Tape may indicate where they are to sit or stand. You may actually want to construct a separate "transition area" where schedules are kept and teach your students to proceed to this area to check their schedules after completing each activity and before proceeding to the next activity.

Avoid Clutter

Because students with autism have difficulty attending to important stimuli, we do not want to confuse them with things to which they do not need to attend. Keep your classroom neat and organized. Use clearly designated cubbies, lockers, or boxes in which students can keep their personal materials, and cue them to do so. You may want to label each box with each student's name or picture, or teach students to respond to certain colors. For example, the materials for Justin are always kept in the red box, and his chair and cubby are marked with red tape. If you use color to cue areas of the classroom for curricular purposes, you should choose a method other than color for organizing student materials (e.g., use the student's picture instead). Attempt to obtain classrooms with enough space so that clutter is avoided. Young students or students with very low cognition will need more visual support. As they become independent in their movements and understand teacher expectations, some visual supports may be faded. We all rely on visual assistance, however, so totally fading visual cues and prompts may not be necessary. Figure 5.3 provides a sample classroom arrangement. Remember that you will need to create your own visual supports that are based on each student's abilities and needs and on the resources available in your school. At-a-Glance 5.2 provides some ideas for visually cueing with physical arrangement.

Visual Support Through Materials

Another way to visually cue and support students with autism is through instructional materials. It is a common educational practice, for example, to hand out written instructions and correct examples with worksheets to ensure that students will complete the worksheet correctly. If your students with autism read, written instructions should also be included—either within their schedules or as a part of the activity—for various instructional tasks. Because many students with autism cannot read, however, teachers should explore other methods for constructing materials that provide visual clarity about what to do. Embedding visual cues within instructional materials is a form of within-stimulus prompting. Sometimes these prompts need to be faded, but not always. As mentioned in Chapter 3, many of us rely on within-stimulus prompts throughout our lives (e.g., IRS forms with lines and boxes

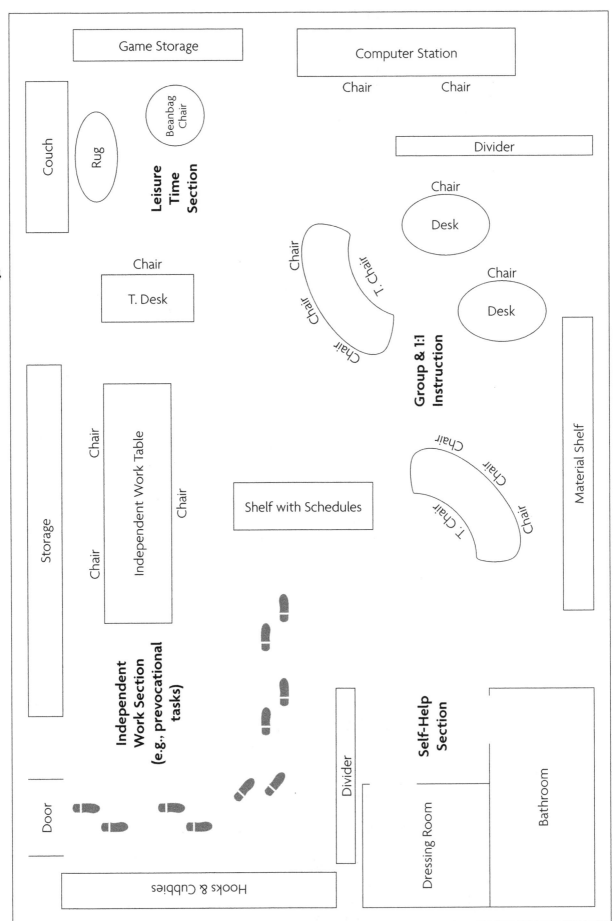

Figure 5.3. Sample classroom arrangement.

At-a-Glance 5.2 Classroom Arrangement as Visual Cues

Use Color for:

- Designating ownership
- Designating curricular expectations
- Organizing materials
- Designating areas of the room

Use Tape for:

- Designating where to sit, stand, or line up
- Designating where to walk
- Creating a personal space for each student
- Designating off-limits areas

Use Dividers for:

- Designating areas of the room
- Masking seductive stimuli
- Providing obstacles to running
- Masking irritating stimuli

Use Furniture for:

- Communicating instructional expectations
- Designating where to walk
- Blocking inappropriate behavior
- Facilitating appropriate behavior
- Increasing independence

indicating what figure to place in each). The thing to remember is that if students (and anyone else) understand what is expected, they are more likely to perform correctly and independently.

There are many ways to communicate expectations through the use of instructional materials. For example, you could draw boxes around individual problems on a math worksheet to help a student decipher which problems are to be completed, or you could provide different colored containers to hold items for a matching task (the student learns to pick one item from the green container and match that item with something from the red container). You might draw circles or paste pictures on a worksheet to cue the student where to place nickels, dimes, quarters, and so forth, next to the correctly printed word. Size might also cue discrimination. For example, when teaching students to identify circles, make all the circles bigger than the triangles and squares.

In the example of a student who is learning to set the table, you could draw the shapes of the spoon, fork, plate, and knife on a plastic placemat so the student is cued where to place the utensils (see Figure 5.4). Or, for a student who is learning to sort nuts and bolts, you could tape pictures of the nuts and bolts on the appropriate containers. Computer or tape recorder on-switches could be colored green for easy identification. Colors, labels, tape, and pictures can all be used to make important

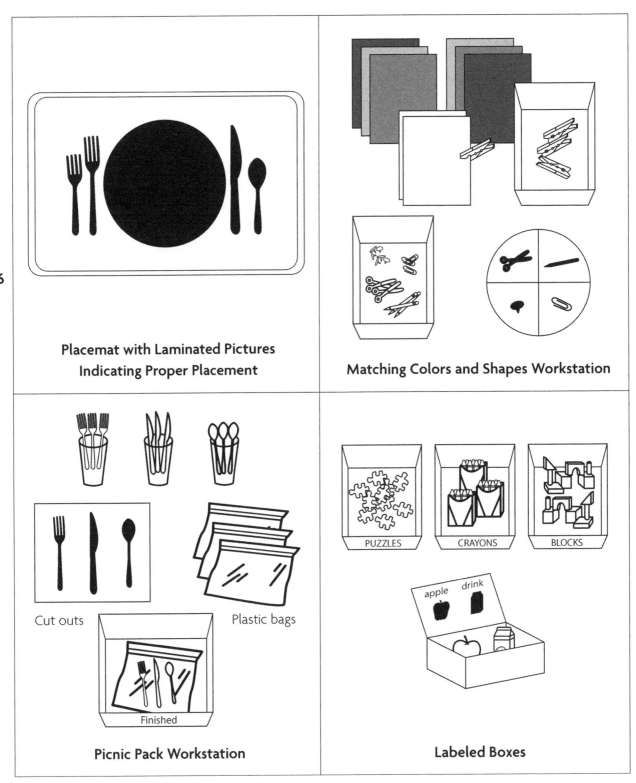

**Placemat with Laminated Pictures
Indicating Proper Placement**

Matching Colors and Shapes Workstation

Cut outs

Plastic bags

Finished

Picnic Pack Workstation

PUZZLES

CRAYONS

BLOCKS

apple   drink

Labeled Boxes

Figure 5.4. Sample instructional materials as visual supports.

stimuli salient; containers, boxes, shelves, and placement of the materials can be used to organize tasks. For example, for a student who is supposed to collate papers, rather than just placing piles of papers on top of the table, place each stack of papers in a box and arrange the boxes from left to right in the desired order. Toileting items might be stored in separate, labeled containers (e.g., toothbrush and toothpaste in one box and soap and washrag in another) so that retrieving and returning appropriate items is visually cued and tasks such as washing the face and brushing the teeth are not confused.

One way of constructing materials for the purpose of visually cueing students is through work systems and jigs (Schopler, Mesibov, & Hearsey, 1995). *Work systems* are constructed to communicate (a) task expectations, (b) how much work should be completed, (c) when the task is completed, and (d) what the student should do after the task is completed. For example, our student who is to complete the nuts-and-bolts sorting task finds a task or activity sequence in a basket of nuts and bolts and two small containers, one taped with a picture of a nut and one with a picture of a bolt. The picture list shows line drawings of someone placing nuts in the container with a nut picture and bolts in the container with the bolt picture. The activity list also depicts an empty basket indicating that all the nuts and bolts should be sorted, leaving none in the basket. The last picture shows the sorted containers back on the shelf and a child checking his or her daily schedule for the next task.

Another work system might be composed of two small boxes, with an empty egg carton placed to the right. Twelve multicolor plastic eggs have been separated into the small boxes (12 egg halves in each). A young student is to work left to right to match same-color egg halves (discrimination) and assemble each (fine-motor skills), and then place each assembled egg in the egg carton until the carton is full (finished). Or a young student may be given a pegboard full of multicolor pegs. To the right of the pegboard are four containers, each of which is papered with a different color. The student is to sort the pegs by color (discrimination) by removing each peg (fine-motor skills) and placing it in the same-color container (discrimination) until the pegboard is empty (finished). For older students, work systems should better approximate actual vocational tasks.

Activity lists can be included with the work systems, or the systems can be set up before the student arrives in the work area. Self-monitoring cards are also a good way to cue students about how much work they need to perform. Each time an item is assembled, for example, the student is to place a round token on a self-monitoring card that contains 20 circles. When all of the circles contain a token, the student knows to stop working. The ability to self-monitor and work independently is important for older students to master for successful employment.

Jigs assist students to complete difficult tasks by modifying equipment or materials and/or providing visual support. For example, if a student has a difficult time holding several papers straight to staple them, she or he might be taught to place the papers in a box with a stapler attached at the left corner. The student then only has to press the stapler down and remove the papers. The box with the stapler attached is called a jig, which is a concrete object that communicates expectations. Other examples of jigs are a paper with the student's name lightly written for tracing for a student who has difficulty writing his or her name and a modified handle for a student who has difficulty using a can crusher. Figure 5.4 illustrates several materials that provide visual supports. In this figure, the left-top quadrant shows a placemat pasted with cut-out shapes to indicate placement of plates and eating utensils. The pasted shapes can be made smaller and eventually removed so the student can set the table with no visual supports.

The right-top quadrant shows two workstations. In the first workstation, students are to match colors (discrimination) by choosing a color paper from the left box, choosing a matching color paper from the right box, and then choosing the same-color clothes pin from the envelope and clipping the papers together (fine-motor skills). The second workstation provides practice for matching objects to pictures. The left-hand box contains various objects. The right-hand round Styrofoam carton has pictures or silhouettes of the objects pasted to the bottoms of each of four compartments. Students are to place each object in the compartment with the appropriate picture (discrimination).

The left-bottom quadrant depicts a prevocational workstation for assembling picnic packets. Plastic eating utensils are placed in cups, and a mat with pictures of each utensil shape placed on it in a consistent order appears below. Students are to place one plastic utensil on each appropriate picture, scoop the three utensils up, and place them in a plastic bag found to the right. They close the bag and place it in the finished box. In this way, the students do not need to remember that one of each utensil goes in the bag. They are guided by the pictures on the mat and only need to learn to place one utensil on each appropriate picture.

The bottom-right quadrant illustrates how each box of materials, and even lunch boxes, should include written and/or picture labels. Students will become more independent in their tasks and activities as they learn to follow visual guides.

Visual Support Through Video and Computers

The use of video-modeled steps to prompt students to perform daily living skills (e.g., hygiene, self-care, community) has been well documented in the literature (Graves, Collins, Schuster, & Kleinert, 2005; Mechling, Pridgen, & Cronin, 2005). Videotapes of nondisabled peers or instructors performing desired task or activity steps are shown to students before they are required to perform the same task themselves. After students watch the entire video, each step usually is cued on the video and set to pause until that particular step is performed. After performing that step, the student is taught to push the play button for the next visual guide. Video can be streamed onto laptop or hand-held computers so that the guides can be used in community or actual contexts (e.g., a kitchen). This is known as computer-based video instruction (CBVI). In some instances, students can watch a video and then perform the entire task. Most often the video will need to be shown in stages, perhaps with additional picture and physical prompts, until the video alone can guide the student's actions. Given the advances in computer video and auditory technology, the inherent motivation to use such technology, and the ease of transporting these supports, CBVI may become one of the most efficient and effective visual support systems.

Additional Visual Supports

There are several other ways to provide visual supports for your students with autism. The following are some suggestions.

Monthly Calendars

Use monthly calendars to indicate what is to occur or not occur each day and who is to be present. Calendars can also be used to indicate what supplies are needed each day. Use pictures, provide line drawings, or print on the calendars to depict important information. For example, each Monday a student is to bring a sack lunch because he will be working in the park and needs to eat outside. The teacher (and parent) can provide a picture of the sack lunch on each Monday of the current month. The student should be taught to refer to the calendar each day. A picture of the bus driver may be placed on the calendar each day and a picture of the substitute bus driver on appropriate days so the student will know there will be a change. Pictures or other indicators can also be placed on calendars to indicate when something has been canceled or changed. This is particularly important for students with autism because they do not react well to surprises. If the student can see when the change will occur, he or she may be better able to continue working without becoming upset.

Task or Activity Sequences

As mentioned before, providing picture or printed sequences can facilitate independent and successful completion of a task or activity. These sequences, like recipes, indicate each behavioral step to be performed and in what order. Remember to teach top–down or left–right orientation and then present sequences in either of these formats. You may want to use such sequences for cueing self-help and domestic activities (e.g., toileting, grooming, cooking), academic activities (e.g., writing, matching), or vocational activities (e.g., assembling, collating, cleaning tables). Sequences can also help students use materials appropriately (e.g., computer use). Teachers might also want to use first–then cards to communicate that certain tasks or steps should be completed first and desired steps or activities will follow. In such a case, you could make a 5-inch × 10-inch card with *First* written on the left, followed by Velcro, with *Then* written next, followed by Velcro. The teacher can Velcro pictures of activities or words in the appropriate order for student guidance. For example, a student is to *first* place plates, forks, and spoons on the table (indicated with a picture) and *then* straighten the chairs (indicated by a second picture). Or, a student is to *first* get his or her coat, don the coat, stand in line (picture sequence), and *then* go outside and play on the swing (picture).

Choice Boards

Allowing students to make choices is a common way to motivate compliance; however, some students with autism will need to be taught how to make choices. Visual supports can assist with choice-making and may increase compliance. Choosing reinforcers might be a good place to start; for example, students may be allowed to choose among several favorite activities during leisure time or among several favorite foods during snack time. Choice boards are constructed to display choices, thus allowing the student to point to, remove, or communicate the item of choice.

Communicating *No*

Many activities might be forbidden to students. In these cases, visual supports can cue students to stay away from, stay out of, or refrain from doing something. The international symbol for *no* (a circle with a line through it diagonally) is often superimposed on an item or on a picture of an item or activity to indicate "off limits." For example, there may be a large red *no* symbol on the closet door, the food cabinet, or the teacher's desk drawer. There may be a large card placed next to the student's desk that illustrates a boy spitting, with a *no* symbol covering it. If students can read, you could post rules in the classroom to indicate, for example, "no climbing" or "no sleeping."

Managing Behavior

Providing rules through visual methods may help your students to behave appropriately (Hodgdon, 1995a, 1999). Use pictures or print to depict rules for using the bathroom, entering and exiting the classroom, replacing materials, and displaying appropriate social behavior. For example, a sequence of appropriate toileting behavior may be displayed on the bathroom wall, or a picture sequence of appropriate lining-up behavior may hang next to the door. A student may be taught to carry a picture sequence cueing him or her to look at friends when they talk, to smile, to listen, and to say "Good-bye" when they are finished talking.

People/Place Locators

Visual cues can also be used to assist students in determining the location of people and places. Hodgdon (1995b) recommended that people locators provide information about the following:

- Who is here today
- Who is not here
- Where someone is
- Who is coming later
- When someone will come
- Who is supposed to come but will not
- Who is not supposed to come but will (p. 58)

For example, the teacher may have paper pockets on the back of the classroom door with a picture of a destination or a person in each (e.g., speech therapist, bus, office secretary, cafeteria, bathroom). When students are to go independently to a destination, they are cued to pull the appropriate picture and take it with them to the destination. At first there should be a picture at the destination site for the student to match. This can be faded so that the picture alone will cue the student where to go or whom to see. Parents may find it useful to have destination pictures of the mall, their church, the bank, the park, and other frequently visited locations. When leaving the house, parents can arrange the pictures in a sequence so that each picture can be removed as the particular location is visited. In this way, children are cued as to where they will be going, in what order, and when they will be returning home. Pictures or symbols of people and locations can also be placed on calendars, for example, so students know that on Thursday they are to go to the gym. Figure 5.5 provides several examples of visual supports.

TEACCH

One well-developed instructional package for students with autism that emphasizes structured classrooms is called Treatment and Education of Autistic and Communication Handicapped Children or TEACCH (Gryzwacz & Lombardo, 1999; Schopler et al., 1995). TEACCH was developed at the University of North Carolina at Chapel Hill in the 1970s and includes many of the principles of ABA (clear S^Ds and prompts, shaping of appropriate behaviors, prompt fading, naturalistic/milieu teaching, and reinforcement). Unlike DTT, however, TEACCH assumes that S^Ds and most prompts are embedded in the classroom and material structure and that reinforcement is achieved through successfully completed and interesting tasks. Drill-and-practice sessions are not present in the TEACCH model. The main components of TEACCH are structured teaching, independent work time and workstations, and vocational skill training.

The program offers parent training for behavior management and intensive teacher training for skills in establishing predictable situations and structuring environments to promote independence. TEACCH promotes the use of visual schedules, predictable routines, and organizational strategies, such as left-to-right sequencing. Unfortunately, some school personnel and parents assume that a good educational program can only include either TEACCH strategies or DTT (aka ABA; Choutka, Doloughty, & Zirkel, 2004), but not both. We highly recommend that teachers use DTT, naturalistic/milieu teaching, *and* structured teaching components as a basis for effective programming. Even using these three instructional models will only

Sample Visual Supports

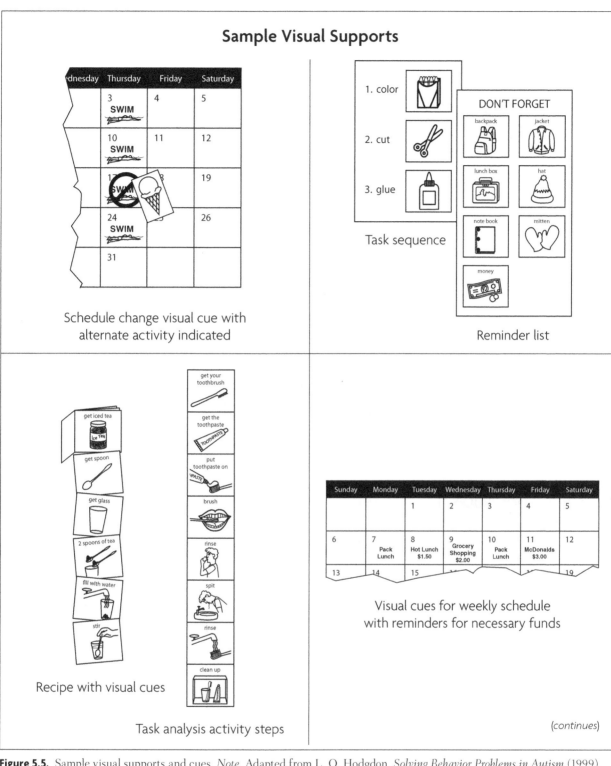

Schedule change visual cue with
alternate activity indicated

Task sequence

Reminder list

Recipe with visual cues

Task analysis activity steps

Visual cues for weekly schedule
with reminders for necessary funds

(continues)

Figure 5.5. Sample visual supports and cues. *Note.* Adapted from L. Q. Hodgdon, *Solving Behavior Problems in Autism* (1999), and *Visual Strategies for Improving Communication* (1995), Troy, MI: QuirkRoberts.

be effective if the following conditions are met: (a) teaching is intensive in terms of the amount of time spent teaching each learning objective, (b) you and your staff are knowledgeable in the use of these techniques, (c) progress data are collected and analyzed, (d) the curriculum is appropriate, (e) teaching emphasizes communication and social skills, and (f) families are included (National Research Council, 2001). Resources 5.1 contains additional information resources for providing structure in your classroom.

Rules and Behavior Guidelines

Figure 5.5. *Continued.*

Summary

Due to cognitive deficits inherent in autism, students with this disorder typically have a difficult time making sense of their world. These students have trouble attending to environmental stimuli and shifting their attention from one contextual variable to another. They appear to be overwhelmed by excessive noise, light, movement, and verbal input. As a result, they are often unmotivated or unable to learn in

Resources 5.1 Resources for Providing Classroom Structure

Dalrymple, N. J. (1995). Environmental supports to develop flexibility and independence. In K. A. Quill (Ed.), *Teaching children with autism: Strategies to enhance communication and socialization* (pp. 243–264). Albany, NY: Delmar.

Dettmar, S., Simpson, R. L., Myles, B. S., & Ganz, J. B. (2000). The use of visual supports to facilitate transitions of students with autism. *Focus on Autism and Other Developmental Disabilities, 15*(1), 163–169.

Downing, J. E., & Peckham-Hardin, K. D. (2001). Daily schedules: A helpful learning tool. *Teaching Exceptional Children, 33*(3), 62–67.

Heflin, L. J., & Alberto, P. A. (2001). Establishing a behavioral context for learning for students with autism. *Focus on Autism and Other Developmental Disabilities, 16*(2), 93–101.

Hodgdon, L. Q. (1995a). Solving social–behavioral problems through the use of visually supported communication. In K. A. Quill (Ed.), *Teaching children with autism: Strategies to enhance communication and socialization* (pp. 265–286). New York: Delmar.

Hodgdon, L. Q. (1995b). *Visual strategies for improving communication: Vol. 1. Practical supports for school and home.* Troy, MI: QuirkRoberts.

Hodgdon, L. Q. (1999). *Solving behavior problems in autism: Improving communication with visual strategies.* Troy, MI: QuirkRoberts.

Mayer-Johnson, R. (1981). *The picture communication symbols book.* Solana Beach, CA: Mayer-Johnson.

McClannahan, L., & Krantz, P. (1999). *Activity schedules for children with autism: Teaching independent behavior.* Princeton, NJ: Woodbine House.

Pierce, K. L., & Schreibman, L. (1994). Teaching daily living skills to children with autism in unsupervised settings through pictorial self-management. *Journal of Applied Behavior Analysis, 27,* 471–481.

Quill, K. A. (1995). Visually cued instruction for children with autism and pervasive developmental disorders. *Focus on Autistic Behavior, 10*(3), 10–22.

Schopler, E., Mesibov, G. B., & Hearsey, K. (1995). Structured teaching in the TEACCH system. In E. Schopler & G. B. Mesibov (Eds.), *Learning and cognition in autism* (pp. 243–268). New York: Plenum Press.

Division TEACCH. (1992). *Independent tasks: Work activities for students with autism and other visual learners.* Chapel Hill: University of North Carolina, School of Medicine, Dept. of Psychiatry.

chaotic settings, preferring instead to withdraw. Because of these cognitive deficits, teachers must provide clarity and support for their students through structure and organization. Such structure and organization should consist of consistent classroom procedures and routines, well-planned daily schedules, visual schedules and activity sequences for individual students, physical arrangements, instructional materials, and other visual supports.

If you are a teacher who is not naturally organized and consistent, you will need to work on those skills. Students with autism do best in highly structured environments. Teachers will need to plan ahead and consider carefully how to develop an environment that promotes learning and discourages inappropriate behavior. Both students and instructional staff will benefit from such structure. Consistency and clear expectations promote a sense of well-being and independent functioning for all of us.

References

Choutka, C. M., Doloughty, P. T., & Zirkel, P. A. (2004). The "discrete trials" of applied behavior analysis for children with autism: Outcome-related factors in the case law. *The Journal of Special Education, 38,* 95–103.

Dalrymple, N. J. (1995). Environmental supports to develop flexibility and independence. In K. A. Quill (Ed.), *Teaching children with autism: Strategies to enhance communication and socialization* (pp. 243–264). Albany, NY: Delmar.

Downing, J. E., & Peckham-Hardin, K. D. (2001). Daily schedules: A helpful learning tool. *Teaching Exceptional Children, 33*(3), 62–67.

Graves, T. B., Collins, B. C., Schuster, J. W., & Kleinert, H. (2005). Using video prompting to teach cooking skills to secondary students with moderate disabilities. *Education and Training in Developmental Disabilities, 40*(1), 34–46.

Gryzwacz, P., & Lombardo, L. (1999). *Serving students with autism: The debate over effective therapies.* Horsham, PA: LRP.

Hodgdon, L. Q. (1995a). Solving social-behavioral problems through the use of visually supported communication. In K. A. Quill (Ed.), *Teaching children with autism: Strategies to enhance communication and socialization* (pp. 265–286). New York: Delmar.

Hodgdon, L. Q. (1995b). *Visual strategies for improving communication: Vol. 1. Practical supports for school and home.* Troy, MI: QuirkRoberts.

Hodgdon, L. Q. (1999). *Solving behavior problems in autism: Improving communication with visual strategies.* Troy, MI: QuirkRoberts.

Mayer-Johnson Co. (1994). *Picture communication symbols combination book.* Solano Beach, CA: Author.

Mechling, L. C., Pridgen, L. S., & Cronin, B. A. (2005). Computer-based video instruction to teach students with intellectual disabilities to verbally respond to questions and make purchases in fast food restaurants. *Education and Training in Developmental Disabilities, 40*(1), 47–59.

National Research Council, Division of Behavioral and Social Sciences and Education, Committee on Educational Interventions for Children with Autism. (2001). *Educating children with autism* (C. Lord & J. P. McGee, Eds.). Washington, DC: National Academy Press.

Schopler, E., Mesibov, G. B., & Hearsey, K. (1995). Structured teaching in the TEACCH system. In E. Schopler & G. B. Mesibov (Eds.), *Learning and cognition in autism* (pp. 243–268). New York: Plenum Press.

Supervision of Teaching Adults

One very important function for teachers of students with autism is that of coordinating and supervising various teaching adults who may also be working with the students. Because students with autism have multiple needs and challenging behaviors, it often "takes a village" to educate them. One or more paraprofessionals may be assigned to help various professionals educate students with low-functioning autism. Sometimes parents or school districts will hire paraprofessionals called "shadows" to provide one-on-one assistance to a particular student. Students with autism may also receive services from one or more of the following professionals:

- speech–language pathologist (SLP)
- occupational therapist (OT)
- physical therapist (PT)
- adaptive physical education (PE) teacher
- school nurse
- school psychologist
- behavior specialist
- job coach

Teachers may also invite community volunteers or mentors, peer tutors, and parents into the classroom to assist with instruction. At times, the adults may outnumber the students. Although students may benefit a great deal from such a low teacher–student ratio, the benefit will quickly diminish if teaching adults are not trained in effective practices.

It falls to teachers to coordinate, train, and/or supervise other adults who are working with their students. This casts teachers into a management role usually not required with other special education populations. In fact, teachers may need to reduce their own direct contact with students to spend time ensuring that all other adults become good teachers and work well together. With more adults providing effective instruction, a larger number of students can be more often engaged. In this chapter, we will address considerations for managing other teaching adults. Getting everyone on the "same page" in terms of the curriculum, instruction, and behavior management should be a major component of the teacher's duties.

Roles and Responsibilities

The various teaching adults assigned to serve students with disabilities represent different professional disciplines and varying levels of training. Teachers should become acquainted with their different professional roles and responsibilities. What follows is a brief description of each type of professional's responsibilities and some information about the education/training for the position. This is just a general description; individual roles and responsibilities will differ across settings and students.

Paraprofessional

Paraprofessionals, also referred to as *teaching assistants, paraeducators,* or *classroom aides,* are individuals hired to assist teachers in their teaching duties, and they work under the teacher's supervision. Most paraprofessionals do not possess college degrees, nor do they have special education training before beginning work (Chopra et al., 2004). Thus, such training often needs to occur on the job. Sometimes paraprofessionals assist the teacher with paperwork, bulletin boards, copying, and organizing the classroom. In the case of students with autism, however, the paraprofessional should deliver instruction as an integral part of the educational team. Because students with autism often require a one-to-one teacher-to-student ratio, paraprofessionals are often called on to instruct individual students for most of the school day. Paraprofessionals may be involved in community-based instruction, inclusion programs, and in-home training programs. They will need to master DTT, naturalistic/milieu teaching, and behavior management techniques. Paraprofessionals will need to be clear about which goals and objectives are targeted, to communicate with a wide variety of people about student progress, and to learn as much as possible about the syndrome of autism. It is absolutely imperative that the teacher and the paraprofessional(s) become an efficient, effective educational team.

Given the need for lower student–teacher ratios for students with autism and the shortage of well-trained special education teachers, training and utilizing paraprofessionals to assist with instruction is highly desirable (National Research Council, 2001). However, we caution against expecting paraprofessionals to teach students if the paraprofessionals do not have prior training in best educational practices and designated curricula. Such a situation is unfair to the paraprofessional (Chopra et al., 2004) and could be detrimental to the students. We also recommend that paraprofessionals be supervised in their instructional duties to ensure that your students with autism are receiving effective instruction all day.

Shadow

Individuals hired to provide one-to-one support for a particular student with autism for part or all of the school day are often referred to as *shadows.* They differ from paraprofessionals in that they are assigned only to one student rather than to a teacher, they typically are trained in DTT, and they may be hired by a student's parents rather than by the school district. Shadows may be expected to provide social opportunities for their charges, promote language production, monitor behavior in inclusive settings, or cue specific responses, such as walking from the bus to the classroom. Although shadows may have specific training in one or two techniques, they usually do not have extensive backgrounds in special education pedagogy. Furthermore, if the shadow is not a school district employee, the lines of supervision may be unclear.

Speech–Language Pathologist

The speech–language pathologist (SLP) should be a key partner in the education of students with autism because of the wide range of speech and language problems inherent in the disability. The SLP is primarily responsible for appraising speech and language functioning, diagnosing problems in these areas, developing goals and objectives to enhance communication, and monitoring progress toward those goals. Speech–language services, called a "related service" under the Individuals with Disabilities Education Act (IDEA, 1990), may include individual therapy sessions, group therapy sessions, naturalistic interventions, counseling and training for family members and school personnel to enhance communicative opportunities and understanding of the impairments, and referral for medical or other professional attention. Using naturalistic/milieu teaching for speech problems—which will be discussed in Chapter 9—involves training speech and language in natural environments based on student interest. Because this is a highly recommended strategy for teaching students with low verbal skills, we suggest that SLPs and teachers coordinate speech and communication goals and training such that they are addressed throughout each day in several settings. The traditional pull-out model in which SLPs work with students in a therapy room for one-half hour a week will probably do little to alleviate language problems for students with low-functioning autism.

SLPs are not interested in just speech production, even though most of their training may have addressed articulation problems. Their primary goal is to improve functional communication. Thus, an SLP should also be able to prescribe augmentative and alternative communication (AAC) systems for students who cannot master speech and train the students in their use. AAC systems may include sign language, vocal output devices, and picture communication. Many SLPs have advanced degrees and many hours of clinical experience. They may not, however, be familiar with the syndrome of autism, DTT, or specific ABA principles.

Occupational Therapist

The occupational therapist (OT) is primarily interested in developing, improving, or restoring independent functioning skills, specifically, the abilities to participate in daily living, recreational, and employment activities. The OT may be interested in strengthening dressing skills, cooking skills, personal hygiene skills, or even writing or typing skills. The responsibilities of an OT, also considered a related service under the IDEA, include assessment of and recommendations for the effective use of materials and appliances at school and home. For example, if you have a student who hates to hold a pencil or pen, the OT may help by adapting the pen with a differently textured grip so it is not repugnant to the student or by exploring other reasons why the student hates to hold the pen. Another example would be a student who chews with his mouth open, drooling food down the front of his shirt. The OT may work with the student to teach a different chewing technique or recommend thickening the food to prevent spillage.

Typically, OTs are trained, through a medical model, to work with individuals who have lost functioning due to illness, injury, or deprivation (e.g., stroke or accidents). They might teach such an individual to function with one hand, for example, or adapt the environment to improve function with the one hand (e.g., provide plates with lips so spearing food with a fork is easier). In the case of autism, OTs may be interested in the typical tactile defensiveness and possible fine-motor clumsiness. OTs may also work with job coaches to adapt job tasks and materials and to train special skills such that individuals can become successfully employed. Some OTs may be interested in *sensory integration techniques*. Believing that the sensory input systems (i.e., visual, tactile, auditory) are not working simultaneously or in an integrated way for individuals with autism, OTs may stimulate one or more systems (e.g., brushing the arms) as a therapy to improve sensory integrative functions and produce adaptive motor responses. The efficacy of sensory integration techniques has been questioned (e.g., Heflin & Simpson, 1998) because of a paucity of empirical studies supporting its use (National Research Council, 2001). However, these techniques may be appealing to children with autism and could be beneficial if their use elicits social interactions, attention, and play. The danger in taking valuable school time to administer questionable therapies lies in the fact that the time is not being used to intensively teach those things that students need to learn. Your IEP team should carefully consider curricula and effective practices supported by research when developing educational plans.

Physical Therapist

Physical therapists (PTs) are interested in the development and maintenance of gross-motor skills, movement, and posture. They, too, are trained through a medical model to prevent motor problems or treat them. Physical therapy, which is another related service, may include massage, prescriptive exercises, swimming, heat treatment, special positioning, and other techniques. Typically, the PT attempts to develop muscular function and reduce pain, discomfort, or long-term physical damage. If your student frequently falls, runs into objects, or has an inefficient walking gait, you may want to consult the PT. You may have a student who not only has autism but also a physical disability, such as cerebral palsy. In this case, the PT may be involved to alleviate the effects of the latter condition. PTs and OTs also complete many hours of clinical experience before receiving a license; however, their experience may not have included school-based programs or specific knowledge of autism.

Adaptive Physical Education Teacher

An adaptive physical education (PE) teacher is a certified PE teacher who has received training in skills for adapting typical physical education activities for students with disabilities. One of our main concerns regarding students with autism is that they lack play skills. Learning to play or engage in leisure-time activities is typically a main goal of any educational program. The adaptive PE teacher might be able to assist the classroom teacher in designing leisure-time activities, especially those that include gross-motor involvement (e.g., ball games) that promote social interaction, communication, mastery of rules, physical exercise, tactile stimulation, and enjoyment. The OT and PT may want to work with the adaptive PE teacher to coordinate their goals and techniques.

School Nurse

The school nurse will be involved with your students if there is a medical need that requires monitoring or if medication needs to be administered. For example, a large number of children with autism develop seizures, so they may need medication or special diets, and they may have seizures while at school. The school nurse will need to develop a rapport with students who must be given medication and/or checked physically. It is also advisable to work with the school nurse to develop strategies for recognizing symptoms of illness when you have students who do not talk or who tend to avoid interaction. Teachers should communicate any changes in behavior or diet and any medication side effects to the school nurse in a timely manner.

School Psychologist

The school psychologist, usually a licensed specialist in school psychology (LSSP), has been trained to conduct standardized assessments for students who are referred for special education services and students who are receiving these services. These individuals are often asked to assess socioemotional and cognitive functioning, participate on planning teams, counsel students, evaluate behavior, assist teachers with behavior management, and administer special programs. School psychologists usually do not have teaching backgrounds, but they may have taken courses in psychology, ABA, counseling, assessment, and consultation strategies. They may or may not know much about autism. The school psychologist will probably be involved with your students when evaluations are required, during meetings that require interpretation of assessment results, and in instances in which student behavior is of concern.

Behavior Specialist

Some school districts hire behavior specialists. Typically, behavior specialists are teachers—usually special education teachers—who have demonstrated effective skills in the area of behavior management or who have received specialized training in ABA and its applications in the school. Sometimes these individuals are certified as behavior specialists or are board-certified behavior analysts (BCBAs), but most are not. Their role is to provide assistance to teachers in dealing with challenging student behavior. Their services might consist of conducting FBAs, training school personnel, working directly with students, and developing behavior plans. Because students with autism often display challenging behavior, the behavior specialist may be a frequent member of the educational team.

Job Coach

The job coach, or employment specialist, is a school employee whose responsibilities are to teach job skills and to place and monitor youth with severe disabilities in community-based employment. A job coach will meet with potential employers and obtain jobs (job development), assess individual students for job skills and aptitude (consumer assessment), assist with securing a job (job placement), train and support the student on the job until she or he can perform independently (job-site training), and monitor as necessary to ensure success. A job coach will usually be part of the planning team for students ages 16 years and older. The job coach might also be involved in adapting work sites and jobs to accommodate the worker's disability. In the case of students with autism, the job coach should be very creative at matching jobs to individual "quirks." For example, a young person who loves to watch washing machines twirl might be very good at using a lettuce shredder at a fast-food restaurant, or a student who is very compulsive about straightening objects and placing them in rows might make a very good library assistant. In any case, the job coach will need to master those strategies that the teacher and SLP have discovered work well with individual students. The job coach may also need to work with both the OT and the PT to adapt materials and job tasks for individual students.

As teachers work with each of these teaching adults, they should strive to build a team; promote consistency, communication, coordination, consultation, and problem solving; and ensure that all teaching adults are able to work effectively with the students. A functional, effective educational team is the basis for everyone's success.

Creating an Educational Team

Team Building

Special education in general is a team endeavor. In the case of a student with autism, a professional team is essential because so many adults are usually involved with the student and because consistent application of educational strategies is highly recommended. Professional team building involves formulating relationships with colleagues that are mutually supportive and positive. Team relationships should be built on trust and respect. There are many strategies for building a team, but all of them involve team members' spending time together, committing to the same goals, and supporting each other in attaining those goals. As a team leader, the teacher should strive to inspire commitment, loyalty, respect, and enthusiasm among team members. This can be done by challenging each team member to do his or her best job and by making members feel that they are important contributors. Encourage team members to talk about themselves, not just the job, and to become interested in each other. Do things together outside of school. Remember birthdays. Make them experts, and give them status.

The teacher should encourage each member to show honest and sincere appreciation to each other for assistance and a job well done. Team members should avoid condemnation, aggression, and criticism. Everyone should smile a lot and appear energetic and positive. Each team member should show respect for others' opinions and try to be sympathetic with other points of view. Team members should admit mistakes quickly and emphatically and apologize when appropriate. Each member should avoid taking credit for others' work and help to reduce stress in the workplace. Most of these strategies will occur naturally if team members develop a spirit of collegiality and generosity. Your students with autism will suffer if teaching adults are indifferent to each other or worse, are hostile. The job, no matter how difficult, will be more appealing if the team is functional, productive, and fun.

Consistency

One of the main reasons that we encourage you to build a team is to ensure consistency in educational practices. Remember that individuals with autism need consistent procedures, routines, cues, S^Ds, and physical arrangements because they tend to memorize each skill, task, or activity rather than transfer learning from one situation to another. In fact, students with autism will usually insist on consistency, showing displeasure when changes are made and/or not responding at all to different stimuli. When more than one person instructs a particular student, which is sure to happen, consistency should be of primary concern. If the teacher cues a student to "Look at me" before beginning a teaching trial, so should the teaching assistant. On the other hand, if that cue has been faded or the objective is to promote generalization, the teaching assistant should no longer give it. If the teacher occasionally reinforces a student for correct toileting behavior or for initiating communication, so should the teaching assistant(s), adaptive PE teacher, SLP, and peers who work with the student. On the other hand, if a teacher ignores attention-getting behavior, such as whining, so should other adults who are working with the student.

Such consistency will occur and be maintained only if specific information is communicated regularly to everyone involved and only if teaching adults are able to adequately perform teaching behaviors. In addition, teaching adults will need to recognize the importance of such consistency and must be willing to work together to achieve it. Even if someone is well trained and informed, it does not mean that he or she is motivated to engage in effective instruction. Motivating and inspiring best practices falls to the teacher.

Communication

Effective communication is the main ingredient for building the team, motivating performance, and ensuring consistency across teaching adults. Effective communication includes giving information in a way that others can hear it, listening to others, and developing problem-solving strategies. Teachers will need to give information about daily/weekly schedules, student progress, curricular expectations, instructional strategies and materials, parent concerns, and administrative concerns. Teachers should also provide feedback about adult performance and reinforcement when things go well. What follows are some suggestions regarding effective communication, some of which were outlined by Gordon (1974).

- Listen well. We recommend that teachers (and other teaching adults) master active listening techniques. It is important to make people feel that they are heard and that what they say has value. When others are speaking, attend to them by making eye contact and using appropriate facial expressions. Communicate interest with your body by leaning forward, nodding, and asking questions. Try to reflect the speaker's feelings and paraphrase the speaker to clarify the message. For example, say things such as, "You seem pretty upset about that," or "Are you saying you want me to help you with this task?" Pay attention to the speaker's body language and behavior. Many times people say one thing (e.g., how happy they are) but communicate something else (e.g., anger). After the conversation, summarize what was discussed and/or decided.
- Speak in a lively way, fluently, and confidently. Communicate in a way that clarifies that you are the team leader but that other members can also take leadership roles. Communicate enthusiasm.
- Use the language of feelings and positive one-liners. For example, respond to comments with "I feel ..." statements or ask, "How does that make you feel?" Give quick feedback using phrases such as "Great smile," "Dynamite technique," or "Super job!"
- Use self-disclosure to help build relationships and keep communication lines open. The more open you are with information, the safer others will feel in sharing personal information.
- Use body language to enhance your message. Body language is usually a more reliable reflection of feelings and intention than are words. Crossed arms, a tight face, and glaring eyes communicate anger and/or defensiveness. Open arms and smiling eyes communicate happiness, relaxation, and contentment. Be sure that your body language is communicating interest and respect.
- Express open-mindedness. Remain open to alternative ideas and suggestions. Refrain from becoming defensive and protective of one certain method, for example. Ask often for other team members' opinions and encourage discussion.
- Give constructive feedback. Just as with students, adults will benefit from feedback about their performance. Feedback is necessary for people to know whether they should continue to behave in certain ways or should change their behavior. Feedback is best given after someone is instructed to behave a certain way and has tried it. Sometimes teachers refrain from giving corrective feedback because they fear hurt feelings or anger; however, it is the teacher's responsibility to ensure that adults are behaving in ways that benefit the students.

On the other hand, teachers should refrain from criticism and scolding, which block productive communication. Ask questions in a conversational tone and listen to the answers. Avoid telling someone that he or she "should" and/or "must" do something and other judgmental phrases. Instead, tell your team members that they "might try" a different technique or "would do well" to do something different. Justify your feedback and use "I" language. Offer assistance if it seems to be needed. Model the behavior you want. Adults also learn well with visual cues, such as notes, arrows, posted reminders, lesson plans, and printed schedules.

• Genuinely reinforce people when they do what you asked. Adults like praise if it is genuine and they earned it. Writing notes of gratitude, using positive facial expressions or body language, and bragging to other people about someone's work will all probably work as reinforcement for your team members.

• Avoid communication roadblocks. Gordon (1974) also outlined communication roadblocks, which are listed in At-a-Glance 6.1. Teachers and other team members should avoid these roadblocks, instead striving to keep lines of communication open and functional.

Coordination, Consultation, and Problem Solving

Once a team is developed, it will be maintained through coordination, consultation, and successful strategies for solving problems. *Coordination* involves activities that aim to organize everyone's job activities. *Consultation* is the provision of information and expertise to one another. *Problem solving* is a systematic process for addressing various types of concerns.

Coordination

Coordinating a team will require organization and communication on the part of the leader. Even a well-formed team will need someone to keep everyone "flying in formation." As the team leader, teachers should have a clear vision of the team's purpose and knowledge about how to achieve it. The main coordination functions of an educational team leader are scheduling, planning, and information sharing. Scheduling activities will most likely include developing daily classroom schedules (see Chapter 5) and preparing for Individualized Education Program (IEP) meetings, parent conferences, and training sessions. Teachers will also need to schedule and conduct team meetings for various purposes.

Communication and coordination will suffer without face-to-face meetings, so we recommend that every effort be made to meet frequently with the entire team to share information, plan, and solve problems, when needed. For example, many districts do not have students attend school on Wednesday afternoons, reserving that time for educational team meetings. Some districts send students home an hour early on Friday so that staff will have time to meet. It will not work well, for example, to have paraprofessionals monitor students or send them to PE while other team members meet because the paraprofessionals and PE teacher need to be in the meetings! Be creative. Find a regular time each week or every other week for the team to meet, and make the meetings productive and fun so people will want to attend. Have clear, realistic, and relevant meeting agendas that are given to each team member. Formulate the agenda for the next meeting and leave time for new agenda items. Summarize the meeting via memo or e-mail to facilitate communication.

Planning is a major function of educational team leaders. Planning will include not only developing, evaluating, and altering IEPs but also setting goals and plan-

At-a-Glance 6.1 Communication Roadblocks

1. **Being overly punitive.** Most people will avoid individuals who punish them severely and regularly. This does not mean that you cannot give constructive feedback, but avoid scolding, harsh criticism, and threats. Also avoid passive–aggressive behaviors, such as withholding necessary information or giving incorrect information, talking negatively about persons behind their back, "forgetting" to invite someone to a meeting or a gathering, or allowing individuals to fail when it could have been prevented.

2. **Showing impatience.** Body language that communicates that you do not want to be having the conversation or that you are uninterested in what is being said is a real turn-off. Remember to communicate interest and attention.

3. **Providing expressions of overconcern.** Communication can be blocked by someone who is too serious or who blows things out of proportion. Take what people are willing to tell you and probe for more information sparingly. Avoid jumping to conclusions without sufficient information.

4. **Arguing.** Arguing about who or what is right is a way to halt communication. Discussions can be useful, but if the goal is to be right and have everyone agree that you are right, arguments may follow. The goal of a discussion is to acquire and digest information. We recommend avoiding topics such as religion or politics that might cause arguments.

5. **Ridiculing or belittling.** Making fun of someone's actions or beliefs may damage a relationship forever. Everyone is to be treated with respect. People need to feel psychologically safe.

6. **Making false promises.** It will not take long for mistrust and miscommunication to appear if false promises are made. Say what you mean and mean what you say. If you follow through on commitments in a timely manner, other persons will probably do the same.

7. **Rejecting the individual.** Be careful to not criticize or reject a person. It is acceptable to correct, change, or request behavior. Comments such as "I prefer that graphs be done every Friday," are very different from statements such as "You're a procrastinator and you need to change!"

Note. Adapted from *T.E.T.: Teacher Effectiveness Training* (pp. 80–87), by T. Gordon, 1974, New York: Peter H. Wyden.

ning for program development and evaluation (within a school or within a district). In addition, each team member may plan for specific professional goals and activities during a given time period. For example, the paraprofessional and the adaptive PE teacher may make a plan to master data collection techniques within the next month through reading and attendance at a workshop. The job coach may plan to have all jobs developed by September 30. Student and program planning will need to occur before the school year begins, perhaps each day or once a week and at the end of semesters or reporting periods. Depending on the purpose, planning can be accomplished in several ways. However, we recommend a multistep process for most planning purposes.

1. Decide where you want to go. If the team is discussing a particular student, what are the long-term goals for that student? If the team is discussing a program, what are the long-range goals for that program?
2. Decide where you are now. What is the student's present level of functioning in each goal area? Where is the program at this stage?
3. Delineate steps, activities, or objectives for reaching the goal from the starting point. What objectives will the student need to master to reach the long-range

goals? What activities will need to be accomplished for the program to reach a target (e.g., obtain new software for the computer)?

4. Assign responsibility for each step, activity, or objective. Who will be involved in teaching the communication objectives? Who will be responsible for the motor objectives? Who will research funding for obtaining necessary resources? Who will meet with the principal to ask for more planning time?

5. Assign a time line for accomplishing each step, activity, or objective. Decide as a team how long each activity will take and arrange to meet again to review progress. For individual students, this is required, but not limited to, once a year. For program development, it may mean meeting once a week or once a month.

Needless to say, this type of coordination will demand regular communication with everyone. If face-to-face meetings are not possible, communicate through notes, e-mail, notebooks, lesson plans, and graphs. It may also be helpful to use visual cues (e.g., smiley faces to cue smiling) and reminders (e.g., "Friday is graph day" posters) and give calendars to everyone at the beginning of the year.

Consultation and Training

Consultation implies that team members are sharing their expertise with each other. This can be done through informal discussions, reading material, or directed training. For example, the SLP may consult with the teacher and paraprofessional(s) on specific naturalistic/milieu teaching techniques, or the OT may consult with other team members about strategies to help a student handle eating utensils.

An important component of consultation—direct training—falls to the teacher. Most other members of the professional team will need to be taught much of the content in this book. We recommend teaching paraprofessionals and other team members who do not know this content the following items:

- characteristics of students with autism,
- DTT and naturalistic/milieu teaching,
- differential reinforcement techniques,
- curriculum development steps,
- formative assessment and graphing strategies,
- effective communication skills,
- planning strategies, and
- problem-solving techniques.

The teacher may refer to references cited in this book for further information for training sessions, and we have provided sample handouts in Appendix B.

The teacher can conduct necessary training either formally (direct instruction with handouts) or informally (discussion and readings). In either case, we recommend visual models. For example, if paraprofessionals conduct naturalistic/milieu teaching sessions well, have the job coach stand by you as you point out the components of the technique while watching the paraprofessional work with a student. The teacher might also want to use video models to instruct teaching techniques. You can either purchase training films (e.g., from PRO-ED, Inc., in Austin, Texas, or Behavior Analysts, Inc., in Pleasant Hills, California) or videotape yourself or someone else who is performing the technique.

It will also help to film each other while teaching individual students so the group members can watch each other and offer feedback. Just as a tennis coach would use videotapes to teach the appropriate way to serve a ball, the teacher can use videotape to train team members how to conduct DTT sessions, and naturalistic/milieu teaching, and/or differential reinforcement. Team members may be reluctant to be filmed, perhaps fearing criticism and ridicule, but if the teacher is the first to be filmed and the subsequent discussion is productive, informative, and reinforcing, other adults will see the benefits of such a training technique.

We also recommend *coaching* team members as they perform specific teaching strategies. For example, if a paraprofessional is learning DTT, the teacher should sit directly behind and close to her or him as he or she works with a student. Give feedback quietly as the paraprofessional performs the steps (e.g., "Good prompt," "No, don't reinforce until he touches his head," "Only give the instruction once"). If the adaptive PE teacher is trying naturalistic/milieu teaching to improve communication, the teacher could stand close to him or her and give feedback as he or she mands and/or models. This on-the-job coaching strategy usually results in better understanding of the fine points of the techniques. Coaching might benefit the SLP, the adaptive PE teacher, the job coach, and parents who are trying to master the teaching strategies.

Once team members have been trained, the teacher can periodically check for proper technique and consistency. Remember that it is the teacher's job to ensure that students are receiving appropriate instruction. Perhaps everyone could be videotaped four or five times a year while working with students. This is a good way to demonstrate that everyone has mastered effective teaching techniques and to ensure consistency across teaching adults.

Problem Solving

In many instances, the team will be called upon to solve problems. Graphs may indicate that a student is regressing or is demonstrating challenging behavior. A parent may request something new for his or her child. A schedule may need to be changed. Team members may become disgruntled about some procedure or aspect of the program. An administrator may request that something different be done. Team members may be drifting apart and not communicating. A team member may leave, or someone new may join the team. In any of these situations, the team may need to meet and proceed through a problem-solving process. If the team has worked together for some time, this will probably be an efficient process. If, on the other hand, the team is new and its members are not functioning well together, this process may take more than one meeting.

Every meeting, regardless of the purpose, needs a leader. We have recommended that the teacher be the team leader, but other adults may want to step up at different times and lead a meeting. For example, the behavior specialist may lead a meeting about challenging behavior. The paraprofessional may lead a meeting about a student's lack of progress. The SLP may lead the discussion about a parent's request. The school psychologist may lead a meeting about the administrator request. The following are common problem-solving steps that may make meetings more efficient and effective. The leader should keep people on track and address each step sequentially and in a timely manner.

1. *Identify the problem.* Problem identification may be the most difficult step. Often, the actual problem is not evident. Team members may think that one thing is the problem (e.g., the schedule is not fair to everyone), when the real problem is that one teaching assistant requires a break earlier in the morning due to physical needs. Taking the time to narrow down and describe the problem often makes it seem less overwhelming, and as a result, solutions easily become apparent. Use a blackboard or butcher paper and make sure that all team members agree on the problem description.

2. *Brainstorm solutions to the problem. Brainstorming* is a process in which individuals rapidly call out solutions without judgment or constraint. Some solutions may seem ridiculous or obviously unachievable, but they should be written down. The process of being ridiculous often leads to more creative solutions. *This is not the time to discuss each solution.* This is just a listing of anything anyone can think of to address the problem. The leader should keep team members from commenting on others' ideas until all ideas have been recorded. Again, we recommend recording the solutions in a place where or in a way such that all group members can see them.

3. *Analyze the solutions in terms of cost and benefit.* During this step, each solution can be addressed in detail. Eliminate ideas that are unsafe, unachievable, or obviously not related to the problem. Conduct a discussion of each remaining solution in terms of the cost (What resources would be needed? How much time would it take? How much would it cost?) and benefits (Is it worth the cost?). At this point, team members have to be realistic about the available resources. They also need to be reminded of the effect of any solution on all constituents. How will the solution affect students, parents, other school personnel, and/or each other?

4. *Pick a solution and plan a course of action (assign responsibilities and time lines).* Settle on a solution, preferably one that is likely to result in success. Plan how the solution is to be accomplished (see the previously mentioned planning steps). Assign responsibility for steps, activities, or objectives in the plan and assign time lines. Agree to a future meeting date to evaluate results.

5. *Implement the solution.* Team members should commit to taking timely action and do so. If additional problems arise, call another meeting or inform other team members of any action taken to correct problems along the way. Solutions that are not implemented in a timely manner are a problem. Meet and try to solve these issues.

6 *Evaluate results.* Many solutions will require data collection and graphs. Certainly, this will not be necessary in the previously mentioned case of the paraprofessional who needs a different break time, but it will be necessary in the case of student regression or inappropriate behavior. Before adjourning the meeting, decide how to evaluate the chosen solution and discuss evaluation data at a follow-up meeting. If the solution did not work, move through the problem-solving steps again. Do not wait too long to evaluate results. If the plan needs to be changed, either call another meeting or change the plan, inform people, and discuss the changes at the next regularly scheduled meeting.

Teaching is actually a series of decisions and problem-solving episodes. Problems will always exist, offering opportunities for developing creative solutions. Do not be discouraged by a problem. It would be best if the same problem does not appear repeatedly, but the appearance of new problems often means progress. Stay flexible, creative, and energetic and accept problems as part of the management task that you have been assigned.

Summary

Teachers of students with autism will typically need to take on a management role because many professionals are assigned to work with their students. The teacher is the best person to develop and lead this professional team because he or she has the responsibility of making sure that the student learns the curriculum and progresses through the IEP. If teachers are to develop and lead the professional team, the teacher will need to be informed about best practices for working with students with autism (e.g., read this book) and will need to understand the roles and responsibilities of each member of the team.

Through effective communication, team-building strategies, coordination, consultation, and problem solving, the teacher can ensure that everyone is working together toward common goals in the students' best interests. Even with the best efforts, however, there may be individuals who do not commit to the goals and who may never become functional, productive team members. At-a-Glance 6.2 lists some personnel characteristics that can disrupt a team's work. A teacher may need to seek help from a school administrator if relationship-building and effective communication techniques do not change adult behavior. Teachers are not trained as administrators, and we do not expect them to deal with challenging personnel issues. However, using some of the strategies described in this chapter will usually result in a very rewarding experience for all team members (and the students) and possibly lifelong friendships.

References

Chopra, R. V., Sandoval-Lucero, E., Aragon, L., Bernal, C., Berg de Balderas, H., & Carroll, D. (2004). The paraprofessional role of connector. *Remedial and Special Education, 25*(4), 219–231.

Gordon, T. (1974). *T.E.T.: Teacher effectiveness training.* New York: Peter H. Wyden.

Heflin, L. J., & Simpson, R. L. (1998). Interventions for children and youth with autism: Prudent choices in a world of exaggerated claims and empty promises: Part II. Legal/policy analysis and recommendations for selecting interventions and treatments. *Focus on Autism and Other Developmental Disabilities, 13,* 212–220.

Individuals with Disabilities Education Act of 1990, 20 U.S.C. § 1400 *et seq.*

National Research Council, Division of Behavioral and Social Sciences and Education, Committee on Educational Interventions for Children with Autism. (2001). *Educating children with autism* (C. Lord & J. P. McGee, Eds.). Washington, DC: National Academy Press.

At-a-Glance 6.2 Personnel Characteristics That May Hamper Team Functioning

- Boredom (does not find joy in the job)
- Incompetence (is unable to master essential skills)
- Indifference (does not care about the goals)
- Sabotage (undermines goals and individuals' performance)
- Noncompliance (refuses to perform, follow directions, or participate in team activities)
- Too much assistance (cannot grasp the concept of building independence and insists on being needed at all times)
- Disparate goals (has goals that conflict with team goals)
- Power hungry (is overcontrolling with students and other team members; must always be right and have own way)
- Uproar (causes problems by spreading incorrect information, gossip, etc.)
- Dependence (refuses to take initiative; only waits to be told what to do)
- Chaos (is uncomfortable when things are going smoothly; prefers chaos, such as noise, tantrums, messy rooms, crises)
- Blocker of team progress (actively or passively works to thwart team activities)

Curriculum Development

In Chapters 2 through 5 we provided information about *how* to teach children and youth with autism such that, given their characteristics, they will most likely learn. We believe, however, that equally important teacher decisions pertain to *what* students should learn. Teachers could be effectively performing all the recommended strategies, but if they are not teaching something that students need to master, the instruction is all for naught. In fact, it is our contention that curricular decisions (what a particular student needs to learn) should precede all other teaching decisions (e.g., how to teach, who should teach, where to teach). In this chapter, we will delineate considerations that affect curriculum development and recommend strategies for developing age-appropriate and individualized curricula.

What a teacher targets to teach is most likely what the students will learn. What the students learn will affect future choices about schooling and how and where they will live and work. For example, a student who is not taught to toilet independently or work without self-injurious behavior may lose the choice of spending time in general education classrooms. Not spending time with age-appropriate peers may limit opportunities to learn language and social skills. In turn, failing to learn language and social skills may limit the student's choice of working in competitive employment situations and living independently. Particularly for students with low-functioning autism who do not learn easily and who need to be taught basic life skills, each curricular decision becomes significant in terms of future outcomes.

A curriculum is usually defined as a course of study and is typically organized in the form of goals and objectives arranged in order of difficulty for several content or skill areas. For most public school students, the course of study includes academic areas (e.g., math, science, social studies) and tool subjects (e.g., reading, writing, spelling) that prepare students for entrance into higher education institutions. The academic curriculum is *standardized,* which means that state education agency personnel develop the curriculum and all students in that state are taught the same things at the same ages. Now mandated under the No Child Left Behind Act (NCLB) of 2001, standardized achievement tests matched to the standardized goals and objectives are regularly administered to ascertain if students are learning the standardized curriculum, and schools are rated as to how well their students perform. General education teachers are trained to teach the standardized curriculum.

Special education requirements in the IDEA, on the other hand, mandate an individualized approach to curriculum development. Based on individual assessments, IEPs are developed for each student and presumably address all relevant areas of instruction. For students who have developmental delays and may have mental retardation, the targeted curricular areas typically include functional domains (e.g., communication, adaptive behavior, social, leisure/recreation, and vocational skills). At-a-Glance 7.1 provides a list of typical curricular areas. Needless to say, there is too little school time to teach all students in all curricular areas. Given time

At-a-Glance 7.1 Public School Curricular Areas

Tool Subjects: reading, writing, spelling, written expression, computer literacy
>   Students use these tools to learn academic and other types of content.

Academic Subject Matter: social studies, math, literature, English, science, foreign languages
>   Mastery of these subjects is required for college entrance.

Fine Arts: art, drama, music
>   Students learn to appreciate aesthetics.

Personal Care: physical education, health
>   Students learn about personal health and develop motor and team skills.

Vocational: industrial arts, cosmetology, home economics, auto mechanics, agriculture, horticulture, distributive education
>   Students master specific work and living skills and learn about good work habits.

Functional Curricular Areas: communication, social interaction skills, community living skills, domestic skills, self-care skills, prevocational and vocational skills, leisure/recreational skills, learning strategies, motor skills
>   Students learn to manage their own basic needs and to live and work as independently as possible.

constraints, IEP teams must make hard choices regarding what students will be taught, and more importantly, what they will *not* be taught.

The difference between general education's approach to curriculum development, with its emphasis on college preparation, and special education's approach, with an emphasis on individualized planning, presents a challenge for IEP teams as they choose curricular goals and objectives. Consider the following challenges:

1. Teaching an academic curriculum to the exclusion of functional skill training may ill-prepare individuals to live and work in their community.
2. Teaching a functional skills curriculum to the exclusion of academic goals may preclude students from successfully performing in general education classrooms, will guarantee the need for special education until graduation, and will preclude entrance into higher education institutions.
3. A program that includes a combination of academic and functional skills goals will also preclude age-appropriate academic performance because students will be receiving less instruction in the academic curriculum than their peers without disabilities.
4. A program that does not include either functional or academic curricula may doom the student to lifelong supervision and possible residential placement.
5. Attempting to teach functional skills in general education settings is difficult because general education teachers are expected to move large numbers of students through the standardized curriculum and are not trained to teach an alternate curriculum. Furthermore, after the first or second grades, there are fewer opportunities to practice functional skills in general education classrooms.

6. Attempting to teach academics in special education classrooms is sometimes difficult because special education teachers typically have not mastered all academic content at the level required to teach it, may not have access to general education materials and textbooks, and may "water down" goals and objectives that seem unattainable for their students.

In spite of these difficult issues, the IEP team must decide the most important content and skills for the student to be taught. The ramifications of choosing an inappropriate curriculum can have lifelong implications; therefore, teachers need to conduct a thoughtful, efficient planning process. We cannot afford to waste instructional time teaching things that will negatively affect students or, worse, not have any effect. Instead, in conjunction with the IEP team, we need to (a) choose important goals and objectives for each student, (b) organize the curriculum into an accessible sequence, (c) refine the objectives in terms of learning levels and task analyses, and (d) develop ways to assess performance within the designated sequence. (We will discuss collecting data for assessment in Chapter 8.)

Curricular Considerations

In this book we are specifically interested in students with low-functioning autism who most likely have delays in language, cognitive, motor, and social development and may lack the prerequisites for mastery of academic subject matter and tool subjects. For these students, we typically focus on functional (i.e., useful) life skills. This does not mean that an academic curriculum would never be appropriate; however, in the individualized IEP deliberations, we recommend targeting skills that will likely enhance ultimate independent functioning in integrated community settings. The following are some guidelines that can assist with this very important task of curriculum development:

1. *Develop a curriculum as a team that includes family members and other adults who are invested in long-term goals.* Having parents and other family members involved in curricular decisions offers several benefits:

- When teachers and parents agree on what needs to be taught, there should be little controversy about how and where it should be taught.
- If teachers and parents both teach and reinforce targeted skills, the student is apt to learn them faster.
- Parents must guide the education of the child throughout his or her school career. Teachers typically only plan for students for 1 year or a few years. Parents need a view of a comprehensive lifelong curriculum.
- Family members often can explain what skills are needed for everyday living. The school perspective tends to be dominated by the general education curriculum.

2. *Choose a curriculum that will facilitate a student's ability to live a productive, fulfilling life.* Take a long-term future view of goals to decide what to teach during the current year. The goal of ultimate independence should guide all current curricular decisions.

3. *The chosen curriculum should result in functional skills.* This means that targeted skills should be useful to the student now and in the future. We assume that a skill is functional if an inability to do it (e.g., dressing, toileting, cooking) means that someone else must do it for the individual. These are important skills to master if independence is to be achieved.

4. *The chosen curriculum should be longitudinal.* Current curriculum goals should be vertically linked to ultimate long-term goals. What is taught in the current year should enhance acquisition of skills that need to be learned in the future. Too often, annual goals are developed without consideration for what an individual ultimately must be able to perform to live and work independently. For example, if a student is to ultimately be able to work in his father's store, it might be best to begin early in his school career to teach him to work around noise and people.

5. *The chosen curriculum should be horizontally integrated.* A horizontally integrated curriculum coordinates goals from several curricular areas. For example, a student who needs to learn to ride a bus will need communication goals (asking for help, asking how much it cost, asking if a seat is taken); motor goals (climbing on the bus, standing while the bus is moving, walking down an aisle, climbing off the bus, putting money in slot); and social skills (sitting still in the seat, smiling in response to someone smiling, saying please and thank you). The speech therapist, teacher, and adaptive PE teacher should not be developing a curriculum in isolation of one another but instead should coordinate what is being taught based on targeted activities, routines, and tasks.

6. *The chosen curriculum should be chronologically age-appropriate.* Consider what activities same-age, same-gender peers perform. Provide similar content in similar settings and use similar materials to that frequented by and used by these peers. For example, adolescents who need to master fine-motor skills need to do so not because they will be putting beads on a string but because they may be making a sandwich, opening a can, or using an electric razor. Match the objectives to these age-appropriate activities and routines.

7. *The chosen curriculum should be community referenced.* Curricular goals and objectives should be developed for an individual with consideration for community standards and expectations. For example, a student living in a farming community may need to learn how to walk along a road safely rather than learn to ride a bus.

8. *The chosen curriculum should include communication and social skills.* We know that characteristics of students with autism include deficits in these two areas. At every opportunity, communication and social goals and objectives should be targeted. You will need to teach communication and language *all* day, as you will learn in Chapter 9. Almost every life activity that you teach will have related language and social requirements, which you should consider as you develop a curriculum. At-a-Glance 7.2 summarizes these considerations.

At-a-Glance 7.2 Curricular Development Considerations

1. Develop curriculum as a team that includes family members and other persons who are invested in long-term goals.
2. Choose a curriculum that will facilitate a student's ability to live a productive, fulfilling life.
3. The chosen curriculum should result in functional skills.
4. The chosen curriculum should be longitudinal.
5. The chosen curriculum should be horizontally integrated.
6. The chosen curriculum should be chronologically age-appropriate.
7. The chosen curriculum should be community referenced.
8. The chosen curriculum should include communication and social skills.

Curriculum Development Process

The curriculum development process that we recommend you use for these very important decisions requires a *discrepancy analysis.* Such a planning process involves three basic steps:

1. determine where you want to end up,
2. determine where you are now, and
3. analyze the discrepancy between the two points in terms of a plan of action.

This means that the curriculum development team should set long-term goals, determine what the student has mastered to date toward those goals, and plan a sequence of objectives that will move the student from his or her current level of functioning to mastery of the long-term goals.

Setting Long-Term Goals

One way to establish long-term goals is to consider *where* the student is to live and work at age 22, when public school services are to end. Establishing *placement goals* will facilitate choosing activity, routine, and skill goals. For example, if a student is to live in a group home and work at a local motel as an adult, she or he will need to learn how to manage her or his own toileting, bathing, and dressing activities; help with cooking and cleaning in the kitchen; get to work on time; make beds; clean bathrooms; manage a paycheck and banking account with assistance; ask for help; and so forth. Such a long-term view of placement goals is called the *criterion of ultimate functioning* (Brown, Nietupski, & Hamre-Nietupski, 1976) and should guide short-term curriculum decisions.

In addition to the ultimate placement goal, it might also be useful to consider *where* the student will have to function *in the next 3 to 5 years.* Vincent, Salisbury, Walter, Gruenwald, and Powers (1980) called this the *criterion of the next environment.* For example, teachers should consider any future transitions to middle school or high school. Knowing that a student will need to walk through crowded hallways without following someone right in front of him or her may dictate what needs to be taught in elementary school. Considering *where* the student *must currently function,* the *criterion of the immediate environment* (Peterson, Trecker, Egan, Fredericks, & Bunse, 1983) also provides information about what the student needs to learn. For example, an 8-year-old needs to function in school, after-school care, Sunday school, and the home. The skills necessary for successful functioning in these placements should be the basis for the curriculum and should guarantee that the curriculum will be individualized.

Letting future goals dictate what will be taught prevents the common errors of letting a textbook or published curriculum guide determine what a student will learn or, worse, haphazardly trying to create things to teach each year. Developing a curriculum based on long-term goals is called *futures planning.* Commercial curricula can be very helpful in this process, but they should best be used only after future goals for individual students have been delineated.

Developing an Individualized Curricular Inventory

Once the long-term and current placement goals are established, we recommend developing an activity- or routine-based curriculum by constructing an *ecological inventory* (Falvey, 1989). At-a-Glance 7.3 lists the steps of an ecological inventory,

At-a-Glance 7.3 Ecological Inventory Steps

1. *List all environments* in which the student must function presently and in the future, such as home, school, group home, motel, or middle school.

2. *List the subenvironments* for *each* of the listed environments. For example, the subenvironments of the school might be the classroom, cafeteria, bathroom, playground, hallway, and bus.

3. *List the activities and/or routines* that would be required for any individual to function success- fully in each subenvironment. For example, in the school bathroom, a student will need to toilet and wash hands. In the home bathroom, he or she will need to bathe, toilet, dress, groom, and clean up.

4. *Task-analyze the activities and/or functional routines* into sequenced substeps or subcomponents.

5. *List the related* communication, motor, cognitive, and social skills that would be necessary for successful completion of each activity or functional routine.

6. *Assess the student using the task analyses* to determine present level of performance in terms of the substeps, and use observational recording to determine present level of performance on discrete or continuous behaviors/skills.

which commences with the curriculum development team, led by the teacher, de-lineating environments in which the target student needs to live, work, and recreate now, 3 years hence, and at age 22. For example, a 9-year-old student currently may need to function at home, school, church, day care, and in the community. In the next 3 years, he or she may also need to function at the community recreation center but no longer need to function at the day-care facility. At 22, he or she may need to function in all those places and the added environment of work. The individual may also be moving to a supervised living situation instead of living at home.

In the next step of the inventory, the team lists all the subenvironments for each target environment. For example, this same student at home must function in the kitchen, dining room, bathroom, bedroom, den, and backyard. In church, he or she must function in the sanctuary, bathroom, and reception hall. Once all the suben-vironments have been identified, the team now lists all the activities and functional routines that the student must perform in each of these subenvironments. In the dining room, for example, the student may have to set the table, eat, and clear the table. In the den, he or she would watch TV, play games, and clean up. Activities are what we call *complex chained skills:* Several related behaviors are chained together to complete a task, such as setting a table or brushing one's teeth. *Functional rou-tines* are also chained behaviors but differ from activities in that they are initiated by natural cues and conclude with a "critical effect" (Neel & Billingsley, 1989, p. 50). For example, a student will go to use the toilet because she or he feels the need (natural cue), and the routine ends when she or he feels better, is dressed, and back at play (critical effect).

Because we recommend conducting this ecological inventory at three different points in time, you can see that the result would be a very comprehensive list of ac-tivities, functional routines, and related skills tailored to a specific student. Even if the team stopped at this point and let the activities/routine lists guide IEP develop-ment, it would probably be a more meaningful curriculum than just ascribing to a commercial curriculum or thinking up something on the spot. Taking the activities/ routine list a few more steps, however, will further assist with the tasks of assessing the student's current level of functioning and keeping track of progress toward designated goals.

Refining the Curriculum

Once a comprehensive list of activities and functional routines is developed, the next step is to break each activity and/or routine down into substeps or subcomponents, which is known as *task analysis*. Learning to create small learning chunks is essential to the curriculum development process. Teachers can practice developing task analyses by watching someone perform activities or routines and noting all of the steps or components. The number of steps in a task will depend on the complexity of the activity or routine. A general rule is to include no more than 15 to 20 steps. Some activities, such as cleaning up after lunch, may only have a few steps, whereas preparing something to eat or drink may have more steps. Figure 7.1 depicts a partial ecological inventory and a task analysis for the current year for a fourth-grade student. Notice that the task analysis is arranged so that assessment data can be gathered about whether a student can perform routine steps and whether he or she needs help to do the steps. The task analysis now becomes an assessment tool to gather information about the student's present level of performance in regard to specific activities and functional routines and also can act as a tool for gathering progress data. Using the task analysis as the initial assessment tool is called *task analytic assessment* (Browder, 2001). We will cover more about collecting and analyzing progress data in Chapter 8. Teachers do not need to develop an analysis for every task. They may also refer to commercial curricula and activity guides for task analyses and skill sequences.

For each task analysis of target activities and functional skills, the teacher now needs to list all the related communication, motor, cognitive, and social skills necessary to perform each task. For example, for a student to participate in an art activity in the classroom, he or she may need to learn to walk while balancing a tub of materials, hold a paint brush, sit straight in a chair, and dip his or her brush in water (motor skills). Furthermore, he or she may need to learn the vocabulary for each of the art supplies and how to ask for assistance (communication skills). Socially, the student will need to learn to stay seated during the activity, to share, and to keep hands to him- or herself. Cognitively, the student may need to be able to identify colors and shapes. These skills are usually what we call *simple discrete behaviors* (e.g., dip brush in water) and *continuous ongoing behaviors* (remain in seat). Assessment of these behaviors and skills will require observational recording, which we will cover in Chapter 8. Figure 7.2 illustrates a partial ecological inventory for two subenvironments in school, with a task analysis for each targeted activity and the related communication, social, motor, and cognitive skills for one of the activities (arrival routine). This ecological inventory process will lead to a detailed, individualized curriculum for each student. The challenge for teachers will be finding the time to develop the inventory.

We envision the curriculum development team (parents, teachers, related service personnel) using butcher paper taped to the wall to diagram all possible environments, subenvironments, and activities for an individual student. We recommend beginning the process with the current year so that parents can see the advantage of thinking about environments and related activities as a basis for the curriculum. Teachers may then suggest thinking about the intermediate and ultimate environments. Do not be surprised, however, if parents are not able to clearly think or talk about where their children may be functioning in the future. Most parents are just trying to get through each day or week, and thinking about future requirements may

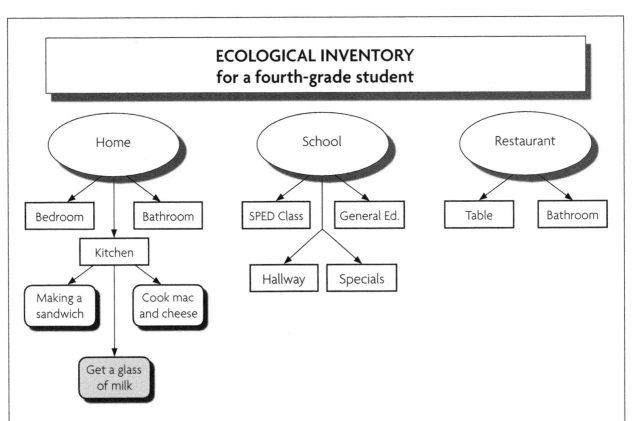

Task Analytic Assessment Form for Getting a Glass of Milk

Task Analysis	Needs Assistance	Needs Verbal Only	Does Without Prompt
Go to kitchen.			
Find the refrigerator.			
Open the refrigerator.			
Locate the milk jug.			
Take the milk out of the refrigerator.			
Set the jug on the counter.			
Take the cap off.			
Locate the cabinet with glasses.			
Take down one glass.			
Set glass on counter beside milk.			
Take milk jug by handle with one hand.			
Take other hand and pick up glass.			
Raise the glass to the top of the milk jug opening.			
Tip milk jug slightly to begin pouring.			
Stop when milk has filled glass half full.			
Place milk jug back on counter.			
Replace milk jug cap.			
Take milk jug by handle and return to refrigerator.			
Return to counter and pick up glass.			
Drink milk.			

Figure 7.1. Partial ecological inventory and task analytic assessment form for the current year for a fourth-grade student.

SCHOOL ENVIRONMENT

Subenvironment: CLASSROOM

Activity 1: Arrival routine

Substeps:
Enter room.
Take off backpack.
Unzip backpack.
Take out notebook.
Put notebook in basket.
Take out lunch.
Put lunch in cubby.
Hang backpack in cubby.
Take off jacket.
Hang up jacket.
Go to lunch choice list.
Indicate lunch choice.*
Go to desk to choose activity.

*Ronald always brings a lunch because he has very particular eating habits.

Activity 2: Choosing activity

Substeps:
Go to desk.
Open activity notebook.
Pick an activity cue.
Take cue to shelf.
Get matching activity.
Put cue on activity box.
Take box to desk.
Sit down.
Take activity out.
Start activity.
Do activity.
Finish activity.
Raise hand.
Wait for teacher.
Tell teacher "Finished."
Put activity in box.
Take activity to shelf.
Put activity on shelf.
Take cue to desk.
Place cue in finished box.
Complete 3 activities.
Take a break.

Activity 3: Cleaning up

Substeps:
S^D "song."*
Stop activity.
Put activity in box.
Take activity to shelf.
Put activity on shelf.
Take cue to desk.
Place cue in finished box.
Go to place on rug.
Sit down.
Wait for class to sit.

*Teacher always uses the same song to cue clean-up time.

Subenvironment: BATHROOM

Activity 1: Using a urinal

Substeps:
Wait for empty urinal.
Move to empty urinal.
Stand facing urinal.
Unsnap pants.
Pull pants down.
Pull down underwear.
Touch toes to urinal.
Urinate.
Flush urinal.
Pull up underwear.
Pull up pants.
Snap pants.
Go wash hands.

Activity 2: Washing hands

Substeps:
Go to sink.
Put hand on tap.
Turn tap on.
Go to soap dispenser.
Put left hand under.
Put right hand on lever.
Push right hand down.
Rub hands with soap.
Put hands under tap.
Rub to remove lather.
Place hand on tap.
Turn tap off.
Dry hands.

Activity 3: Drying hands*

Substeps:
Go to blower.
Put hand under nozzle.
Rub hands in wind.
Count to 10 slowly.
Leave bathroom.

*If Ronald will have access to other drying apparatus, these should be taught as well.

Figure 7.2. Partial ecological inventory for two current school subenvironments, with a task analysis for each targeted activity and related communication, social, motor, and cognitive skills for one of the activities (i.e., arrival routine).

(continues)

137   Curriculum Development

RELATED SKILLS FOR ARRIVAL ROUTINE

Substeps:	Communication Skills*	Social Skills	Fine Motor Skills	Gross Motor Skills	Cognitive Skills
enter room take off backpack		walk in line		walk, open door slide pack off arms	
unzip backpack take out notebook put notebook in basket		hands to self	grasp and pull zipper grab notebook release notebook	pull zipper pull out notebook walk to basket	recognize notebook recognize basket
take out lunch put lunch in cubby hang backpack in cubby			grab lunch release lunch position loop for hook	pull out lunch walk to cubby lift pack to hook	recognize lunch choose his cubby hang pack on correct hook
take off jacket hang up jacket			unzip, unbutton, etc.	maneuver jacket off walk to cubby, lift jacket	choose cubby and hangs jacket
go to lunch choice list	uses signs to tell choice	wait for his turn		walk	locate list
indicate lunch choice		move only his picture	pick his picture, place it on lunch list		recognize lunch cues and his picture, make appropriate choice
go to desk to choose activity				walk	
	*Throughout the routine, he needs to understand teacher's cues as well as how to ask for help.				

Figure 7.2. *Continued.*

be very difficult. Present the future placement goal activity as "where they hope or dream" their child may be functioning and assure them that the team is just making a best guess about these things. If, given time constraints and team nonparticipation, you are able to develop an inventory only for the current year, it will still be well worth your time and will greatly benefit your students.

Determining What to Teach This Year

Once the comprehensive activity/routine list, task analyses, and related skills are delineated, the team should decide which of these things the student might need to learn first. Parents may have definite opinions about what they would like their child to master in a given school year. Other team members (OT, PT, SLP) may also provide input about what should be taught first. At-a-Glance 7.4 lists some considerations when deciding what to teach first.

Choosing Academic Goals

For students who need to primarily learn skills leading to functional independence, academic goals—if they are targeted—tend to be in the areas of reading, writing, and basic math. These might be appropriate goals for some students but may not be appropriate for others, and thus take time away from teaching more meaningful and functional goals. We must make sure we are using instructional time to teach what is most important for each student to learn. Westling and Fox (2004) recommended five primary considerations in determining the appropriateness of academic goals:

1. *Consider the student's age and the remaining amount of school time.* Younger students may benefit more from academic goals while older students may most need to learn functional living and vocational skills.

2. *Consider the amount of success in mastering academic goals to date.* If the student has received effective instruction in academic goals and has yet to master them, the IEP team may need to reevaluate the appropriateness of those goals in comparison to other functional curriculum components that may have been excluded.

3. *Consider what academic skills might be necessary for functioning in relevant environments.* Relate academic skills to the targeted activities and functional routines delineated

At-a-Glance 7.4 Considerations for What to Teach First

Teach things that family members think are important.

Teach skills that require the most supervision so the student can perform them independently.

Teach activities and routines that the individual performs frequently (e.g., eating, toileting, talking, school routines).

Teach skills that prevent problem behavior (e.g., functional communication and social behavior that elicit reinforcement).

Teach simple skills and then move to complex skills.

Teach skills that will ensure safety (crossing street, using a stove properly).

Teach initial learning behaviors: compliance, attending, imitation, visual and auditory discrimination.

in the ecological inventory. For example, shopping may require some knowledge of reading functional labels and counting money. Riding a bus may require reading the bus destinations or schedule, telling time, and counting the correct change for a bus ticket.

4. *Consider the relative value of academic skills to other functional skills.* Remember that in curriculum development the important considerations are not only what you choose to teach students but also what you do *not* choose to teach. What you do not teach will probably not be learned. Consider which skills will make it most likely that the individual will access integrated living, working, and recreational settings now, in the near future, and ultimately.

5. *Consider the wishes of the student and his or her family in terms of academic skills.* If the student and/or family members wish for the student to learn academic skills after participating in a futures planning process, such as the ecological inventory, and answering the four previous considerations, serious consideration should be given to these wishes.

Determining Current Functioning Level Within a Curriculum

Once functional activities, routines, related skills, and/or academic skills have been targeted, the teacher should conduct an assessment to determine to what degree the student can currently perform those targets. The teacher might use a task analytic assessment (see Figure 7.1) in which he or she would observe the student performing an activity or routine and mark each step on the task analysis in terms of the amount of assistance needed to perform it. Another method for assessing current performance level is to refer to commercial curricula and activity guides, many of which also include assessment instruments. Using an established curricular sequence (either from an ecological inventory or a commercial guide) for assessment purposes is known as *curriculum-based assessment* (CBA).

Teachers may also assess present level of functioning by using formal measures such as adaptive behavior scales, speech and language assessments, social skills assessments, and academic readiness and skill assessments. Resources 7.1 lists some common adaptive behavior scales and academic assessment instruments. Although formal assessments and CBAs from commercial curricula may provide information about the student's present functioning in several domains relative to chronological-age peers or to the published curricula, these instruments may provide little information about what the student still needs to learn to, for example, be able to work at the motel down the road in his or her hometown. We do, however, recommend using commercial curricula and activity guides to develop IEPs when there is no time to conduct an ecological inventory. We also recommend that teachers use the curricula and/or guides for obtaining task analyses and skill sequences relative to ecological inventory results. Appendix C provides information about several commercially available functional curricula; activity guides; and basic communication, social skills, and academic curricula. Many of these curricula come with CBA profiles. Just remember that it is still up to the teacher to relate any curriculum choices or assessment results to an individual student's current, intermediate, and ultimate placement goals.

Units of Instruction

Teachers should now organize their curriculum into clear *units of instruction* for each student. This means you should avoid simply teaching splinter skills, instead incorporating skill training into units based on specific activities (e.g., riding a bus),

Resources 7.1 Adaptive Behavior Scales and Academic Assessment Instruments

Adaptive Behavior Scales and Developmental Inventories

Adaptive Behavior Assessment System–Second Edition (ABAS-II). Harrison and Oakland (2004). San Antonio, TX: Harcourt Assessment.

AAMR Adaptive Behavior Scales (ABS; 2nd ed.). Nihira, Leland, and Lambert (1993). Austin, TX: PRO-ED.

Pyramid Scales. Cone (1984). Austin, TX: PRO-ED.

Scales of Independent Behavior–Revised (SIB-R). Bruininks, Woodcock, Weatherman, and Hill (1985). Allen, TX: DLM Teaching Resources.

Vineland Adaptive Behavior Scales (Vineland-II; 2nd ed.). Sparrow, Balla, and Cicchetti (1984). Circle Pines, MN: American Guidance Service.

Commercial Academic Assessments

AIMS: Pre-reading Kit. Early (1986). Elizabethtown, PA: Continental Press.

Brigance Diagnostic Inventories. Brigance (1983, 1999). North Billerica, MA: Curriculum Associates.

Diagnostic Achievement Battery (3rd ed.). Newcomer (2001). Austin, TX: PRO-ED.

Early Learning Accomplishments Profile. Grover, Piminger, and Sanford (1988). Winston-Salem, NC: Kaplan Press.

Learning Accomplishments Profile (Diagnostic ed.). LeMay, Giffen, and Sanford (1977). Chapel Hill, NC: Chapel Hill Training Outreach Program.

Peabody Individual Achievement Test. Marwardt (1997). Circle Pines, MN: American Guidance Service.

Test of Early Reading Ability–Third Edition (TERA-3). Reid, Hresko, and Hammill (2001). Austin, TX: PRO-ED.

Test of Early Written Language–Second Edition (TEWL-2). Hresko, Herron, and Peak (1996). Austin, TX: PRO-ED.

Woodcock-Johnson Tests of Achievement. Woodcock and Johnson (1989). Allen, TX: DLM Teaching Resources.

Woodcock Reading Mastery Test. Woodcock (1997). Circle Pines, MN: American Guidance Service.

routines (e.g., eating lunch), themes (e.g., "transportation," "our community," "people in our lives"), work tasks (e.g., greenhouse maintenance, cleaning motel rooms), social skills lessons (e.g., "making friends"), or some other organization. The units should integrate goals and objectives across curricular domains and help ensure that the discrete skills that are taught to students will be meaningful. Teaching skills through units of instruction helps students to generalize their skills, gives them multiple opportunities to practice skills, helps teaching adults organize their time and understand why students need to learn targeted skills, and facilitates student motivation to learn because the learning unit will have a purpose. Hopefully, you choose these units of instruction based on (a) a futures planning process that includes family and student input, where appropriate, and (b) the curricular considerations presented in this chapter.

Writing Goals and Objectives

Having thoughtfully developed individualized and functional targets for individual students, the teacher is now ready to write down a list of goals and objectives. We encourage teachers to develop what we call *behavioral* or—as you learned in Chapter 2—*operational* goals and objectives so that targeted outcomes are clear to all of the persons involved and so that progress data can be easily gathered. Because teaching how to write good behavioral goals and objectives is beyond the scope of this book, we refer the reader to Alberto and Troutman (2006) for more detail.

Basically, an instructional goal communicates what the teacher intends to teach during one school year, as mandated by the IDEA. We write annual goals, for example, "Johnny will complete grooming routines independently," or "Angela will increase the quantity and quality of peer interactions." Goals are generally broad statements about what the student is expected to master and what the teacher intends to teach.

Learning objectives communicate short-term, intended instructional outcomes. There may be several objectives written for each goal. Objectives identify behaviors and responses that the student is to perform to indicate that learning has occurred. A well-written objective has four parts:

1. *Identify the learner* so we know who is intended to learn. For example, "Ivan will recite . . ." or "Hannah will name . . ."

2. *State the target behavior* such that it can be observed and counted (as we noted in Chapter 2). Typically, only one behavior is targeted per objective. In the case of teaching a routine or activity that contains many chained behaviors, the objective can state that the student is to "perform all steps of the attached task analysis." Each step would not need a specific objective. Operational behaviors include verbs such as *point to, say, sign, pick up, sit down, place on, state, complete, bring to,* and *carry.* You want to avoid verbs such as *appreciates, accepts, knows, understands, thinks, tells* the difference, and so forth, because you cannot reliably observe when those things are taking place. Operationally defining target behaviors takes practice. Examples of good questions to ask yourself are the following: Could a stranger read this and understand exactly what the learner is to do? Could two people count this target and get close to the same count?

3. *State the condition* under which the learner is to perform the behavior. Target responses are often dependent on certain conditions before they can be emitted. Other times, it is necessary to be clear about when, where, and with whom you expect the student to emit the behavior, for example, "On the playground, Jeremy will . . ."; "After rising in the morning, Peggy will . . ."; "Given the verbal cue 'put in', Alice will . . ."; or "Asked to tell what sound the (cow, dog, bear, cat) makes, James will . . ."

4. Last, the objective needs to contain a *mastery criterion statement.* When will you know the student has mastered the targeted response or behavior? How many behaviors (e.g., 10 conversations this week), how accurate does the behavior need to be (e.g., 7 of 10 correct trials 3 days in a row), or how long does the behavior have to last (e.g., remains in seat 20 consecutive minutes each circle time for 2 weeks) to denote mastery? The criterion statement will give you information about how to develop progress data sheets and when to note that the objective has been mastered so you can target another objective. The more specifically you write all components of the objectives, the easier it will be to collect progress data and to communicate to all teaching adults exactly what the learner is to be taught.

Learning Levels

An important component of writing goals and objectives is to consider at what learning level a student needs to master the target behavior. *Learning levels* refer to depth of knowledge or skill mastery. For example, *listing* the previous components of a behavioral objective shows some knowledge on your part, but not as much knowledge as it would take for you to *define* each component. More knowledge would be needed for you to actually *write* objectives correctly, and even more knowledge would be needed for you to *analyze* the process of writing objectives such that you could *teach* someone else how to do it.

For the purpose of writing goals and objectives for students with autism, we refer to Alberto and Troutman's (2006) "hierarchy of response competence" (p. 73). New first-time learning occurs at the *acquisition level.* Mastering a response at the acquisition level means that the student can produce the target response at least a few times over a few days. An example would be "When cued by the teacher to 'put in,' Sarah puts the blocks in the box 5 of 6 trials for 3 consecutive days." We say that Sarah has acquired the behavior of "putting in."

The next response level is *fluency.* Now we want to see the student produce the behavior at a faster rate over a longer period of time. For the next month, we now want Sarah to put the blocks in the box every time she is cued. At the *maintenance level,* we want the student to maintain the rate of response production over a long period of time. For the rest of the semester, Sarah now can put the blocks in every time the teacher cues her.

At the *generalization level,* the student will respond under varied conditions (called *stimulus generalization*) and/or vary the manner in which he or she performs the behavior (called *response generalization*). For stimulus generalization, Sarah will put the blocks in the box when anyone cues her to do it in the classroom or at home. She also will produce the behavior to various cues, such as "Put the blocks up," "Clean up the blocks," "Put the blocks in the box," and "Clean up our toys." Response generalization would have Sarah not just putting the blocks in the container one at a time when told but gathering together several blocks and dumping them in the box or maybe even asking for help with the task as she puts the blocks away. Because we are talking about a hierarchy, the implication is that the student must master responses at the lower learning levels before mastering responses at the higher levels. Thus, a student would have to be able to ask for an ice cream cone each time he or she wants it at home before we might expect that he or she would ask for it at school or in the mall.

The conditions and criteria statements in an objective need to reflect at which learning level a student needs to show competence. Criteria statements target a relatively few mastered responses at acquisition level over a short period of time, a higher rate of responding over a longer period of time at fluency, and the same rate of responding over a semester or a year at maintenance levels. At the generalization level, criteria statements may revert to fluency targets, but the condition statements are changed (stimulus generalization). Once fluency is mastered under the different conditions, the criteria statements reflect not only the changed conditions but also maintenance criteria.

Teaching at various learning levels requires teachers to adjust prompting and reinforcement schedules, which we discussed in Chapters 2 and 3. Acquisition learning requires heavy prompting and thick reinforcement schedules. Fluency requires prompt and reinforcement fading. Maintenance requires no prompting and a thin, unpredictable reinforcement schedule. Generalization might initially require more prompts and reinforcement, with rapid fading of both. As mentioned in Chapter 3, we recommend that teachers use DTT to teach students who are learning at the acquisition and fluency levels but move to probe trials and naturalistic/milieu teaching (see Chapter 4) for teaching at the maintenance and generalization levels.

We recommend that teachers explain the hierarchy of response competence to parents to acquaint them with the complexity of targeting and teaching exactly what their child needs to learn. It will also help parents to understand what is written on their child's IEP and why it takes a while to fully master a skill or chained behaviors through all learning levels.

A Word About Generalization

We really have not finished teaching our students until they can generalize their responses across conditions and cues. It does little good to teach a student to brush his or her teeth at school if he or she does not do it at home, or to teach a student to initiate conversations in the classroom if he or she does not do it in the cafeteria. For almost everything you teach, you will have to teach to generalization. In Chapter 3 we taught you to loosen stimulus control (change the S^Ds), and in Chapter 4 we taught you to use naturalistic/milieu teaching to promote generalization. Other strategies for promoting generalization are listed in Focus Here 7.1. Teachers should be sure to write generalization objectives when students are ready for that level of learning and should use these specified strategies for teaching to mastery.

Focus Here 7.1 Strategies for Teaching to Generalization

1. **Loosen stimulus control (S^D).** Once the student acquires a response to one S^D, present other relevant S^Ds, use different reinforcers, and have the student vary the original response. For example, give different verbal cues, have different people give the cues, cue in different settings, and use different materials. This will prevent the student from becoming *stimulus bound* (producing a response only in the presence of one specific condition).

2. **Implement a successful teaching program in other settings.** If the student is responding to trials that require sign language at school, have the parents conduct the same type of trials at home. This technique will require you to train adults as well as the student.

3. **Make the training setting more like the generalized setting.** If you are teaching self-help skills at school, modify the classroom and/or bathroom to approximate the bedroom/bathroom in the child's home. The student will be more likely to produce the response in both settings. You may also want to take familiar items (e.g., a timer or a favorite stim toy) from the training setting to the generalized setting.

4. **Introduce natural reinforcers.** Move the student away from contrived reinforcers. Naturalistic/milieu teaching facilitates this move. Teach skills, activities, and routines that result in a critical effect or natural reinforcement for the student, such as requesting (manding) what he or she wants (results in the desired item) or smiling and making eye contact (results in positive interactions). You may need to teach students with autism to recognize natural reinforcers (e.g., hugs) as something positive. You may also need to train adults in various settings to reinforce frequently for appropriate responses.

5. **Reinforce generalized behavior.** Every teaching adult should be prompting responses in generalized settings and providing frequent reinforcement when those responses occur. Snacktime and lunchtime are excellent opportunities to prompt and reinforce communication and self-help responses. Playtimes are excellent opportunities to prompt and reinforce social skills.

Summary

In this chapter we discussed a very important teacher task: developing an individualized, functional curriculum based on futures planning. The care you take in choosing what to teach a student will affect that student's choices now and in the future in terms of living and working opportunities. A well-developed curriculum will also facilitate decisions about the best instructional strategies to use and the best place for the learner to be taught targeted goals. The better you become at specifying what the student is to learn, the easier it will be for you to teach it and for the learner to master it. Well-written goals and objectives will also facilitate the collection of progress data (i.e., formative assessment). The next chapter will address formative assessment methods to confirm that your instruction in the designated curriculum has been effective. Once you have established an appropriate curriculum, you must utilize effective instructional strategies and regularly check to ensure that the learner is progressing toward mastery.

References

Alberto, P. A., & Troutman, A. C. (2006). *Applied behavior analysis for teachers* (7th ed.). Columbus, OH: Merrill/Prentice Hall.

Browder, D. M. (2001). *Curriculum and assessment for students with moderate and severe disabilities.* New York: Guilford Press.

Brown, L., Nietupski, J., & Hamre-Nietupski, S. (1976). Criterion of ultimate functioning and public school services for severely handicapped students. In M. S. Thomas (Ed.), *Hey, don't forget about me! New directions for serving the severely handicapped* (pp. 2–15). Reston, VA: Council for Exceptional Children.

Falvey, M. A. (1989). *Community-based curriculum: Instructional strategies for students with severe handicaps* (2nd ed.). Baltimore: Brookes.

Neel, R. S., & Billingsley, F. F. (1989). *IMPACT: A functional curriculum handbook for students with moderate to severe disabilities.* Baltimore: Brookes.

No Child Left Behind Act of 2001, 20 U.S.C. 70 § 6301 *et seq.* (2002)

Peterson, J., Trecker, N., Egan, I., Fredericks, H. D. G., & Bunse, C. (1983). *The teaching research curriculum for handicapped adolescents and adults: Assessment procedures.* Monmouth, OR: Teaching Research.

Vincent, L. J., Salisbury, C., Walter, G., Gruenwald, L. J., & Powers, M. (1980). Program evaluation and curriculum development in early childhood special education: Criteria of the next environment. In W. Sailor, B. Wilcox, & L. Brown (Eds.), *Methods of instruction for severely handicapped students* (pp. 303–328). Baltimore: Brookes.

Westling, D. L., & Fox, L. (2004). *Teaching students with severe disabilities* (3rd ed.). Columbus, OH: Merrill/Prentice Hall.

Collecting Progress Data

8

Directly related to curriculum development is the very important teacher responsibility of regularly collecting information regarding how well and how quickly a student masters the targeted objectives. If we cannot document that a student has mastered the designated goals and objectives, we cannot show that we have taught. Parents, school administrators, and the general public want to know that teachers are teaching and students are learning. In fact, the NCLB mandates that states document adequate student progress (and school progress) through end-of-year test performance. For students who learn slowly, progress is documented via more specific direct performance measures.

Another reason for collecting progress data has to do with making instructional decisions. If students are not appropriately progressing toward mastery of the curriculum, instructional strategies might need to be adjusted, the curriculum might need to be broken into smaller chunks, and/or prerequisites might need to be addressed. Conversely, if slow, steady progress goes unnoticed because no data are collected, teachers may unnecessarily change a teaching program that is actually working. Finally, regular measurement of student progress can prevent teaching adults and parents from becoming discouraged. Progress data may provide adult reinforcement for the difficult work of teaching.

Once teachers have specified target behaviors or responses in their behavioral objectives and stated to what mastery level a student is to progress (as discussed in Chapter 7), they should develop data collection procedures and forms to measure target responses over time. The collected progress data should then be visually represented (e.g., on a graph) for communication purposes and to assist teachers in adjusting instructional strategies as needed. The graphs should illustrate what responses are expected, what responses are produced, and the criterion for mastery as stated in the instructional objectives or related task analysis. Teachers should also develop a structure for maintaining these graphs matched to targeted objectives for accountability purposes.

Progress Data Collection Techniques

You should choose a method of measuring behavior based on what behavior has been specified for a particular objective. In Chapter 2, we noted that there are two main ways of measuring behavior: permanent product recording and observational recording. In permanent product recording, you count some permanent change in the environment caused by a behavior as an indicator that the behavior occurred. For example, you can count written responses (permanent changes to the paper) as an indicator that the student spelled his or her name correctly. You could count the number of assembly tasks completed as an indicator that the student followed all steps to put together the picnic package. You could check the student's plate after lunch to determine the amount and nature of uneaten food. The benefit of permanent product recording is that you do not have to be observing when the behavior occurs to obtain a record of whether it occurred and how well it was performed. Because not all responses and behaviors that you want to teach result in permanent products (e.g., speech responses), you will need to also master observational recording techniques.

We discussed observational recording in detail in Chapter 2. Remember that with observational recording, you must be observing as the student responds and must be making some notation about that response as it occurs. Three of the most commonly used types of observational recording, which we listed in Chapter 2, are event recording, duration recording, and latency recording. You use event recording to measure simple, discrete behaviors and to record the number of times a behavior occurred. If the response is restricted to some particular S^D (e.g., following directions, where you must have a direction for the student to respond), you will have to count both the response and the number of opportunities (S^Ds) to respond.

Figure 8.1 shows a sample form for both event and restricted event recording. If you are counting simple unrestricted discrete behaviors (e.g., initiating social interactions), you can place a hash mark each time the student performs that behavior. You could easily create a form similar to the one shown in Figure 8.1 or use other surfaces that can be marked. Many teachers put masking tape on their wrist and mark on the tape. At the end of the session or day, put the date and total time of observation on the tape and stick it on a piece of paper. In this way you will have data from multiple days or sessions on one sheet of paper. On any recording form, note how long you observed and leave the opportunities section blank if there is no required S^D. Figure 8.2 shows an event recording form for verbal responses. You

---

Instructions: Record *unrestricted events* (discrete behaviors) by placing hash marks in the Responses column. Leave the Opportunities column blank. Record *restricted events* (an S^D is required) by placing data in all columns.

STUDENT: Annie

RESPONSE: Retrieves calendar picture after task completed

Date	Obs. Time	Responses	Opportunities	% Opportunities Correct
9-17	10:00–12:00	ⵜⵜⵜ ///	10 tasks	80%
9-18	9:30–10:30	ⵜⵜⵜ /	8 tasks	75%

Figure 8.1. Event and restricted event–recording form.

Instructions: Figure percentage of total vocalizations that are spontaneous appropriate responses and transfer to a graph. You may adapt this form to have each column signify a different place (for one student) or multiple students (same behaviors).

STUDENT: Henry

OBJECTIVE: During lunch, while sitting with same-age peers, Henry will spontaneously emit the following verbal behaviors, as appropriate: verbal requests for and descriptions of items, initiations of verbal interactions, and verbal protests.

Date	11-5	11-16	Fifth-grade Table	Fourth-grade Table	Henry	Annie
Requests	//	////				
Describes						
Verbally initiates	//	//////				
Verbally protests						
Screams		//				
Percentage of vocalizations that are spontaneous appropriate utterances	100	83				

Figure 8.2. Event recording form for discrete verbal responses.

can create your own version by adapting it for behavior counts in separate settings or situations or for simultaneously counting behaviors of multiple students. Simply change the headings for the columns as depicted in the figure. In any of these cases, it is still an event recording form.

If you are counting the number of steps completed for complex chained behaviors (activities and routines), you can list the steps and make a notation next to each step about whether it occurred. There are also ways to use event recording to note whether prompts were used to elicit the response and even what type of prompts were used. Figure 8.3 (and the corresponding blank form in the appendix to this chapter) is an example of such a data collection form. Notations of the type of prompts appear next to each step (V = verbal, M = model, P = full physical, + indicates correct unprompted, − indicates incorrect). Each column is a training session. The percentage indicators in the left-most column allow you to graph the percentage of correct responses per session right on the data collection form. For the first session, Ann independently completed 1 of the 10 steps (Step 5), or 10% of the total number of steps. The first graph point is placed next to the 10% indicator for that session. These graph points are connected across sessions to form a line graph showing Ann's progress over time.

Another event recording form is provided in Figure 8.4, with the blank version in the appendix to this chapter. A number denotes the type of prompt used for each

Instructions: Indicate correct or incorrect responses or type of prompt used next to each step. Compute the percentage of steps completed correctly with no prompts for each session and indicate relative to percentages provided on left.

Behavior: Open bar-press door   **Name:** Ann   **Mastery:** 100% / 2-3 days

Step	7	8	9	10	11	14	15	16	17	18	21	22	23	24	25	28	29	30
10. Step clear of door.	V	+	+	V	+	V	+	+	+	+	+	+	+	+	+	+	+	+
9. Release door.	M	M	−	M	V	M	M	−	V	+	V	+	+	+	+	+	+	+
8. Step forward.	P	P	−	P	M	P	P	−	M	M	M	V	+	+	+	+	+	+
7. Release left hand.	P	V	−	M	M	M	M		V	V	V	V	−	V	+	V	V	+
6. Hold door w/right hand.	P	P	−	M	M	M	M	−	M	M	M	V	−	V	V	M	V	−
5. Release right hand.	+	+	+	+	+	+	+	+	+	+	+	+	+	+	+	+	+	+
4. Step forward again.	V	M	−	+	+	+	+	+	+	+	+	+	+	+	+	+	+	+
3. Step forward.	V	V	−	V	V	V	V	−	+	+	+	+	+	+	+	+	+	+
2. Push bar down.	V	V	−	V	V	V	V	−	V	V	V	V	−	+	V	V	+	+
1. Grasp bar.	P	P	−	P	P	P	P	−	M	P	M	M	−	M	M	M	V	−

%

Dates: September   7 8 9 10 11 14 15 16 17 18 21 22 23 24 25 28 29 30

Date	Trend	Decision

Types of prompts: V = verbal, M = model, P = full physical, + = correct unprompted, − = incorrect

Figure 8.3. Event recording with prompt notations for a task analysis, with graphing option. *Note.* Adapted from *Assessment of Individuals With Severe Disabilities: An Applied Behavior Approach to Life Skills Assessment* (2nd ed., p. 115), by D. M. Browder, 1991, Baltimore: Paul H. Brookes. Copyright 1991 by Paul H. Brookes Publishing Co. Adapted with permission.

Instructions: Fill in the task analysis steps in the first column on the left. Color in a circle to indicate level of prompting, with 5 indicating an independent correct response. Connect colored circles to show progress toward less assistance for each task analytic step.

STUDENT: _Steve_ **DOMAIN:** _Work Training_

ENVIRONMENT: _Local Market_ **MAJOR ACTIVITY:** _Bread Stocking_

LEVEL OF PROMPTS:

5 Independent 4 Verbal 3 Gesture 2 Partial physical 1 Full physical

Task Steps		Jan. 15	Jan. 17						
Ask boss which color tie to pull.	5	○	○	○	○	○	○	○	○
	4	●	○	○	○	○	○	○	○
	3	○	●	○	○	○	○	○	○
	2	○	○	○	○	○	○	○	○
	1	○	○	○	○	○	○	○	○
Find spot—match package color and label.	5	○	●	○	○	○	○	○	○
	4	○	○	○	○	○	○	○	○
	3	●	○	○	○	○	○	○	○
	2	○	○	○	○	○	○	○	○
	1	○	○	○	○	○	○	○	○
Match shelf label.	5	●	●	○	○	○	○	○	○
	4	○	○	○	○	○	○	○	○
	3	○	○	○	○	○	○	○	○
	2	○	○	○	○	○	○	○	○
	1	○	○	○	○	○	○	○	○
Fresh bread in back, older in front.	5	○	○	○	○	○	○	○	○
	4	●	●	○	○	○	○	○	○
	3	○	○	○	○	○	○	○	○
	2	○	○	○	○	○	○	○	○
	1	○	○	○	○	○	○	○	○
Front row—fresh on bottom, old on top.	5	○	●	○	○	○	○	○	○
	4	●	○	○	○	○	○	○	○
	3	○	○	○	○	○	○	○	○
	2	○	○	○	○	○	○	○	○
	1	○	○	○	○	○	○	○	○
Check that bread is neatly stacked.	5	●	●	○	○	○	○	○	○
	4	○	○	○	○	○	○	○	○
	3	○	○	○	○	○	○	○	○
	2	○	○	○	○	○	○	○	○
	1	○	○	○	○	○	○	○	○
Stack empty bread trays.	5	○	○	○	○	○	○	○	○
	4	○	○	○	○	○	○	○	○
	3	○	●	○	○	○	○	○	○
	2	●	○	○	○	○	○	○	○
	1	○	○	○	○	○	○	○	○
Front bread, tortillas, bakery items—fill row.	5	●	●	○	○	○	○	○	○
	4	○	○	○	○	○	○	○	○
	3	○	○	○	○	○	○	○	○
	2	○	○	○	○	○	○	○	○
	1	○	○	○	○	○	○	○	○

Figure 8.4. Event recording with numbered prompt notations, with graphing option.

step of the work-training activity. Each column is a different day. Simply color in the circle next to the appropriate number depicting the prompt you used and connect these circles across sessions. The goal is to have all 5s or independent responses for each step. It is useful to collect prompting data to show progress toward independent responding.

You will use duration recording for continuous, ongoing behaviors to determine how long a behavior lasts (e.g., attending to a work task), as we noted in Chapter 2. Figure 8.5 is a form for collecting duration data. (A blank duration recording form is provided in the chapter appendix.) A third observational recording technique that might be of interest for measuring some behaviors is *latency recording. Latency* is the time between the S^D and the beginning of a response. For example, you might be interested in teaching a student to come to circle time within 10 seconds of when you ring the bell, or you might be interested in how long it takes a student to begin his or her workstation task once he or she sits down. The time between the bell sounding and the student coming to the circle, and the time between sitting down and beginning work, are what we call latency. To record latency data, you can create your own recording form, modifying it as needed. Figure 8.6 offers an example of a latency recording form. You could graph the total latency time per day to show progress toward the objective criterion (i.e., within 10 seconds for 10 consecutive days).

Finally, when you are teaching objectives at the fluency level, you may want to collect rate data. Remember that rate relates behavior to time. For example, you might be interested in how fast a student copies his or her letters. In this case, you would count the number of letters the student copies, the amount of time it took to copy them, and then divide the number of behaviors by the total time to get a "number of letters per second/minute/hour," depending on what you divided by (seconds/minutes/hours). Figure 8.7 displays rate data, and a blank form is provided in the chapter appendix.

Developing Recording Forms

Developing a progress-recording form does not have to be a tedious process. For your convenience, we have provided some samples of forms in the figures and corresponding blank data collection forms in the chapter appendix. The forms you use need to match what you have written in your objective; thus, almost all commercially available data recording forms may need to be modified, depending on the targeted behavior(s), what aspect of the behavior you are trying to teach, the learning level, and the mastery criterion. Generally, data collection forms will be formulated as follows:

- General event recording forms for single or multiple behaviors, as in Figures 8.1 and 8.2

- Task analytic forms depicting prompts, as in Figure 8.3, 8.4, and 8.8

- General duration and latency forms, as in Figures 8.5 and 8.6

- Trial-by-trial forms depicting controlled presentations and prompts, as in Figures 8.9, 8.10, and 8.11

- Naturalistic/milieu teaching forms depicting natural S^Ds and prompts, as in Figures 8.12 and 8.13

Some forms have places for graphing on the data recording form itself, as in Figure 8.3. Figure 8.8 is another form that includes a graphing component. In this figure, each of the steps in lunch and recess are listed to the left. Codes for the

Instructions: Enter dates and the time the target behavior begins and stops. Total the time and enter in the last column. Total all times for the target behavior for the day and graph as either number of minutes/seconds or percentage of minutes/seconds on a separate line graph.

Student: Erin

Objective: Erin will remain playing with one other student for 10 consecutive minutes during play station time for 4 of 5 days this week.

Time(s) observed: 10:00–10:30 each day

Sessions or Days	Begins Behavior	Stops Behavior	Total Time
Monday October 20	10:00 10:03 10:10	10:02 10:08 10:19	2 mins 5 mins 9 mins
			Total for day: 16 mins
Tuesday October 21	10:00 10:07	10:05 10:20	5 mins 13 mins
			Total for day: 18 mins
Wednesday October 22			
			Total for day:
Thursday October 23			
			Total for day:
Friday October 24			
			Total for day:

Figure 8.5. Duration recording form.

various levels of assistance are shown at the bottom. By simply connecting the circled levels after each response, you can create a graph of your data for each step. (A blank form is provided in the chapter appendix.) For many of the forms you will use, however, you will be required to develop accompanying graphs, as we indicated in Chapter 2.

For trial-by-trial sessions, at a minimum you should plan to count the number of trials you conduct for each objective and the number of correct unprompted responses. It is also wise to keep track of the number and nature of the prompts you use for each trial and those trials that were incorrect, whether prompted or not. Figure 8.9 is an example of a trial-by-trial data form with prompt codes. For each session, you should note the S^D, date, and the expected response for that objective in the left column. Several objectives can be addressed on this form (or you could record data for several students regarding the same objective, in which case you will need to add names in the far left column). The type of response is divided into

Student: Donald

Objective: Donald will begin his math assignment within 10 seconds of the teacher saying, "Start your math work now," each math period for 10 consecutive days.

Times observed: 9:50–11:30

Sessions or Days	S^D: Teacher Says, "Start Work"	Begins Response: Working on Math	Total Time
Monday Sept. 22	9:56:20	9:57:00	40 secs
Tuesday Sept. 23	10:01:10	10:01:15	5 secs
Wednesday Sept. 24	10:00:13	10:10:20	10 mins, 7 secs
Thursday September 25	10:05:00	10:05:09	9 secs
Friday September 26	10:10:15	10:10:23	8 secs

Figure 8.6. Latency recording form.

Instructions: Record the total observation time and the total number of behaviors/responses emitted during that time. Divide the number of behaviors by the observation time in seconds, minutes, or hours to obtain the rate.

Student: Joseph

Dates: March 21–25

Objective: Joseph will copy three letters per minute during writing time each session this week.

	Monday	Tuesday	Wednesday	Thursday	Friday
Time: Secs/mins/hrs	10 minutes	10 minutes	9 minutes	9 minutes	8 minutes
# of behaviors: # of letters	7	12	13	20	20
Rate: # behaviors/ time	#: .7 letters Per minute	#: 1.2 letters Per minute	#: 1.4 letters Per minute	#: 2.2 letters Per minute	#: 2.5 letters Per minute

Figure 8.7. Rate data form.

Instructions: Circle the code depicting the level of assistance and connect the circles for a per-step graph.

Student: Kirsten   **Observation times:** Lunch time

Objective: Kirsten will complete the 4-step task analysis for eating lunch independently for 5 consecutive weeks.

Task Steps	Level of Assistance									
Carries lunch through cafeteria line	3	3	③—③		3	3	3	3	3	3
	②	2	2	2	②	2	2	2	2	2
	1	①	1	1	1	1	1	1	1	1
	U	U	U	U	U	U	U	U	U	U
Selects table and greets peers	3	③—③		3	③	3	3	3	3	3
	②	2	2	②	2	2	2	2	2	2
	1	1	1	1	1	1	1	1	1	1
	U	U	U	U	U	U	U	U	U	U
Cleans up after finished eating	3	3	3	3	3	3	3	3	3	3
	2	2	2	②—②		2	2	2	2	2
	1	①—①		1	1	1	1	1	1	1
	Ⓤ	U	U	U	U	U	U	U	U	U
Walks to playground and joins group	3	3	3	③	3	3	3	3	3	3
	2	②—②		2	②	2	2	2	2	2
	①	1	1	1	1	1	1	1	1	1
	U	U	U	U	U	U	U	U	U	U
Dates	4-2	4-5	4-6	4-8	4-9					

Rating Codes:

(3) Completes step independently

(2) Requires one verbal reminder to complete step

(1) Requires physical prompting

(U) Unable to complete step

Figure 8.8. Task analytic data form with prompt levels and graphing.

correct and incorrect sections on the data sheet, and codes for the type of prompt assistance are provided at the top of the form. Simply place the prompt code in either the correct or incorrect sections for each trial. If the trial is unprompted, the response will be marked with a + in the correct column and a / in the incorrect column. Count the number of responses marked with only a + (unprompted correct), compute the percentage of total trials that were marked with a +, and note this on an accompanying line graph. (A blank form is provided in the chapter appendix.)

Figure 8.10 illustrates another trial-by-trial form in which the prompt codes are preprinted so that you will just need to circle the type of prompt in either the correct or incorrect columns. If the response is unprompted, circle + if it is correct and − if it is incorrect. The task description is provided at the top (you can record three tasks

Instructions: Mark the code for the type of prompt for prompted trials in either the correct or incorrect sections. For unprompted trials, mark + in correct section or / in incorrect section. Figure the percentage of all trials that were unprompted and correct (+). This percentage will be transferred to a graph. Several trial-by-trial tasks could be recorded on this sheet for one student or one objective for multiple students.

Student Name: _Patrick_

Setting: _1-1, classroom_

Code:

Correct = +	Full physical = FP	Verbal = V
Incorrect = /	Partial physical = PP	
No response = NR	Gesture = G	

Task	Correct					Incorrect					% correct
S^D: Give me	PP	PP	PP	+	G	NR	PP	/	/		10%
Response: Hand appropriate object (block, car, doll)	G										
Date: Sept. 3	Comments: watch for prompt dependence					Comments: most trouble with *car*					
S^D:											
Response:											
	Comments:					Comments:					
Date:											
S^D:											
Response:											
	Comments:					Comments:					
Date:											
S^D:											
Response:											
	Comments:					Comments:					
Date:											
S^D:											
Response:											
	Comments:					Comments:					
Date:											

Figure 8.9. Trial-by-trial data sheet.

Instructions: This sheet can work for multiple tasks for one student or, with slight modifications, one task for each of multiple students. Circle a + if trial is correct unprompted, a − if unprompted and incorrect. Circle the type of prompt for correct responses and for incorrect responses. Total correct, unprompted trials and transfer to a graph as a raw number or percentage correct.

Date: October 29   **Student:** Sylvia

Setting: Classroom 1-2

Correct: +   Incorrect: −

Prompts: PP = Physical   GP = Gestural   VP = Verbal

	Task: "What comes first?" 5 objects arranged in varying order		Task:		Task:	
	Date: Oct. 29		**Date:**		**Date:**	
Trials	**Correct**	**Incorrect**	**Correct**	**Incorrect**	**Correct**	**Incorrect**
1	+ PP GP (VP)	− PP GP VP	+ PP GP VP	− PP GP VP	+ PP GP VP	− PP GP VP
2	(+) PP GP VP	− PP GP VP	+ PP GP VP	− PP GP VP	+ PP GP VP	− PP GP VP
3	+ PP GP VP	(−) PP GP VP	+ PP GP VP	− PP GP VP	+ PP GP VP	− PP GP VP
4	+ PP GP VP	− PP GP (VP)	+ PP GP VP	− PP GP VP	+ PP GP VP	− PP GP VP
5	(+) PP GP VP	− PP GP VP	+ PP GP VP	− PP GP VP	+ PP GP VP	− PP GP VP
Total correct:	2/5					
Comments	Looks at favorite object.					

Figure 8.10. Trial-by-trial data sheet with preprinted codes.

on this sheet), and trials run vertically. Graph the percentage of unprompted correct trials (those marked with a +). (A blank form is provided in the chapter appendix.)

A simple trial-by-trial form is provided in Figure 8.11. Each column can represent a teaching session for one task or objective, with the date of the session at the top of the column. This particular form allows for eight sessions with three students. After each trial, circle the number in the column if it was correct (unprompted) and put a slash mark through it if it was incorrect or required a prompt. At the end of the session, total the correct responses and place a box around that number. The

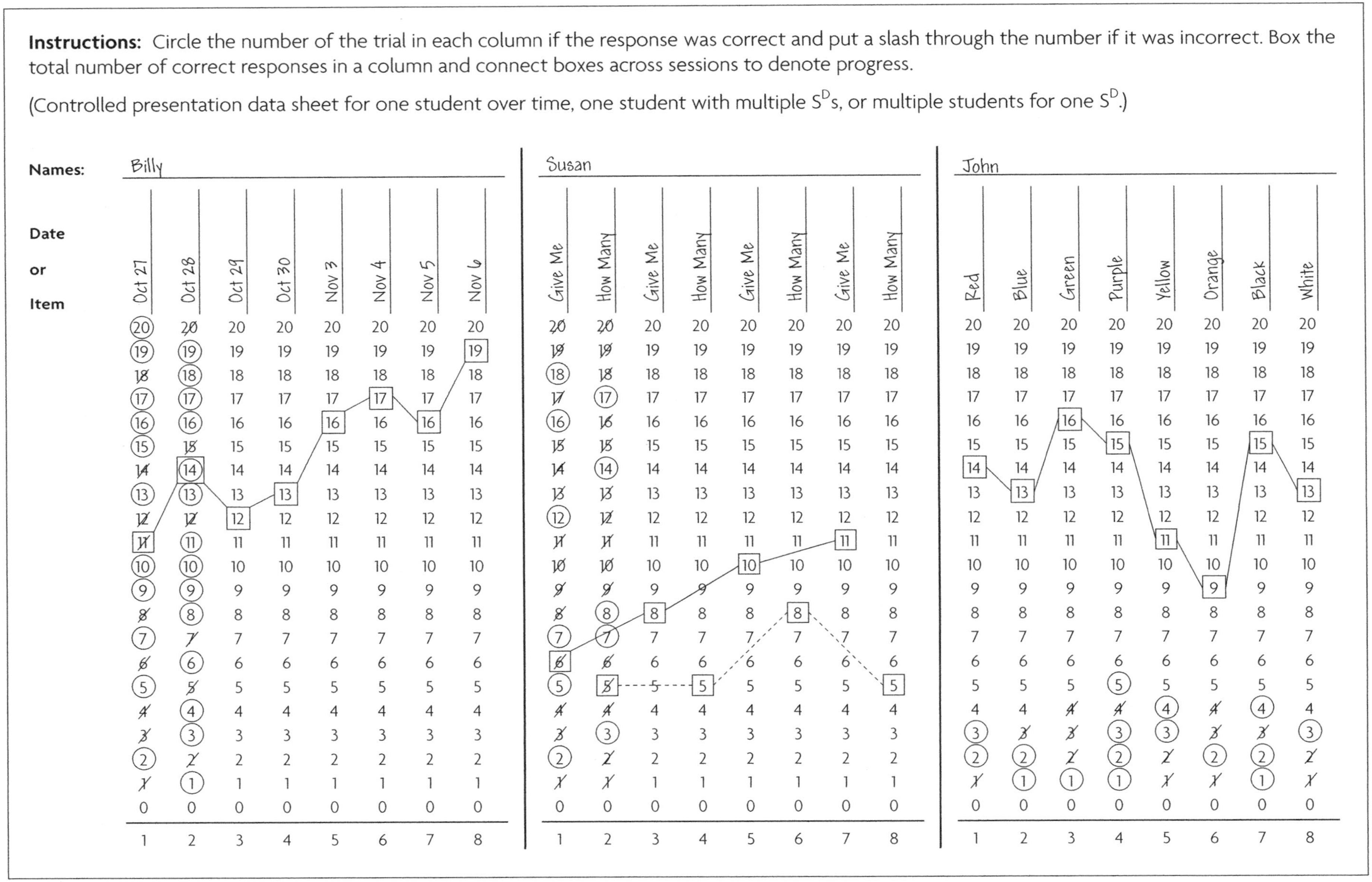
Instructions: Circle the number of the trial in each column if the response was correct and put a slash through the number if it was incorrect. Box the total number of correct responses in a column and connect boxes across sessions to denote progress.
(Controlled presentation data sheet for one student over time, one student with multiple S^Ds, or multiple students for one S^D.)
Names:
Billy
Susan
John
Date
or
Item
Oct 27
Oct 28
Oct 29
Oct 30
Nov 3
Nov 4
Nov 5
Nov 6
Give Me
How Many
Red
Blue
Green
Purple
Yellow
Orange
Black
White

Figure 8.11. Data collection sheet for use with controlled presentations. *Note.* Adapted from "A Multi-Purpose Data Sheet for Recording and Graphing in the Classroom," by R. Saunders and K. Koplik, 1975, *AAESPH Review.* Copyright 1975 by The Association for the Severely Handicapped. Adapted with permission.

October 27 session for Billy shows that he had 11 correct unprompted responses (11 numbers were circled). Connect the boxed numbers for a graph to depict progress. Note that information about types of prompts is not available on this form. You can, however, adapt the form to have each column represent a different task or S^D for each student. (A blank form is provided in the chapter appendix.)

For naturalistic/milieu teaching sessions, you will want to count the number of spontaneous language responses and note the conditions under which each response was produced. You will also want to note which strategy was necessary if the response was not spontaneous. Figure 8.12 is a recording form for three students. For each student, there are three possible language targets. Michael is working on

Date: _____

Student: Michael		
Setting	Times	Prompts/ Conseq.
TARGET 1	"want" + noun	
Breakfast	//	S, TD
Group	/	MQ
TARGET 2	new noun labels	
math	/	M
hall	/	M
transition		
bus	/	M/T (peer)
TARGET 3	_____	

Student: Kristie		
Setting	Times	Prompts/ Conseq.
TARGET 1	photo + label	
breakfast	///	MQ, MQ, MQ
sm. grp.	/	M/T
TARGET 2	request assistance	
arrival	/	S/T
departure	/	S/T
TARGET 3	_____	

Student: Caryn		
Setting	Times	Prompts/ Conseq.
TARGET 1	two words	
group	/	S/T
math	/	TD
TARGET 2	action verbs	
group	/	M/T
self-help	/	M/T
transition	/	M/T
TARGET 3	req. assistance	
	"help please"	
breakfast	/	MQ/T
self-help	/	TD/T

Setting: Specify activity when response occurred

Times: Use slash for each occurrence

Prompts: (Record one symbol for each occurrence)

M = Model, S = Spontaneous, T = Acknowledged by adult or peer, MQ = Mand or question, TD = Time delay

Figure 8.12. Naturalistic/milieu teaching progress data form. *Note.* Adapted from "Functional Language," by A. P. Kaiser. In M. E. Snell (Ed.), *Instruction of Students With Severe Disabilities* (p. 354), Upper Saddle River, NJ: Prentice Hall. Copyright 1993 by Prentice Hall. Adapted with permission.

saying or signing "want" plus a noun (what he wants) and labeling new things and people. Kristie and Caryn have different target objectives. At the bottom of the form are codes for the teaching strategies, spontaneous responses, and whether someone acknowledged the language response. For each target there are three columns: one to note the language context, one to note frequency of responses, and one to note the type of teaching strategy or whether it was spontaneous and acknowledged. At breakfast, Michael had two instances of saying "want" plus a noun. The first was spontaneous (S) and the second required a time delay (TD) from the teaching adult. During math, Michael said one new noun label that required a model (M) from the teaching adult. You would want to graph the percentage of language responses that are spontaneous (spontaneous/total responses) per target per day. (A blank form is provided in the chapter appendix.)

A second naturalistic/milieu teaching form is provided in Figure 8.13. In this form, the codes for teaching strategies are defined at the top and preprinted next to each target. Each column represents a language context, with room to record multiple utterances or signs. Circle the teaching strategy used or S (spontaneous) for each time the student requests the target. Compute the percentage of spontaneous requests per target and depict these percentages on a graph. (A blank form is provided in the chapter appendix.)

For any form that you develop or use, provide a space for the student's name, the setting, the date and time of observation, the objective and/or S^D, and response description. In some instances, you may want to show totals or percentages of behaviors or minutes per session or day. On some forms you may want spaces for comments or a description of the actual behavior (e.g., you write the entire phrase or sentence the student used to describe the TV show because you are teaching him or her to use complete sentences and more adjectives). On some forms you may want to be able to record behaviors of more than one student or in more than one setting. Each of the sample forms in the chapter appendix includes directions for use.

Remember that you will choose or develop a recording form based on what you have targeted in your objectives and how you wrote your mastery criteria. You need to be able to tell from your data that the student met your specified criteria. For example, if you have targeted simple discrete behaviors or steps of chained behaviors, you will probably want an event recording form. If the response cannot occur without a specific S^D (i.e., restricted event), you will need a form with a column to record opportunities to respond. If your criteria statement gives a number of times, it implies event recording. If the statement pertains to a length of time, that implies duration recording. The more information you can obtain from your form, the more useful it will be for your teaching decisions and adjustments.

When to Collect Progress Data

We would not expect a teacher to collect data on every student response all day. You will need to make choices about when to collect data and how much data to collect. As a general rule, we recommend that you frequently collect data on acquisition objectives. You may want to make some notations each day or several times a week to make sure that the student is adequately responding to your prompts and reinforcers. Because we recommend that more-frequent, intense instruction occur for acquisition learning, there should be multiple opportunities for you to collect such data.

When teaching at the fluency level, you may just need to collect data on an objective one to three times a week to ensure that the rate of responding is increasing. For maintenance, you will check (what we call *probe*) every once in a while (e.g., once a month) to make sure the student can still produce the behavior. For

Instructions: Circle the type of naturalistic/milieu teaching prompt needed or circle spontaneous (S). Transfer the percentage of utterances that were spontaneous to graph.

Student: Susie

Objective: Susie will spontaneously request the listed items or situations as she needs them during the school day.

Date: January 15

MM: Mand–Model   M: Model   TD: Time Delay   S: Spontaneous

Utterance	Setting			
	Snack	**Lunch**	**Class Time**	**Gym**
Food	⟨MM⟩ M TD S	MM ⟨M⟩ TD S	MM M TD S	MM M TD S
	⟨MM⟩ M TD S	MM ⟨M⟩ TD S	MM M TD S	MM M TD S
	MM ⟨M⟩ TD S	MM M ⟨TD⟩ S	MM M TD S	MM M TD S
	MM M ⟨TD⟩ S	MM M TD ⟨S⟩	MM M TD S	MM M TD S
	MM M TD ⟨S⟩	MM M TD ⟨S⟩	MM M TD S	MM M TD S
	MM M ⟨TD⟩ S 1/6	MM M TD S 2/5	MM M TD S	MM M TD S
Toy	MM M TD S	MM M TD S	MM ⟨M⟩ TD S	MM M ⟨TD⟩ S
	MM M TD S	MM M TD S	MM M ⟨TD⟩ S	MM M TD ⟨S⟩
	MM M TD S	MM M TD S	MM M TD ⟨S⟩	MM M TD ⟨S⟩
	MM M TD S	MM M TD S	MM M TD ⟨S⟩	MM M TD ⟨S⟩
	MM M TD S	MM M TD S	MM M TD S	MM M TD S
	MM M TD S	MM M TD S	MM M TD S 2/4	MM M TD S 3/4
More	MM ⟨M⟩ TD S	MM M TD ⟨S⟩	MM M TD S	MM M TD S
	MM M ⟨TD⟩ S	MM M TD ⟨S⟩	MM M TD S	MM M TD S
	MM M TD ⟨S⟩	MM M TD S	MM M TD S	MM M TD S
	MM M TD ⟨S⟩	MM M TD S	MM M TD S	MM M TD S
	MM M TD S	MM M TD S	MM M TD S	MM M TD S
	MM M TD S 2/4	MM M TD S 2/2	MM M TD S	MM M TD S
Toilet	MM M TD S	⟨MM⟩ M TD S	⟨MM⟩ M TD S	MM M TD S
	MM M TD S	MM M TD S	MM M TD S	MM M TD S
	MM M TD S	MM M TD S	MM M TD S	MM M TD S
	MM M TD S	MM M TD S	MM M TD S	MM M TD S
	MM M TD S	MM M TD S	MM M TD S	MM M TD S
	MM M TD S	MM M TD S 0	MM M TD S 0	MM M TD S

(⟨ ⟩ indicates a circled code on the form.)

Figure 8.13. Naturalistic/milieu progress data form with preprinted codes.

generalization, you may need more frequent data at first, then once a week, and then just probes. You might decide to collect data on the responses of Students A, B, and C on Mondays and Wednesdays and other student responses on the other days, or you might want to assign certain objectives to certain days (e.g., self-help objectives Monday–Wednesday). Once you have gathered your data, you need to create a graph. If your data form does not have the option of graphing directly onto it, you will need to develop a separate graph. (We provide information on how to construct a line graph in Chapter 2, so you may want to review that section.) Figure 8.14 shows

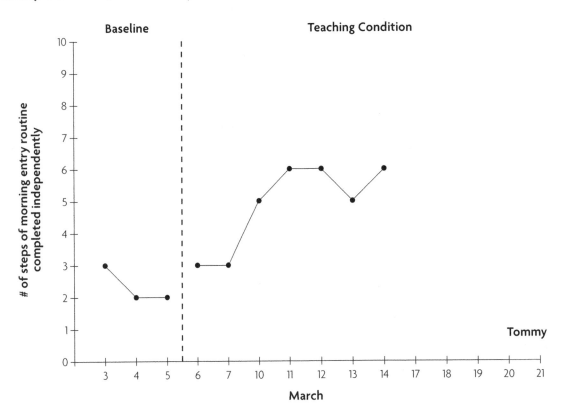

Entering Classroom Routine (10-step task analysis)

Student: Tommy

Teaching Condition: 1-3 ratio as students enter classroom

Mastery Criterion: 5 consecutive days

Objective: Tommy will independently complete all steps of the 10-step task analysis for entering the classroom each day for a week.

Figure 8.14. Sample progress data line graph.

a sample line graph for progress data in which student progress toward mastering a 10-step morning routine is depicted. Your graphs should be self-explanatory and neat, whether constructed by hand or with a computer.

There are many advantages to constructing graphs to display your progress data. First, it is much easier to communicate exactly what the student has accomplished through a visual presentation. You will want to communicate this information to parents, other family members, related service personnel, and other members of your teaching team. You may also want to share graphs with school administrators. Second, it is much easier for you and your teaching team to make instructional decisions after viewing a progress graph than it would be by looking at piles of data collection sheets. If the progress trend is not adequate, you will need to adjust your instructional strategies or your curricular objective. Third, graphs take up less space and allow for a filing system that is useful and clear.

Collecting data and graphing will take time. Train all teaching adults to collect data and construct line graphs, and set a time for the entire team to graph progress data each week. Each person could be responsible for a certain number of students, or each person might graph data for one or two curricular domains (e.g., communication and gross-motor) for all of the students. If one person on the team likes graphing, perhaps that person could be scheduled to graph while the other members continue to work with the students. Use this time to analyze your graphs and make sure all students are progressing as expected.

Notebook Files

Before the year begins, teachers should think about a system for maintaining their assessment and progress data. One way to easily organize curricular and progress information is to develop a notebook for each student. In each student's notebook place dividers depicting curricular domains or areas. In the front of the notebook place the ecological or other initial assessment results and targets for that year. Behind each divider place a list of annual goals or objectives for that domain, lesson plans, and/or task analyses, and behind that place the progress graph. This way, anyone could pick up a student's notebook and know what you intend to teach, how you determine to teach those things, the student's initial performance levels, and his or her current progress for each objective being addressed.

Figure 8.15 shows a sample notebook file. Dividers are labeled with the main curricular domains. Included are a divider for comprehensive assessment information and one for behavioral expectations. Behind each divider is a lesson plan with corresponding progress graphs (not data sheets). You may also include samples of the student's work. In your behavioral expectations section, you'll want to include a functional behavioral assessment (FBA), a related behavior intervention plan (BIP), a reinforcer survey, and a baseline/intervention graph for targeted behaviors (see Chapters 11 and 12 for more information about these items).

Clarity about what students are being taught, why they are being taught those things, and whether they are learning what they are being taught makes all other teaching decisions (e.g., placement, teaching strategy, schedule) easier. All teaching adults should have access to student's progress notebooks and should be familiar with the contents. Share the notebooks frequently with parents and other family members. If they understand exactly what is being taught and why, they are more likely to help teach those things outside of school. As we have pointed out, the more opportunities for students to be prompted, to be reinforced, and to practice, the faster they will learn and maintain those skills.

Summary

In this chapter we discussed strategies for collecting data related to students' progress, and we provided several data collection forms to facilitate that task. Decisions about recording techniques, forms, and graphs are directly related to specific learning objectives. Well-written objectives clearly communicate what needs to be counted and recorded. However, data collection activities should make sense in terms of instruction. We do not want you to collect data just to say you have done so. The data you collect should be useful to you and your teaching team by indicating whether your instruction is effective or, if not, what components are in need of adjustment.

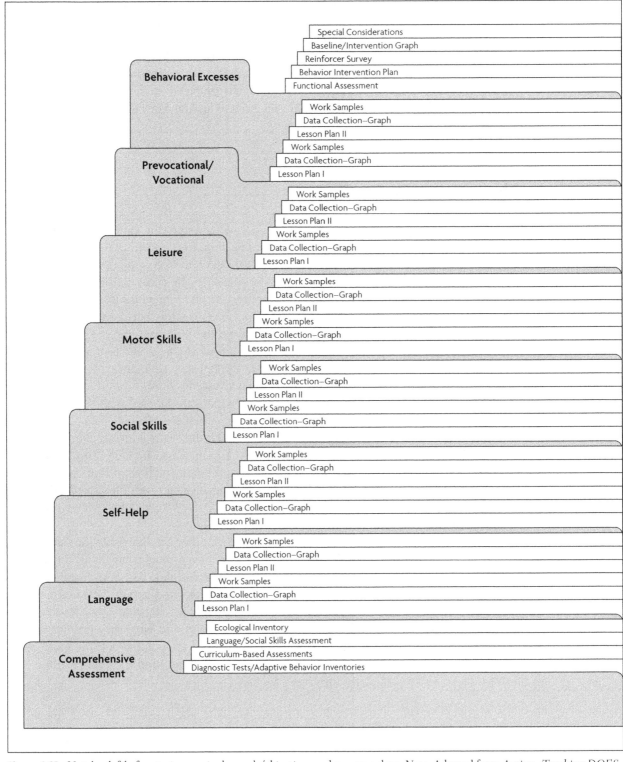

Figure 8.15. Notebook file for storing curricular goals/objectives and progress data. *Note.* Adapted from *Autism: Teaching DOES Make a Difference,* by B. Scheuermann and J. Webber, 2002, Belmont, CA: Wadsworth. Copyright 2002 by Wadsworth Publishing. Adapted with permission.

Progress data are the only reliable way to confirm that the learner is learning or to cue you that the learner is not learning. In the first situation, congratulate yourself and your team and celebrate with the student. In the latter case, immediately adjust your teaching strategies and/or the curriculum or task analyses. Above all, do not "fly blind," not knowing whether your students are progressing or, worse, make no changes when the student fails to progress. Finally, we recommended establishing a notebook file for the purpose of storing curricular and progress data. Easy access to this information will facilitate instructional decisions and communication about students' educational programs.

Appendix:
Progress Data Collection Forms

Event Recording With Prompt Notations for a Task Analysis, With Graphing Option

Event Recording With Numbered Prompt Notations, With Graphing Option

Duration Recording Form

Rate Data Form

Task Analytic Data Form With Prompt Levels and Graphing Option

Trial-by-Trial Data Sheet

Trial-by-Trial Data Sheet With Preprinted Codes

Data Collection Sheet for Use With Controlled Presentations

Naturalistic/Milieu Teaching Progress Data Form

Naturalistic/Milieu Progress Data Form With Preprinted Codes

Event Recording With Prompt Notations
for a Task Analysis, With Graphing Option

Instructions: Indicate correct or incorrect responses or type of prompt used next to each step. Compute the percentage of steps completed correctly with no prompts for each session and indicate relative to percentages provided on left.

Behavior: _____ **Name:** _____ **Mastery:** _____

%

Dates:

Date	Trend	Decision

Types of prompts: V = verbal, M = model, P = full physical, + = correct unprompted, − = incorrect

Note. Adapted from *Assessment of Individuals With Severe Disabilities: An Applied Behavior Approach to Life Skills Assessment* (2nd ed., p. 115), by D. M. Browder, 1991, Baltimore: Paul H. Brookes. Copyright 1991 by Paul H. Brookes Publishing Co. Adapted with permission.

Event Recording With Numbered Prompt Notations, With Graphing Option

Instructions: Fill in the task analysis steps in the first column on the left. Color in a circle to indicate level of prompting, with 5 indicating an independent correct response. Connect colored circles to show progress toward less assistance for each task analytic step.

STUDENT: _____   DOMAIN: _____

ENVIRONMENT: _____   MAJOR ACTIVITY: _____

LEVEL OF PROMPTS:

5 Independent   4 Verbal   3 Gesture   2 Partial physical   1 Full physical

Task Steps									
	5	○	○	○	○	○	○	○	○
	4	○	○	○	○	○	○	○	○
	3	○	○	○	○	○	○	○	○
	2	○	○	○	○	○	○	○	○
	1	○	○	○	○	○	○	○	○
	5	○	○	○	○	○	○	○	○
	4	○	○	○	○	○	○	○	○
	3	○	○	○	○	○	○	○	○
	2	○	○	○	○	○	○	○	○
	1	○	○	○	○	○	○	○	○
	5	○	○	○	○	○	○	○	○
	4	○	○	○	○	○	○	○	○
	3	○	○	○	○	○	○	○	○
	2	○	○	○	○	○	○	○	○
	1	○	○	○	○	○	○	○	○
	5	○	○	○	○	○	○	○	○
	4	○	○	○	○	○	○	○	○
	3	○	○	○	○	○	○	○	○
	2	○	○	○	○	○	○	○	○
	1	○	○	○	○	○	○	○	○
	5	○	○	○	○	○	○	○	○
	4	○	○	○	○	○	○	○	○
	3	○	○	○	○	○	○	○	○
	2	○	○	○	○	○	○	○	○
	1	○	○	○	○	○	○	○	○
	5	○	○	○	○	○	○	○	○
	4	○	○	○	○	○	○	○	○
	3	○	○	○	○	○	○	○	○
	2	○	○	○	○	○	○	○	○
	1	○	○	○	○	○	○	○	○
	5	○	○	○	○	○	○	○	○
	4	○	○	○	○	○	○	○	○
	3	○	○	○	○	○	○	○	○
	2	○	○	○	○	○	○	○	○
	1	○	○	○	○	○	○	○	○
	5	○	○	○	○	○	○	○	○
	4	○	○	○	○	○	○	○	○
	3	○	○	○	○	○	○	○	○
	2	○	○	○	○	○	○	○	○
	1	○	○	○	○	○	○	○	○

Duration Recording Form

Instructions: Enter dates and the time the target behavior begins and stops. Total the time and enter in the last column. Total all times for the target behavior for the day and graph as either number of minutes/seconds or percentage of minutes/seconds on a separate line graph.

Student:

Objective:

Time(s) observed:

Sessions or Days	Begins Behavior	Stops Behavior	Total Time
			Total for day:
			Total for day:
			Total for day:
			Total for day:
			Total for day:

Rate Data Form

Instructions: Record the total observation time and the total number of behaviors/responses emitted during that time. Divide the number of behaviors by the observation time in seconds, minutes, or hours to obtain the rate.

Student:

Dates:

Objective:

	Monday	Tuesday	Wednesday	Thursday	Friday
Time: Secs/mins/hrs					
# of behaviors:					
Rate: # behaviors/ time	#: Per _____	#: Per _____	#: Per _____	#: Per _____	#: Per _____

Task Analytic Data Form With Prompt Levels and Graphing Option

Instructions: Circle the code depicting the level of assistance and connect the circles for a per-step graph.

Student: **Observation times:**

Objective:

Task Steps	Level of Assistance									
	3 2 1 U	3 2 1 U	3 2 1 U	3 2 1 U	3 2 1 U	3 2 1 U	3 2 1 U	3 2 1 U	3 2 1 U	3 2 1 U
	3 2 1 U	3 2 1 U	3 2 1 U	3 2 1 U	3 2 1 U	3 2 1 U	3 2 1 U	3 2 1 U	3 2 1 U	3 2 1 U
	3 2 1 U	3 2 1 U	3 2 1 U	3 2 1 U	3 2 1 U	3 2 1 U	3 2 1 U	3 2 1 U	3 2 1 U	3 2 1 U
	3 2 1 U	3 2 1 U	3 2 1 U	3 2 1 U	3 2 1 U	3 2 1 U	3 2 1 U	3 2 1 U	3 2 1 U	3 2 1 U
	3 2 1 U	3 2 1 U	3 2 1 U	3 2 1 U	3 2 1 U	3 2 1 U	3 2 1 U	3 2 1 U	3 2 1 U	3 2 1 U
	3 2 1 U	3 2 1 U	3 2 1 U	3 2 1 U	3 2 1 U	3 2 1 U	3 2 1 U	3 2 1 U	3 2 1 U	3 2 1 U
	3 2 1 U	3 2 1 U	3 2 1 U	3 2 1 U	3 2 1 U	3 2 1 U	3 2 1 U	3 2 1 U	3 2 1 U	3 2 1 U
	3 2 1 U	3 2 1 U	3 2 1 U	3 2 1 U	3 2 1 U	3 2 1 U	3 2 1 U	3 2 1 U	3 2 1 U	3 2 1 U
	3 2 1 U	3 2 1 U	3 2 1 U	3 2 1 U	3 2 1 U	3 2 1 U	3 2 1 U	3 2 1 U	3 2 1 U	3 2 1 U
	3 2 1 U	3 2 1 U	3 2 1 U	3 2 1 U	3 2 1 U	3 2 1 U	3 2 1 U	3 2 1 U	3 2 1 U	3 2 1 U
	3 2 1 U	3 2 1 U	3 2 1 U	3 2 1 U	3 2 1 U	3 2 1 U	3 2 1 U	3 2 1 U	3 2 1 U	3 2 1 U
Dates										

Rating Codes:

(3) Completes step independently

(2) Requires one verbal reminder to complete step

(1) Requires physical prompting

(U) Unable to complete step

Trial-by-Trial Data Sheet

Instructions: Mark the code for the type of prompt for prompted trials in either the correct or incorrect sections. For unprompted trials, mark + in correct section or / in incorrect section. Figure the percentage of all trials that were unprompted and correct (+). This percentage will be transferred to a graph. Several trial-by-trial tasks could be recorded on this sheet for one student or one objective for multiple students.

Student Name: _____

Setting: _____

Code: Correct = +   Full physical = FP   Verbal = V
       Incorrect = /   Partial physical = PP
       No response = NR   Gesture = G

Task	Correct					Incorrect					% correct
S^D:											
Response:											
	Comments:					Comments:					
Date:											
S^D:											
Response:											
	Comments:					Comments:					
Date:											
S^D:											
Response:											
	Comments:					Comments:					
Date:											
S^D:											
Response:											
	Comments:					Comments:					
Date:											
S^D:											
Response:											
	Comments:					Comments:					
Date:											

Trial-by-Trial Data Sheet With Preprinted Codes

Instructions: This sheet can work for multiple tasks for one student or, with slight modifications, one task for each of multiple students. Circle a + if trial is correct and unprompted, a − if unprompted and incorrect. Circle the type of prompt for correct responses and for incorrect responses. Total the correct, unprompted trials and transfer to a graph as a raw number or percentage correct.

Date: _____   **Student:** _____

Setting: _____

Prompts: Correct: +   Incorrect: −
PP = Physical   GP = Gestural   VP = Verbal

Trials	Task: Date: Correct	Incorrect	Task: Date: Correct	Incorrect	Task: Date: Correct	Incorrect
1	+ PP GP VP	− PP GP VP	+ PP GP VP	− PP GP VP	+ PP GP VP	− PP GP VP
2	+ PP GP VP	− PP GP VP	+ PP GP VP	− PP GP VP	+ PP GP VP	− PP GP VP
3	+ PP GP VP	− PP GP VP	+ PP GP VP	− PP GP VP	+ PP GP VP	− PP GP VP
4	+ PP GP VP	− PP GP VP	+ PP GP VP	− PP GP VP	+ PP GP VP	− PP GP VP
5	+ PP GP VP	− PP GP VP	+ PP GP VP	− PP GP VP	+ PP GP VP	− PP GP VP
6	+ PP GP VP	− PP GP VP	+ PP GP VP	− PP GP VP	+ PP GP VP	− PP GP VP
7	+ PP GP VP	− PP GP VP	+ PP GP VP	− PP GP VP	+ PP GP VP	− PP GP VP
8	+ PP GP VP	− PP GP VP	+ PP GP VP	− PP GP VP	+ PP GP VP	− PP GP VP
Total correct:						
Comments						

Data Collection Sheet for Use With Controlled Presentations

Instructions: Circle the number of the trial in each column if the response was correct and put a slash through the number if it was incorrect. Box the number of correct responses in a column and connect boxes across sessions to denote progress.

(Controlled presentation data sheet for one student over time, one student with multiple S^{D}s, or multiple students for one S^D.)

Names: _____

Date
or
Item

1	2	3	4	5	6	7	8
20	20	20	20	20	20	20	20
19	19	19	19	19	19	19	19
18	18	18	18	18	18	18	18
17	17	17	17	17	17	17	17
16	16	16	16	16	16	16	16
15	15	15	15	15	15	15	15
14	14	14	14	14	14	14	14
13	13	13	13	13	13	13	13
12	12	12	12	12	12	12	12
11	11	11	11	11	11	11	11
10	10	10	10	10	10	10	10
9	9	9	9	9	9	9	9
8	8	8	8	8	8	8	8
7	7	7	7	7	7	7	7
6	6	6	6	6	6	6	6
5	5	5	5	5	5	5	5
4	4	4	4	4	4	4	4
3	3	3	3	3	3	3	3
2	2	2	2	2	2	2	2
1	1	1	1	1	1	1	1
0	0	0	0	0	0	0	0
1	2	3	4	5	6	7	8

(The grid of numbers 20 down to 0 and trial labels 1–8 repeats in three sections across the sheet.)

Note. From "A Multi-Purpose Data Sheet for Recording and Graphing in the Classroom," by R. Saunders and K. Koplik, 1975, *AAESPH Review.* Copyright 1975 by The Association for the Severely Handicapped. Reprinted with permission.

Collecting Progress Data

Naturalistic/Milieu Teaching Progress Data Form

176

Date: _____

Student: _____			Student: _____			Student: _____		
Setting	**Times**	**Prompts/ Conseq.**	**Setting**	**Times**	**Prompts/ Conseq.**	**Setting**	**Times**	**Prompts/ Conseq.**
TARGET 1 _____			**TARGET 1** _____			**TARGET 1** _____		
_____	_____	_____	_____	_____	_____	_____	_____	_____
_____	_____	_____	_____	_____	_____	_____	_____	_____
_____	_____	_____	_____	_____	_____	_____	_____	_____
_____	_____	_____	_____	_____	_____	_____	_____	_____
_____	_____	_____	_____	_____	_____	_____	_____	_____
_____	_____	_____	_____	_____	_____	_____	_____	_____
TARGET 2 _____			**TARGET 2** _____			**TARGET 2** _____		
_____	_____	_____	_____	_____	_____	_____	_____	_____
_____	_____	_____	_____	_____	_____	_____	_____	_____
_____	_____	_____	_____	_____	_____	_____	_____	_____
_____	_____	_____	_____	_____	_____	_____	_____	_____
_____	_____	_____	_____	_____	_____	_____	_____	_____
_____	_____	_____	_____	_____	_____	_____	_____	_____
TARGET 3 _____			**TARGET 3** _____			**TARGET 3** _____		
_____	_____	_____	_____	_____	_____	_____	_____	_____
_____	_____	_____	_____	_____	_____	_____	_____	_____
_____	_____	_____	_____	_____	_____	_____	_____	_____
_____	_____	_____	_____	_____	_____	_____	_____	_____

Setting: Specify activity when response occurred

Times: Use slash for each occurrence

Prompts: (Record one symbol for each occurrence)

M = Model, S = Spontaneous, T = Acknowledged by adult or peer, MQ = Mand or question, TD = Time delay

Note. Adapted from "Functional Language," by A. P. Kaiser. In M. E. Snell (Ed.), *Instruction of Students With Severe Disabilities* (p. 354), Upper Saddle River, NJ: Prentice Hall. Copyright 1993 by Prentice Hall. Adapted with permission.

Naturalistic/Milieu Progress Data Form With Preprinted Codes

Instructions: Circle the type of naturalistic/milieu teaching prompt needed or circle spontaneous (S). Transfer the percentage of utterances that were spontaneous to graph.

Student:

Objective:

Date:

MM: Mand–Model   M: Model   TD: Time Delay   S: Spontaneous

Utterance	Setting			
	MM M TD S	MM M TD S	MM M TD S	MM M TD S
	MM M TD S	MM M TD S	MM M TD S	MM M TD S
	MM M TD S	MM M TD S	MM M TD S	MM M TD S
	MM M TD S	MM M TD S	MM M TD S	MM M TD S
	MM M TD S	MM M TD S	MM M TD S	MM M TD S
	MM M TD S	MM M TD S	MM M TD S	MM M TD S
	MM M TD S	MM M TD S	MM M TD S	MM M TD S
	MM M TD S	MM M TD S	MM M TD S	MM M TD S
	MM M TD S	MM M TD S	MM M TD S	MM M TD S
	MM M TD S	MM M TD S	MM M TD S	MM M TD S
	MM M TD S	MM M TD S	MM M TD S	MM M TD S
	MM M TD S	MM M TD S	MM M TD S	MM M TD S
	MM M TD S	MM M TD S	MM M TD S	MM M TD S
	MM M TD S	MM M TD S	MM M TD S	MM M TD S
	MM M TD S	MM M TD S	MM M TD S	MM M TD S
	MM M TD S	MM M TD S	MM M TD S	MM M TD S
	MM M TD S	MM M TD S	MM M TD S	MM M TD S
	MM M TD S	MM M TD S	MM M TD S	MM M TD S
	MM M TD S	MM M TD S	MM M TD S	MM M TD S
	MM M TD S	MM M TD S	MM M TD S	MM M TD S
	MM M TD S	MM M TD S	MM M TD S	MM M TD S
	MM M TD S	MM M TD S	MM M TD S	MM M TD S
	MM M TD S	MM M TD S	MM M TD S	MM M TD S
	MM M TD S	MM M TD S	MM M TD S	MM M TD S

Teaching Language and Communication Skills

The most important curricular area for students with autism involves language and communication skills. Mastery of language allows us to acquire knowledge, form relationships, indicate preferences, and live and work independently. Without effective language skills, our quality of life would be seriously compromised and our long-term outcomes negatively affected. Students with autism manifest many language problems that are directly related to delays in learning and interacting and are often the cause of problem behaviors. Inappropriate behaviors in turn may limit interactions with verbal peers and adults, which limits opportunities to learn language. You can see that such a cycle is educationally nonproductive. For these reasons, teaching students effective communication and language skills should be a priority in any school program.

Language Characteristics

In Chapter 1 we discussed some basic language characteristics of students with autism. Suffice it to say that they often have severe language delays and problems in most language areas. In addition, one of the most devastating characteristics is a *lack of communicative intent,* which means low or no motivation to communicate. Thus, the task of teaching language and communication skills will be difficult. A common assumption about communication is that people will not be able to communicate unless they know how to respond and are motivated to do so (Michael, 1993). It is likely that students with autism are missing both of these components. Motivating them to communicate and attending to "teachable moments" when they appear naturally motivated to communicate will be essential considerations for effective language instruction.

We also pointed out that students with autism have problems in both *receptive* and *expressive* language. Receptive difficulty means that an individual fails to understand what others are telling him or her. Receptive language problems may include an inability or refusal to attend to auditory stimuli, which limits receptive vocabulary. Furthermore, these individuals tend to have restricted interests, so they are not very motivated to attend to their environment in general, which is how people typically learn new vocabulary. Students with autism may fail to use the context to obtain meaning for unfamiliar words, and they struggle to infer meanings from new words because of their failure to generalize from past learning.

Expressively, students with low-functioning autism may (a) be *mute* (nonverbal) or have few verbal skills, (b) be verbal but *echolalic* (echo others' speech), or (c) speak but have problems with *articulation, grammar, intonation, and functional language* (i.e., only requesting and protesting, not commenting, conversing, explaining). They may also manifest problems with *pragmatics* (the social effectiveness of language). Verbal students with autism typically may fail to (a) respond to other's verbal interactions, (b) take turns speaking, (c) listen, and (d) move off of favorite topics (e.g., trains, washing machines). They may display speech that does not seem to fit with current situations. What they say may seem to "come out of the blue." For example, you may be teaching a student to identify the emotions of people in pictures. You show a picture of someone who is sad and ask, "What is he feeling?" Your student says, "Let's go riding in the green Volvo." Although you might be able to figure out why he or she said this phrase (e.g., communicating that he or she does not know the answer to your question), such responses will do little to effectively communicate meaning and sustain social interactions. Unfortunately, individuals who fail to develop effective communication may resort to challenging behaviors (e.g., tantrums, self-injurious behavior, aggression, whining, crying) as a mode of communication.

As you can tell, teaching your students with autism to communicate well will be a challenging task, but it is a very important one. The more you know about teaching speech and language, and the more time you spend teaching language skills, the better able you will be to address these problems and positively affect your students' opportunities and outcomes.

Components of Language

Before you can teach language, you first need to understand its components. Language consists of a very complex set of behaviors that most children seem to learn easily. Once you begin to assess the skills of someone who has great difficulty with the process, you will realize how remarkable it is that most 4-year-olds have mastered verbal language. The major components of language are *form* (the type of communicative response), such as speech, sign, tantrums, or pointing, and *function* (the communicative purpose or intent). Examples of purposes include requesting things they want to obtain, responding to others' social initiatives, seeking comfort, expressing interest in the environment, conversing or commenting about experiences, protesting things they do not like, and initiating and maintaining social interactions (Neel & Billingsley, 1989). Most researchers agree that for students who manifest severe language delays, teaching effective forms for communicating multiple functions is more important than requiring a particular way of communicating.

There are various schools of thought about the composition of language and how it best develops. These theories are derived from developmental models and from the behavioral model. Because we are deriving our recommendations in this book from the behavioral model (ABA), we will present B. F. Skinner's (1957) analysis of language as a basis for what you should be assessing and teaching your students. In Chapter 2 you learned that the A–B–C model explains human behavior as a function of antecedents and consequences. This model is based on Skinner's (1938) theory of *operant conditioning*. According to Skinner, an *operant behavior* is a voluntary behavior that humans can control, such as eating, walking, writing, signing, and talking. Operant behaviors are differentiated from *reflexive behaviors,* which are not under voluntary control. An example would be blinking when something gets in your eye.

Because Skinner was interested primarily in operant (voluntary) behaviors, he provided an analysis of language in similar terms. He referred to language as *verbal behavior* in an attempt to differentiate his analysis from the analyses of developmental theorists and in keeping with the idea that such responses are a function of environmental influences (i.e., antecedents and consequences) rather than internal maturational processes (Miguel, Petursdottir, & Carr, 2005). According to Skinner, verbal behavior achieves reinforcement through someone else's actions (asking for something gets someone to produce it), whereas nonverbal behaviors achieve reinforcement through mechanical action (picking something up; Skinner, 1957). Defined this way, verbal behavior not only includes speech responses, but also refers to gesturing, writing, reading, signing, and so forth.

Skinner (1957) classified verbal behavior into functional categories that he called *verbal operants*. Each verbal operant, which as a group provide the basis for teaching effective communication, needs to be explicitly taught. Mastering one functional category will not guarantee mastery of the other categories. Assessing and teaching verbal operants has been shown to be an effective language training program for students with autism (Sundberg & Michael, 2001).

It is important to understand that it is not how we say something (form) but the intention behind our communication responses (function) that is most important in language acquisition. For example, let's consider the word *banana*. The word is understandable, but from a functional—or pragmatic—perspective, there are several reasons why you might utter this word. You could do the following:

1. ask for a banana,
2. tell someone there is a banana on that tree over there,
3. repeat the word *banana* when someone else says it,
4. make the sign for *banana* when someone shows you how,
5. hand someone a banana when asked to do so,
6. answer "Banana" when someone asks you what you put on your cereal,
7. point to a banana when someone asks, "Show me something that is a fruit," and
8. describe the properties (healthy, contains potassium) of a banana when you see one in the store.

Students with severe language delays seldom acquire the ability to communicate all these possibilities unless we explicitly teach them how to do so. Too often, students with autism are only taught to point to pictures or objects on cue, label items or picture when cued, and make a few requests. Teaching your students to use language for many functions will enhance their personal and social proficiency and increase their ability to learn in general (Partingen, 2007).

Verbal Operants

In this section we have listed and described Skinner's functional categories, or verbal operants, that are recommended for early language learners. These categories should be reflected in your language assessment and your curriculum (what you prompt and teach). Fortunately, commercial curricula based on verbal operants are available. We will review one such curriculum as an example.

Skinner's Expressive Categories

1. *Echoic.* An echoic is simply vocal imitation. Someone says something and the learner imitates what was said. Usually, some type of social reinforcer ("Good," "That's right") follows the response. For example, the teacher points to another child and says, "Sam." The learner repeats "Sam." Sam and the teacher smile.

2. *Motor imitation.* The learner imitates motor movement made by someone else. For example, a speech therapist sticks out her or his tongue and the learner produces the same

behavior. Usually, this is followed by social reinforcement. Or, a teacher could make the sign for water and the student imitates that sign and then obtains praise and a drink of water.

3. *Mand.* Mand is probably short for the word *command* or *demand.* It means to make a request. The antecedent in this case has to be something the learner wants (e.g., yogurt). He says, "Yogurt please" (mand) and usually receives what he wants (reinforcement).

4. *Tact.* Tact could be short for *contact* or *tactile.* *Tact* means to label or name objects, events, relationships, properties, and so forth (perhaps as a result of sensual stimulation, such as smell or sight). Adjectives and prepositions are also tacts. For example, a teacher holds up a pair of glasses, and the learner says, "Glasses." Or, the teacher sprays a scent, and the learner shouts, "Lemon!" A tact is usually followed by social reinforcement.

5. *Intraverbal.* An *intraverbal* is responding to someone else's verbal behavior with a response that does not directly match (echoic) what the other person said. An intraverbal is conversational and includes answering "Wh–" questions. For example, the teacher says, "What did you watch on TV last night?" and the student replies, "I watched cartoons." Or, the teacher says, "It's cold outside," and the learner says, "Maybe it will snow." Usually the learner responses are followed by social reinforcement (e.g., more comments and conversation).

Skinner's Receptive Categories

1. *Receptive language.* The learner follows directions (nonverbal behavior) or complies with another person's mands. Reinforcement is usually social; for example, a teacher tells the learner to line up at the door, the learner complies, and the teacher nods.

2. *Receptive by feature, function, and class (RFFC).* The learner can identify items in the environment when provided with a description of them. For example, a teacher says, "Show me your backpack," and the student points to his or her backpack. Or, the teacher says, "Get the big red ball," and the student retrieves it. Usually, the reinforcement is social.

These categories are not arranged in a hierarchy in which mastery of one category is required before moving to another. Sundberg and Partington (1998) recommended that you teach across verbal operants, depending on the skill level of the student. For example, you do not have to teach a child to label (tact) something or point to it on command before he or she could ask for it (mand). As a matter of fact, these authors also recommend that manding (requesting) be the first category taught because the motivation to communicate is highest when making a request for something desirable (a reinforcer). Remember that motivating students with autism to communicate is a high priority. Also, manding develops very early in typically developing infants, who cry as a way of asking for food, comfort, or interaction. Shaping an acceptable form for manding (speech or sign instead of whining or crying) will also be a key component of early language training.

Assessing Language and Communication

Before commencing with teaching, you will need to assess your students to determine in which functional contexts the students currently respond and something about their preferred response forms. One curriculum based on ABA theory that provides information about assessing and teaching language skills, is the *Assessment of Basic Language and Learning Skills–Revised* (ABLLS-R; Partington, 2007). We believe that you may find it helpful for assessing and teaching verbal operants to students with low language skills. Appendix C lists additional commercial curricula, not necessarily based on ABA, that may also be helpful for assessing and teaching language.

Assessment of Basic Language and Learning Skills

The ABLLS-R was inspired by Skinner's analysis of verbal behavior and includes an assessment system, a task analytic curriculum guide, and a progress tracking system. It is composed of a protocol for scoring students' assessed responses and recording progress data and a guide explaining how to score the protocol, analyze scores, and develop an IEP. The ABLLS-R targets language and other basic skills deemed necessary for students to be able to learn from their routine experiences without depending on the presence and assistance of teaching adults. The targeted skills consist of the following:

- response motivation,
- attention to verbal and nonverbal stimuli,
- generalization skills,
- use of spontaneous language,
- functional language skills,
- academic skills,
- self-help skills, and
- motor skills.

The assessment is criterion-referenced, with items arranged in an approximate developmental sequence (Partington, 2007).

The ABLLS-R assessment, which is conducted over several weeks, uses interview data, observational recording, and the presentation of several tasks. Scores are assigned according to a scoring rubric for assessing student responses to designated tasks (e.g., "The student will be able to use adjectives that describe objects"; 0–4 scoring, with 0 = *cannot perform*, 4 = *labels using at least 20 adjectives with three colors, two shapes and two sizes*). Interview questions are also provided for each task so that the score can be obtained without having the student complete every task (e.g., can the student identify properties of objects [color, size, shape texture, length, etc.]?). Each task has enough scoring rows for an initial assessment and three annual follow-up assessments. Assessment scores are transferred to a progress grid so that it can be easily determined which skills have been mastered, are still in progress, and cannot currently be performed. As students master designated skills, the grid can be color coded to reflect progress.

Once assessment data are obtained, the authors recommend that objectives be chosen based on "a set of basic learner skills such that he will 'learn to learn'" (Partington & Sundberg, 1998, p. 15). These basic learner skills fall into 15 categories, which are listed in At-a-Glance 9.1.

The guide provides recommendations for choosing objectives from the various categories and writing IEPs for early and advanced learners. The profile provides a user-friendly method for recording progress data. In a separate book, Sundberg and Partington (1998) offered specific teaching strategies, such as DTT and naturalistic/milieu teaching. Figures 9.1 and 9.2 illustrate two lesson plans for teaching verbal operants specified in the ABLLS-R.

At-a-Glance 9.1 ABLLS-R Basic Learner Skills

A. **Cooperation and Reinforcer Effectiveness:** Child must be able to respond to instructor-controlled reinforcers and intermittent reinforcement schedules

B. **Visual Performance:** Matching, sorting, putting together puzzles, sequencing visually, and so forth, with more and more complex arrays of stimuli

C. **Receptive Language:** Following instructions under various conditions, selecting designated items or pictures by label or by feature, function, and/or class

D. **Motor Imitation:** Gross- and fine-motor imitation, mouth-movement imitation

E. **Vocal Imitation (Echoic):** For students who cannot echo speech sounds or need to improve articulation and prosody

F. **Requests (Mands):** Making various requests from simple to complex (e.g., spontaneously asking for items, actions, information throughout the day)

G. **Labeling (Tacts):** Labeling objects, people, pictures, actions, and so forth; use of adjectives, pronouns, and possessives

H. **Intraverbals:** Describing action sequences, answering "Wh–" questions

I. **Spontaneous Vocalizations:** Using language skills (requests, labels, echoing, adding to comments) across contexts

J. **Syntax and Grammar:** For students who can produce phrases, instruction about verb tense, conjunctions, and so forth

K. **Play/Leisure Skills:** Playing appropriately with objects and others; imaginative play, cooperative play

L. **Social Interaction Skills:** Using language skills with peers, sharing, making social initiations, engaging in conversations

M. **Group Instruction:** Group participation, with imitation, labeling, receptive language tasks, and acquisition of new language skills

N. **Classroom Routines:** Lining up, remaining on-task, making transitions, waiting

O. **Generalized Responding:** Displaying learned responses across settings, people, materials, tasks, and varying behaviors, as necessary

Note. Adapted from *The Assessment of Basic Language and Learning Skills–Revised*, by J. W. Partington, 2007, Los Angeles: Western Psychological Services. Adapted with permission.

Additional Assessment Strategies

Although we recommend the ABLLS-R because it is specifically based on Skinner's (1957) analysis of verbal behavior, you can certainly assess and teach verbal behavior without it. For example, teachers can develop a simple assessment matrix for determining the current level of performance pertaining to language functions and forms. Figure 9.3 is a sample function–form matrix. An adult who knows the child well should complete the assessment (a reproducible version is located in the appendix to this chapter). Notice that challenging behaviors can be a form of communication for children. (As we noted before, it is a good idea to assume initially that challenging behaviors have a communicative function.)

You can also obtain assessment information using an ecological inventory, as described in Chapter 7. By listing the associated speech and language skills for each activity or functional routine that you delineate for a student, you will be able to compile a list of language objectives that are guaranteed to be useful to particular students. When you are listing the associated language skills, be sure to include both receptive and expressive verbal operants, especially mands, tacts, and intraverbals. While observing the student in current contexts, note what types of communicative

NET LESSON PLAN—Early Learner

ACTIVITY	WHAT CHILD WILL TALK ABOUT

Reading a book:
 	
A favorite book:
 	
  Thomas the Train
  Barney
  Teletubbies
 	
A book with lots of simple pictures inside
	MANDS (REQUESTS):
	
	Child mands to: "open book" when child has an interest to look inside
	                  "turn page" when child wants to see the next page
	                  "go back" when child wants to see the previous page
	                  "move your hand" as you cover a favorite picture
	
	TACTS (LABELS):
	
	Child labels all favorite characters in response to "Who is this?"
	Child labels common items in response to "What is this?"
	Child labels the body parts of the characters in the book. You then ask, "What's this?" as you point to a body part on yourself.
	
	RECEPTIVE:
	
	Child follows lots of receptive commands:
	
	  "Touch Barney." "Show me Baby Bop."
	  "Touch the cup." "Point to the spoon."
	  "Touch something mommy drives." (car)
	  "Turn the page."
	  "Touch your eyes."
	
	INTRAVERBALS (WH– QUESTIONS)
	
	  "What is something you read?"
	  "Tell me something you eat."
	  "What says choo choo?" (as you're reading *Thomas the Train* book).

Figure 9.1. Early language learner lesson plan for teaching verbal operants in the natural environment. From V. J. Carbone, *Teaching Verbal Behavior to Children With Autism and Related Disabilities* (2004, March). Workshop presented in Austin, Texas. Reprinted with permission.

forms (e.g., vocalizations, signs, gestures, challenging behaviors) are currently used and for what purpose each form is used.

Finally, you can obtain assessment information from formal language assessments. Your SLP may be able to assist with formal assessments. Resources 9.1 lists some commercially available language assessments, including the ABLLS-R. You might find that some of these instruments are based on a different analysis of language than the one we presented. You will want your assessment categories to match what you will be teaching, so choose your assessment methods with that in mind.

Choosing the Best Form of Communication

When we talk about the form of communication, we are referring to *how* the student communicates. The preferred communication form is speech, or vocal responses, because almost everyone understands, uses, and models speech; speech does not

NET LESSON PLAN–Intermediate

ACTIVITY	WHAT CHILD WILL TALK ABOUT
Watching a favorite video	**MANDS (REQUESTS):** Manding using full sentences Use a variety of carrier phrases. **TACTS (LABELS):** Tacts using full sentences Tacts all characters. Tacts colors of characters and clothing (e.g., "Tell the color of Charlie Brown's shirt."). Tacts position (e.g., "Where is Snoopy?"). **RECEPTIVE:** Points to or touches things by size (e.g., "Touch the big ball."). Receptively identifies things by feature, function, or class. **INTRAVERBALS (WH– QUESTIONS)** Answers wh– questions. "What is he wearing on his head?" "Why is he wearing that on his head?" "How did he get to school?"

Figure 9.2. Intermediate language learner lesson plan for teaching verbal operants in the natural environment. From V. J. Carbone, *Teaching Verbal Behavior to Children With Autism and Related Disabilities* (2004, March). Workshop presented in Austin, Texas. Reprinted with permission.

take long to produce (it's efficient); and it is readily available in all settings. We recommend that every effort be made to teach students to produce vocal responses. The probability that a student will acquire speech is higher if intensive instruction starts at a young age (National Research Council, 2001). Even with intensive instruction, many students with autism have a very difficult time learning to talk, as we noted earlier. Also, it is *very important* to teach students functional communication, no matter what the form, to prevent the development of challenging behavior and to facilitate continual learning. That said, if students cannot easily learn to talk, they may need to be taught to use *augmentative and alternative communication* (AAC) systems. In choosing language forms, keep in mind the following three important goals:

1. provide students with a functional way to spontaneously communicate across settings and people,
2. ensure that students are able to continue to acquire vocabulary and language functions within the communication system, and
3. choose a system that likely will enhance speech acquisition (Mirenda, 2003).

Augmentative and Alternative Communication Systems

AAC systems are defined as "the supplementation or replacement of natural speech and/or writing using aided and/or unaided symbols" (Lloyd, Fuller, & Arvidson,

Instructions: Place a check mark in the boxes for all communication forms used for a particular function.

Student: Timothy   Date: 10-3-01   Respondent: Jane Grey

Function	Multiple Words	One-Word Speech	One-Word Sign	Multiple Signs	Points to Pictures	Gestures/Pointing	Uses Other's Hands	Proximity	Grabs	Gives Object	Gazing	Shakes Head	Facial Expression	Whining/Crying	Self-Injurious Behavior	Tantrum	Aggression	Other
Mands/Requests																		
Food							✓		✓		✓			✓				
Objects							✓		✓									
Activity								✓					✓					
Attention							✓	✓					✓	✓	✓			
Assistance							✓											
Interaction								✓		✓	✓		✓					Touches
Protests																		
Change														✓		✓	✓	
Place or person													✓	✓		✓	✓	
Task, activity													✓	✓			✓	runs
Food												✓	✓	✓				
Expresses																		
Confusion													✓	✓				
Frustration														✓		✓		
Anger																	✓	
Happiness						✓	✓						✓					
Greeting							✓			✓			✓					
Describes																		
Objects																		N/A
People																		N/A
Events																		N/A
Responds to																		
Social initiatives																		
Peers																		ignores
Adults								✓		✓	✓		✓					
Initiates interaction with																		
Peers						✓	✓	✓						✓				
Adults							✓	✓		✓	✓		✓					
Family						✓	✓	✓		✓	✓		✓	✓ happy				

Figure 9.3. Assessment of language function and form.

Resources 9.1 Examples of Commercially Available Language Assessments

The Assessment of Basic Language and Learning Skills—Revised (ABLLS-R)
  Western Psychological Services
  12031 Wilshire Blvd.
  Los Angeles, CA 90025-1251

Clinical Evaluation of Language Fundamentals, 4th ed. (CELF-4)
  Harcourt Assessments, Inc.
  19500 Bulverde Rd.
  San Antonio, TX 78259

Communication and Symbolic Behavior Scales (CSBS)
  Paul H. Brookes
  PO Box 10624
  Baltimore, MD 21285

Environmental Language Inventory
  Charles E. Merrill
  445 Hutchinson Ave.
  Columbus, OH 43235

Fluharty Preschool Speech and Language Screening Test, 2nd ed.
  PRO-ED
  8700 Shoal Creek Blvd.
  Austin, TX 78757-6897

Goldman-Fristoe Test of Articulation, 2nd ed. (G-FTA-2)
  American Guidance Service
  Publishers Building
  Circle Pines, MN 55014

Khan-Lewis Phonological Analysis, 2nd ed. (KLPA-2)
  American Guidance Service
  Publishers Building
  Circle Pines, MN 55014

"Let's Talk" Inventory for Adolescents
  Charles E. Merrill
  445 Hutchinson Ave.
  Columbus, OH 43235

Peabody Picture Vocabulary Test, 4th ed. (PPVT-4)
  American Guidance Service/Pearson Assessment
  Publishers Building
  Circle Pines, MN 55014

Preschool Language Scale, 4th ed. (PLS-4)
  Harcourt Assessments, Inc.
  19500 Bulverde Rd.
  San Antonio, TX 78259

Psychoeducational Profile, 3rd ed. (PEP-3)
  PRO-ED
  8700 Shoal Creek Blvd.
  Austin, TX 78757-6897

Receptive–Expressive Emergent Language Scale, 3rd ed. (REEL-3)
American Guidance Service/Pearson Assessment
Publishers Building
Circle Pines, MN 55014

Test of Adolescent and Adult Language, 2nd ed. (TOAL-2)
PRO-ED
8700 Shoal Creek Blvd.
Austin, TX 78757-6897

Test of Early Language Development, 3rd. ed. (TELD-3)
PRO-ED
8700 Shoal Creek Blvd.
Austin, TX 78757-6897

Test of Language Development–Primary, 4th ed. (TOLD-P:4)
PRO-ED
8700 Shoal Creek Blvd.
Austin, TX 78757-6897

Token Test for Children, 2nd ed. (TTFC-2)
PRO-ED
8700 Shoal Creek Blvd.
Austin, TX 78757-6897

1997, p. 524). AAC systems may be used to enhance (i.e., augment) existing verbal ability or to act as the individual's primary mode of expressive communication (i.e., alternative system). AAC can also be used to augment students' receptive language (Mirenda & Erickson, 2000). For example, teachers can use pictures in conjunction with verbal instructions to help students understand expectations and directions. *Aided* AAC systems require that individuals use supplementary materials or equipment (e.g., electronic voice-output aids, communication boards, pictures, concrete objects) to be able to communicate. An *unaided* system does not require supplementary equipment or materials. Sign language and gesturing are examples of unaided systems.

Since the 1970s, AAC systems have been developed and successfully utilized with students with low verbal ability (Mirenda, 2003). The following are several examples of aided systems.

1. *Visual–Spatial Symbols.* In Chapter 5 we discussed the use of concrete objects and pictures to visually guide students through their environment, schedule, and activities. Pictures, line drawings, and concrete objects can also be used for communicative purposes. Because many individuals with autism and PDD seem to respond well to static visuals, using visual–spatial symbols seems like a natural fit (Mirenda, 2001). The most commonly used symbols are the *Picture Communication Symbols* (Mayer-Johnson Co., 1994), but photographs and nonspecific graphic symbols have also been used. The symbols or objects can be used on a communication board, in a communication book, in a wallet or notebook, and/or with voice-output devices. The student may be required to point to the object or symbol when trying to express something or may be required to exchange the object or symbol, as with the *Picture Exchange Communication System* (PECS; Frost & Bondy, 1994). Based on ABA techniques, the PECS program teaches individuals to initiate interactions and exchange pictures with others as a means of requesting (manding), tacting, commenting, and gathering information.

2. *Assistive Technology.* As mandated in the IDEA, assistive technology must be provided to special education students when they cannot learn without it. For expressive communication, the most commonly used assistive technologies are *voice output communication aids* (VOCAs). These are portable devices that can produce computerized speech at the touch of a button or with the use of other types of switches. Visual–spatial symbols or printed words are arranged on the activation display, and speech responses can be programmed into the device at will. Students are taught to scan the symbols, select what they want to say, and push a specific symbol to activate the designated speech responses (e.g., mands, greetings, comments, tacts). The more expensive devices can be programmed for multiple, more-specific speech responses.

Sign language is the most commonly used unaided AAC system for students with autism. Students can be taught to mand, tact, converse, and comment with American Sign Language (ASL; Sundberg & Partington, 1998). In the 1970s and 1980s, *total,* or *simultaneous, communication* was commonly taught to children with autism. In total communication, students are taught to speak and sign simultaneously while teaching adults also speak and sign simultaneously (e.g., Brady & Smouse, 1978). Current research supports the thinking that teaching sign language promotes vocal responses (Mirenda, 2003; Tincani, 2004).

Choosing an AAC System

When choosing an AAC system, discuss the following questions with parents, family members, and SLPs:

1. Is the system portable? Is it easy for the student to access the system at all times?
2. Does the system accommodate a wide variety of vocabulary and language functions?
3. Can others easily understand the system?
4. Is it easy to prompt responses with the system?
5. Is the student motivated to use the system?

As you might imagine, there are advantages and disadvantages with each of the AAC systems that we have listed. Remember that the main goal is to provide a means for students to spontaneously and effectively communicate in generalized situations. Unaided systems are the easiest to access in a wide variety of situations. For example, if a student were playing at recess, cleaning tables, or doing an art project, it would be much easier and quicker to make a comment or request with ASL than having to obtain a picture or a VOCA. Signs can be used from a distance and are easily portable. On the other hand, not many people use signs (provide models) or understand ASL, so communicating with sign language may not be effective except with a few select "listeners."

Some argue that sign language is easier for students with autism to learn because it only requires the student to form a sign as opposed to scanning an array of pictures and then selecting the picture (Michael, 1985). On the other hand, use of an aided system in which the student chooses a picture or symbol is a much easier motor response than forming specific manual signs. Because students with autism often have fine-motor delays, they may not easily acquire manual signs. VOCAs provide a more understandable output feature and attain attention better than just pictures or sign language (Sigafoos, O'Reilly, Seely-York, & Edrisinha, 2004); however, they are expensive and perhaps more cumbersome to transport than pictures or communication boards. For aided systems to be effective, they must be readily available to the communicator. Sign language would always be readily available.

Both sign language and aided language systems are easier to prompt than speech. Like speech, sign language has the advantage of being a comprehensive language system with few limits on the number of language functions that can be produced. Aided systems are limited in the number of available pictures or symbols, the ability to depict abstract concepts, the number of speech responses that can be programmed, and so forth. Fortunately, it appears that aided language systems also facilitate speech development (Mirenda, 2003).

Perhaps the most functional system would be an aided/unaided combination (Sigafoos & Drasgow, 2001). Functionality of a particular system may depend on the situation. We all use multimodal communication (verbal and nonverbal) to enhance understanding, so it would make sense that multiple communicative strategies might also be useful to our students. In addition, because of the previously listed advantages and disadvantages of AAC systems, using more than one system may overcome these limitations. Students could be taught to use more than one system simultaneously (e.g., sign and speech, pictures and signs) or multiple systems conditionally (i.e., just when they need to use the systems). For example, if a student wants to make a request and the communication board is not available, he or she could use a manual sign, or if the listener does not respond to the sign, the student could seek out his or her pictures. With multimodal communication systems, you will have to teach your students when they should use each mode and how to use them.

Determining which AAC systems to teach is a difficult challenge for teachers, SLPs, and parents. Further consideration should be given to

1. the student's current and future communicative needs;
2. the student's current abilities in regard to receptive and expressive communication, response to symbols, sensory issues, and motor skills;
3. characteristics of the listening community (parents, peers, family members) for each student; and
4. possible communicative barriers (Mirenda, 2001).

We refer the reader to Reichle, York, and Sigafoos (1991) for specific information about AAC assessments and teaching strategies.

If a student is echoic and learns mands and tacts fairly easily, speech is probably the preferred mode. If echoic responses are not forthcoming and the student is young, you might want to try manual signs with speech. If fine-motor skills are a problem, consider a VOCA or picture system. If the student is older, but has few speech responses, try sign language with an aided system (Sundberg & Partington, 1998). Remember that the goal is to teach your students to communicate effectively and efficiently across settings and with many people.

Teaching Strategies

The two major instructional strategies for teaching language and communication skills are DTT (discussed in Chapter 3) and naturalistic/milieu teaching (described in Chapter 4). We recommend using DTT for teaching new skills and naturalistic/milieu teaching for maintenance and generalization of skills. As a general rule, use DTT when drill-and-practice is needed and use naturalistic/milieu strategies at every possible opportunity. Prompting and reinforcing students for producing language responses in naturally occurring situations will make the skills functional. In addition to matching teaching strategies to levels of learning (see Chapter 7), Sundberg and Partington (1998) recommended specific teaching strategies for instructing each verbal operant. We discuss some of their recommendations next.

Manding

It is usually recommended that you initially teach early language learners to mand (i.e., request a reinforcer) for things they want (Sundberg & Partingen, 1998). Individuals are naturally motivated to mand because it usually results in something desirable. Because individuals with autism are not often motivated to communicate, we need to take advantage of this type of motivation to initially elicit language responses. Producing a mand is dependent on the existence of a reinforcing stimulus (e.g., object, food, activity that they want). Environmental conditions that evoke attention and motivation to act are known as *establishing operations* (EOs). For example, being hungry is an EO for fixing a meal, asking for food, stealing food, buying food, and so forth (whatever has worked for you in the past). Being full, on the other hand, is an EO for refraining from any of the above responses. Seeing a favorite stim toy may be an EO for a student to grab it, point to it, whine, sign "toy," or say, "I want the toy." To teach your students to mand, you will have to have various powerful reinforcers (EOs) present to keep the students highly motivated to make requests. The following are some considerations for teaching mands:

1. Conduct a reinforcer survey to determine what might motivate students to make requests and obtain those items. Make note of the times of day when the student might be most motivated to make requests. For example, during snack or mealtime, most students are motivated to request foods or drink or help with opening wrappers. Right after mealtime, however, may *not* be a time when the student is highly motivated to mand.

2. Use decreasing assistance or most-to-least prompts (see Chapter 3) to obtain requesting responses in the presence of EOs. For students who are not imitating or echoing, you might consider initially using sign language because it is easy to prompt physically and to model.

3. Fade physical prompts first and then models. Add a second mand for a different item and ask the student to indicate what he or she wants from the two items (e.g., ball or music). *Remember* that you must have EOs, which means you must teach words, signs, or pictures for those items that an individual student is motivated to request.

4. For students who can imitate signs or speech, or who can point to pictures, verbally prompt them to "say" the word. For example, you would ask, "What do you want—chip?" (perhaps point to a picture or make the sign for the word *chip*). You would next fade out the model (*chip*), then use time delay and wait for a request for up to 5 seconds before prompting with the question, "What do you want?" The goal is to have the students spontaneously request without dependence on teacher prompting.

5. Add signs and/or words for additional items that the student is motivated to request. Add these words at a pace that does not cause confusion.

6. Create a classroom environment that stimulates students to make requests multiple times throughout the day (see Chapter 4 for ways to stimulate manding). Take note of things that interest students and prompt them to mand at every opportunity. At the same time, do *not* reward inappropriate mands (e.g., whining, crying, throwing a tantrum, grabbing). Not rewarding such mands is called *extinction*.

7. Use multiple, intensive trials for new learning. Intersperse practice situations at the fluency level. Use naturalistic/milieu teaching to establish generalization across situations, people, and settings.

Motor Imitation

For early learners, gross-motor imitation is fairly easy to teach. You would present the S^D, "Do this," and physically prompt, for example, hands up, hands out, hands together, waving. You should fade the physical prompts so that motor imitation occurs fluently. When correct responses are emitted, praise the response and have the student mand for a reinforcer (e.g., "I want a chip," "I want a raisin").

Verbal Imitation

Teaching students to echo verbal responses is difficult. At first, you will need to reinforce any vocalizations the student emits and then gradually shape the vocalizations into recognizable sounds and words. Because you cannot physically prompt verbal responses, you will need to rely on multiple trials of "Say _____," and reinforcing better approximations from the student. If echoic responses do not form, consider teaching the student to use an AAC system in conjunction with speech.

Receptive Language

For receptive language, you will first want to teach students to follow simple directions, such as "Sit down," "Come here," "Come to the table." Physically prompt the responses and reinforce the student when they are correct. Use multiple, intensive trials interspersed with motor imitation and mands, if possible. Second, teach students to point to or show you the items that you label. This way, you can teach students to identify objects, pictures, words, and adjectives (e.g., colors, size). Third, teach students to match visual stimuli to the command, "Match this," or "Put with same." Teaching visual discrimination is an important component for further cognitive responding (e.g., reading).

Last, you will teach students to identify stimuli by feature, function, and class (RFFC). Now you are asking students to "point to the one that you ride to school (bus)" (function) or "show me the one that is soft (feather)" (feature) or "point to the one that is a flower (daisy)" (class). Begin with visual and verbal prompts (point to the correct item) with multiple trials. Fade the prompts, deliver the S^{D}s at a more rapid pace, and increase the complexity of the stimuli (e.g., given a picture of animals, say, "Find the ones that are mammals").

Tacting

Once students can echo words or imitate signs, mand for desired items, and point to pictures and objects, you might be ready to teach tacting or labeling. When you ask, "What is this [or that]?" the student will say or sign what it is. Sundberg and Partington (1998) made the following recommendations for teaching tacts:

1. Begin with words that are important or relevant in the child's life. It might be that you begin with items that the student has already learned to mand (e.g., *toy*). You would say, "What is this?" [toy]
2. Choose items for which everyone agrees on the label (e.g., *ball*) and that are easy to discriminate from other objects.
3. Choose developmentally appropriate and easy to say/sign responses.

4. Choose words that are functional and are frequently modeled (e.g., *eat*). You would say, "What is the boy doing?" [eating]
5. Avoid words that might have a negative connotation (e.g., *shower*).

As with other responses, use models and prompts within multiple trials and then fade prompts (including asking, "What is this?"), and provide opportunities to practice in the natural environment. You can combine tacting and RFFCs in trials, for example, by requesting the student to "point to the one you find in the kitchen" [pan] and then asking, "What do you find in the kitchen?" The student should say or sign *pan*.

Intraverbals

As we noted previously, *intraverbals* are responses to others' verbal behaviors without just echoing or following directions. For example, someone says, "It's my birthday today." The listener replies, "Happy birthday; what will you do today?" The response is related but not echoic. Intraverbals lead to conversational skills. Once your students reach fluency on many mands and tacts, you can begin teaching intraverbals using a fill-in-the-blank strategy. For example, you might say, "After you finish your sandwich, you will eat your _____" [cookie], or "It's time to go _____" [outside]. Prompt initial responses, fade prompts, and provide practice opportunities in trials and naturally occurring situations. Eventually, you should ask Wh– questions (e.g., "What do you jump on?" "Who made your lunch?" "What did you watch on TV?").

To keep your students motivated to learn new language functions, pay attention to interest levels and pacing. For example, during DTT you should

1. intersperse various verbal operants to prevent boredom and allow students to become comfortable when responding to multiple verbal stimuli;
2. try to avoid multiple consecutive trials for one specific response;
3. for new learners, keep the pace fairly slow, initially using many prompts using powerful reinforcers; and
4. as students begin responding, increase the pace of the trials, fade prompts, and fade reinforcers.

It is especially important for language training to use a combination of DTT and naturalistic/milieu teaching so that language responses are prompted and reinforced in natural settings and situations. It is also very important that all teaching adults commit to teaching language and communication at every opportunity, *all* day.

Additional Teaching Strategies

In addition to DTT and naturalistic/milieu teaching strategies, teachers might also consider *observational learning*, in which students learn language by watching and listening to other peers or adults. If teachers reinforce peers for emitting responses, it is very likely that other students will imitate the behaviors. You might also consider using video models and prompting students to imitate what they see. Remember, however, that for many students with autism imitating others does not come easily, so you will need to make a concerted effort to teach them to attend to models and prompt them to imitate what they see.

Expansion is another method of facilitating language development (Rappaport, 1996). When a student initiates a verbal behavior, repeat the response and add one or two words, then have the student repeat the expanded response. For example, a student points and says, "Washing machine." You might reply, "A big white washing machine," and then have the student repeat the expanded phrase. Expansion might also help you teach prosody through modeling correct intonation and voice level. Neel and Billingsley (1989) recommended teaching language within *functional routines*. By embedding mands, tacts, and intraverbals into regular routines, students will learn self-help, social, and language skills in a meaningful context. For example, José might be taught to prepare for lunch by asking permission to go to the sink, going to the sink, washing his hands, asking the teacher for his lunch, lining up, telling a peer what is in his lunchbox, asking a peer what's in her lunchbox, walking down the hall, and so forth.

Koegel (1995) recommended teaching students to make *queries* to enhance spontaneous verbal interactions:

1. Teach *What's that?* Put items in a sack and prompt the student to ask, "What's that?" After the response, open the sack, remove the item, and reinforce the student. Eventually fade the prompts. In this way, the student can learn new vocabulary by asking others, "What's that?"
2. Teach *where* questions. Place objects in various locations and ask the student, "Where is it?" The student will soon be able to ask others where things are (mands).
3. Teach *whose* questions. Hold up an item and have the student ask, "Whose is it?" Before getting the object, the student must repeat the possessive (e.g., *mine, yours, Allie's*).
4. Teach *What happened?* Use interactive toys and prompt the student to ask, "What happened?" after, for example, something pops up. Also require the child to answer using the past tense (e.g., "The puppet popped up"). Reinforce correct responses.

Hughes et al. (2000) suggested providing low-verbal students with a *communication book* containing pictures of activities, people, and things that the student enjoys and may wish to talk about. Peer partners are trained to make comments about the pictures, ask a question about the pictures, and wait for the target student to respond. More prompting by teachers or peers might initially be necessary, depending on the target student's verbal skills. Eventually, prompts should be faded.

Finally, teachers should concentrate on establishing language-rich environments (at school and home) that stimulate students to communicate. For example, in Chapter 4 we listed several strategies for motivating students to mand (e.g., giving choices, placing desired items out of reach, leaving the student unfulfilled). We also listed things to avoid in developing a language-rich environment (e.g., failing to attend to students, giving too much assistance, failing to teach at opportune moments). We recommend that you review Chapters 3 and 4 in regards to teaching language and communication skills. Intensive language instruction, especially for young children, has been found to positively affect all other educational outcomes (National Research Council, 2001). As a teacher, you may do nothing as important as teaching your students to effectively communicate.

Summary

Remember that your goal is to teach students *how* to communicate in a variety of situations and to *motivate* them to do so spontaneously. You must be careful to choose initial communicative responses that are meaningful and result in reinforcers. If you do not, your students with autism may be very resistant to your instruction. We recommend teaching verbal operants (e.g., mands, tacts, intraverbals) as a basis for your curriculum. You also need to carefully consider communicative form. The mode of communication should be relatively easy, quick, and understandable, so you will need to work with the SLP and the student's parents to choose a reasonable combination of effective communication systems. Teach language using DTT and naturalistic/milieu strategies, paying attention to intensive drill-and-practice and generalization of skills. Finally, create a language-rich environment by providing multiple EOs (antecedents that motivate language production), training all teaching adults to prompt and reinforce communicative responses, and committing to teaching language at every possible opportunity.

References

Brady, D. O., & Smouse, A. D. (1978). A simultaneous comparison of three methods for language training with an autistic child: An experimental single case analysis. *Journal of Autism and Childhood Schizophrenia, 8,* 271–279.

Frost, L., & Bondy, A. S. (1994). PECS: *The picture exchange communication system training manual.* Newark, DE: Pyramid Educational Consultants.

Hughes, C., Rung, L., Wehmeyer, M., Agran, M., Copeland, S. R., & Hwang, B. (2000). Self-prompted communication book use to increase social interactions among high school students. *Journal of The Association for Persons with Severe Handicaps, 25,* 153–166.

Koegel, L. K. (1995). Communication and language intervention. In R. L. Koegel & L. K. Koegel (Eds.), *Teaching children with autism* (pp. 17–32). Baltimore: Brookes.

Lloyd, L. L., Fuller, D. R., & Arvidson, H. H. (Eds.). (1997). *Augmentative and alternative communication: A handbook of principles and practices.* Boston: Allyn & Bacon.

Mayer-Johnson Company. (1994). *The picture communication symbols combination book.* Solana Beach, CA: Author.

Michael, J. (1993). Establishing operations. *The Behavior Analyst, 16,* 191–206.

Michael, J. (1985). Two kinds of verbal behavior plus a possible third. *The Analysis of Verbal Behavior, 3,* 1–4.

Miguel, C. F., Petursdottir, A. I., & Carr, J. E. (2005). The effects of multiple-tact and receptive-discrimination training on the acquisition of intraverbal behavior. *The Analysis of Verbal Behavior, 21,* 27–42.

Mirenda, P. (2001). Autism, augmentative communication, and assistive technology: What do we really know? *Focus on Autism and Other Developmental Disabilities, 16,* 141–151.

Mirenda, P. (2003). Toward functional augmentative and alternative communication for students with autism: Manual signs, graphic symbols, and voice output communication aids. *Language, Speech and Hearing Services in Schools, 34,* 203–216.

Mirenda, P., & Erickson, K. A. (2000). Augmentative communication and literacy. In A. M. Wetherby & B. M. Prizant (Eds.), *Autism spectrum disorders: A transactional approach* (pp. 333–369). Baltimore: Brookes.

National Research Council, Division of Behavioral and Social Sciences and Education, Committee on Educational Interventions for Children with Autism. (2001). *Educating children with autism* (C. Lord & J. P. McGee, Eds.). Washington, DC: National Academy Press.

Neel, R. S., & Billingsley, F. F. (1989). *IMPACT: A functional curriculum handbook for students with moderate to severe disabilities.* Baltimore: Brookes.

Partington, J. W. (2007). *The assessment of basic language and learning skills–revised (ABLLS-R).* Los Angeles, CA: Western Psychological Services.

Rappaport, M. (1996). Strategies for promoting language acquisition in children with autism. In C. Maurice, G. Green, & C. Luce (Eds.), *Behavioral intervention for young children with autism* (pp. 307–319). Austin, TX: PRO-ED.

Reichle, J., York, J., & Sigafoos, J. (1991). *Implementing augmentative and alternative communication: Strategies for learners with severe disabilities.* Baltimore: Brookes.

Sigafoos, J., & Drasgow, E. (2001). Conditional use of aided and unaided AAC: A review and clinical case demonstration. *Focus on Autism and Other Developmental Disabilities, 16,* 152–161.

Sigafoos, J., O'Reilly, M., Seely-York, S., & Edrisinha, C. (2004). Teaching students with developmental disabilities to locate their AAC device. *Research in Developmental Disabilities, 25,* 371–383.

Skinner, B. F. (1938). *The behavior of organisms.* New York: Appleton-Century-Crofts.

Skinner, B. F. (1957). *Verbal behavior.* New York: Appleton-Century-Crofts.

Sundberg, M. L., & Michael, J. (2001). The benefits of Skinner's analysis of verbal behavior for children with autism. *Behavior Modification, 25,* 698–724.

Sundberg, M. L., & Partington, J. W. (1998). *Teaching language to children with autism or other developmental disabilities.* Danville, CA: Behavior Analysts.

Tincani, M. (2004). Comparing the Picture Exchange Communication System and sign language training for children with autism. *Focus on Autism and Other Developmental Disabilities, 19,* 152–163.

Appendix:

Assessment of Language Function and Form

Instructions: Place a check mark in the boxes for all communication forms used for a particular function.

Student: _____ Date: _____ Respondent: _____

Function	Form																	
	Multiple Words	One-Word Speech	One-Word Sign	Multiple Signs	Points to Pictures	Gestures/Pointing	Uses Other's Hands	Proximity	Grabs	Gives Object	Gazing	Shakes Head	Facial Expression	Whining/Crying	Self-Injurious Behavior	Tantrum	Aggression	Other
Mands/Requests																		
Food																		
Objects																		
Activity																		
Attention																		
Assistance																		
Interaction																		
Protests																		
Change																		
Place or person																		
Task, activity																		
Food																		
Expresses																		
Confusion																		
Frustration																		
Anger																		
Happiness																		
Greeting																		
Describes																		
Objects																		
People																		
Events																		
Responds to																		
Social initiatives																		
Peers																		
Adults																		
Initiates interaction with																		
Peers																		
Adults																		
Family																		

Socialization and Inclusion

As we noted in Chapter 1, a cardinal feature of children and youth with autism is their dislike of social contact and their poor social interaction skills. While most children seek interaction with peers and adults, children with autism prefer to be left alone. In fact, it appears that social interactions are uncomfortable for them, sometimes to the point of being painful. This does not mean, however, that we should avoid interactions with these students or allow them to avoid social experiences with peers and other adults. On the contrary, to be successful in mainstream environments, these students must learn to tolerate social interactions and to engage in expected social behavior.

Socialization Characteristics of Students With Autism

Children and youth with autism typically have impairments in a number of areas related to socialization, including motivation, social communication, specific social skills, empathy, and joint attention. Focus Here 10.1 describes each of these areas and offers examples. All of these deficit areas combine to make improving social behavior one of the more challenging aspects of teaching students with autism. To design effective social intervention programs, practitioners must recognize the complexity of social behavior and the nature of the deficits that contribute to impairments in this area for children with autism.

Socialization and Inclusion

One of the most important things to remember when addressing the socialization needs of students with autism is that socialization skills, more than any other curricular area, are best taught in natural settings to better achieve generalization of these skills. For students with autism, *natural settings* in schools may mean general education environments.

Since its inception in 1975, the Individuals with Disabilities Education Act (IDEA) has required students with disabilities to be educated in the *least restrictive environment* (LRE), which means the setting most like general education in which the student's educational needs can be met (Heward, 2006). This practice, originally called *mainstreaming,* has more recently been referred to as *inclusion* and has produced fierce debate about the extent to which students with disabilities should

Focus Here 10.1 Socialization Characteristics of Students With Autism

1. **Lack of motivation.** Most individuals with autism are not motivated by social activities. In fact, typically their motivation is to *avoid* such activities. Because of this and the additional problem of communication deficits, students with autism may use some inappropriate behaviors for the purpose of avoiding or escaping social interactions (see Chapter 11 for a more complete discussion of the purposes of challenging behavior). For example, Sean predictably engages in self-injurious behavior, such as hitting his head and biting his fist, when peers try to play with him. Abby engages in a more subtle example of social avoidance: She simply does not make eye contact, even when directly addressed and prompted to orient her face toward the speaker. Abby keeps her eyes averted.

2. **Lack of social communication skills.** As noted in Chapter 9, children with autism have significant deficits in pragmatic aspects of language and communication. Characteristic problems with social communication include the following:

- not using language for social purposes, such as to greet, converse, inquire, explain, or for humor

- not recognizing social cues and conventions, such as facial expressions, other individuals' preferred or disliked topics of conversation, conversational turn-taking, and personal space

- lack of expression, clarity, and variation in voice tone and word usage

- lack of interest in communication, such as providing only one- or two-word responses, and then only when absolutely necessary

3. **Deficits in specific social skills.** Most children with autism fail to learn basic social skills, such as taking turns, greeting and responding to greetings, giving and receiving hugs, using toys appropriately, and sharing toys and materials. This is not surprising, given that most children learn these skills through informal channels, such as trial-and-error, informal feedback, and social shaping. These types of informal learning experiences are the least effective for children with autism. With proper interventions, however, they can learn to use expected skills in socially appropriate contexts.

4. **Lack of empathy and perspective-taking.** One of the most frustrating aspects of working with students with autism is their apparent lack of empathy or concern for other people. Most children would visibly respond to seeing an adult who is crying or angry. Children with autism, on the other hand, usually provide no clue that they are aware of anything out of the ordinary, perhaps because they are unable to understand that other people feel and think differently than they do (theory of mind). In fact, they usually do not even acknowledge another person's presence. Such lack of emotional response is difficult for teachers and parents. It is highly reinforcing for us when a child seeks a hug, shows joy upon catching sight of us, or is sad to leave us. Working with or parenting children who seldom or never show these responses can create an emotional void that adults must learn to not take personally.

5. **Lack of joint attention.** This is one of the four primary social symptoms of autism described in the *Diagnostic and Statistical Manual of Mental Disorders–Fourth Edition* (American Psychiatric Association, 2000), and is considered a differentiating characteristic for autism (National Research Council, 2001). *Joint attention* is a social experience attended to by two or more people simultaneously. For example, a child watching something funny on television may turn to his parent and laugh, and then turn back to the TV, as if to share the humor with the parent. Students playing with a special toy may look back and forth between the toy and the teacher with verbal and nonverbal expressions of enjoyment. Most adults, upon encountering a powerful stimulus (e.g., a good joke, a beautiful painting, a disturbing site, a surprise), will look at other people who are sharing the same experience and smile, nod, shake their heads, or display other appropriate, shared responses. Students with autism, even if they voluntarily attend to social stimuli, characteristically do not seek to share social experiences with other people.

be educated with their nondisabled peers. Some researchers and educators argue that inclusion means that all students, regardless of disability, are to be educated in general education classrooms full-time, a concept sometimes referred to as *full inclusion* (Stainback & Stainback, 1992). Some schools have adopted this approach, going so far as to eliminate some or all separate (i.e., pull-out) special education classes. In these schools, special education teachers function primarily as (a) consultants to general education teachers, (b) co-teachers in general education classes, or (c) full- or part-time direct-service providers to students with autism and other disabilities within the general education classroom.

Other professionals believe that some students with disabilities need separate educational environments for at least part of the day to effectively meet their individual educational needs (Hallahan & Kauffman, 1995). We are of the opinion that no one educational setting, including general education, is appropriate for *all* students, especially students with autism. We strongly support maintaining a continuum of educational services and placements for students with disabilities, including separate special education classes. More important, this is what U.S. law requires. Our experiences with students with low-functioning autism has led us to the conclusion that it is often difficult to adequately address all of their curricular and behavioral needs in a general education classroom. This is particularly true in secondary schools, where the general education curriculum is highly specialized and departmentalized and classes are often large, noisy, and demanding. For these students, a separate special education classroom may be essential to providing individualized instruction in the wide range of curricular areas for maximizing independent functioning.

Furthermore, we believe that placement in general education does not serve students with autism well when that placement requires the full-time presence of a teacher or paraprofessional working side by side with the student to prompt and reinforce appropriate behavior and also manage inappropriate behavior. In our opinion, this type of arrangement has the effect of further isolating the student and highlighting the student's differences. In addition, research has indicated that such an arrangement may actually interfere with natural social exchanges and may teach the student to become dependent on prompts (Giangreco & Broer, 2005; Odom & Strain, 1986; Strain & Fox, 1981).

Finally, we argue that aggressive, self-abusive, or extreme noncompliant or self-stimulatory behavior in students with autism must be eliminated or reduced to near-zero levels prior to placing these students in general education classrooms. Not doing so creates the risk that the student with autism will significantly disrupt the general education environment, potentially resulting in less favorable attitudes toward him or her. Another risk is that he or she will be ostracized or made fun of by nondisabled peers because of the atypical behavior. Still another risk is that a nondisabled peer may be hurt. All of these situations must be avoided.

On the other hand, we acknowledge that some educational needs of students with autism are best met in integrated environments. For example, teaching socialization, communication, and play skills in separate environments without nondisabled peers to initiate, guide, and reinforce use of appropriate skills (that is, to provide natural contexts for use of desired skills) would probably be of little benefit. For most individuals, social environments are rich with cues about how to behave, including expected social and communicative behavior, immediate feedback about behavior, and strong reinforcement for appropriate behavior. Many general education contexts offer these naturally occurring events, which can be used as resources for socialization programs for students with autism (we will describe how to do this in later sections of this chapter).

Boutot, Guenther, and Crozier (2005) provided support for using naturalistic settings to increase social behavior. They compared the use of DTT and naturalistic/ milieu teaching to increase play skills in a 4-year-old boy with autism. In the DTT phases, the child was given a mand ("Do this") and a model to engage in a specific play behavior. If he did not respond, he was given physical and verbal prompts. Peers were present, but did not participate in the DTT sessions. In the naturalistic/milieu sessions, the tutor and same-age peers interacted with the student with autism by modeling, describing, and encouraging the targeted play skills. During the naturalistic/milieu phases, the child exhibited significantly more nonprompted play skills than during the DTT phases. Furthermore, he exhibited more independent play skills following the naturalistic/milieu phases than he did following the DTT phases. This study indicated that certain skills may be more successfully taught in general education (e.g., naturalistic) contexts, in which nondisabled peers are involved in initiating, modeling, and reinforcing appropriate social behaviors.

For students with low cognition, we argue that the best educational program provides a combination of intensive, individualized instruction in specialized curricular areas and placement in age-appropriate mainstream environments for practicing and initiating social and communication skills. General education contexts should be carefully chosen with each student's individual goals in mind. For example, it will probably be of little benefit for a high school student with autism to participate in an English or algebra class unless college is a goal for that student or socialization is a regular part of the curriculum in that class. Similarly, an elementary-age student with autism would probably not be well served by participating in a spelling lesson with a general education class if she or he does not need to learn to spell at this point and there are no socialization opportunities in the activity. Even if spelling is an instructional goal for that student, the large-group format may not be the most effective approach.

Students with autism should participate in the natural social or nonacademic environments of general education if such participation will encourage and facilitate language and socialization. For high school students, this might mean lunch in the cafeteria, homeroom, art or physical education classes, after-school clubs, or extracurricular activities, such as dances and athletic events. For elementary students, target environments could include morning groups, story time, library time, recess, lunch, assemblies, physical education, art, and music.

We believe that the most effective programs for students with autism are designed to meet students' individual instructional needs rather then being based on the latest popular approach. In other words, curriculum should drive placement, meaning that curricular goals should be established first and then the instructional approaches and contexts to most effectively meet those goals should be determined. We are suspicious of any program that purports to meet all students' needs in a single setting, whether that setting is special education or general education.

Strategies for Teaching Socialization Skills

Socialization interventions are a critical component of programs for students with autism. The most effective programs use a combination of teacher-mediated and peer-mediated interventions and pay careful attention to generalization. We describe specific strategies for each of these concerns in this section.

Whatever socialization interventions you choose, paying attention to a few general guidelines will increase the quality of your program (see Focus Here 10.2). Because these are universal guidelines that are applicable to all ages and functioning

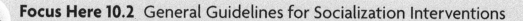

Focus Here 10.2 General Guidelines for Socialization Interventions

1. **Begin socialization interventions as early as possible.** The younger the child, the more likely these interventions will have lasting effects on overall development.

2. **Use ecological assessment and inventories to identify socially valid skills as targets for intervention.** Social skills will only be useful if they are important for success in environments in which the child functions. This means teaching social behaviors that are exhibited and reinforced by nondisabled peers, such as informal ways of interacting, topics of conversation, or use of slang, and using social materials that are preferred by nondisabled peers, such as videogames, gum and candy, and MP3 players or DVD players. See Chapter 7 for more information on ecological inventories.

3. **Teach skills both directly and in contexts in which they are needed.** Given the fact that students with autism do not automatically generalize newly learned skills, there is no purpose in teaching social skills in socially isolated settings. For example, teaching a social skills lesson in the special education classroom only for students with autism will not teach them how to initiate social overtures to nondisabled peers or how to respond to such initiations. Skills therefore should be taught in the contexts in which they are most needed. Not only is this approach more meaningful, but students will also be more likely to use those skills in those contexts when instructional interventions are withdrawn.

4. **Teach pivotal behaviors.** See Focus Here 10.3 for more information on critical pivotal behaviors. These are behaviors that serve a wide range of purposes for the student. Teaching a few pivotal behaviors will help prepare the student to manage many different social situations. For example, a student who learns to initiate and maintain interactions should be able to use that pivotal behavior in the classroom, in unstructured social situations at school, on the job, at home, and in the community.

5. **Focus on quality socialization experiences** (Simpson, Myles, Sasso, & Kamps, 1991). Social interactions that occur out of context, such as teaching greetings during a group lesson, are not useful even if they occur at high rates. Instead, focus on providing high-quality socialization experiences during natural times and in natural contexts. For example, simply placing a child with autism in a general education classroom all day for purposes of socialization will probably not improve his or her overall socialization skills. A better option would be to include the child in naturally occurring general education social contexts, such as lunch, recess, or center time, after teaching general education peers how to initiate and maintain social interactions and to prompt and reinforce appropriate responses.

6. **Reduce inappropriate behavior** (Simpson et al., 1991). Inappropriate behavior will interfere with socialization in several ways. First, students with autism who exhibit stereotypic, self-injurious, tantrum-like, or aggressive behaviors will undoubtedly receive fewer initiations from peers. Second, such behaviors might subject the student to name-calling or taunts from peers. Finally, such behaviors distract from the naturally occurring rhythm of social contexts, especially because the teacher will probably have to intervene.

levels, they are an important first step in addressing socialization deficits. In addition, following them will facilitate generalization of social skills.

Teacher-Mediated Interventions

Given that students with autism typically lack specific social skills, it follows that one component of a social skills program should be *direct instruction* of needed skills. This strategy might involve traditional teacher-led instruction using a commercial social skills curriculum. Resources 10.1 lists examples of curricula and other materials that can be used to guide social skills instruction. When selecting a curriculum, teachers should examine the skills it addresses to determine if those are the skills that are required in the social environments in which students participate. Also,

Resources 10.1 Commercially Available Social Skills Curricula

ACCEPTS (elementary) and ACCESS (secondary)
　　Austin, TX: PRO-ED Publishing (www.proedinc.com)
ASSET: A Social Skills Program for Adolescents
　　Champaign, IL: Research Press (www.researchpress.com)
Comic Strip Conversations
　　Arlington, TX: Future Horizons (www.futurehorizons-autism.com)
Getting Along with Others: Teaching Social Effectiveness to Children
　　Champaign, IL: Research Press (www.researchpress.com)
The Hidden Curriculum: Practical Solutions for Understanding Unstated Rules in Social Situations
　　Shawnee Mission, KS: Autism Asperger Publishing Co. (www.asperger.net)
My Social Stories
　　Book, PA: Jessica Kingsley
The New Social Story Book
　　Arlington, TX: Future Horizons (www.futurehorizons-autism.com)
The Original Social Story Book
　　Arlington, TX: Future Horizons (www.futurehorizons-autism.com)
Scripting: Social Communication for Adolescents
　　Eau Claire, WI: Thinking Publications (www.thinkingpublications.com)
Skillstreaming in Early Childhood
Skillstreaming the Elementary School Child
Skillstreaming the Adolescent
　　Champaign, IL: Research Press (www.researchpress.com)
Social Skills Intervention Guide
　　Circle Pines, MN: American Guidance Service (www.agsnet.com)
The Social Skills Picture Book: Teaching Play, Emotion, and Communication to Children with Autism
　　Arlington, TX: Future Horizons (www.futurehorizons-autism.com)
Social Skills Stories: Functional Picture Stories for Readers and Nonreaders K–12
　　Solana Beach, CA: Mayer-Johnson
Social Skills Strategies
　　Eau Claire, WI: Thinking Publications (www.thinkingpublications.com)
Social Star: Peer Interaction Skills
　　Greenville, SC: Thinking Publications (www.thinkingpublications.com)
The Tough Kid Social Skills Book
　　Longmont, CO: Sopris West (www.sopriswest.com)

(*Note.* See Appendix C of this book for additional social skills curricula.)

because most social skills curricula are not developed specifically for students with autism, keep in mind that you might need to adjust the presentation style, language, and activities recommended in the curriculum.

A direct-instruction approach might also involve teaching target skills in the highly structured and predictable environment of the special education classroom by using either naturalistic/milieu teaching or a DTT approach. For example, the teacher would give a cue (e.g., "Hi, Stevie"); prompt the appropriate response, if needed (e.g., "Stevie, what do you say?"); reinforce or correct the student's response; and record the trial as correct or incorrect on a data sheet. Once students meet the criterion on each target skill, instruction should move to real-life environments (naturalistic/milieu teaching, use of mand–model or time delay). In the case of Stevie, the teacher might greet him as he exits the bus and record whether he responds without prompting. On the way to the classroom, the teacher would record Stevie's responses to greetings from other teachers and peers.

One interesting approach to skills instruction that has proven effective for students with autism is *pivotal response training* (PRT; L. K. Koegel, Koegel, Harrower, & Carter, 1999; L. K. Koegel, Koegel, Shoshan, & McNerney, 1999; R. L. Koegel et al., 1989). Given that it would be impossible to teach students with autism all of the separate behaviors needed for successful socialization, PRT instead focuses on teaching what Koegel et al. (1989) called "pivotal behaviors," which they described as behaviors that are used in a wide range of situations and therefore are essential for generalization. Sample pivotal behaviors are described in Focus Here 10.3.

The language and communication deficits of students with autism may make the language aspects of social interactions difficult for them, especially social exchanges that are more complicated than simply initiating or returning a greeting. To account for this, a variation of the direct-instruction approach involves giving students *instructional scripts* to use as they are learning basic social skills (Breen, Haring, Pitts-Conway, & Gaylord-Ross, 1985; Gaylord-Ross, Haring, Breen, & Pitts-Conway, 1984; Goldstein & Cisar, 1992). By removing the potential obstacle of having to decide what to say, social scripts allow students to focus on other aspects of the social exchange. Social scripts can be developed for situations that have wide applicability. For example, secondary students might be taught a script for initiating a conversation with peers (e.g., "Hi, what's up? Have you seen any good movies lately?"). Elementary students could be taught a script for initiating a request to play (e.g., "Hi. Do you want to play with me?"). Scripts can be used for a variety of play activities.

Another teacher-mediated technique that is also a naturalistic/milieu approach is *antecedent prompting* (Simpson, Myles, Sasso, & Kamps, 1991). In this approach, the teacher or other adult uses time delay combined with one or more of the prompt procedures described in Chapter 3 to cue the student to exhibit appropriate social behaviors. For example, during centers in Ms. Jacobs' first-grade class, a peer tells Hodari to look at the tower he built. Ms. Jacobs waits a few seconds and when Hodari fails to respond, she uses a mand–model: "Hodari, look at the tower! Say, 'That's a tall tower!'" Antecedent prompting can be an effective intervention to increase social behaviors in natural contexts, but because this is not typically a naturally occurring social phenomenon, certain cautions must be observed.

1. Be certain the student knows the expected social behavior. If not, this must first be taught (using DTT, for example) before antecedent prompting in natural contexts will be effective.
2. Prompt only if the student fails to respond within a given time (time delay). Be careful not to prompt when it is not needed.
3. Use the lowest-level prompt needed to cue the desired behavior. Remember, the goal should be to interfere as little as possible with the naturally occurring social context. Intrusive prompts, such as full physical prompts, violate this rule.

Focus Here 10.3 Pivotal Behaviors

These are behaviors that have applicability in a wide range of social situations (Koegel & Koegel, 1995). Pivotal behaviors might include the following:

- **Joint attention.** For example, teach the student to ask questions about a story that is being read to her or reinforce the student for glancing at another student or adult during a video or other observed activity.

- **Initiating and maintaining interactions.** This means teaching skills that help achieve these goals. These skills might include greeting others, using conversational encouragers ("Really?" "Uh-huh," nodding), asking questions, smiling at other people, and complimenting them.

- **Functional communication skills.** Given that the majority of social experiences involve some form of communication, social communication should be considered a pivotal behavior. Functional communication for social purposes would include initiating greetings and other verbal interactions, responding to greetings and other initiations, asking questions, and making comments on shared social experiences during those experiences.

- **Self-management behaviors.** Self-management includes self-monitoring both inappropriate behaviors targeted for reduction (e.g., self-stimulatory, self-injurious) and appropriate behaviors that need to be increased (e.g., social skills, communication skills). For example, teaching a student to self-monitor how many greetings he or she initiates during the walk from the bus to the classroom or how many people he or she compliments during lunch may facilitate generalization of these skills to novel situations.

- **Motivation.** This involves increasing students' motivation to interact with environmental stimuli. This is a pivotal behavior because as students' motivation increases, actual interactions increase.

- **Responsiveness to multiple cues.** An important pivotal behavior is responding to complex stimuli. Teaching students to respond to complex cues enhances learning and helps avoid the problem of *stimulus overselectivity*, which is the tendency of children with autism to focus on discrete, often irrelevant stimuli, such as recognizing a *toy* as only a small item with wheels while ignoring the many other relevant stimuli that constitute *toys*. Students with autism who learn to respond to varied forms of cues should be able to function more independently than students who associate a single cue with a single response.

4. Fade prompts quickly and monitor for prompt dependence. If you think a student is waiting for a prompt before he or she will respond, add a reinforcer for unprompted responding or switch to another technique.

One final teacher-mediated technique is *social stories*. A variation on antecedent prompts, social stories are brief stories that convey expected responses to social situations encountered by the student (Gray & Garand, 1993). A social story consists of three components, typically presented in two to five total sentences: (a) one or more descriptive sentence(s), which explain the social situation the student will encounter; (b) directive sentence(s), which describe what the student should do; and (c) perspective sentence(s), which convey the feelings of the people involved. These sentences are put in a written format that is appropriate for the student, along with picture cues or icons, if needed. The story is then presented to the student immediately before the social situation; that is, the teacher or other adult reads the story to the student and shows the pictures, perhaps even requiring the student to practice the target behavior described in the story (Scott, Clark, & Brady, 2000). Social stories and scripts are most effective with students who have language abilities, can memorize and/or read, and can remember scripts. Social stories should be individualized for each student and for various social situations. The following is an example of a social story:

At lunch, I sit with Caitlyn and Sam, my friends from Ms. Hunter's class.

When I see Caitlyn, I say, "Hi, Caitlyn," and when I see Sam, I say, "Hi Sam."

Caitlyn says, "Hi, Anna!" and Sam says, "Hi, Anna!"

I like to talk to Caitlyn and Sam, and they like to talk to me.

One aspect of socialization that is characteristically weak or lacking in children with autism is play behaviors. Given that play is an important mechanism through which young children learn social, language, motor, and cognitive skills (Gitlin-Weiner, Sandgrund, & Schaefer, 2000; Saracho & Spodek, 1998), failure to engage in typical play behaviors may deprive students with autism of opportunities to learn and practice these skills. One socialization goal for children with autism thus should probably be age-appropriate play skills. Any of the socialization interventions described in this chapter—or the instructional interventions described in Chapters 3 and 4—can be used to teach play skills. As Boutot and her colleagues (2005) demonstrated, however, involving typical peers as models for teaching play skills may be more effective than teaching those skills in isolation.

Peer-Mediated Interventions

As the name implies, *peer-mediated interventions* involve the use of carefully selected, trained *peer confederates* to initiate, prompt, and reinforce social behaviors in students with autism. Research has suggested this to be an effective strategy for increasing social behavior in students with autism of all ages (Haring & Breen, 1992; Odom & Strain, 1986; Sasso, Mundshenk, Melloy, & Casey, 1998) and one that naturally facilitates generalization of skills. Lee, Odom, and Loftin (2007) also noted that increasing social interactions with peers through the use of peer confederates may result in improvements in other behaviors, including increases in play and language behaviors and reductions in challenging behaviors.

Many studies have examined the efficacy of using peers as socialization mediators for children with autism. Using typically developing peers has been shown to be an effective intervention for facilitating social communication skills (Garrison-Harrell & Kamps, 1997) and social interactions (Garfinkle & Schwartz, 2002). Other studies have demonstrated that peer confederate groups that include both typically developing children and other children with autism can (a) effectively increase interactive play behaviors and reduce stereotypic, isolated play (Wolfberg & Schuler, 1993) and (b) improve social communication skills (Loncola & Craig-Unkefer, 2005).

Peer Confederate Skills That Should Be Taught

Engaging peers to improve social behaviors in children with autism requires that the peers be taught to use the following skills:

1. *Social initiations*—peers are taught how to gain the attention of the student with autism and are given recommended initiations to be used in specific social situations. For example, initiations might include an invitation to share a toy or snack, an invitation to join in an activity, or a question about a familiar topic.
2. *Prompts*—peers are taught prompting procedures to use to cue the student with autism to respond or exhibit other socially appropriate behavior.
3. *Maintaining social interactions*—peers are taught how to keep a social exchange going beyond the initiation. Although this simply involves ongoing use of other skills (i.e., prompts and reinforcement), peers should be taught that continued intrusiveness and insistence on social behavior will probably be necessary to keep the student with autism engaged.
4. *Reinforcement*—peers are taught specific reinforcement strategies for individual students. Reinforcers should be as natural as possible, such as high fives or praise, while still being effective for the student with autism.

Steps for Teaching Peer-Mediated Interventions

To use peer-mediated interventions, we suggest the following steps:

1. *Select and train peers.* Some evidence has indicated that using high-status peers may produce higher levels of social behavior from students with autism and may facilitate additional social interactions from other, untrained peers (Sasso & Rude, 1987). Research has also shown that training students in strategies for eliciting and reinforcing social behavior in their peers with autism is an essential step (Gonzalez-Lopez & Kamps, 1997; Kamps et al., 2002). Careful consideration must be given to selecting peers, deciding what skills to teach them, and ensuring that they are proficient in those skills prior to implementing a peer-mediated intervention.

2. *Designate specific situations for intervention.* Logical choices are naturally occurring situations, such as lunch, play and leisure activities, and so forth. Kamps and her colleagues have also shown that cooperative groups involving trained peer confederates and students with autism can result in increased social behavior on the part of the students with autism (Kamps, Barbetta, Leonard, & Delquadri, 1994; Kamps et al., 2002). Choosing situations for intervention should be a function of (a) the goals for the student with autism, (b) age of the students (e.g., naturally occurring social situations may be preferable for secondary students), and (c) factors unique to each situation, for example, a noisy, overcrowded cafeteria may render that setting undesirable for socialization interventions for some students with autism.

3. *Assign peer confederates to students with autism in those situations.* It may be best to assign no more than one peer confederate to each student with autism (Sasso et al., 1998). Assigning more than one may result in the peer confederates interacting more with one another than with the student with autism.

4. *Monitor and adjust the intervention as needed.* If data indicate unchanged social behaviors in your student with autism, or if problems arise (e.g., the student with autism refuses to respond or exhibits inappropriate behavior), changes must be made in the peers' prompts or reinforcers or another intervention may need to be used first (e.g., teacher antecedent prompting or direct instruction of skills).

Focus Here 10.4 provides a description of an interesting peer-mediated social intervention called the Partners at Lunch (PAL) Club. The goal of the PAL Club was not simply to increase the use of social behaviors by students with disabilities but

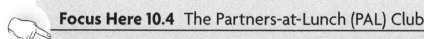

Focus Here 10.4 The Partners-at-Lunch (PAL) Club

The Partners-at-Lunch Club—also known as the PAL Club—was developed by Breen, Lovinger, and Haring (Haring & Ryndak, 1994) for secondary students with severe disabilities. They recruited non-disabled peers to spend one to three lunch periods per week with a student with disabilities. Also, both the peer confederates and their partners with disabilities met after school one afternoon each week as part of the PAL Club. During PAL Club time, in which a teacher was present, students engaged in leisure activities with one another. In addition, the teacher used this time to check on progress of the lunch interactions and to help students problem-solve, if needed.

also for them to develop friendships with their nondisabled peers. This is a worthy goal for all peer-mediated social interventions. Attaining this goal means that teachers should look beyond simply increasing discrete skills in students with autism and attempt to create opportunities that foster real interpersonal relationships. Although students with autism will probably never have the type of friendships that occur between nondisabled peers, research on the socialization interventions described in this chapter has shown that these students can become more socially oriented and initiate more social interactions when given appropriate interventions.

Facilitating Generalization of Social Skills

Because students with autism seldom spontaneously generalize target skills, teachers must carefully plan and implement strategies to ensure that generalization occurs. The following strategies, along with the recommendations from Focus Here 10.2, will help this to occur.

- *Teach pivotal behaviors.* This is especially important because pivotal behaviors are so versatile and will positively affect many other responses. Pivotal behaviors facilitate generalization of desired classes of behaviors, such as social skills and communication skills.
- *Use naturalistic/milieu teaching.* As noted in Chapter 4, this refers to (a) teaching skills in the contexts in which they are needed; (b) taking advantage of natural teaching opportunities; (c) arranging motivating S^Ds on a regular basis; and (d) using antecedent prompting, manding, and time-delay techniques. Unlike nondisabled peers, for students with autism, teaching must occur *all the time* and *in all contexts,* not just in the classroom.
- *Use peer confederates in natural social contexts.* Because the goal is for students with autism to develop connections with their peers, the peers must be a part of socialization interventions, for two reasons. First, research has indicated that peers can elicit higher quality social responses from students with autism than can teachers (Sasso & Rude, 1987). Second, without special instruction on how to effectively interact with students with autism, it is unlikely that many peers will naturally know how to do so. Social interactions with students with autism are not naturally reinforcing; it takes intrusion and perseverance to evoke responses.
- *Teach students to attend to social models.* Students must be taught to watch others for social cues and to imitate the types of behaviors being exhibited by those models.
- *Teach other persons to expect social behavior from your students with autism and how to prompt that behavior, if needed.* General education teachers, parents, paraprofessionals,

cafeteria workers, and other adults can all be taught to use simple prompting techniques to cue desired responses.

• *Teach other persons to recognize socialization attempts.* The social behaviors of children and youth with autism will probably be somewhat awkward, even after intervention and practice. It is important to teach adults and peers who may be in a position to reinforce socialization attempts to recognize those attempts when they occur in generalization settings. For example, a child with autism may approach a peer and reach for the truck the peer is holding. An untrained peer might simply turn away from this initiation or hand the truck over without trying to extend the interaction. A trained peer, on the other hand, could say, "Oh, you want to play! Sit down and I'll roll the truck to you," and maintain the interaction.

• *Teach others to reinforce social behavior that occurs in natural contexts.* Most people, even educators, do not think to reinforce expected social behavior. Students with autism need this reinforcement, so anyone who may interact with your students should be taught to recognize and reinforce social behaviors.

• *Teach students to recognize reinforcement they may encounter in social situations.* Most social reinforcement is subtle (e.g., a smile, a nod, facial expressions). Teaching these more subtle forms of reinforcement probably means pairing them with more intrusive forms during structured teaching situations and then gradually fading the more intrusive ones.

Summary

Socialization and communication may be the two most important areas for intervention for children and youth with autism. Without skills in these areas, children are destined to a life of isolation and dependence. Research has clearly shown that students with autism *can* learn to be active participants in social interactions. However, attaining this goal means careful application of a combination of strategies that have been proven to be effective for this purpose. The strategies described in this chapter qualify for such purposes. In general, socialization interventions should focus on teaching socially flexible behaviors in natural contexts by using peers and other individuals to initiate and extend social attempts. As with all teaching for these students, socialization interventions must be intense, carefully planned, and pervasive. The results of these efforts, however, may provide more rewards for everyone involved than in any other area of the curriculum.

References

American Psychiatric Association. (2000). *Diagnostic and statistical manual of mental disorders* (4th ed., text rev.). Arlington, VA: Author.

Boutot, E. A., Guenther, T., & Crozier, S. (2005). Let's play: Teaching play skills to young children with autism. *Education and Training in Developmental Disabilities, 40*(3), 285–292.

Breen, C., Haring, T. G., Pitts-Conway, V., & Gaylord-Ross, R. (1985). The training and generalization of social interaction during break time at two job sites in the natural environment. *Journal of the Association for Persons with Severe Handicaps, 10*(2), 41–50.

Garfinkle, A. N., & Schwartz, I. S. (2002). Peer imitation: Increasing social interactions in children with autism and other developmental disabilities in inclusive preschool classrooms. *Topics in Early Childhood Special Education, 22*, 26–38.

Garrison-Harrell, L., & Kamps, D. (1997). The effects of peer networks on social-communicative behaviors for students with autism. *Focus on Autism and Other Developmental Disabilities, 12*, 241–255.

Gaylord-Ross, R. J., Haring, T. G., Breen, C., & Pitts-Conway, V. (1984). The training and generalization of social interaction skills with autistic youth. *Journal of Applied Behavior Analysis, 17,* 229–247.

Giangreco, M. F., & Broer, S. M. (2005). Paraprofessionals in inclusive schools: Are we addressing symptoms or causes? *Focus on Autism and Other Developmental Disabilities, 20,* 10–26.

Gitlin-Weiner, K., Sandgrund, A., & Schaefer, C. (2000). *Play diagnosis and assessment* (2nd ed.). New York: Wiley.

Goldstein, H., & Cisar, C. L. (1992). Promoting interaction during sociodramatic play: Teaching scripts to typical preschoolers and classmates with disabilities. *Journal of Applied Behavior Analysis, 25,* 265–280.

Gonzalez-Lopez, A., & Kamps, D. (1997). Social skills training to increase social interaction between children with autism and their peers. *Focus on Autism and Other Developmental Disabilities, 12*(1), 2–14.

Gray, C., & Garand, J. (1993). Social stories: Improving responses of students with autism with accurate social information. *Focus on Autistic Behavior, 8*(1), 1–10.

Hallahan, D. P., & Kauffman, J. M. (1995). From mainstreaming to collaborative consultation. In J. M. Kauffman, & D. P. Hallahan (Eds.), *The illusion of full inclusion* (pp. 5–18). Austin, TX: PRO-ED.

Haring, T. G., & Breen, C. G. (1992). A peer-mediated social network intervention to enhance the social integration of persons with moderate severe disabilities. *Journal of Applied Behavior Analysis, 25,* 319–334.

Haring, T. G., & Ryndak, D. (1994). Strategies and instructional procedures to promote social interactions and relationships. In E. C. Cipani & F. Spooner (Eds.), *Curricular and instructional approaches for persons with severe disabilities* (pp. 289–321). Needham Heights, MA: Allyn & Bacon.

Heward, W. L. (2006). *Exceptional children.* Upper Saddle River, NJ: Pearson/Prentice Hall.

Kamps, D. M., Barbetta, P. M., Leonard, B. R., & Delquadri, J. (1994). Classwide peer tutoring: An integration strategy to improve reading skills and promote peer interactions among students with autism and general education peers. *Journal of Applied Behavior Analysis, 27*(1), 49–61.

Kamps, D., Royer, J., Dugan, E., Kravits, T., Gonzalez-Lopez, A., Garcia, J., et al. (2002). Peer training to facilitate social interaction for elementary students with autism and their peers. *Exceptional Children, 68*(2), 173–187.

Koegel, L. K., Koegel, R. L., Harrower, J. K., & Carter, C. M. (1999). Pivotal response intervention I: Overview of the approach. *Journal of the Association for the Severely Handicapped, 24,* 174–185.

Koegel, L. K., Koegel, R. L., Shoshan, Y., & McNerney, E. (1999). Preliminary long-term outcome data. *Journal of the Association for Persons with Severe Handicaps, 24,* 186–198.

Koegel, R. L., & Koegel, L. K. (1995). *Teaching children with autism: Strategies for initiating positive interactions and improving learning opportunities.* Baltimore: Brookes.

Koegel, R. L., Schreibman, L., Good, A., Cerniglia, L., Murphy, C., & Koegel, L. K. (1989). *How to teach pivotal behaviors to children with autism: A training manual.* Unpublished manuscript, University of California at Santa Barbara.

Lee, S., Odom, S. L., & Loftin, R. (2007). Social engagement with peers and stereotypic behavior of children with autism. *Journal of Positive Behavior Interventions, 9,* 67–79.

Loncola, J. A., & Craig-Unkefer, L. (2005). Teaching social communication skills to young urban children with autism. *Education and Training in Developmental Disabilities, 40*(3), 243–263.

National Research Council, Division of Behavioral and Social Sciences and Education, Committee on Educational Intervention for Children with Autism. (2001). *Educating children with autism.* (C. Lord & J. P. McGee, Eds.). Washington, DC: National Academy Press.

Odom, S. L., & Strain, P. S. (1986). A comparison of peer-initiation and teacher-antecedent interventions for promoting reciprocal social interaction of autistic preschoolers. *Journal of Applied Behavior Analysis, 19*(1), 59–71.

Saracho, O. N., & Spodek, B. (1998). Preschool children's cognitive play: A factor analysis. *International Journal of Early Childhood Education, 3*(2), 67–76.

Sasso, G. M., Mundshenk, N. A., Melloy, K. J., & Casey, S. D. (1998). A comparison of the effects of organismic and setting variables on the social interaction behavior of children with developmental disabilities and autism. *Focus on Autism and Other Developmental Disabilities, 13*(1), 2–16.

Sasso, G. M., & Rude, H. A. (1987). Unprogrammed effects of training high-status peers to interact with severely handicapped children. *Journal of Applied Behavior Analysis, 20*(1), 35–44.

Scott, J., Clark, C., & Brady, M. (2000). *Students with autism.* San Diego, CA: Singular.

Simpson, R. L., Myles, B. S., Sasso, G. M., & Kamps, D. M. (1991). *Social skills for students with autism.* Reston, VA: Council for Exceptional Children.

Stainback, S., & Stainback, W. (1992). *Curriculum considerations in inclusive classrooms: Facilitating learning for all students.* Baltimore: Brookes.

Strain, P. S., & Fox, J. (1981). Peer social initiations and the modification of social withdrawal: A review and future perspectives. *Journal of Pediatric Psychology, 6,* 417–433.

Wolfberg, P. J., & Schuler, A. I. (1993). Integrated play groups: A model for promoting the social and cognitive dimensions of play with children with autism. *Journal of Autism and Developmental Disorders, 23,* 467–489.

CHAPTER 11

Functional Behavioral Assessment

In the previous chapters we have discussed ways to arrange the environment, develop curricula, teach and enhance various skills, and prepare others to assist with the teaching. When teachers have organized classrooms, well-developed curricula, and use effective instructional techniques, students—even students with autism—are usually responsive to instruction and demonstrate appropriate behavior in the classroom. In other words, the strategies and techniques we have discussed to this point can act to prevent students from acting inappropriately. However, even with the most dedicated and effective instruction, students with autism may present challenging behavior. Chapters 11 through 14 present information that will assist in reducing such behaviors if they occur. We advise first considering whether or not previously recommended educational components are in place before developing elaborate behavior reduction interventions. For students with autism, such thoughtful environmental, curricular, and instructional antecedents may be the best behavior management approach. For challenging behaviors that manifest despite these measures, school personnel will need to master additional ABA techniques.

Developing interventions for challenging behaviors without first conducting a functional behavior assessment (FBA) is like implementing remedial academic instruction for a student without first determining the student's specific deficits. For example, punishing Megan for refusing to do her long division problems will be unsuccessful if the reason she is refusing is because she does not yet know how to solve long division problems. Similarly, punishing Colt for biting his hand when he does not want to do something will be unsuccessful if he bites his hand because he has no other way to express refusal.

The 1997 amendments to IDEA included, for the first time in this legislation, a requirement to use FBA and *positive behavioral interventions and supports* (PBIS) to address problem behaviors. We will discuss PBIS (also called *positive behavioral supports,* or PBS) further in Chapter 12, but essentially, PBIS refers to a philosophy of preventing and managing challenging behavior by relying on preventive measures, instructional interventions, high levels of attention to appropriate behaviors, and positive behavioral reductive strategies. The first step in designing PBIS interventions for challenging behaviors is to conduct an FBA to identify (a) when and where the behavior is likely to occur and (b) the function(s) associated with the challenging behavior(s). This information is then used to design positive, preventative, and instructional interventions to reduce the problem behaviors. Interventions that are not based on FBA are less likely to be effective in reducing the problem behavior.

The IDEA requires the use of FBA under certain narrowly defined conditions (i.e., when a student's educational placement is changed due to challenging behavior). Even if this requirement had not been included in IDEA, it is good practice to use an FBA as a tool in designing interventions for challenging behaviors, because it will increase the probability that your interventions will be successful.

Like ABA, FBA is based on certain assumptions (Foster-Johnson & Dunlap, 1993; O'Neill et al., 1997). Knowing these assumptions, and relying on them to guide your responses to challenging behaviors, will aid you in designing interventions for those behaviors. The assumptions are as follows:

1. *Challenging behavior serves a purpose (function) for the student.* Challenging behavior may be the only way the child has to get what he or she wants, to avoid or escape unpleasant situations, or to communicate something. This is a very important concept and one of the main goals of FBA: to identify the function of the challenging behavior. FBA data will help you pinpoint what a student may be getting or avoiding as a result of the challenging behavior. Some behavioral functions are easier to identify than others. Remember that children with autism frequently have unusual or unexpected likes and dislikes. For example, if uncomfortable situations (e.g., being asked to do certain tasks) are removed when the student throws a tantrum, the function of the tantrum may be to avoid situations, tasks, or even people. Determining the function of the challenging behavior will help you develop an effective intervention, one that teaches the student an alternative, acceptable way to achieve the same outcome. We explain how to identify behavioral functions in this chapter.

2. *Behavior is related to specific antecedents and consequences in the immediate environment.* Challenging behaviors occur in response to particular antecedent stimuli, and they are maintained by consequences that follow the behavior (e.g., escape a disliked task, obtain a desired item). Thus, as we discussed in the A–B–C model in Chapter 2, both antecedents and consequences influence behavior. FBA will help you identify antecedent and consequent stimuli that may be contributing to challenging behaviors.

3. *Behavior may be affected by conditions other than immediate antecedents.* Sometimes events or conditions that are not immediately connected in time and place to the behavior in question may affect the behavior. These conditions are called *setting events.* Setting events can be internal or external to the student. Internal setting events might include pain, hunger, fatigue, illness, boredom, or dislike of a task. External setting events could be a long bus ride, a noisy gym, a flickering light, or a change in schedule. These conditions set the stage for problematic behavior but do not necessarily cause the behavior. For example, a student who has a sinus infection may refuse to do tasks that she or he typically enjoys. Another example would be a disrupted schedule that may increase the likelihood that a student will be irritable and noncompliant. Although we as educators can manipulate some setting events to reduce their influence on students' behaviors, many setting events will be beyond our control. Simply knowing how a given setting event affects a student, however, can help us make decisions about behavioral interventions. For example, we cannot control the fact that a student has a cold, but knowing that she tends to engage in higher levels of stereotypic behaviors when she has a cold may help us to remember to increase reinforcement for appropriate alternatives. We might allow her quicker access to self-stimulatory time when she asks appropriately, or allow her to engage in self-stimulation for slightly longer than usual, or reduce the number of disliked tasks.

4. *Challenging behavior may be the result of organic causes.* Why children with autism develop self-injurious and stereotypic behaviors has been the subject of much research. A definitive cause has yet to be identified, but it seems clear that much of this behavior is biologically based, that is, stemming from a genetic basis (Symons, Butler, Sanders, Feurer, & Thompson, 1999), a neurochemical basis (National Research Council, 2001; Symons & Thompson, 1997; Thompson, Symons, Delaney, & England, 1995), or environmental toxins (Centers for Disease Control, 2006). For example, Thompson et al. (1995) showed that some self-injurious behavior actually produces neurochemical changes. These changes become the basis for ongoing self-injurious behavior; that is, the individual "learns" to engage in the inappropriate behavior to produce that neurochemical response.

One indicator that organic forces are at play is the effectiveness of some medications in controlling aggression, hyperactivity, and stereotypic behaviors. Of course, every medication carries significant potential side effects, including possible increases in challenging behaviors. For example, stimulants (often prescribed for hyperactivity) may actually worsen some symptoms of autism, especially self-stimulatory behaviors (National Research Council, 2001). Educators should know what medications their students are taking and watch for possible side effects. This means working closely with parents as children are placed on medication and including medical personnel (e.g., school nurse, child's pediatrician or psychiatrist) in any discussion regarding challenging behaviors that may be related to medication side effects.

Despite the growing research base substantiating the organicity of self-injurious and stereotypic behaviors, effective behavioral interventions will still be necessary (National Research Council, 2001). In fact, Schroeder, Bickel, and Richmond (1986) suggested that children do not outgrow such behaviors, and that without specific interventions, these types of behaviors will worsen as the child gets older.

How to Conduct a Functional Assessment

In conducting an FBA, you are trying to determine what is triggering a behavior, what might be reinforcing a behavior, and/or what a student might be trying to communicate with the behavior. Finding these answers involves six basic steps, which are to:

1. gather indirect data about the student's behavior and contextual variables (e.g., setting events, antecedents, consequences) associated with that behavior;
2. conduct direct observations of the challenging behaviors in the contexts in which those behaviors are most likely to occur;
3. analyze data, looking for patterns that suggest possible antecedents to the challenging behaviors and functions of those behaviors;
4. develop hypotheses about when a challenging behavior is likely to occur and the possible functions of the behavior;
5. develop and implement one or more interventions based on those hypotheses; and
6. monitor interventions and adjust them as needed.

Step 1. Gather Indirect Data About the Behavior and the Context(s) in Which It Occurs

This step involves using interview forms or checklists to obtain input from people who are familiar with the student. The goal is to determine perceptions of contextual variables associated with target behaviors and possible functions of those behaviors. Teachers, paraprofessionals, parents, and related service providers are among the individuals you might want to contact. Several instruments exist for guiding these interviews; we will describe three. (A blank copy of each of the forms described in this chapter is provided in the appendix at the end of this chapter.) The first tool for gathering indirect assessment data is the *Brief Functional Assessment Interview* (BFAI; Murdock, O'Neill, & Cunningham, 2005), which solicits information about the behaviors of concern, predictors (conditions under which those behaviors are likely to occur), maintaining functions of the behaviors, and setting events associated with them. A diagram of setting events, antecedents, the behaviors, and the maintaining function provides a clear visualization of the variables that may be affecting the behavior. The BFAI may be used to interview others, or individuals can complete the form on their own. A sample BFAI showing information for Jason, a 10-year-old boy with autism, is presented in Figure 11.1.

Brief Functional Assessment Interview Form

Instructions:

1. Identify those individuals who have the most current and extensive knowledge about the student (teachers, therapists, paraprofessionals, parents, trainers, etc.).

2. Either interview those individuals using the BFAI or ask each person to complete a BFAI independently.

3. Encourage respondents to be as specific and detailed as possible in their responses.

Student: Jason   **Date:** 10/12

Behavior(s) of Concern:

    (1) self-injurious behavior (hitting head, chest, biting hands or arms)

    (2) self-stimulatory behaviors (rocking, flapping hands, staring at lights, making noises, spinning objects)

    (3) crying

Predictors: (when, where, with whom, with what) (Routine)

    (1) Jason attempts to hit or bite himself when asked to use signs to communicate and when in public areas where a lot of people are present.

    (2) Jason tries to self-stim when he is not engaged or when he does not like the task or activity.

    (3) Jason cries when he wants something, especially when he is in crowded areas and wants to go back to the classroom.

Maintaining Function(s): (attention, objects/food, avoid demands/tasks, avoid social contact, obtain activity)

    (1) he avoids signing or escapes environment or activity

    (2) sensory stimulation (boredom) or escape

    (3) escape, communication

What Makes it Worse (Setting Events): (sleep, diet, schedule, home problems, constipation)

    Behaviors are all worse when he doesn't feel well, or when he is hungry or tired.

Summary Statement (Define by Routine)

Setting Event ⟶	Predictor ⟶	Problem Behavior ⟶	Maintaining Function
Not feeling well Hungry	In cafeteria, hall, play-ground, etc. Asked to sign	Hits or bites self Cries	Avoidance/escape

Setting Event ⟶	Predictor ⟶	Problem Behavior ⟶	Maintaining Function
Not feeling well Hungry	In cafeteria, hall, etc. Asked to complete a dis-liked task or participate in a disliked activity	Cries	Avoidance/escape

Figure 11.1. Brief functional assessment interview form–completed. *Note.* Adapted from "A Descriptive Comparison of Teacher Teams' Perceptions of Student Behavior to Results of Functional Assessments," by S. G. Murdock, 2000, Unpublished master's thesis, Dept. of Special Education, University of Utah. Adapted with permission.

Another tool, the *Functional Behavioral Assessment Inventory* (Florida Center on Self-Injury, 2002b), gathers much of the same information but uses a more focused questioning format to obtain important information. This instrument poses questions regarding challenging behaviors, contexts in which those behaviors occur, possible functions, target replacement behaviors, communication skills, potential reinforcers, and previous interventions used. Figure 11.2 shows an example of this inventory as completed by Jason's teacher.

Finally, the *Functional Analysis Screening Tool* (FAST; Florida Center on Self-Injury, 2002a) poses 16 yes/no questions. Responses are compiled to provide an indication of potential functions of challenging behaviors. A sample FAST completed by Jason's teacher is shown in Figure 11.3.

Once you gather information from each person who has regular contact with the student, you must consider all the data, looking for patterns of when and where challenging behaviors are likely to occur and possible functions of those behaviors.

Step 2. Conduct Observations in Contexts Associated With the Challenging Behaviors

In addition to indirect data, you must also directly observe the student in contexts in which the challenging behavior predictably occurs, which should have been identified in Step 1. We recommend using one of two forms for this purpose (see the appendix at the end of the chapter for blank copies of each form). One form that is easy to use is a simple Antecedent–Behavior–Consequence (A–B–C) Report, or anecdotal report, which is a written description of everything that happens concerning the student during a specific period that is associated with direct antecedents and consequences (see Figure 11.4; Bijou, Peterson, & Ault, 1968). The A column on the report allows the observer to record antecedents related to the target student, the B column is for recording the target student's observable behaviors, and the C column is for recording consequences or events that follow the behavior(s). To conduct an observation using the A–B–C Report form, first note on the form the environmental conditions: who is present; activities that occur during your observation; any unusual circumstances, such as the student has a cold or a new student is present; and the time you start and finish the observation. As you observe, simply make a written record of everything you see, along with the time of each entry. You should simply write what you see; do not interpret, draw conclusions, or make assumptions. At a minimum, your observation should be as long as one activity and the transitions before and after that activity. You may need to observe the student much longer than that to obtain an adequate sample of the behavior and the related contextual variables. In addition, you may need to observe the student over several days to get a complete picture of the student's behavior as it relates to all the different environmental variables.

Once you are finished with the observation, review the A–B–C Report. Alberto and Troutman (2006) recommended looking for answers to the following questions:

What is the student doing that is inappropriate?

How frequently does this inappropriate behavior occur?

Are there consistent patterns of reinforcement of or punishment for that inappropriate behavior?

Are there identifiable antecedents to the inappropriate behavior?

Are there patterns to the antecedents?

Are there recurring chains of specific antecedents, behaviors, and consequences?

Are there possibilities for intervention?

(text continues on p. 223)

Functional Behavioral Assessment Inventory

I. General Information

Name: _Jason_____ Sex: (M) F   Date of Birth: _10-23-95_____

Class/Residence: _Ms. Scott's class_____ Date of Interview: _2-10_____

Informant/Relationship: _Teacher_____ Interviewer: _Mr. Jacobs_____

II. Problem Behavior Identification

Instructions: List up to three problem behaviors of concern. Describe each in clear, objective terms.

1. _self-stim ⟶ rocking, flapping hands, staring at lights, noises_____

2. _self-injury ⟶ hitting head & chest, biting hands, arms_____

3. _crying_____

III. Dimensions of Problem Behavior

Instructions: Circle the appropriate frequency and severity indicators for each problem behavior. Use the following criteria for severity: Mild (disruptive, but not dangerous), Moderate (destructive to physical environment), Severe (poses physical danger to student or others).

	Frequency	**Severity**
1.	(Hourly)/ Daily / Weekly / Less often	Mild / Moderate /(Severe)
2.	(Hourly)/ Daily / Weekly / Less often	Mild /(Moderate)/ Severe
3.	(Hourly)/ Daily / Weekly / Less often	Mild /(Moderate)/ Severe

IV. Critical Situations

1. Describe the situations in which problem behavior is <u>most</u> likely to occur.

   Days/times: _any time he is left alone_____ Setting: _any time teachers are not attending to him_

   Persons present: _____ Activity: _any; lunch; group activities_____

   What is usually happening to the person right <u>before</u> the problem behavior occurs?

   _left alone or unengaged; asked to sign; in crowded area_____

   What happens to the person right <u>after</u> the problem behavior occurs?

   _mild reprimand "No stim, Jason"; task ends; returns to classroom_____

2. Describe the situations in which problem behavior is <u>least</u> likely to occur.

   Days/times: _____ Setting: _classroom_____

   Persons present: _classmates_____ Activity: _working with teacher or paraprofessional_

   (continues)

Figure 11.2. Completed functional behavioral assessment inventory. *Note.* Adapted from *Functional Behavioral Assessment Inventory,* by the Florida Center on Self-Injury, 2002, Gainesville, FL: Author. Copyright 2002 by the Florida Center on Self-Injury. Adapted with permission.

V. Daily Schedule

Instructions: Fill in the student's daily schedule. For each time period, indicate the setting (e.g., classroom, cafeteria), activity taking place (e.g., morning group, lunch), and whether problem behavior is likely or unlikely to occur during each time period.

Time	Setting	Activity	Behavior (circle)
7:00	classroom	Breakfast	Likely **(Unlikely)**
8:00		Morning group	**(Likely)** Unlikely
9:00		Individual work time	Likely **(Unlikely)**
10:00		Break	**(Likely)** Unlikely
11:00		Adapted P.E.	**(Likely)** Unlikely
12:00		Lunch	**(Likely)** Unlikely
1:00		Leisure time	Likely **(Unlikely)**
2:00		Jobs	Likely **(Unlikely)**
3:00		Bus	**(Likely)** Unlikely
4:00			Likely Unlikely
5:00			Likely Unlikely
6:00			Likely Unlikely
7:00			Likely Unlikely
8:00			Likely Unlikely
9:00			Likely Unlikely
10:00			Likely Unlikely
Later			Likely Unlikely

Does the problem behavior occur more often/less often (circle) on weekends? If so, elaborate.

N/A

VI. Functions of Problem Behavior

Instructions: Items A–D assess possible functions of the problem behavior. Read each question under each letter and circle the item if the answer to the question is "yes." Enter the total number of items circled in each section.

A. Function: Access to Attention or Preferred Activities (Positive Reinforcement)

①. Does the person engage in this behavior when (s)he is being ignored or when the caregiver is paying attention to someone else?

2. Does the person engage in this behavior when preferred games or toys are taken away?

③. Does the person usually get preferred activities (leisure items, snack, etc.) when (s)he engages in this behavior?

④. Is the person usually well behaved while (s)he is getting lots of attention or when (s)he has access to preferred toys/games?

___3___ Total number of circled items

(continues)

Figure 11.2. *Continued.*

B. Function: Escape from Task Demands (Negative Reinforcement)

1. Is the person usually noncompliant when asked to perform a task?

② Does the person frequently engage in this behavior when asked to perform a task?

③ Is the person usually given a "break" from work when this behavior occurs?

4. Is the person usually well behaved when there are no task requirements present?

___2___ Total number of circled items

C. Function: Sensory Stimulation (Automatic Reinforcement)

① Does this behavior occur repeatedly (for long periods of time) and usually in the same way?

② Does the person engage in this behavior when no one is around or watching?

③ Does the person engage in this behavior even though no one pays attention to it?

④ Does it appear that the behavior provides some type of sensory stimulation?

___4___ Total number of circled items

D. Function: Pain Attenuation (Automatic Reinforcement)

1. Does the person have a history of recurrent illness (e.g., ear infections, allergies, dermatitis)? If so, please list: ___No___

2. Does the person have any other periodic physical difficulties (e.g., irregular sleep or diet)? If so, please list: ___No___

③ Does the person engage in this behavior more often when ill?

4. If the person has medical problems and they are treated, does this behavior usually go away?

___1___ Total number of circled items

VII. **Replacement Behaviors**

Instructions: For behaviors 1–3 (from Part II), list one or more alternative replacement behaviors.

Problem Behavior	Replacements
1. self-stim	teach hand isometrics; teach Jason to ask for stim time
2. SIB	teach a communicative skill (ask for break, ask to leave) other than signs
3. crying	(see SIB)

VIII. **Communication Skills**

Instructions: Answer the following three questions that assess how the student communicates.

1. Indicate the person's primary form of communication:

_____ Speech _____ Signs _____ Gestures   Other: _behavior_

(continues)

Figure 11.2. *Continued.*

2. How does the person communicate to others a want or need (for attention, food, etc.)?

cries, self-injures

3. How does the person communicate a desire to stop an ongoing activity?

same

IX. Preferences

List persons, activities, games or toys, and foods that the student seems to like and that might be used as reinforcers to strengthen appropriate behavior.

1. Preferred persons: _Ms. Scott, Ms. Gonzalez, Mr. Cameron_

2. Leisure activities or hobbies: _swing, trampoline_

3. Games or toys: _lava lamp, stress balls, Play-Doh_

4. Foods, snacks, drinks: _cheese, yogurt, potato chips, apple juice_

X. Previous Interventions

On a separate page, provide a summary of interventions that have been tried in the past and note their effects on the problem behavior. Include descriptions of procedures, dates, and a summary of behavioral data.

Intervention	Dates	Effectiveness
Self-stimulatory behaviors		
Redirection to another activity	August–October	Produced brief cessation in self-stim behaviors, but behaviors typically quickly (e.g., within 5 minutes) resumed.
Self-injury		
Redirection to another activity	August–September	Produced brief cessation in self-injurious behaviors, but behaviors typically quickly (e.g., within 5–10 minutes) resumed.
Time-out (teacher or para-professional turned away from student for 30 seconds)	Late September–November	No change in frequency or duration of self-injurious behaviors
Move student to another activity	mid-November–January	Self-injurious behavior stops if new activity is a preferred activity. If new activity is not a liked activity, self-injurious behavior typically resumes within minutes.
Crying		
Ignore	All year	High levels of crying, usually during disliked activities. Less likely to cry when left alone.

Figure 11.2. *Continued.*

Figure 11.4 shows a completed A–B–C Report for Jason. Examine the report shown in Figure 11.4 and then answer each of these questions based on the data provided. Our answers to the six questions are provided at the end of Figure 11.4. How did your responses compare to ours?

Another tool for gathering direct observation data is the *Structured A–B–C Analysis Form* (Florida Center on Self-Injury, 1996). To use this form, which is shown in Figure 11.5, list the specific problem behaviors in the appropriate section at the

FAST

Functional Analysis Screening Tool

Instructions:

1. Identify those individuals who have the most current and extensive knowledge about the student (e.g., teachers, therapists, paraprofessionals, parents, trainers).
2. Either interview those individuals using the FAST or ask each person to complete a FAST independently.
3. In the "Problem Behavior Information" section, respondents should check the problem behaviors that apply to the student and then provide operational definitions for each checked behavior. For the remaining items, the respondent should be as specific as possible in answering questions.
4. In the last part of the FAST, the respondent simply circles "Yes," "No," or "N/A" (not applicable) for each item.
5. At the end of the survey, circle the number of each item that was answered "Yes" to identify probable functions of behavior.

Client: _Jason_____   Date: _2-10_____

Informant: _Teacher_____   Interviewer: _____

To the Interviewer: The FAST identifies factors that may influence problem behaviors. It should be used only for screening purposes as part of a comprehensive functional analysis of the behavior. Administer the FAST to several individuals who interact with the client frequently. Then use the results as a guide for conducting direct observations in several different situations to verify suspected behavioral functions and to identify other factors that may influence the problem behavior.

To the Informant: Complete the sections below. Then read each question carefully and answer it by circling "Yes" or "No." If you are uncertain about an answer, circle "N/A."

Informant–Client Relationship

1. Indicate your relationship to the person: _____ Parent _✓_ Instructor
   _____ Therapist/Residential Staff   (Other) _____

2. How long have you known the person? _2_ Years _6_ Months

3. Do you interact with the person daily? _✓_ Yes _____ No

4. In what situations do you usually interact with the person?
   _✓_ Meals   _✓_ Academic training
   _✓_ Leisure   _✓_ Work or vocational training
   _✓_ Self-care (Other) _____

Problem Behavior Information

1. Problem behavior (check and describe)
   _____ Aggression _____
   _✓_ Self-Injury _bites, hits self_____
   _✓_ Stereotypy _rocks, flaps hands, stares at lights_____
   _____ Property destruction _____
   _____ Other _____

(continues)

Figure 11.3. Completed functional analysis screening tool. *Note.* Adapted from *The Functional Analysis Screening Tool,* by the Florida Center on Self-Injury, 2002, Gainesville, FL: Author. Copyright 2002 by the Florida Center on Self-Injury. Adapted with permission.

2. Frequency: __✓__ Hourly _____ Daily _____ Weekly _____ Less Often

3. Severity: __✓__ Mild: Disruptive but little risk to property or health

_____ Moderate: Property damage or minor injury

_____ Severe: Significant threat to health or safety

4. Situations in which the problem behavior is <u>most</u> likely:

Days/Times _____

Settings/Activities __hallway, cafeteria, playground_____

Persons present __many other children_____

5. Situations in which the problem behavior is <u>least</u> likely:

Days/Times _____

Settings/Activities __individual work time_____

Persons present __Teacher_____

6. What is usually happening to the person right <u>before</u> the problem behavior occurs?

__asked to sign; left alone; in a crowded environment_____

7. What usually happens to the person right <u>after</u> the problem behavior occurs?

__end task; mild reprimand; allowed to return to classroom_____

8. Current Treatments

_____

_____

_____

_____

1. Does the person usually engage in the problem behavior when (s)he is being ignored or when caregivers are paying attention to someone else?	(Yes) No N/A
2. Does the person usually engage in the problem behavior when requests for preferred activities (games, snacks) are denied and or when these items are taken away?	Yes (No) N/A
3. When the problem behavior occurs, do you or other caregivers usually try to calm the person down or try to engage the person in preferred activities?	(Yes) No N/A
4. Is the person usually well behaved when (s)he is getting lots of attention or when preferred items or activities are freely available?	(Yes) No N/A
5. Is the person resistant when asked to perform a task or to participate in group activities?	Yes (No) N/A
6. Does the person usually engage in the problem behavior when asked to perform a task or to participate in group activities?	(Yes) No N/A
7. When the problem behavior occurs, is the person usually given a "break" from tasks?	(Yes) No N/A
8. Is the person usually well behaved when (s)he is not required to do anything?	Yes (No) N/A
9. Does the problem behavior seem to be a "ritual" or habit, repeatedly occurring the same way?	(Yes) No N/A
10. Does the person usually engage in the problem behavior even when no one is around or watching?	(Yes) No N/A

(continues)

Figure 11.3. *Continued.*

11.	Does the person prefer engaging in the problem behavior over other types of leisure activities?		(Yes) No N/A
12.	Does the problem behavior appear to provide some sort of "sensory stimulation?"		(Yes) No N/A
13.	Does the person usually engage in the problem behavior more often when (s)he is ill?		(Yes) No N/A
14.	Is the problem behavior cyclical, occurring at high rates for several days and then stopping?		Yes (No) N/A
15.	Does the person have recurrent painful conditions, such as ear infections or allergies? If so, please list. _____		Yes (No) N/A
16.	If the person is experiencing physical problems, and these are treated, does the problem behavior usually go away?		Yes No (N/A)

Scoring Summary

Circle the number of each question that was answered "Yes."

Items Circled "Yes"	Total	Potential Source of Reinforcement
(1) 2 (3) (4)	3	Social (attention/preferred items)
5 (6) (7) 8	2	Social (escape)
(9) (10) (11) (12)	4	Automatic (sensory stimulation)
(13) 14 15 16	1	Automatic (pain attenuation)

Figure 11.3. *Continued.*

top. Record the date and time of the observation and then simply use checkmarks to record behaviors that occurred during that observation, locations, activity, antecedents, and consequences. After all observations have been completed, antecedent and consequence data are summarized by recording the number of checkmarks occurring in each line in the antecedent and consequence boxes and totaling the columns under each function (positive reinforcement–attention, positive reinforcement–materials, etc.). The column with the highest total suggests potential functions for challenging behaviors. Figure 11.5 shows a completed *Structured A–B–C Analysis Form* for Jason.

Step 3. Analyze Data

The purpose of data collection is to identify setting events that may increase the likelihood of the challenging behavior, antecedents that are likely to trigger it, and functions of the challenging behavior. Analysis isn't complicated; we recommend literally spreading each data form (interviews, checklists, observations) in front of you and examining data sources by reading each one consecutively, looking for patterns and repetitions. For example, on her interview form, Daniel's teacher wrote that Daniel often cries and tries to hit himself when asked to use sign language. In two observations, this behavior was noted on five separate occasions. The fact that the antecedent of being asked to sign was noted in multiple places in the data is strong

A–B–C Report Form

Name: Jason   **Date/Time of observation:** 2/12, 9:30 – 11:20

Place observation occurred: classroom, hallway, recess

Activities observed: snack, morning play, trial teaching with 2 other students

Configuration of environment where student was observed: snack: table with 6 other children;

play: carpet area with all students; trial teaching: table

Number of students/adults present: 7 students; teacher, 2 paraprofessionals

T = Teacher; P = paraprofessional; J = Jason; S = other students

Time	Antecedent	Behavior	Consequence
9:30	1. T passing out snack items, requires each student to communicate his or her choice (crackers or fruit, juice or milk).	2. At his turn, J looks away from T, moans loudly and rocks. 4. Cries, continues to rock.	3. T: "Jason, if you want snack, show me your signs."
	5. T: "Jason, what do you want?"	6. J cries, bites hand. 8. J cries, hits head.	7. P physically prompts J's signs. 9. T: "J, no hitting! No snack if you don't ask the right way!"
	10. T reissues mand.	11. J cries, hits head.	12. T: "Sorry, J, no snack. Go to carpet."
9:40	13. T and Ps supervise S in snack.	14. J sits on carpet alone.	
9:43	15. T and Ps still at snack table.	16. J rocks and flaps hands.	17. T: "J, no flapping!"
9:45		18. J continues rocking and flapping.	19. P sits with J and begins engaging him with stacking blocks, then knocking them over.
		20. J participates in block activity for 7 minutes.	
9:52	21. T and Ps help S line up.	22. J complies.	
	23. Class moves through hall to music with first-grade class. No other S in hall.	24. J quiet.	
9:53	25. Other classes enter hall for passing.	26. J cries, mouths hand.	
	27. Class continues walking.	28. J cries, hits head, bites hand; continues all the way to music room.	
9:55	29. S enter class, other class already there, seated in circle on carpet. T and Ps direct S to places on carpet (interspersed among other S). Music teacher hands out rhythm instruments. S play with instruments while Music T is getting organized.	30. J puts hands on ears, rocks.	
10:05	31. Music T begins song, directs students to use instruments in time with music.	32. J cries, hits head.	33. P sitting next to J says, "Its fun, J! Play your tambourine!"
10:10		34. J continues crying, hitting head.	35. P tries to help J play tambourine.
		36. J continues crying, hitting.	37. P tries to stop hitting by holding J's hands.

(continues)

Figure 11.4. Completed antecedent–behavior–consequence (A–B–C) report form and summary. *Note.* Adapted from *Applied Behavior Analysis for Teachers* (7th ed.), by P. A. Alberto and A. C. Troutman, 2006, Upper Saddle River, NJ: Merrill/Prentice Hall. Copyright 2006 by Pearson Education, Inc. Adapted with permission.

Time	Antecedent	Behavior	Consequence
10:20	38. P takes J out of music class and returns to classroom.	39. J walks quietly, plays on computer in room.	
10:40	40. Other S return to room; T takes J and 2 S to table for math/language trials; T gives cue for each S in turn to count items (blocks, sticks, spoons, etc.) and place in box. J required to use signs for counting.	41. J waits turn quietly.	
	42. T: "J, count the spoons."	43. J touches spoons.	44. T: "No, J, count the spoons. Use your signs."
	45. T provides model (points to each spoon and signs number).	46. No response	47. T physically prompts J's signs.
		48. J moans and rocks.	49. J completes count with T assistance. T assists J in putting spoons in box.
	50. T completes trials with two other S.	51. J quiet.	52. T: "J, I like the way you're sitting!"
	53. T gives mand for J to count.	54. J moans.	55. T begins physical prompt.
		56. J cries, hits head.	57. T uses full physical prompt to get J to finish task.
	Trials continue in same manner for 15 minutes.		
10:55	58. T takes J and other S to puzzle table.	59. J works on puzzle.	
11:03		60. J continues to work on puzzle.	61. P: "J, good job on that puzzle! You're almost finished!"
	Jason continues to work on puzzles until 11:20, at which time teacher and paraprofessionals begin helping with bathroom and washing hands for lunch.		

Data Summary Questions:

A. What is the student doing that is inappropriate?

- hitting and biting self
- crying
- self-stimming

B. How frequently does this inappropriate behavior occur?

- frequently under certain conditions (see C.)

C. Are there consistent patterns of reinforcement of or punishment for that inappropriate behavior?

- the self-stim or self-injurious behavior (SIB) is usually (not always) interrupted by the teacher or aide
- a mild reprimand was given for one instance of self-stim and one instance of SIB

D. Are there identifiable antecedents to the inappropriate behavior?

- when in crowded or noisy situations (lunchroom, hall)
- when peer buddy tries to interact with him
- when asked to respond to language questions

(continues)

Figure 11.4. *Continued.*

E. Are there patterns to the antecedents?

- data strongly suggest that loud or crowded environments are consistent antecedents for target inappropriate behaviors
- requests for language responses almost always produced SIB and/or crying

F. Are there recurring chains of specific antecedents, behaviors, and consequences?

- when Jason is left alone → he self-stims → adults stop him
- when Jason is in the hall or cafeteria → he cries and hits himself or bites his hand → he is removed from the situation
- when Jason is asked to sign responses to questions → he hits or bites self and cries → either no response, or he is allowed to noncomply

G. Describe possibilities for intervention

- reduce time Jason must wait with nothing to do

Hall, cafeteria:

- do not require Jason to walk in hall or eat lunch in cafeteria during crowded times
- allow Jason's lunch buddy to eat lunch with Jason in the classroom
- use social stories to help prepare Jason for the hall and cafeteria conditions
- provide differential reinforcement [see Chapter 12 for an explanation of how to do this] for appropriate behaviors in the hall and cafeteria. For example, carry Jason's favorite stim toy to lunch so that he understands that if he does not hit or bite, he may play with the toy when he is finished eating.

Language:

- use differential reinforcement to reinforce Jason for correct signed responses
- for each correct signed response (at first), allow him to hold his stim toy for 30 seconds
- if he hits or bites, hold his hands and firmly say, "No hurting, Jason," and then repeat cue
- teach Jason to sign that he wants to stop working
- only end sessions after a compliant response

Figure 11.4. *Continued.*

support for the teacher's hypotheses: "Daniel is likely to cry and try to hit himself when asked to sign" and "Daniel cries and tries to hit himself when asked to sign to avoid interaction or communication" or "Daniel does not like to sign."

Step 4. Develop Hypotheses

Using all the data you have collected, the next step is to develop hypotheses about the following items:

- setting events and specific antecedents that typically precede a challenging behavior;
- the function of the behavior: to get something, avoid something, or communicate something (At-a-Glance 11.1 lists potential functions of challenging behavior, along with possible indicators for each function);
- possible skill deficits related to the challenging behavior (for students with autism, these commonly will be in the areas of communication, interpersonal relationships, or self-control); and
- possible biological causes of behavior as determined by medical reports, information from parents, or the child's response to medication.

Structured A–B–C (Antecedent–Behavior–Consequence) Analysis Form

Individual: Jason

Residence: _____

Instructions: Use this form to identify situational factors related to the occurrence of behavior problem. Each time a target behavior occurs, record the date, time, and your initials. Use check marks to identify target behavior, location, activity, and what happened immediately before and after the behavior.

Data on antecedents (As) and consequences (Cs) are summarized in the boxes below. As and Cs are organized under likely behavioral functions (Note: Some As or Cs may reflect more than one function). In each box, enter the number of times an A or C was checked (use the arrows as guides). Enter the overall totals at the bottom of each column.

Date 10-23	7:10	7:30	8:03	8:10	8:19	9:00	9:15	9:42	10:03	11:13
Staff HS										
Behavior (list specific problem):										
1. Hitting head	✓					✓	✓		✓	✓
2. Biting hands and arms			✓			✓	✓		✓	✓
3. Flapping hands	✓	✓	✓	✓			✓			
Location where behavior occurred:										
Residence										
Worksite										
School Classroom	✓	✓	✓	✓	✓	✓	✓			
Outside										
Community outing										
Other: School-gym								✓		
General activity in progress:										
Leisure/solitary (TV, music, etc.)	✓									
Leisure/social (with another person)				✓			✓			
Meal (preparation, eating, clean up)	✓									
Self-care or household chore										
Academic, work, or training activity		✓	✓	✓		✓				
Alone: Engaging in leisure activities				✓	✓					
Other: Socialization & motor activities								✓		
Immediate antecedent (A):										
Ignored by staff or staff walked away					✓			✓		
Leisure material or food removed/denied										
Other request denied						✓				
Given instruction/prompt to work		✓	✓	✓			✓		✓	
Provoked by peer										
None (individual alone/doing nothing)	✓							✓		✓
Immediate consequence (C):										
Attention, response block, told to "stop"	✓				✓	✓		✓		
Redirected to another area/activity			✓	✓		✓				
Leisure material/food given										
Work requirement terminated									✓	
Staff walked away										
Staff did nothing	✓	✓	✓				✓			✓

Summary boxes (behavioral functions):

	Pos. Reinf. (attention)	Pos. Reinf. (materials)	Neg. Reinf. (escape)	Auto Reinf. (sensory)
Antecedent (A)	3	0 / 1	5 / 1	3
Consequence (C)	3 / 2	2 / 0	1 / 0	0 / 5
TOTAL	11	3	7	8

Figure 11.5. Structured Antecedent–Behavior–Consequence (A–B–C) Analysis Form. *Note.* Adapted from *Structured A–B–C Analysis*, by the Florida Center on Self-Injury, 1996, Gainesville, FL.: Author. Copyright 1996 by the Florida Center on Self-Injury. Adapted with permission.

At-a-Glance 11.1 Potential Functions of Challenging Behavior and Corresponding Indicators

Function	Indicator
Communication	Behavior increases or intensifies when desired objects are in view, but student cannot access them.
	Behavior occurs when asked to do disliked tasks.
	Behavior occurs in response to interruption in routine or schedule, or when a preferred ritual is interrupted.
	Examples: • Student tantrums if his or her desk is moved or if favorite lunch drink is unavailable. • Student acts aggressively toward a substitute teacher if his or her regular teacher is absent. • Student cries if bad weather dictates that he or she must go to the gym for recess instead of outside.
Sensory stimulation (for self-injurious and self-stimulatory behaviors)	Behavior increases when student is not otherwise engaged or when the environment is not stimulating.
Negative reinforcement (escape or avoidance)	Behavior occurs when student is presented with disliked tasks or when near people he or she does not like.
Positive reinforcement	Behavior increases when the student wants a desired item and gets it as a result of the behavior.
	Behavior occurs when teacher or other adult moves away.

For example, when dealing with self-injurious behavior, Carr (1977) recommended that the child be screened for (a) Lesch-Nyhan or deLange syndrome if the behavior involves finger, lip, or tongue biting and (b) otitis media if the student displays head banging.

Figure 11.6 lists hypotheses that reflect the data shown in Jason's data forms. Note the format that we used for developing these hypotheses. This system involves using one box for each component of the equation (antecedent, behavior, actual consequence, hypothesized function) and a separate set of boxes for each hypothesis. We find this approach to be an efficient way to develop hypotheses from a variety of data.

A word of caution: Be sure to rely on your data in forming hypotheses. For each hypothesis, ask yourself, "Where in the data is this hypothesis supported?" You should be able to identify at least one, and preferably more than one, specific item from the data to support each hypothesis. The more places that the data support a hypothesis, the stronger the hypothesis.

For example, Ms. Sperry is a behavior specialist who was consulted to provide suggestions for managing Jorge's tantrums. After reviewing the FBA data that she had gathered, Ms. Sperry hypothesized that Jorge exhibited tantrums to get preferred foods (anything with a soft texture) at snack time and lunch or items that he uses for self-stimulatory behavior during work and play time. These hypotheses were supported in both the indirect and direct data. On the BFAI form, Jorge's mother indicated that she tries to make him eat a wide variety of foods, but when he tantrums, she removes the food she has given him and allows him to have his mashed potatoes,

Hypothesis Development Form

Instructions: Use a separate line for each different challenging behavior. In the first box, enter the antecedent(s) commonly associated with that behavior. In the second box, describe the behavior. In the third box, describe typical consequences that follow the behavior. Finally, note possible functions of the problem behavior.

Hypotheses

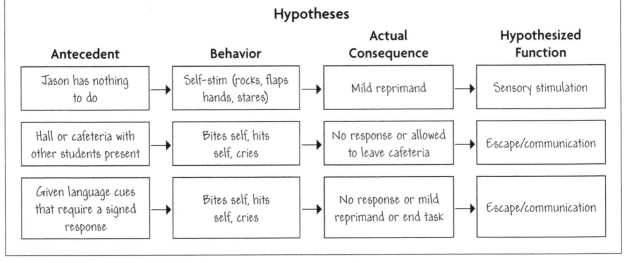

Antecedent	Behavior	Actual Consequence	Hypothesized Function
Jason has nothing to do	Self-stim (rocks, flaps hands, stares)	Mild reprimand	Sensory stimulation
Hall or cafeteria with other students present	Bites self, hits self, cries	No response or allowed to leave cafeteria	Escape/communication
Given language cues that require a signed response	Bites self, hits self, cries	No response or mild reprimand or end task	Escape/communication

Figure 11.6. Hypothesis development form.

pudding, ice cream, or other soft food. During one observation, Ms. Sperry observed Jorge's teacher give Jorge the crackers that other students were having for snack, but when he started to cry and hit his head, the teacher took away the crackers and allowed him to have a small cup of pudding instead. In addition, multiple instances during three separate observations indicate that when Jorge begins to tantrum, he is given the objects that he likes to use to engage in self-stimulatory behavior (e.g., pieces of string or yarn, limp pieces of paper). Ms. Sperry's hypothesis is likely to be correct because she has multiple sources of data to support that hypothesis.

Step 5. Develop an Intervention Plan

Your hypotheses statements should now guide development of one or more interventions. At-a-Glance 11.2 lists generic interventions, including some for specific functions. These should not be used as a blueprint for your own interventions but rather as a tool to stimulate creative thinking about individualized interventions for your students.

There are two important considerations in planning interventions. First, identify a competing behavior as a replacement for each targeted problem behavior. The competing replacement behavior should be one that either is currently in the student's repertoire or can be easily taught and that will more appropriately serve the same function as the problem behavior. Second, ensure that interventions reflect hypotheses from the FBA. This may mean that you change current antecedents that cue problem behaviors, teach new behaviors for possible skill deficits reflected by each behavior, and/or design reinforcers to reflect the hypothesized functions of each behavior. The closer the intervention plan reflects assessment findings, the more likely the intervention is to be successful.

At-a-Glance 11.2 Sample Interventions

Modify Antecedents

- Ensure clear, concise directions.
- Provide picture schedules.
- Provide picture cues.
- Use timers to delineate required length of tasks.
- Provide shorter tasks.
- Change task pace (e.g., present S^Ds and trials quicker and avoid downtime between activities).
- Ensure that tasks are functional for student.
- Increase clarity in environment (e.g., use visual cues to delineate where student is to sit, wait, line up).
- Change task order (e.g., present less desirable tasks before preferred activities).
- Ensure consistency across all adults who are working with the student.

Teach New Behaviors That Reflect Functional Behavior Assessment (FBA) Data About Possible Skill Deficits

- Communication skills, especially how to make requests and how to refuse
  - *Functional Communication Training* (Carr & Durand, 1985; Durand & Merges, 2001) is a strategy in which the communicative intent of the challenging behavior is identified through FBA and a functional communicative behavior is taught and reinforced. At first, the new communication behavior should produce the same consequences as the original challenging behavior. For example, when Anthony tired of an activity, he began to cry and bite his hand. This almost always resulted in his teacher removing the task or taking Anthony away from the activity. The teacher taught Anthony to point to his "Stop" card to communicate that he wanted the activity to end. Each time Anthony points to his "Stop" card, the task or activity is terminated. Anthony's new communicative behavior thus produces the same consequence as his previous behaviors of crying and biting his hand.
  - In another example, Halle was taught to sign "Play" when she wanted to play with her favorite stim toy. In the past, when Halle wanted her toy, she either jumped up and ran to where it was kept and/or screamed and cried. To reinforce Halle as she learns to ask for her toy, the teacher gives her the toy for a brief time as soon as she signs an approximation of "Play."
- Waiting skills
- Interpersonal skills (e.g., sharing a toy, taking turns, sitting in a group)
- Appropriate forms of self-stimulation (see Chapter 2)

Provide Reinforcers for Replacement Behaviors Based on Function of the Challenging Behavior

- Reinforcers based on attention-seeking behaviors:
  - Use enthusiastic praise, clapping, a brief tickle, or other social reinforcers for appropriate behavior.
  - Ensure that appropriate behavior receives more attention than inappropriate behavior.
- Reinforcers based on sensory stimulation–seeking behaviors:
  - Allow student to engage in self-stimulatory behavior contingent upon task completion or compliance with adult directives.
  - Allow student to use alternative self-stimulatory toys/activities contingent upon task completion or compliance (see At-a-Glance 2.4 for ideas).
- Reinforcers based on escape or avoidance behaviors:
  - Allow student to avoid or stop an activity contingent upon appropriate expression of refusal (e.g., allow student to stop an activity when he or she points to the "Stop" picture card).

Note. Remember that when you first start teaching replacement behaviors, you will use frequent reinforcement and then gradually lessen the amount of reinforcement as the student moves to fluency and maintenance of the behavior.

Sometimes, one of the hardest steps in intervention planning is thinking of interventions to match functions. At-a-Glance 11.2 should facilitate this process, as will interventions described in Chapters 12 and 14. Of course, all of the information presented throughout this book potentially relates to designing interventions. For example, two main considerations in addressing challenging behavior are the following: Does the student have language? Does he or she use an efficient communication system? If the answer to either or both of these is no, the strategies described in At-a-Glance 11.2 and other communication strategies described in Chapter 9 should be a starting point in dealing with challenging behaviors.

We find it helpful to use the *Behavior Management Analysis Chart* (Webber & Wheeler, 1995) shown in Figure 11.7 to plan interventions. This form is a simple way to organize interventions by antecedent modifications, teaching of new behaviors, or changing of consequences. Our form shows possible interventions that reflect the hypotheses from Figure 11.6. In Chapter 12, we show how this form can also serve as a basis for a formal behavior intervention plan.

Step 6. Monitor the Interventions

Use the measurement techniques described in Chapter 2, along with the forms in Chapter 13, to monitor target replacement (competing) behaviors as well as the behaviors targeted for reduction. If the behavior(s) do not change in the desired direction after a reasonable time (e.g., 1 to 5 days) of faithfully using the interventions, you may need to adjust the intervention (i.e., change some aspect of it, such as the type of reinforcer you are using), develop a new intervention based on a different hypothesis, or collect additional functional assessment data and develop new hypotheses.

Summary

Functional assessment is a critical step in designing effective interventions for the behavioral excesses of students with autism because they often cannot communicate wants, needs, or feelings. We must do our best to figure out what needs are being met through challenging behaviors so we can match the interventions to what we know about the contributing factors. Because these children have significant skill deficits, their inappropriate behaviors are often the only way they have of getting their needs met. The older the child becomes without acquiring language and communication abilities, the more likely it is that he or she will display problem behavior. Failure to recognize events that support challenging behaviors and act upon these events will probably mean that behavior intervention plans will do little to reduce challenging behaviors.

Two subsequent chapters will provide further guidance for dealing with challenging behavior. Chapter 12 deals with specific strategies for reducing challenging behaviors, while Chapter 14 describes interventions for common problem behaviors exhibited by students with autism, including noncompliance, aggression, and self-injurious behavior. Conscientious application of the ABA principles presented in Chapter 2, careful use of the FBA methods described in this chapter, attention to students' communication needs as discussed in Chapter 9, and consideration of the strategies presented in Chapters 12 and 14 should give teachers a toolbox full of effective methods for preventing and responding to the challenging behaviors exhibited by students with autism.

Behavior Management Analysis Chart

Instructions: List the problem behavior in the "Behavior" column. In the "Reason" column, note hypotheses for that behavior. List appropriate functional replacement behaviors in the "Alternate Behavior" column. In the "Antecedent Interventions" column, describe all antecedent interventions that will be used to prevent the behavior or cue or prompt the alternate behavior(s). Finally, list consequences, including reinforcement interventions for the alternate behavior(s) and behavior reductive interventions for the challenging behaviors. Create a separate section for each challenging behavior (that is, each column should be completed for each challenging behavior).

Behavior	Reason	Alternate Behavior	Antecedent Interventions	Consequences
Self-hitting, self-biting	Escape language tasks; communicate dislike of language tasks	• Teach Jason to ask for a break; • Give Jason a squeeze ball to hold during language	• Timer to mark brief periods required for work • Use visual schedule to show preferred activity after language • Social story before language • Present questions that lead to reinforcement for him to respond to (e.g., "Do you want juice or milk?" "Do you want to play music or build Legos?"	• Allow Jason the reinforcer when he signs his response with no biting or hitting. • DRO for no biting and no hitting • If he hits or bites, gently prompt his hands to his lap and say, "No biting," or "No hitting."
Self-biting or hitting, crying	To avoid loud noise and activity in hall and cafeteria	Sign "Too loud," or "Leave, please," or teach him to point to or present picture/symbol cards to express these wishes	• Social story before going into hall and cafeteria • Allow him to wear headphones at first • Allow him to carry favorite toy	• Allow him to return to room if he asks correctly. • DRO for no self-injurious behavior • Differential reinforcement for walking, interacting with lunch buddy
Self-stim (spinning objects, flapping hands)	Boredom	• Use sensory toys appropriately • Ask for favorite toys	• Partial verbal prompt • Provide preferred toys (e.g., dreidel)	• Provide toy when he asks appropriately. • Mild reprimand for stim

Figure 11.7. Behavior management analysis chart. *Note.* Adapted from "Managing Difficult Student Behaviors," by J. Webber and L. Wheeler, 1995, San Marcos, TX: Center for Initiatives in Education, Southwest Texas State University. Adapted with permission.

References

Alberto, P., & Troutman, A. (2006). *Applied behavior analysis for teachers* (7th ed.). Englewood Cliffs, NJ: Merrill/Prentice Hall.

Bijou, S. W., Peterson, R. F., & Ault, M. F. (1968). A method to integrate descriptive and experimental field studies at the level of data and empirical concepts. *Journal of Applied Behavior Analysis, 1,* 175–191.

Carr, E. G. (1977). The motivation of self-injurious behavior: A review of some hypotheses. *Psychological Bulletin, 84,* 800–816.

Carr, E., & Durand, V. M. (1985). Reducing behavior problems through functional communication training. *Journal of Applied Behavior Analysis 18*(2), 111–126.

Centers for Disease Control. (2006). *Brick Township autism investigation.* Retrieved April 17, 2007, from http://www.atsdr.cdc.gov/HAC/PHA/brick/bti_p1.html

Durand, V. M., & Merges, E. (2001). Functional communication training: A contemporary behavior analytic intervention for problem behaviors. *Focus on Autism and Other Developmental Disabilities, 16,* 110–119.

Florida Center on Self-Injury. (1996). *Structured A–B–C Analysis.* Gainesville, FL: Author.

Florida Center on Self-Injury. (2002a). *The functional analysis screening tool.* Gainesville, FL: Author.

Florida Center on Self-Injury. (2002b). *Functional behavioral assessment inventory.* Gainesville, FL: Author.

Foster-Johnson, L., & Dunlap, G. (1993). Using functional assessment to develop effective, individualized interventions for challenging behaviors. *Teaching Exceptional Children, 25*(3), 44–50.

Murdock, S. G., O'Neill, R. E., & Cunningham, E. (2005). A comparison of results and acceptability of functional behavioral assessment procedures with a group of middle school students with emotional/behavioral disorders (E/BD). *Journal of Behavioral Education, 14*(1), 5–18.

National Research Council, Division of Behavioral and Social Sciences and Education, Committee on Educational Interventions for Children with Autism. (2001). *Educating children with autism* (C. Lord & J. P. McGee, Eds.). Washington, DC: National Academy Press.

O'Neill, R. E., Horner, R. H., Albin, R. W., Sprague, J. R., Storey, K., & Newton, J. S. (1997). *Functional assessment and program development for problem behavior.* Pacific Grove, CA: Brooks/Cole.

Schroeder, S. R., Bickel, W. K., & Richmond, G. (1986). Primary and secondary prevention of self-injurious behaviors: A life-long problem. *Advances in Learning and Behavioral Disabilities, 5,* 63–85.

Symons, F. J., Butler, M. G., Sanders, M. D., Feurer, I. D., & Thompson, T. (1999). Self-injurious behavior and Prader-Willi syndrome: Behavioral forms and body locations. *American Journal of Mental Retardation, 104*(3), 260–269.

Symons, F. J., & Thompson, T. (1997). Self-injurious behavior and body site preference. *Journal of Intellectual Disability Research, 41*(6), 456–468.

Thompson, T., Symons, F. J., Delaney, D., & England, C. (1995). Self-injurious behavior as endogenous neurochemical self-administration. *Mental Retardation and Developmental Disabilities Research Review, 1*(2), 137–148.

Webber, J., & Wheeler, L. (1995). *Managing difficult student behaviors.* San Marcos, TX: Center for Initiatives in Education.

Appendix:
Functional Behavioral Assessment Forms

Brief Functional Assessment Interview Form
Functional Behavioral Assessment Inventory
Functional Analysis Screening Tool (FAST)
Antecedent–Behavior–Consequence (A–B–C) Report
Structured A–B–C (Antecedent–Behavior–Consequence) Analysis Form
Hypothesis Development Form
Behavior Management Analysis Chart

Brief Functional Assessment Interview Form

Instructions:

1. Identify those individuals who have the most current and extensive knowledge about the student (teachers, therapists, paraprofessionals, parents, trainers, etc.).

2. Either interview those individuals using the BFAI or ask each person to complete a BFAI independently.

3. Encourage respondents to be as specific and detailed as possible in their responses.

Student: **Date:**

Behavior(s) of Concern:

Predictors: (when, where, with whom, with what) (Routine)

Maintaining Function(s): (attention, objects/food, avoid demands/tasks, avoid social contact, obtain activity)

What Makes it Worse (Setting Events): (sleep, diet, schedule, home problems, constipation)

Summary Statement (Define by Routine)

Setting Event ⟶	Predictor ⟶	Problem Behavior ⟶	Maintaining Function

Note. Adapted from "A Descriptive Comparison of Teacher Teams' Perceptions of Student Behavior to Results of Functional Assessments," by S. G. Murdock, 2000, Unpublished master's thesis, Dept. of Special Education, University of Utah. Adapted with permission.

Functional Behavioral Assessment Inventory

I. General Information

Name: _____ Sex: M F Date of Birth: _____

Class/Residence: _____ Date of Interview: _____

Informant/Relationship: _____ Interviewer: _____

II. Problem Behavior Identification

Instructions: List up to three problem behaviors of concern. Describe each in clear, objective terms.

1. _____

2. _____

3. _____

III. Dimensions of Problem Behavior

Instructions: Circle the appropriate frequency and severity indicators for each problem behavior. Use the following criteria for severity: Mild (disruptive, but not dangerous), Moderate (destructive to physical environment), Severe (poses physical danger to student or others).

	Frequency	Severity
1.	Hourly / Daily / Weekly / Less often	Mild / Moderate / Severe
2.	Hourly / Daily / Weekly / Less often	Mild / Moderate / Severe
3.	Hourly / Daily / Weekly / Less often	Mild / Moderate / Severe

IV. Critical Situations

1. Describe the situations in which problem behavior is <u>most</u> likely to occur.

   Days/times: _____ Setting: _____

   Persons present: _____ Activity: _____

   What is usually happening to the person right <u>before</u> the problem behavior occurs?

   _____

   What happens to the person right <u>after</u> the problem behavior occurs?

   _____

2. Describe the situations in which problem behavior is <u>least</u> likely to occur.

   Days/times: _____ Setting: _____

   Persons present: _____ Activity: _____

V. Daily Schedule

Instructions: Fill in the student's daily schedule. For each time period, indicate the setting (e.g., classroom, cafeteria), activity taking place (e.g., morning group, lunch), and whether problem behavior is likely or unlikely to occur during each time period.

Time	Setting	Activity	Behavior (circle)	
7:00	_____	_____	Likely	Unlikely
8:00	_____	_____	Likely	Unlikely
9:00	_____	_____	Likely	Unlikely
10:00	_____	_____	Likely	Unlikely
11:00	_____	_____	Likely	Unlikely
12:00	_____	_____	Likely	Unlikely
1:00	_____	_____	Likely	Unlikely
2:00	_____	_____	Likely	Unlikely
3:00	_____	_____	Likely	Unlikely
4:00	_____	_____	Likely	Unlikely
5:00	_____	_____	Likely	Unlikely
6:00	_____	_____	Likely	Unlikely
7:00	_____	_____	Likely	Unlikely
8:00	_____	_____	Likely	Unlikely
9:00	_____	_____	Likely	Unlikely
10:00	_____	_____	Likely	Unlikely
Later	_____	_____	Likely	Unlikely

Does the problem behavior occur more often/less often (circle) on weekends? If so, elaborate.

_____

_____

VI. Functions of Problem Behavior

Instructions: Items A–D assess possible functions of the problem behavior. Read each question under each letter and circle the item if the answer to the question is "yes." Enter the total number of items circled in each section.

A. Function: Access to Attention or Preferred Activities (Positive Reinforcement)

1. Does the person engage in this behavior when (s)he is being ignored or when the caregiver is paying attention to someone else?

2. Does the person engage in this behavior when preferred games or toys are taken away?

3. Does the person usually get preferred activities (leisure items, snack, etc.) when (s)he engages in this behavior?

4. Is the person usually well behaved while (s)he is getting lots of attention or when (s)he has access to preferred toys/games?

_____ Total number of circled items

B. Function: Escape from Task Demands (Negative Reinforcement)

   1. Is the person usually noncompliant when asked to perform a task?

   2. Does the person frequently engage in this behavior when asked to perform a task?

   3. Is the person usually given a "break" from work when this behavior occurs?

   4. Is the person usually well behaved when there are no task requirements present?

   _____ Total number of circled items

C. Function: Sensory Stimulation (Automatic Reinforcement)

   1. Does this behavior occur repeatedly (for long periods of time) and usually in the same way?

   2. Does the person engage in this behavior when no one is around or watching?

   3. Does the person engage in this behavior even though no one pays attention to it?

   4. Does it appear that the behavior provides some type of sensory stimulation?

   _____ Total number of circled items

D. Function: Pain Attenuation (Automatic Reinforcement)

   1. Does the person have a history of recurrent illness (e.g., ear infections, allergies, dermatitis)? If so, please list: _____

   2. Does the person have any other periodic physical difficulties (e.g., irregular sleep or diet)? If so, please list: _____

   3. Does the person engage in this behavior more often when ill?

   4. If the person has medical problems and they are treated, does this behavior usually go away?

   _____ Total number of circled items

VII. Replacement Behaviors

Instructions: For behaviors 1–3 (from Part II), list one or more alternative replacement behaviors.

Problem Behavior	Replacements
1. _____	_____
	_____
2. _____	_____
	_____
3. _____	_____
	_____

VIII. Communication Skills

Instructions: Answer the following three questions that assess how the student communicates.

1. Indicate the person's primary form of communication:

   _____ Speech _____ Signs _____ Gestures   Other: _____

2. How does the person communicate to others a want or need (for attention, food, etc.)?

_____

3. How does the person communicate a desire to stop an ongoing activity?

_____

IX. Preferences

List persons, activities, games or toys, and foods that the student seems to like and that might be used as reinforcers to strengthen appropriate behavior.

1. Preferred persons: _____

2. Leisure activities or hobbies: _____

3. Games or toys: _____

4. Foods, snacks, drinks: _____

X. Previous Interventions

Provide a summary of interventions that have been tried in the past and note their effects on the problem behavior. Include descriptions of procedures, dates, and a summary of behavioral data.

Intervention	Dates	Effectiveness

Note. Adapted from *Functional Behavioral Assessment Inventory,* by the Florida Center on Self-Injury, 2002, Gainesville, FL: Author. Copyright 2002 by the Florida Center on Self-Injury. Adapted with permission.

F A S T

Functional Analysis Screening Tool

Instructions:

1. Identify those individuals who have the most current and extensive knowledge about the student (e.g., teachers, therapists, paraprofessionals, parents, trainers).
2. Either interview those individuals using the FAST or ask each person to complete a FAST independently.
3. In the "Problem Behavior Information" section, respondents should check the problem behaviors that apply to the student and then provide operational definitions for each checked behavior. For the remaining items, the respondent should be as specific as possible in answering questions.
4. In the last part of the FAST, the respondent simply circles "Yes," "No," or "N/A" (not applicable) for each item.
5. At the end of the survey, circle the number of each item that was answered "Yes" to identify probable functions of behavior.

Client: _____   Date: _____

Informant: _____   Interviewer: _____

To the Interviewer: The FAST identifies factors that may influence problem behaviors. It should be used only for screening purposes as part of a comprehensive functional analysis of the behavior. Administer the FAST to several individuals who interact with the client frequently. Then use the results as a guide for conducting direct observations in several different situations to verify suspected behavioral functions and to identify other factors that may influence the problem behavior.

To the Informant: Complete the sections below. Then read each question carefully and answer it by circling "Yes" or "No." If you are uncertain about an answer, circle "N/A."

Informant–Client Relationship

1. Indicate your relationship to the person: _____ Parent _____ Instructor

   _____ Therapist/Residential Staff   (Other) _____

2. How long have you known the person? _____ Years _____ Months

3. Do you interact with the person daily? _____ Yes _____ No

4. In what situations do you usually interact with the person?

   _____ Meals   _____ Academic training

   _____ Leisure   _____ Work or vocational training

   _____ Self-care   (Other) _____

Problem Behavior Information

1. Problem behavior (check and describe)

   _____ Aggression _____

   _____ Self-Injury _____

   _____ Stereotypy _____

   _____ Property destruction _____

   _____ Other _____

2. Frequency: _____ Hourly _____ Daily _____ Weekly _____ Less Often

3. Severity: _____ Mild: Disruptive but little risk to property or health

   _____ Moderate: Property damage or minor injury

   _____ Severe: Significant threat to health or safety

4. Situations in which the problem behavior is <u>most</u> likely:

Days/Times _____

Settings/Activities _____

Persons present _____

5. Situations in which the problem behavior is <u>least</u> likely:

Days/Times _____

Settings/Activities _____

Persons present _____

6. What is usually happening to the person right <u>before</u> the problem behavior occurs?

_____

7. What usually happens to the person right <u>after</u> the problem behavior occurs?

_____

8. Current Treatments

_____

_____

_____

1.	Does the person usually engage in the problem behavior when (s)he is being ignored or when caregivers are paying attention to someone else?	Yes	No	N/A
2.	Does the person usually engage in the problem behavior when requests for preferred activities (games, snacks) are denied and or when these items are taken away?	Yes	No	N/A
3.	When the problem behavior occurs, do you or other caregivers usually try to calm the person down or try to engage the person in preferred activities?	Yes	No	N/A
4.	Is the person usually well behaved when (s)he is getting lots of attention or when preferred items or activities are freely available?	Yes	No	N/A
5.	Is the person resistant when asked to perform a task or to participate in group activities?	Yes	No	N/A
6.	Does the person usually engage in the problem behavior when asked to perform a task or to participate in group activities?	Yes	No	N/A
7.	When the problem behavior occurs, is the person usually given a "break" from tasks?	Yes	No	N/A
8.	Is the person usually well behaved when (s)he is not required to do anything?	Yes	No	N/A
9.	Does the problem behavior seem to be a "ritual" or habit, repeatedly occurring the same way?	Yes	No	N/A
10.	Does the person usually engage in the problem behavior even when no one is around or watching?	Yes	No	N/A
11.	Does the person prefer engaging in the problem behavior over other types of leisure activities?	Yes	No	N/A
12.	Does the problem behavior appear to provide some sort of "sensory stimulation?"	Yes	No	N/A
13.	Does the person usually engage in the problem behavior more often when (s)he is ill?	Yes	No	N/A

14. Is the problem behavior cyclical, occurring at high rates for several days and then stopping?	Yes No N/A	
15. Does the person have recurrent painful conditions, such as ear infections or allergies? If so, please list. _____	Yes No N/A	
16. If the person is experiencing physical problems, and these are treated, does the problem behavior usually go away?	Yes No N/A	

Scoring Summary

Circle the number of each question that was answered "Yes."

Items Circled "Yes"	Total	Potential Source of Reinforcement
1 2 3 4	_____	Social (attention/preferred items)
5 6 7 8	_____	Social (escape)
9 10 11 12	_____	Automatic (sensory stimulation)
13 14 15 16	_____	Automatic (pain attenuation)

Antecedent–Behavior–Consequence (A–B–C) Report Form

Instructions:

1. Determine the most appropriate times to observe the student. Students should be observed in contexts and during times of the day when challenging behaviors are most likely to occur.

2. Someone other than the persons responsible for teaching the student or interacting with the student at those times should conduct the observation. The teacher cannot teach and conduct an *A–B–C Report* at the same time. The paraprofessional who is assisting the student during lunch would not be able to simultaneously conduct an A–B–C observation of the student's lunch behaviors. Observations can be done by other teachers, behavior specialists, school psychologists or educational diagnosticians, or even the teacher or paraprofessional if the observation is being conducted in settings where other adults have responsibility for the student (e.g., speech and language therapy, adapted physical education).

3. Complete the information at the top of the form (date and time, place, activities, etc.).

4. Note times of each behavior. It may be helpful to add seconds to the time notation to help track frequency and duration of behaviors.

5. In the "Antecedent" column, write down each antecedent event that relates to the student you are observing (e.g., instructions given, peer interactions directed to student, transitions, or any other event that involves the student).

6. In the "Behavior" column, describe the student's behavior in response to each antecedent. Note only what you <u>see</u>; you should not include any interpretations or conclusions.

7. In the "Consequences" column, record what happens after each instance of the student's behavior.

8. It is a good idea to number each entry so that when you are reviewing the information, you can determine the correct sequence of events.

9. Observe for at least one complete activity, preferably including the transitions before and after the activity.

10. Complete 3 to 5 separate observations over several days using the *A–B–C Report* format.

11. For each *A–B–C Report*, answer the questions at the end of the report with as much detail as possible using information from the report.

A–B–C Report Form

Name: _____ Date/Time of observation: _____

Place observation occurred: _____

Activities observed: _____

Configuration of environment where student was observed: _____

_____

Number of students/adults present: _____

Time	Antecedent	Behavior	Consequence

Data Summary Questions:

A. What is the student doing that is inappropriate?

B. How frequently does this inappropriate behavior occur?

C. Are there consistent patterns of reinforcement of or punishment for that inappropriate behavior?

D. Are there identifiable antecedents to the inappropriate behavior?

E. Are there patterns to the antecedents?

F. Are there recurring chains of specific antecedents, behaviors, and consequences?

G. Describe possibilities for intervention.

Note. Adapted from *Applied Behavior Analysis for Teachers* (7th ed.), by P. A. Alberto and A. C. Troutman, 2006, Upper Saddle River, NJ: Merrill/Prentice Hall. Copyright 2006 by Pearson Education, Inc. Adapted with permission.

Structured A–B–C (Antecedent–Behavior–Consequence) Analysis Form

Instructions:

1. Determine the most appropriate times to observe the student. Students should be observed in contexts and during times of the day when challenging behaviors are most likely to occur.

2. Someone other than the persons responsible for teaching the student or interacting with the student at those times should conduct the observation. Observations can be done by other teachers, behavior specialists, school psychologists or educational diagnosticians, or even the teacher or paraprofessional if the observation is being conducted in settings where other adults have responsibility for the student (e.g., speech and language therapy, adapted physical education).

3. In the "Behavior" section, describe up to three challenging behaviors using specific descriptions.

4. In the next two sections, you may add locations and/or general activities that pertain to the student being observed. Write these on the lines titled "Other."

5. Each time a target behavior (one of the three listed in the Behavior section) occurs, record the date, time, and your initials (NOTE: if only one person conducts the observations, such as the teacher, initials are not necessary).

6. Check the behavior(s) that occurred, then place check marks in each box corresponding to the situational factors related to the behavior: location, general activities, immediate antecedents, and immediate consequences. More than one item can be checked in each section.

7. After the observation, summarize the data from the Antecedents and Consequences sections. Count the number of checks entered on each line under Immediate Antecedents and Immediate Consequences. Record the total for each line in the box at the far right that corresponds to that line (use the arrows as guides).

8. Finally, add the numbers entered in each of the behavioral function columns (e.g., Positive Reinforcement–Attention; Positive Reinforcement–Materials) and enter the totals in the boxes in the TOTAL line.

9. The function columns with the highest totals indicate potential functions for the challenging behaviors exhibited by the student.

Structured A–B–C (Antecedent–Behavior–Consequence) Analysis Form

Individual: _____

Residence: _____

Instructions: Use this form to identify situational factors related to the occurrence of behavior problem. Each time a target behavior occurs, record the date, time, and your initials. Use check marks to identify target behavior, location, activity, and what happened immediately before and after the behavior.

Data on antecedents (As) and consequences (Cs) are summarized in the boxes below. As and Cs are organized under likely behavioral functions (Note: Some As or Cs may reflect more than one function). In each box, enter the number of times an A or C was checked (use the arrows as guides). Enter the overall totals at the bottom of each column.

Date

Time

Staff

Behavior (list specific problem):

1.

2.

3.

Location where behavior occurred:

Residence

Worksite

School

Outside

Community outing

Other:

General activity in progress:

Leisure/solitary (TV, music, etc.)

Leisure/social (with another person)

Meal (preparation, eating, clean up)

Self-care or household chore

Academic, work, or training activity

Alone (sitting in bed, etc.)

Other:

Immediate antecedent (A):

Ignored by staff or staff walked away

Leisure material or food removed/denied

Other request denied

Given instruction/prompt to work

Provoked by peer

None (individual alone/doing nothing)

Immediate consequence (C):

Attention, response block, told to "stop"

Redirected to another area/activity

Leisure material/food given

Work requirement terminated

Staff walked away

Staff did nothing

	Pos. Reinf. (attention)	Pos. Reinf. (materials)	Neg. Reinf. (escape)	Auto Reinf. (sensory)

TOTAL

Note. From *Structured A–B–C Analysis*, by the Florida Center on Self-Injury, 1996, Gainesville, FL: Author. Copyright 1996 by the Florida Center on Self-Injury. Adapted with permission.

Copyright 2008 by PRO-ED, Inc.

Functional Behavioral Assessment

249

Hypothesis Development Form

Instructions: Use a separate line for each different challenging behavior. In the first box, enter the antecedent(s) commonly associated with that behavior. In the second box, describe the behavior. In the third box, describe typical consequences that follow the behavior. Finally, note possible functions of the problem behavior.

Hypotheses

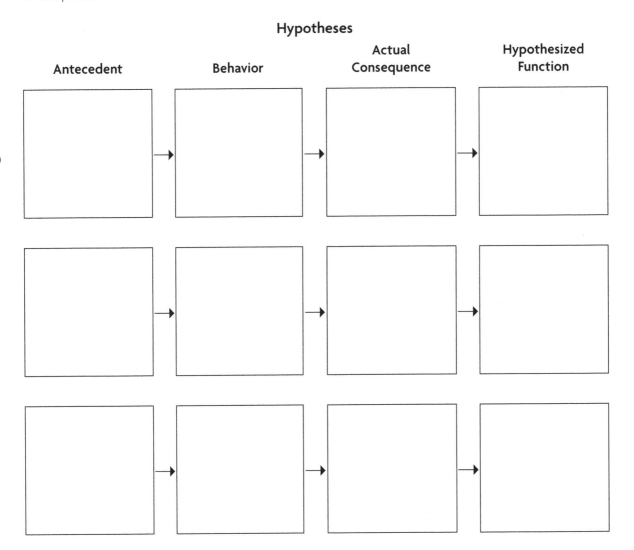

Behavior Management Analysis Chart

Instructions: List the problem behavior in the "Behavior" column. In the "Reason" column, note hypotheses for that behavior. List appropriate functional replacement behaviors in the "Alternate Behavior" column. In the "Antecedent Interventions" column, describe all antecedent interventions that will be used to prevent the behavior or cue or prompt the alternate behavior(s). Finally, list consequences, including reinforcement interventions for the alternate behavior(s) and behavior reductive interventions for the challenging behaviors. Create a separate section for each challenging behavior (that is, each column should be completed for each challenging behavior).

Behavior	Reason	Alternate Behavior	Antecedent Interventions	Consequences

Note. From "Managing Difficult Student Behaviors," by J. Webber and L. Wheeler, 1995, San Marcos, TX: Center for Initiative in Education, Southwest Texas State University. Adapted with permission.

Reducing Challenging Behaviors

Given the potential long-term damaging effects of challenging behaviors, teachers and IEP teams must make reducing or eliminating these behaviors through the use of ethical and effective methods a top priority. As discussed in Chapter 11, the first step in dealing with challenging behavior is to conduct a functional behavioral assessment (FBA) of the behavior and then use that information to develop a behavior intervention plan (BIP) based on positive behavioral supports (PBS). This chapter will describe in more detail interventions that can be used as an approach based on positive behavioral interventions and supports (PBIS) to reduce unwanted behaviors exhibited by children with autism.

Positive Behavioral Supports

We view PBS as the evolution and expansion of ABA into broader, more systemic, and more preventive applications. Anderson, Albin, Mesaros, Dunlap, and Morelli-Robbins (1993) described the following four critical elements of PBS:

1. an emphasis on instructive strategies, prevention, and interventions based on hypotheses;
2. an emphasis on treatments and supports that include multiple interventions;
3. criteria for success, including changes in quality of life; and
4. use of long-term supports.

We discuss PBS here for several reasons. First, the philosophy of this book and the strategies presented throughout it reflect PBS. It is important to understand that PBS is as much a way of thinking about behavior (e.g., behavior is the result of skill deficits, behavior serves a purpose) as it is a set of methods. Second, the extent to which all adults in the life of a child with autism rely on PBS techniques will facilitate generalization and enhance overall success for the child. Children of all abilities, but especially children with high levels of challenging behavior, do better in environments that provide support for appropriate behavior, teach expected behavior, and provide frequent and powerful reinforcement for appropriate behavior. Finally, PBS is much more effective than isolated, punitive interventions.

Behavior Intervention Plans

BIPs for children whose behavior interferes with their learning or with the learning of other children were first required under the 1997 amendments to IDEA. BIPs are only as good as the process used to develop them: They can be just another piece of paper in a child's special education folder or a useful, effective tool for preventing and managing challenging behavior. The first step in developing a BIP is to conduct an FBA and develop hypotheses based on the resulting data (see Chapter 11). One or more interventions are then designed to address each hypothesis.

A BIP should include the following components:

- target behavior(s) to reduce or eliminate, with criteria
- hypothesis (or hypotheses) for each behavior
- target replacement behaviors, or behaviors to increase, with criteria
- antecedent strategies
- new skills to be taught
- consequence strategies (consequences for reducing problem behaviors and increasing replacement behaviors)

Figure 12.1 shows an example of a BIP for Jason, whose FBA data were presented in Chapter 11. Note that this behavior intervention plan is based on the Behavior Management Analysis Chart from Chapter 11. We have simply added those components that should be part of a BIP, such as criteria. Most special education programs use their own BIP forms. Regardless of the type of form used, IEP teams should ensure that all the components we have listed are included on the form. (A sample blank BIP is provided in the appendix to this chapter.)

In the following sections we present specific strategies for each of the components that should be included in a BIP. These are not intended to be exhaustive, nor are they intended to be used as a "choice list" from which IEP teams will pick and choose for a particular student. Instead, we suggest these ideas as starters for teachers and other team members from which to develop functionally based, individualized interventions.

Regardless of the intervention techniques used, any behaviors targeted for reduction should be monitored frequently, using objective measures. We discussed data collection in Chapter 2 and explained data collection for monitoring progress in Chapter 8. In Chapter 13, we will explain specifically how to monitor behaviors targeted for reduction and will provide multiple examples of forms that can be used for this purpose.

Antecedent Strategies for Preventing Challenging Behaviors

The most effective strategy for managing challenging behaviors is to prevent their occurrence. Antecedent strategies are preventive in nature because they set the stage for desired behaviors and reduce the likelihood of inappropriate behaviors. The most important antecedent strategy is a comprehensive, appropriate educational program that relies on PBIS. The strategies listed in At-a-Glance 12.1, and the curricular and instructional recommendations from Chapters 3 through 10 may function as setting events for appropriate behaviors and for preventing challenging behaviors.

Arguably, the most critical element of the setting event strategies described in At-a-Glance 12.1 is the use of individualized communication methods. Research has overwhelmingly shown that challenging behaviors are directly connected to deficits in communication skills and that improving communication skills can reduce challenging behaviors and maintain those reductions over time (National Research

Behavior	Reasons/ Hypotheses	Criteria	Alternate Behavior	Criteria	Antecedent Interventions	New Skills to Teach	Reinforcement Strategies	Behavior Reduction Strategies
Self-hitting or biting during language or other disliked tasks	Escape language tasks; communicate dislike of language tasks	0 instances per day	Ask for a break	80% of time	• Give Jason a squeeze ball to hold during language • Timer to mark brief periods required for work • Use visual schedule to show preferred activity after language • Social story before language	• Point to "stop" or "break" card	• Allow Jason the reinforcer when he signs his response with no biting or hitting	• DRO for no biting and no hitting • If he hits or bites, gently prompt his hands to his lap and say "No biting" or "No hitting"
Self-hitting, self-biting, crying in cafeteria and public places	To avoid loud noise and activity in busy places	0 instances per day	Sign (or point to picture card) "Too loud" or "Leave, please"	80% of time	• Social story before going into hall and cafeteria • Allow him to wear headphones at first • Allow him to carry favorite toy	• Sign or point to cards to indicate "Too loud" or "Leave, please"	• Allow him to return to room if he asks correctly	• DRO for no SIB • Differential reinforcement for walking, interacting with lunch buddy
Self-stim (spinning objects, flapping hands)	Boredom	< 5 instances per day	• Use sensory toys appropriately • Ask for favorite toys	• 10 consecutive minutes per session • 4 requests per day	• Partial verbal prompt • Provide preferred toys (e.g., dreidel)	• Appropriate play with sensory toys • Ask for toys using signs or picture cards	• Provide toy when he asks appropriately	• Mild reprimand for stim

Figure 12.1. Sample behavior intervention plan. *Note.* DRO = differential reinforcement of other behaviors; SIB = self-injurious behavior.

At-a-Glance 12.1 PBS Interventions for Setting Events

Curriculum

Teach the following:

- functional communication skills and use of AAC systems when appropriate
- socialization and social awareness skills
- play or leisure skills
- work skills
- adaptive and self-help skills
- physical exercise
- appropriate alternatives for challenging behaviors

Instruction

Use the following instructional strategies:

- discrete trial teaching (DTT)
- naturalistic/milieu teaching strategies
- high levels of student engagement
- low teacher–student ratios
- unambiguous cues and instructions
- high levels of feedback for student responses

Structure

Ensure a clear and predictable environment by using:

- picture schedules
- picture communication systems that cue expected behavior
- color coding for tasks (e.g., all work materials have a red dot), individual students (e.g., all materials that Eddie needs have a green dot), or area (e.g., work area is bordered with yellow tape, and tables are covered with yellow paper; leisure area carpet is purple, and shelves are lined with purple paper)
- clearly delineated spaces (e.g., footprints on the floor to show where students are to line up; tape on the floor to designate spots where students are to sit)
- jigs for vocational tasks
- a clear schedule that is followed consistently
- clear routines (e.g., for completing tasks, using the rest room, moving from one area of the room to another)
- clear, concise instructions
- timers to signal how long a task will last
- mechanical signals (e.g., "cricket clickers") to cue students to stop an activity

Council, 2001). Communication interventions are so essential that we devoted all of Chapter 9 to strategies for teaching language and communication skills.

While setting events set the stage for certain behaviors, antecedents—especially S^Ds—cue specific behaviors. Some antecedents occur naturally as part of the environment; these often set the stage for inappropriate behavior but usually can be modified to elicit more appropriate behavior. For example, a student who screams in an attempt to avoid his or her assigned task of vacuuming because he or she doesn't like the sound of the vacuum cleaner could be allowed to wear headphones and lis-

At-a-Glance 12.2 Antecedent-Based Interventions for Increasing Desired Behaviors

Naturally Occurring Antecedents That May Trigger Undesired Behaviors	Possible Modification
Environmental antecedents	
Noisy cafeteria	Have student wear headphones to listen to preferred music or sounds during lunch; gradually reduce the use of headphones by requiring student to sit for increasingly longer periods of time before putting headphones on; have students wear soft earplugs
Crowded bus-loading area	Provide clearly marked space where student is to wait; provide picture cues of student waiting and then boarding bus; provide preferred activity for student to engage in while waiting
Schedule antecedents	
Waiting	Provide clearly marked area where student goes when waiting is required (e.g., special chair) and indicators of wait time (e.g., timer)
Disruption in schedule (e.g., fire drill, visitor)	Provide preferred object for student to hold during disruption; practice disruptions in schedule
Task antecedents	
Disliked task	Require student to work on task for a brief time; gradually increase the time required to work; follow task with preferred activity
	Modify task to make it more agreeable
	Examples: a student who dislikes getting hands wet when washing dishes could wear gloves; a student who dislikes working puzzles could work a puzzle created from a picture of a favorite stim-toy
Verbal antecedents	
Verbal directions	Give directions using another form of communication, such as sign language or pictures; use if-then format for instructions
Saying "no"	Change the way you deny a request (e.g., "Oh, you want . . . You can have it after . . . , when you . . .")

ten to music while completing the task. At-a-Glance 12.2 provides a list of antecedents that may trigger problem behavior and ideas for modifying those antecedents.

Sometimes a simple change in the antecedents of a problem behavior is all that is needed to reduce or eliminate it. For example, what appears to be noncompliance may actually be the result of vague or complicated instructions. Punishing a child for not following those directions would not help him or her learn what to do under similar circumstances in the future. Instead, the logical and most effective intervention would be for the teacher to give clearer, more concise directions. The FBA will help pinpoint contextual variables that contribute to inappropriate behavior. Focusing on these antecedents is a form of antecedent-based PBS.

Consequence Strategies for Reducing Challenging Behaviors

We will now describe ABA strategies for reducing or eliminating undesirable behavior. These strategies should be only one component of a comprehensive program that includes high levels of structure, consistently used individualized communication systems for each student, and frequent reinforcement of target replacement behaviors. Reliance on effective antecedent interventions and reinforcement interventions will lessen the need for behavior reduction methods.

The behavior reduction strategies we describe are presented in the order in which they generally should be used; that is, less intrusive and less aversive procedures, such as differential reinforcement, should be applied first. If these procedures are ineffective in reducing inappropriate behavior, more direct reduction procedures can be used (e.g., response cost, time-out). The most aversive procedures, which include aversive consequences and overcorrection, are not considered positive behavioral supports and should only be used if (a) all other strategies have not reduced target behaviors to desired levels and (b) the student's IEP team determines that such strategies are warranted. We explain how to use recommended behavior reduction interventions in the following sections. We also discuss problems associated with non-PBS interventions.

Differential Reinforcement

Differential reinforcement is a highly effective set of procedures in which reinforcement is used to reduce or eliminate target behaviors. Reinforcement is delivered (a) for behaviors that are desirable alternatives to the inappropriate behavior, (b) for periods of time during which the inappropriate behavior does not occur, or (c) when the inappropriate behavior does not exceed a specified criterion. If inappropriate behaviors continue to be exhibited despite high levels of antecedent structure and reinforcement, one or more of the three types of differential reinforcement procedures should be implemented. Focus Here 12.1 describes how to implement each differential reinforcement system.

Differential Reinforcement of Incompatible Behavior (DRI)
This strategy involves reinforcing one or more behaviors that are incompatible with the target inappropriate behavior. The student receives reinforcement for the appropriate behavior(s) (e.g., quiet mouth) and gets no reinforcement (i.e., extinction) for the inappropriate behavior (e.g., screaming). For example, the teacher might give D'John a piece of cracker and praise for each stack of papers he collates; however, when he self-stims by dangling a piece of paper in front of his eyes, the teacher might remove the paper and turn away from D'John for a brief time.

The advantage of DRI is that it expands students' repertoires of appropriate behaviors. A potential disadvantage is that the inappropriate behavior may be so self-reinforcing that it is difficult to find an equally powerful external reinforcer.

Differential Reinforcement of Communicative Behavior (DRC)
This is a specialized form of DRI and is a very good procedure to use for students with autism because of their language deficits. DRC is essentially functional communica-

Focus Here 12.1 How to Implement Differential Reinforcement Systems

Differential Reinforcement of Incompatible Behavior (DRI)

1. Select a behavior for reinforcement that is incompatible or at least a close alternative to the inappropriate behavior. According to Alberto and Troutman (2006), target replacement behaviors should meet the following guidelines:
   - is already in the student's repertoire, that is, the student should already exhibit the replacement behavior
   - reflects the function of the inappropriate behavior (the reason why the student exhibits the inappropriate behavior) as identified through functional assessment (e.g., if functional assessment indicates that the function is escape or avoidance, the replacement behavior should allow the student an appropriate way to avoid a situation or task, such as say or sign, "I don't want to")
   - should result in more frequent reinforcement than does the inappropriate behavior
2. Decide what reinforcer will be used.
3. Reinforce each time the replacement behavior occurs while giving no attention or other forms of reinforcement to the inappropriate behavior.

Differential Reinforcement of Communicative Behavior (DRC)

1. Use functional assessment to determine what the student may be attempting to communicate via the challenging behavior.
2. Teach a functional communicative alternative (using an appropriate communication system for the student, such as words, pictures, or signs). The student should be taught to use this communication alternative at a time other than when the challenging behavior is occurring; that is, you do not want to try to teach a student to sign "No" when she or he is in the middle of a tantrum or refusing to work. Teach the communicative word or phrase at a neutral time, perhaps by using contrived situations to encourage the desired response. For example, you might present to a student who dislikes cookies and then prompt the student to communicate "No." As soon as the student does this, provide praise and remove the cookie.
3. Once the communicative alternative has been taught, use naturalistic/milieu teaching techniques (see Chapter 4) to help the student use the new form of communication in real-life situations.
4. At first, every instance of appropriate communication must be reinforced. That may mean that the student is allowed to avoid disliked tasks if she or he communicates an appropriate form of refusal (e.g., signs "No") rather than displaying the inappropriate behavior.
5. Eventually, you will teach the student that even appropriate communication does not guarantee access to desired outcomes. This is a gradual process. In the case of our student who tantrums to express refusal, once she or he is consistently signing "No" to refuse, we may require her or him to engage in the target activity for 30 seconds and then allow her or him to leave. Once the student can do that, we will require a minute of engagement before stopping, and so forth. Throughout this time, we sometimes allow the student to completely avoid the activity when she or he signs "No." This form of intermittent reinforcement will help ensure maintenance of the communicative skill over time.

Differential Reinforcement of Other Behaviors (DRO)

1. Determine the frequency with which the target behavior is exhibited (i.e., count how many times the behavior occurs in a specified period of time).
2. Set a DRO interval for reinforcement that is shorter than the current rate of the inappropriate behavior. For example, according to his teacher's data, Kip screamed about every 15 minutes. She therefore set his initial DRO interval at 5 minutes. Travis, on the other hand, tried to bite his peers

about every 30 seconds during the 20-minute daily group time, so his teacher placed Travis on a 10-second initial DRO interval.

3. Monitor the specified intervals—a timer is useful for this purpose—and deliver reinforcement at the end of each interval during which the target behavior was not emitted.

4. Should the target behavior occur, reset the timer (i.e., the interval begins again). As the student is successful with ever-increasing intervals during which the target behavior does not occur, the DRO intervals should gradually be increased. For example, Kip's teacher might move from 5-minute intervals to 10 minutes, then 15, then 20, and then 30, until Kip is able to go an entire day, or whatever length of time is considered appropriate, with no instances of the target behavior. Depending on the behavior and the student, you might also use a consequence, such as a mild reprimand or time-out, before resetting the timer. If Kip screams, for example, you might say, "No screaming, Kip. No juice until you work quietly."

Differential Reinforcement of Lower Levels of Behavior (DRL)

1. Determine baseline levels of the target behavior.

2. Set the initial level allowed for reinforcement. This might be an average of baseline data or just slightly below the highest baseline point. The point is you want to set a criterion level that ensures that the student will be successful.

3. Count each instance of the behavior during a specified time (e.g., teaching session, lunch).

4. At the end of the session, reinforce the student if the total number of behaviors is equal to or below the predetermined criterion.

5. After 3 days of meeting that criterion, lower it slightly.

6. Continue until your goal for the behavior has been attained: The behavior either is not occurring—it has been reduced to zero levels—or is occurring at manageably low levels.

tion training as described in Chapter 11. Because this procedure differentially reinforces students for appropriate communicative behavior, it may be the procedure of choice if a functional assessment indicates that the student's inappropriate behavior is for the purpose of communication. A student who is self-injuring to communicate refusal, for example, may be reinforced for signing "No" or for using whatever form of communication is appropriate for that student. Signing "No" would result in immediate reinforcement—the disliked task would be removed—whereas self-biting would produce no reinforcement, and the teacher would redirect the student to sign "No." Eventually the student would gradually be taught to continue working for longer periods of time even when he or she appropriately communicates "No."

When using DRC (or any intervention), it is important to use a reinforcer that reflects the function of the challenging behavior. For example, if FBA data suggest that the challenging behavior is used to obtain sensory reinforcement, the student should be taught a way to ask (e.g., using picture cards, sign language, or an augmentative communication device) for that sensory reinforcement. When the student uses an appropriate mand, he or she is given the reinforcer (e.g., a sensory toy). Likewise, if FBA data indicate that the function of the challenging behavior is to obtain a favorite food or drink, when the student uses an appropriate mand, he or she should immediately receive the requested food or drink.

During the early stages of implementation of any intervention, including establishing new communicative behaviors through DRC, the student should be reinforced each time the desired behavior occurs (i.e., continuous schedule of reinforcement). As the student becomes more fluent in the communicative behavior, the reinforcement schedule should be thinned to a planned intermittent schedule. Eventually, the goal should be for naturally occurring reinforcement to maintain the behavior. That is, at times the child uses an appropriate mand and receives the reinforcer, but at other times he or she mands but does not get the reinforcer, perhaps because it is not a good time or place to engage in the reinforcing activity, because the reinforcer is not available, or because the student must first complete certain tasks.

Some professionals have theorized that most challenging behaviors in students with autism are communicative in nature. For this reason, all challenging behavior should be assessed for communicative intent. If you determine that a student is using challenging behavior to communicate, you should teach a functional communicative alternative and reinforce it by using DRC. Because the student's needs are now being met when he or she uses appropriate communication, challenging behaviors that he or she previously used to meet those needs should lessen in number or disappear. This makes DRC one of the most effective behavior reduction strategies available to teachers of students with autism.

Differential Reinforcement of Other Behaviors (DRO)

In this procedure, also known as *differential reinforcement of zero rates of behavior,* a student is reinforced for increasingly longer periods of time during which the target inappropriate behavior is not exhibited. For example, a student might be given a small sip of juice every 5 minutes (or more or less, depending upon the student) during which she or he does not bite her- or himself. A potential problem with DRO is that the student receives reinforcement contingent only upon the nonoccurrence of the target inappropriate behavior, regardless of any other behaviors the student exhibits during that time. So, the student is reinforced for not biting his or her hand during a 5-minute period, even if the student screams or engages in self-stimulatory behavior during that time. Another potential problem with DRO is that it does not teach a student more appropriate replacement behaviors or more appropriate ways of getting his or her needs met. If an inappropriate behavior is functioning as a way to get a need met for a student, eliminating that behavior may result in exhibition of another inappropriate behavior that serves the same purpose. DRO may be an appropriate intervention for a behavior that is dangerous, extremely destructive, or disruptive or for one that occurs at such a high frequency that it is difficult to redirect the child to other tasks.

Differential Reinforcement of Lower Levels of Behavior (DRL)

This remaining differential reinforcement system allows for gradual reduction of undesired behaviors. Students are reinforced when the number or duration of target inappropriate behaviors is less than a predetermined criterion. DRL is an effective strategy to use with behaviors that are not dangerous or highly disruptive. To illustrate DRL, we will use the example of Sheila, who persistently asks about snack or lunch ("Can I have snack?" "I want lunch," etc.) even when she is not hungry. Sheila's teacher, Mr. Preston, uses nonrestricted event recording to count the number of times Sheila asks about snack or lunch between 8:30 A.M. and 11:30 A.M. On Monday, she asks 57 times; on Tuesday, she asks 48 times; and on Wednesday, she asks 64 times. Mr. Preston implements DRL to reduce Sheila's asking behavior to no more than 3 questions per morning. Initially, given her baseline average of 56, he determines that she can ask 55 questions and still earn her reinforcer (ice cream). If she asks more than 55 questions between 8:30 and 11:30, she will not receive any ice cream. He uses a hand-held digital counter to keep track of the number of questions about snack or lunch that Sheila asks. Sheila meets her criterion on the second day of intervention. After 3 consecutive days of meeting the criterion, Mr. Preston lowers the number of questions allowed to 45. Once Sheila is successful at this level for 3 consecutive days, Mr. Preston lowers the criterion to 35 questions. This process continues until Sheila is asking no more than 3 questions per morning.

Differential reinforcement interventions are an effective way to reduce challenging behaviors. DRI and DRC are particularly advantageous as interventions because they teach the student a replacement behavior while simultaneously reducing the challenging behavior. However, other behavior reduction interventions may be needed, particularly for severe challenging behaviors. These other techniques, described in the following sections, must be used in conjunction with reinforcement of desired behaviors, perhaps by using them combined with one or more differential reinforcement interventions.

Extinction

Extinction reduces behavior by withholding the maintaining reinforcer (usually attention) for that behavior. Because children with autism typically are not reinforced by attention, extinction may not be an appropriate behavior reduction strategy for these students, and it should be used cautiously. Not attending to the student will only be effective if the maintaining reinforcer for the target behavior is the teacher's attention. For example, if the student's inappropriate behavior is for the purpose of getting the teacher's attention, extinction may be an effective intervention.

More often, extinction is used for students with autism when the reinforcer is obtaining stimulatory input. This is called *sensory extinction* and includes techniques such as those listed in At-a-Glance 12.3.

To implement extinction, you should operationally define both the target behavior to be placed on extinction and the maintaining reinforcer. When the behavior occurs, you should not allow this reinforcer to occur. At the same time, however, you should allow for that reinforcer (or a similar substitute) for alternative replacement behaviors.

Extinction typically reduces behavior more slowly than other procedures. In addition, a behavior that is put on extinction will often get worse before it gets better because the child initially tries harder to get the reinforcer. For example, if a teacher uses extinction for inappropriate giggling that has been maintained by attention, the student may escalate to other, more serious behaviors (e.g., screaming, self-abuse) to try to get the teacher's attention. The following are two good guidelines for using extinction:

1. It should not be used with self-abusive or aggressive students.
2. It should always be used in conjunction with one or more differential reinforcement techniques.

The following techniques are based on the assumption that a negative consequence occurs that is contingent upon inappropriate behavior. These techniques may produce certain side effects of which you need to be aware, including aggression or self-injurious behavior, tantrums, and escalation of the inappropriate behavior. For this reason, these techniques should be used sparingly and only when other methods have proven ineffective in reducing or eliminating the challenging behavior. In addition, these techniques must never be used in isolation. Always use them in conjunction with reinforcement of appropriate, functional replacement behaviors.

Response Cost

This procedure involves removing previously acquired reinforcers contingent upon target inappropriate behaviors. Each of us has experienced response cost: paying

Stereotypic Behaviors That Produce Auditory Stimulation

- Making noises with mouth or tongue — Have student listen to music or other sounds through headphones or earbuds
- Spinning objects — Cover hard surfaces (e.g., desks or tables where student sits) with a rubber material (such as a pad that is used to keep rugs from slipping), carpet, or cloth

Stereotypic Behaviors That Produce Gustatory (Taste) Stimulation[a]

- Tasting, chewing, or licking — Mask the taste of target objects with a flavor that student dislikes (e.g., if student puts work materials in his mouth, sprinkle flavor extracts, lemon juice, or other disliked flavors on each material student uses)
- Chewing or sucking on fingers — Have student wear mittens or latex gloves

Stereotypic Behaviors That Produce Olfactory (Smell) Stimulation

- Sniffing objects — Have student carry a handkerchief scented with a favorite scent; mask the scent of those objects that the student is most likely to sniff by sprinkling them with something in a scent student does not like (e.g., cologne, flavor extracts, vinegar)

Stereotypic Behaviors That Produce Proprioceptive Stimulation

- Rocking — Have student wear a weighted vest
- Flapping hands or arms — Have student wear light wrist weights
- Flicking fingers — Have student wear gloves or mittens
- Bouncing on toes — Have student wear ankle weights

Stereotypic Behaviors That Produce Tactile Stimulation

- Touching objects — Have student wear gloves or mittens
- Hitting self with hand — Have student wear soft, padded gloves
- Hitting head against objects — Have student wear padded helmet; cover target objects with foam padding, plush material, or other soft material

Stereotypic Behaviors That Produce Visual Stimulation

- Flicking fingers — Have student wear mittens; turn off lights in the room or draw the blinds
- Turning light off and on — Disconnect the light switch

---

[a]An interesting application of sensory extinction for gustatory self-stimulatory behavior was reported by Rincover (1981). The target student swallowed and regurgitated his food, then ate it. Rincover speculated that this was because he liked the flavor. To mask (or more accurately, interfere with) the flavor of regurgitated food, treatment consisted of adding lima beans, a food the student disliked, to the regurgitated food. The student attempted to eat the regurgitated food despite the lima beans, but spit it out each time, eventually giving up.

a fine for speeding or late library books, having to work through lunch to finish paperwork that should have been completed earlier, or losing recess as a result of misbehavior in the classroom. Examples of response cost include removing tokens (if you are using a token system for appropriate behaviors), removing all or part of an activity reinforcer (e.g., the student loses 1 minute of access to favorite music for each instance of self-abuse), or removing a material reinforcer (e.g., the student's favorite toy is removed for 1 minute each time he or she engages in self-stimulatory behavior while playing with it).

Like tokens, response cost is somewhat abstract in nature. For this reason, it may not be the reductive procedure of choice for very young children or children with low cognitive levels. If you choose to use response cost, be sure that removal of the token, material, or activity occurs in close proximity to the inappropriate behavior. You should also briefly explain the reason for the removal. For example, Brandon earns a plastic chip for each set of papers he collates correctly. At the end of the task, Brandon may exchange chips for access to headphones to listen to his favorite music. If Brandon interrupts his work to self-stim, or self-stims while listening to music, his teacher says, "No stim, Brandon!" and removes a chip or turns off the music for 30 seconds. Focus Here 12.2 lists steps for using response cost.

A caution is needed here. Because many children with autism like only a few things in life, we want to be careful not to take these few things away from them. They already withdraw. We want them to *want* to be with us and in the world, and the few external stimuli they like may be the only things connecting them with the external environment.

Time-Out

Time-out means the student is denied access to reinforcement for a specific period of time. During the time-out period, the student is given no attention and should not have access to any toys, activities, or other students. There should be a clear distinction between time-in and time-out: Students should want to be in the time-in situation, but not in time-out. Ironically, most children with autism *prefer to be left alone,* so exclusionary and seclusionary time-outs should be used with caution, and the effects should be monitored closely. However, as Itard illustrated with the boy, Victor (Lane, 1976), time-out can be used effectively for students with autism.

Time-out has a number of different forms. The less exclusionary forms are easy to use and have widespread acceptability (Kazdin, 1980a, 1980b). At-a-Glance 12.4 lists forms of time-out described by Scheuermann and Webber (2002). You should always try the least exclusionary forms first and only move to more exclusionary forms if the student's IEP team determines it is necessary.

If it is decided that time-out is the appropriate behavior reduction procedure, following a few easy guidelines—listed in Focus Here 12.3—will help ensure effectiveness. Always remember that for students with autism, for whom social interaction is not typically appealing, time-out may actually serve as a reinforcer rather than a punisher. Be sure to monitor the effects of any behavior reduction intervention.

Aversives

Aversives refer to anything the child dislikes that is presented as a consequence for inappropriate behavior. The only aversive we advocate that teachers use is a brief, stern reprimand. Too often, we see educators who want to try aversives for severely challenging behavior without first using more positive approaches to reduce that behavior.

For students with autism, a stern reprimand can be an effective way to gain the child's attention when he or she is engaging in inappropriate behavior. You should give a reprimand from no more than 3 feet away from the student, using a loud voice (not yelling) and few words. For example, Keneisha engages in a particularly intense

Focus Here 12.2 How to Use Response Cost

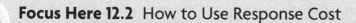

1. Use operational terms to clearly define the behavior(s) that will be targeted with response cost.

2. Identify what the student will lose contingent upon the inappropriate behavior(s) (e.g., tokens, minutes of free time, loss of an object). If the student is on a simple token system, he might lose a token for each instance of the target inappropriate behavior. For example, Kayla engages in a particularly distasteful self-stimulatory behavior: she plays with her saliva. Kayla's teacher is using a combination of interventions to eliminate this behavior: DRO and response cost. Kayla's teacher sets the timer for 2-minute intervals. At the end of 2 minutes, if Kayla has not touched her saliva, the teacher places a Goldfish® in a six-section egg carton. When all six sections contain a cracker, Kayla may eat the crackers. However, if she touches her saliva during the interval, the teacher responds with a firm, "No spit!" as she moves Kayla's hand away from her mouth and removes a cracker from a section of the egg carton.

    A student who is not using a token system might lose a small amount of reinforcement time. For example, Jacob's teacher uses a timer in which the time remaining is shown as a colored section. This timer indicates how much reinforcement time Jacob earns during work time; for each task that Jacob completes, he earns 2 minutes of reinforcement time (the teacher adds 2 minutes onto the timer after each completed task). However, if Jacob hits or bites himself, the teacher takes away 1 minute of reinforcement time by moving the timer display backward by one minute. At the end of work time, Jacob earns reinforcement time for as many minutes as are indicated on the timer.

    Of course, because of the abstract nature of response cost, the forms of response cost described previously may be inappropriate for many students with autism, especially those who have forms of low-functioning autism. A more concrete form of response cost may be effective for these students. For example, Todd, a student with LFA, engages in mild forms of noncompliance: he cries briefly and puts his hand in his mouth when asked to do disliked activities such as transitions or doing his daily grooming activities. When giving him a direction to move from one activity to the next or to comb his hair, brush his teeth, or other grooming activities, his teacher shows him his picture schedule that has an "if-then" card next to each activity. If Todd completes the activity with no crying, then he gets a few minutes with his favorite stim-toy (a small piece of an old blanket). However, if Todd cries, the teacher shows him the "if-then" card and removes the picture of the blanket as she says, "No crying, Todd," and then turns away for a few seconds. When she turns back, if Todd has stopped crying, she puts the blanket picture back on the card and says, "Good, Todd! If you comb hair, then you get blanket!"

    If you are unable to devise a concrete form of response cost, or if your students do not even understand the concrete form, you may need to use a different technique.

3. Determine how many tokens or minutes of reinforcement time will be removed contingent upon the target inappropriate behavior. It is very important not to over-punish the behavior by removing too much of the reinforcer. Even a few seconds of lost reinforcement time may be sufficient.

4. If you use response cost, ensure that you provide a way for the student to earn back lost reinforcement time, tokens, or desired items. Remember, we always want to maintain strong motivation for our students to respond appropriately to the stimuli we provide. If a student loses all of his reinforcement time and there is no provision for him to easily or quickly earn this back, his motivation to respond will probably disappear. It will be more appealing to engage in self-stimulatory behavior (or other inappropriate behaviors) since he no longer has anything to gain by controlling that behavior.

5. Design a clear, visible method of communicating to the student how the system works, and let the student know when the response cost intervention is applied. Utilize one of the forms of visual structure that were described in Chapter 5.

6. Implement the system. When the target behavior occurs, use a mild reprimand (e.g., "No") and tell the student what the consequence is. For example, "No hitting. I take the squishy ball."

7. Monitor the effects of the response cost system. If the target behavior does not improve (i.e., occur less frequently, for shorter durations, or with less intensity), either modify the response cost intervention (e.g., increase the "fine" for the misbehavior), add a stronger reinforcer for a desired alternative behavior, or use another behavior reductive intervention instead of response cost.

form of self-injurious behavior. When she does this, her teacher quickly moves close to her, firmly says "Keneisha! No hitting!" and physically prompts Keneisha's hands back to the task. In addition, the teacher systematically reinforces incompatible behaviors, such as working on her assigned task without SIB.

At-a-Glance 12.4 Types of Time-Out

- **Signal**—ribbon on wrist or red card on desk that indicates reinforcers are not forthcoming
- **Visual Screen**—briefly (1–2 seconds) cover student's eyes to mask visual input
- **Head Down**—head down on desk for a brief time
- **Removal**—remove materials or toys for a period of time
- **Teacher Turnaway**—the person working with the student turns away from the student for a brief time, contingent upon target inappropriate behavior
- **Contingent Observation**—the student's chair is pushed slightly away from the group or activity
- **Time-Out Chair**—the student sits in a specially designated "time-out" chair in a particular place
- **Time-Out Square**—the student sits inside a square (approximately 2 ft × 2 ft) space on the floor that has been outlined using masking or brightly colored tape
- **Time-Out Rug**—the student sits on a small rug or carpet samples (especially flexible in that rug or carpet can be taken on field trips or used in other parts of the school or playground)
- **Screen**—the student sits behind a screen or partition
- **Time-Out Room**—the student is placed in an empty room that is used only for time-out (easily misused); to avoid misuse, Gast and Nelson (1977) suggested the following guidelines:
    1. The room should be at least 6 ft × 6 ft in size.
    2. The room should have proper ventilation and lighting (preferably recessed, with the switch outside the room).
    3. The room should have no objects or fixtures with which students could harm themselves.
    4. There should be a way for teachers or staff members to monitor a student both visually and auditorily.
    5. The room should not be locked.

You should also obtain parents' permission before using a time-out room. Also, we do not recommend the use of time-out rooms for children and youth with autism, especially if they have low cognition. Less exclusionary forms of time-out—combined with other behavioral procedures—should enable teachers to effectively manage behavioral excesses. Be aware that exclusion may actually act as a reinforcer for a child with autism.

Note. From *Autism: Teaching DOES Make a Difference* (p. 56), by B. Scheuermann and J. Webber, 2002, Belmont, CA: Wadsworth. Copyright 2002 by Wadsworth Group. Adapted with permission.

Focus Here 12.3 How to Use Time-Out

1. Use operational terms to clearly identify the target inappropriate behavior(s) that will be targeted with time-out.

2. Use the simplest, least exclusionary forms of time-out. Remember that time-out must be easily implemented or it will not be used.

3. Use brief time-outs. Even the old adage of 1 minute per year of age is probably too long for most students. The distinction between time-in and time-out—not the length—determines the effectiveness of time-out: Even a 30-second time-out can be effective. As a test before using exclusionary or seclusionary time-out with a student, whoever is planning the procedure should sit in the designated time-out spot for the designated length of time. If it feels too long (e.g., you get bored, restless, impatient), it is probably too long for students.

4. When the misbehavior occurs, say only, "That's (describe the behavior). Time-out," and direct the student to the designated time-out place. This must be done every time the behavior occurs.

5. Ignore inappropriate behavior (e.g., screaming, crying) during the time-out. When the time-out is over, simply say "Time-out is over. Back to (activity)," and direct the student back to the activity that he or she was doing prior to the time-out. Under no circumstances should the child be allowed to escape a required activity because of misbehavior and the resulting time-out.

We caution against the use of aversives for three reasons. First, sometimes what we think is aversive is actually a reinforcer for students with autism; that is, they may like what we consider to be aversive. An example would be using physical restraint as a reductive procedure, because some students may like the deep muscle pressure they experience during restraint. Second, there are a wide range of nonaversive (i.e., positive, supportive) strategies that are highly effective at increasing desired behaviors and reducing challenging behaviors. We have described these strategies throughout this book. Finally, some aversives pose risk to the student or teacher (i.e., physical restraint). This reason alone should be sufficient to ensure that you rely on other types of interventions.

Overcorrection

Overcorrection involves one of two procedures designed to (a) reduce the target inappropriate behavior and (b) establish appropriate behaviors (Maag, 1999). In each form, if the student misbehaves, he or she is required to engage in an appropriate behavior multiple times. *Positive practice overcorrection* means that contingent upon the target inappropriate behavior, the student is required to repeatedly exhibit an appropriate alternative behavior related to the behavioral infraction. For example, when Billy hits someone, he is required to shake hands with 15 different people. In *restitutional overcorrection,* the student is required to fix damage resulting from misbehavior. For example, if Toni spits, she must get a sponge, wet it, and wipe off all surfaces in the area where she spat.

According to Scheuermann and Webber (2002), overcorrection should be used judiciously, for several reasons. First, the appropriate behavior must be practiced under close adult supervision, even necessitating manual guidance if the student will not perform the behavior independently. Because of this, the student receives high levels of attention. While not typically a maintaining function for the behaviors of students with autism, attention that results from overcorrection may be a source of reinforcement for an inappropriate behavior.

Second, overcorrection procedures have the potential for being very time-consuming for both the staff person and the student. Time spent in overcorrection is time away from instruction unless the positive practice behavior is one that needs instruction and practice. This should be a consideration when deciding whether to use overcorrection. Finally, overcorrection sometimes results in escalation of the student's inappropriate behavior: The student may resist or refuse, go limp during manual guidance, and so forth. Teachers should anticipate this possibility and determine whether the manual guidance needed to complete the procedure under these circumstances will be reinforcing to the student.

Overcorrection can effectively reduce challenging behavior, but it should only be used after other, less-intrusive interventions have failed. Overcorrection should also always be used in conjunction with instruction in and reinforcement of desired behaviors, particularly replacement behaviors.

Other Interventions for Reducing Challenging Behaviors

Advances in medical and pharmaceutical research have resulted in beneficial medications that treat some of the behaviors associated with autism. A thorough discussion of the medications used for these purposes is beyond the scope of this text. However, if you have a student who takes any medications, you should research them, especially as it relates to what they are used for; administration instructions, even if you do not administer the medication; and potential side effects. You should also be aware of interactions among medications and interactions between medications and diet. Drug and/or dietary interactions may actually cause problem behavior. If you have conducted a thorough, systematic FBA and find that problem behaviors occur across settings, under many conditions, and with no clear function, you might want to look at medication effects and advise parents to check with the child's doctor. Check with your school nurse, the child's parents, a pharmacist, or other sources that we have listed in Resources 12.1.

Summary

For inexperienced or undertrained teachers, the challenging behaviors displayed by children with autism can be frightening and distressing. Furthermore, these behaviors have the potential to seriously limit the child's opportunities for typical living and learning conditions. Fortunately, reducing those behaviors is a manageable task, provided that you use the methods described in this chapter. Most important in the prevention of challenging behaviors is to create clear, predictable, and consistent environments and to teach effective communication and socialization strategies. If additional strategies are needed, the antecedent modification techniques and behavior reduction strategies described in this chapter in all likelihood will effectively address the problem. All of these strategies, with the exception of aversives and overcorrection, fall under the umbrella term of *positive behavioral supports* and would meet IDEA requirements regarding use of PBS.

Of course, like any tools, these strategies must be used correctly and consistently to achieve the desired outcomes. Some of the behavior reduction techniques, par-

Resources 12.1 Sources for Information About Medication

Books

Brown, R. T., & Sawyer, M. G. (1998). *Medications for School Age Children.* New York: Guilford Press.

Tsai, L. (2001). *Taking the Mystery Out of Medications in Autism/Asperger's Syndromes.* Arlington, TX: Future Horizons.

Online Articles

Autism spectrum disorders. (2007, Feb.). Available at www.nimh.nih.gov/publicat/autism.cfm

Grandin, T. *Evaluating the Effects of Medication.* Available at http://www.autism.org/temple/meds.html

Sweeney, D. (2003). *An Update on Psychopharmacologic Medication: What Teachers, Clinicians, and Parents Need to Know.* Available at http://www.ldonline.org/article15700

Waltz, M. (2002). *Autism Spectrum Disorders: Finding a Diagnosis and Getting Help* (Appendix E). Available at http://www. oreilly.com

Journal Articles

Forness, S., Walker, H., & Kavale, K. (2003). Psychiatric disorders and treatments: A primer for teachers. *Teaching Exceptional Children, 36*(2).

Forness, S. R., Sweeney, D. P., & Toy, K. (1996). Psychopharmacologic medication: What teachers need to know. *Beyond Behavior, 7*(2), 4–11.

Sweeney, D. P., Forness, S. R., Kavale, K. A., & Levitt, J. G. (1997). An update on psychopharmacologic medication: What teachers, clinicians and parents need to know. *Intervention in School and Clinic, 33*(1), 4–21, 25.

Web Sites

National Institutes of Health Medline Plus (http://www.nlm.nih.gov/medlineplus/druginformation.html)

Healthy Place (http://www.healthyplace.com/medications/index.asp)

PsyWeb Mental Health Site (http://www.psyweb.com/Drughtm/jsp/menus/psydrugs.jsp)

Autism Center: Medication (http://www.patientcenters.com/autism/news/med_reference.html)

AutismLink (http://www.autismlink.com/pages/autism_medications/)

---

ticularly time-out and overcorrection, have great potential for misuse. In addition, students with autism tend to have different, idiosyncratic responses to techniques than do other students. Be sure you apply all of these techniques correctly and that you monitor the effects of any intervention on the target behavior. If the behavior does not change in the desired direction in a very short period of time, either the intervention is not being used correctly or a different intervention is needed. For maximum results, use these techniques judiciously as part of a comprehensive educational program.

References

Alberto, P., & Troutman, A. (2006). *Applied behavior analysis for teachers* (7th ed.). Englewood Cliffs, NJ: Merrill/Prentice Hall.

Anderson, J. L., Albin, R. W., Mesaros, R. A., Dunlap, G., & Morelli-Robbins, M. (1993). Issues in providing training to achieve comprehensive behavioral support. In J. Reichle & D. P. Wacher (Eds.), *Communicative alternatives to challenging behaviors* (pp. 262–406). Baltimore: Brookes.

Gast, D., & Nelson, C. M. (1977). Time out in the classroom: Implications for special education. *Exceptional Children, 43,* 461–464.

Kazdin, A. E. (1980a). Acceptability of alternative treatments for deviant child behavior. *Journal of Applied Behavior Analysis, 13,* 259–273.

Kazdin, A. E. (1980b). Acceptability of time out from positive reinforcement procedures for disruptive child behavior. *Behavior Therapy, 11,* 329–344.

Lane, H. (1976). *The wild boy of Aveyron.* Cambridge, MA: Harvard University Press.

Maag, J. W. (1999). *Behavior management.* San Diego, CA: Singular.

National Research Council, Division of Behavioral and Social Sciences and Education, Committee on Educational Interventions for Children with Autism. (2001). *Educating children with autism* (C. Lord & J. P. McGee, Eds.). Washington, DC: National Academy Press.

Rincover, A. (1981). *How to use sensory extinction.* Austin, TX: PRO-ED.

Scheuermann, B., & Webber, J. (2002). *Autism: Teaching DOES make a difference.* Belmont, CA: Wadsworth.

Appendix:

Behavior Intervention Plan (BIP)

Name: _____

Date: _____

Behavior	Reasons/ Hypotheses	Criteria	Alternate Behavior	Criteria	Antecedent Interventions	New Skills to Teach	Reinforcement Strategies	Behavior Reduction Strategies

Note. From "Managing Difficult Student Behaviors," by J. Webber and L. Wheeler, 1995, San Marcos, TX: Center for Initiative in Education, Southwest Texas State University. Adapted with permission.

Collecting Data for Monitoring Behaviors Targeted for Reduction

Children and youth with autism characteristically exhibit one or more challenging behaviors, including self-injurious behaviors, self-stimulatory behaviors, noncompliance, and aggression. These behaviors—perhaps more than any other characteristic excesses or deficits—are most likely to interfere with the student's success and must be addressed efficiently and effectively. Teachers must know whether interventions being used to reduce challenging behaviors are in fact producing sufficient reductions in those behaviors; however, the nature of these behaviors makes it difficult to determine through informal observation alone whether interventions are working. Precise, objective data are needed to accurately determine whether a targeted behavior is improving or is improving quickly enough to warrant continued use of the intervention.

As we noted in Chapter 2, behavior is measured using either permanent product recording or observational recording. The nature of challenging behaviors usually means that observational recording should be used. Observational recording systems include event recording, to count discrete behaviors, and duration recording, to measure how long a behavior occurs. Once you have determined which measurement system is appropriate for the target behavior, you will need a form on which to record raw data. In this chapter, we provide many examples of data collection forms that are appropriate for recording raw data gathered on behaviors targeted for reduction. The next step in the monitoring process is to determine whether your raw data need to be converted to a rate or a percentage. Finally, either raw data or converted data should be graphed to allow for easy visual inspection. (We discussed data conversion and graphing procedures in Chapter 2.) Graphs are essential for monitoring behaviors targeted for reduction because they quickly reveal that behavior is not reducing or weakening or that it is not changing in a timely fashion. If either of these is the case, the intervention should be reevaluated and modified or changed, if necessary. Graphs also allow for easy communication about target behaviors among team members.

Forms for Event Recording

Event recording is the appropriate measurement system for behaviors that have a discrete start and end, for behaviors that do not occur over long periods, and for behaviors that do not occur so rapidly that it is impossible to count each instance of the behavior. Restricted event recording is used for event-type behaviors that only occur in response to a discriminative stimulus. For example, Zach throws items when given a direction to do a task he dislikes. Will does not initiate after being given a directive. Amalia usually tries to bite or pinch peers who walk or sit within arm's length of her. Figures 13.1 through 13.3 show examples of restricted event recording

Instructions: Note each occurrence of the specified stimulus and each occurrence of the target behavior. Calculate the percentage of occurrences (number of occurrences of the target behavior divided by the total occurrences of the stimulus × 100).

STUDENT: _Zach_

TARGET BEHAVIOR: _Throwing items when asked to complete a task (e.g., throwing puzzle pieces, spoons, toothbrush)_

OBSERVATION PERIOD: _9:30–9:45 (Play Time)_

Date	Stimulus	Target Behavior	Calculation	Percentage
	Items Given (e.g., puzzle piece to place in puzzle, Magnetix or Lego to attach, Mr. Potato Head part to affix)	Instances of Throwing (any instance of item tossed out of hand and not used as directed)		of Items Thrown
2/12	~~HHH~~ ~~HHH~~ ~~HHH~~	~~HHH~~ ///	$\frac{8}{15} \times 100$	53
2/13	~~HHH~~ ~~HHH~~ ~~HHH~~ //	~~HHH~~ ~~HHH~~	$\frac{10}{17} \times 100$	58
2/14	~~HHH~~ ~~HHH~~ //	~~HHH~~ ////	$\frac{9}{12} \times 100$	75

Figure 13.1. Restricted event recording sample form (with calculations).

forms used with these three students. Blank versions of these forms are provided in the chapter appendix. Note that for restricted events, you must count both the stimulus and the behavior. Pay particular attention to Figure 13.3. The form used in this figure allows for collection of multiple behaviors, in this case, multiple related behaviors. This format may be useful if a student exhibits several behaviors that need to be monitored. We will provide other examples of forms that can be used to measure multiple behaviors or behaviors in more than one student throughout the chapter.

Behaviors that can occur at any time (i.e., do not occur in response to a discriminative stimulus) are called unrestricted events. These behaviors are counted by simply recording each time the behavior occurs during the observation period. Figures 13.4 through 13.6 offer examples of data collection forms that can be used for unrestricted event behaviors. Note that Figure 13.6 is a data collection form that allows the user to simultaneously chart and graph data. In addition, Figure 13.7 is an example of a form for measuring more than one unrestricted event behavior during each observation session. This form also allows for counting behaviors during multiple activities during the day.

While many teachers like to use a form to monitor unrestricted event behaviors, another option is to count these behaviors using a hand-held digital counter. We find these devices to be extremely useful during teaching. A hand-held counter allows you to effortlessly count target behaviors while attending to students. In addition, you do not need to keep track of pencils and data-recording forms. The hand-held counter can be kept in your hand, hung on a lanyard around your neck, or clipped to your belt or a clipboard. Hand-held counters are inexpensive, so you might wish to

Instructions: Place a check mark for each occurrence of the stimulus and a boxed check mark for each occurrence of the behavior.

STUDENT: Will

TARGET BEHAVIOR: Noncompliance (not initiating following a direction within 15 seconds of direction)

OBSERVATION PERIOD: 1:30–2:30 (afternoon workstations)

✓ = direction given

☑ = compliance not initiated within 15 seconds

Date	Behaviors							Percentage
								of noncompliant responses
4-8	✓ ✓	☑	☑	☑ ✓	✓ ✓	☑	✓ ✓	$\frac{4}{11} = 36\%$
4-9	✓ ✓	✓ ✓	☑ ✓	☑ ✓	☑ ✓	☑ ✓	☑	$\frac{5}{13} = 39\%$
4-10	☑ ✓	✓ ✓	☑ ✓	☑ ✓	☑ ✓	☑	☑ ✓	$\frac{6}{13} = 46\%$
4-11	☑ ✓	☑ ✓	☑ ☑	☑ ✓	☑ ✓	☑	☑	$\frac{8}{12} = 67\%$
4-12	Absent							

Figure 13.2. Restricted event recording sample form (with calculations).

keep one or more counters in each teaching location in the room and provide each teaching adult with a counter. (These counters may be purchased online through Amazon.com [use the search term *tally counters*]).

Forms for Duration Recording

Duration recording measures how long a behavior occurs. Duration recording forms are simple: They require only notations of start and stop times for the target behavior. Total duration is then noted in minutes and/or seconds. Examples of duration recording forms are shown in Figures 13.8 and 13.9. (Figure 13.9 is another example of a combined data collection and graphing form.)

Another option for measuring the duration of behaviors is to simply use a stopwatch. Start the watch when the behavior begins and stop it when the behavior ends. Most stopwatches allow for cumulative time recording. Thus, you could measure each instance of the target behavior with the stopwatch but simply record (and graph) the cumulative total number of minutes and/or seconds for each observation

Instructions: Determine a code for each target behavior being monitored (up to four behaviors). Record these codes in the shaded boxes. Begin recording on the next line. Note the date, then place a check each time the stimulus occurs. Place a check mark or tally mark in the column corresponding with the target behavior. After the observation period ends, calculate the percentage for each behavior (number of occurrences of the behavior divided by the total number of stimuli × 100) and record the percentage in columns.

STUDENT: Amalia

TARGET BEHAVIOR: Pinching or biting peers, or attempting to pinch or bite peers who sit, play, or walk within 2 feet of Amalia

OBSERVATION PERIOD: 10:30–10:50 (transition from snack to play area, leisure time)

Date	Stimulus: ✓ = peer walks, sits, or stands within 2 feet of Amalia	Student responses: Amalia's Response P = pinched B = bit AP = Attempted to pinch AB = Attempted to bite				Percentage of occurrences for each response pinches, bites, pinching attempts, and biting attempts			
Codes for Student Responses:		(1) P	(2) B	(3) AP	(4) AB	(1) P	(2) B	(3) AP	(4) AB
Monday, 3/10	✓✓✓✓✓✓✓	//			///	25%	0%	0%	37.5%
Tuesday, 3/11	✓✓✓✓✓	/		//		20%	0%	40%	0%
Wednesday, 3/12	✓✓✓✓✓✓✓✓✓	/		///	////	11%	0%	33%	44%
Thursday, 3/13	✓✓✓✓✓✓	/		//	/	17%	0%	33%	17%
Friday, 3/14	✓✓✓✓✓✓✓		/	////	///	0%	14%	51%	43%

Figure 13.3. Multiple restricted event recording sample form.

period. Figure 13.10 is a recording form for noting total number of minutes and/or seconds accumulated during an observation period. Of course, if you are monitoring cumulative time, it is not necessary to use this form. Instead, you could simply graph the total number of minutes and/or seconds at the end of each recording period.

Forms for Recording Multiple Behaviors or Monitoring Behaviors in Multiple Students

Classrooms are busy environments, and teachers—especially teachers of students with autism—have many demands on their time and attention. Data collection therefore

Instructions: Note each activity occurring during the data collection periods and the time in minutes/seconds of the data collection period. Place a check mark in the "Occurrences" column each time the target behavior occurs. Calculate the rate by dividing the total number of occurrences by the total number of minutes and/or seconds of the data collection period.

STUDENT: _Carson_

TARGET BEHAVIOR: _Hitting head with open palm_

DATA-COLLECTION PERIOD: _morning centers, lunch, afternoon work session_

✓ = Target Behavior			
Activity	Time	Occurrences	Rate (occurrences/units of time)
Wednesday morning centers	8:00–8:17	✓✓✓✓✓✓✓✓✓✓✓✓✓✓✓✓	.94 hits per minute
Monday lunch	11:30–11:55	✓✓✓✓✓✓✓	.28 hits per minute
Monday afternoon work session	1:45–2:05	✓✓✓✓✓✓✓✓✓✓✓✓✓✓✓✓ ✓✓	1.8 hits per minute

Figure 13.4. Unrestricted event recording sample form (rate of occurrences).

Instructions: Note the date and the time of each data collection session. In the "Notations of Occurrences" column, place a check mark or tally mark each time the target behavior occurs. Enter the total number of occurrences in the "Total Occurrences" column.

STUDENT: _Jason_

TARGET BEHAVIOR: _Shaking hands or flicking fingers between eyes and light source_

Date	Time	Notations of Occurrences	Total Occurrences
10/27	9:30–10:30	‖‖ ‖‖ ////	14
10/18	9:30–10:30	‖‖ ‖‖ ‖‖ //	17
10/19	9:30–10:30	‖‖ ‖‖ ‖‖ ‖‖	20
10/20	9:30–10:30	‖‖ ‖‖ ///	13

Figure 13.5. Unrestricted event recording sample form (total occurrences).

Instructions: Use a new column for each data collection period (each column represents one data collection period). Each time the target behavior occurs, cross out the next number in the column (beginning with 1). If the target behavior does not occur during the data collection period, cross off "zero" in the column. Chart the data by connecting the last number crossed out in each column.

STUDENT: Sergio

TARGET BEHAVIOR: Placing arm or hand in mouth

DATA-COLLECTION PERIOD: Individual work time (9:30–9:50)

25	25	25	25	25	25	25	25	25	25	25	25
24	24	24	24	24	24	24	24	24	24	24	24
23	23	23	23	23	23	23	23	23	23	23	23
22	22	22	22	22	22	22	22	22	22	22	22
21	21	21	21	21	21	21	21	21	21	21	21
20	20	20	20	20	20	20	20	20	20	20	20
19	19	19	19	19	19	19	19	19	19	19	19
18	18	18	18	18	18	18	18	18	18	18	18
17	17	17	17	17	17	17	17	17	17	17	17
16	16	16	16	16	16	16	16	16	16	16	16
15	15	15	15	15	15	15	15	15	15	15	15
14	14	14	14	14	14	14	14	14	14	14	14
13	13	13	13	13	13	13	13	13	13	13	13
12	12	12	12	12	12	12	12	12	12	12	12
11	11	11	11	11	11	11	11	11	11	11	11
10	10	10	10	10	10	10	10	10	10	10	10
9	9	9	9	9	9	9	9	9	9	9	9
8	8	8	8	8	8	8	8	8	8	8	8
7	7	7	7	7	7	7	7	7	7	7	7
6	6	6	6	6	6	6	6	6	6	6	6
5	5	5	5	5	5	5	5	5	5	5	5
4	4	4	4	4	4	4	4	4	4	4	4
3	3	3	3	3	3	3	3	3	3	3	3
2	2	2	2	2	2	2	2	2	2	2	2
1	1	1	1	1	1	1	1	1	1	1	1
0	0	0	0	0	0	0	0	0	0	0	0

Date: 10/27 10/28 10/29 | 10/30 11/1 11/2 11/3 11/4

Baseline | Intervention

Figure 13.6. Self-graphing data collection chart for unrestricted event recording.

should be as easy and unobtrusive as possible. One possibility for streamlining data collection is to monitor more than one target behavior in an individual student during a single observation period or simultaneously monitor the same target behavior in multiple students. Of course, this type of data collection requires the observer to be at what we call the "fluency" level in terms of data collection skills; that is, the data collector should be able to monitor a single behavior easily and accurately

Instructions: List each target behavior to be monitored in the column on the left. List up to four activities during which data will be collected in the four boxes under "Activities." During each activity, record a check mark or tally mark in the appropriate row each time one of the target behaviors occurs. At the end of the day, record the daily total for each target behavior in the column at the right.

DATE: _9-24_

STUDENT: _Hodari_

OBSERVER: _Ms. Hall_

Target Behavior	Activities				Total Daily Occurrences per Behavior
	Breakfast (8:00–8:25)	Grooming (8:30–8:45)	Morning Work (9:40–10:00)	Afternoon Language (1:30–1:45)	
Gouging (using fingernails to scratch or attempt to scratch any part of own body)	✓ ✓		✓ ✓ ✓ ✓ ✓ ✓	✓ ✓ ✓ ✓ ✓ ✓ ✓ ✓ ✓	17
Flapping arms and/or hands		✓ ✓ ✓	✓ ✓ ✓ ✓	✓	8
Spinning or attempting to spin objects	✓ ✓ ✓ ✓ ✓		✓ ✓ ✓	✓	9
Total Occurrences per Activity	7	3	13	11	

Figure 13.7. Sample form for recording multiple unrestricted event behaviors over multiple activities.

before trying to monitor multiple behaviors. We recommend that teachers who are new to data collection focus on one behavior per student. Once you become more fluent in data collection (that is, you can record data quickly while attending to other teaching tasks at the same time), you can begin monitoring multiple target behaviors or multiple students simultaneously.

Easy-to-use forms can facilitate monitoring multiple behaviors or students. Figures 13.2, 13.7, 13.11, and 13.12 are examples of forms for monitoring multiple target behaviors in one student. Figures 13.13 and 13.14 are formats for monitoring the same behavior or different behaviors in more than one student.

Developing and Using Data Collection Forms

The forms we have provided may be suitable or adaptable for your data collection needs. However, if you need to design your own data collection form, be sure to follow the instructions that we provided in Chapter 8. It is particularly important to match your form to the data collection system that you are using and to the target behavior(s).

Once you have forms for each target behavior, you must teach other adults how to (a) record data and (b) use the forms correctly. This is best done by first clearly

Instructions: Each time the target behavior occurs, record the start time and end time and then note the total duration of each instance.

STUDENT: _Armando_

TARGET BEHAVIOR: _Amount of time student engages in tantrum. Tantrums include_ _any of the following: screaming, crying, lying on floor, kicking floor or furniture._

OBSERVATION PERIOD: _Afternoon work period (2:00–2:40)_

DATE	START	STOP	DURATION
1/19	2:00	2:01	1 min.
	2:07	2:10:30	3 min., 30 sec.
	2:32	2:32:30	30 sec.
1/20	2:08	2:10	2 min.
	2:23	2:26:45	3 min., 45 sec.
1/21	2:14	2:22	8 min.

Figure 13.8. Duration recording sample form.

explaining what constitutes occurrences of the target behavior. Next, have anyone who will be expected to collect data join you in recording data while observing the target student. During this observation period, each person records data on his or her own form. When the observation period ends, compare your data with those of each of the other observers. The data listed on each person's form should match your data with 80% or greater accuracy. Less than 80% accuracy in data comparison may mean that the definition of the target behavior is unclear, the data collection procedure needs to be clarified, or the person is unclear on how to use the form. You should address the problem and then provide further practice until each data collector reaches at least 80% agreement with your data while measuring a behavior simultaneously with you.

At the end of each data-recording session, or at least at the end of the day, all raw data must be converted, if needed, and graphed. As we have stated several times before, graphing is an essential step in data collection. In this chapter, we have provided two examples of data collection forms that are self-graphing (i.e., recording the data actually produces a graph). However, not all data collection needs are appropriate for self-graphing forms. Before graphing data, refer to our directions in Chapter 2 regarding when to convert data and how to graph them. To test your graphing skills, you can practice graphing the data we provided in Figures 13.1, 13.3, and 13.8 and then compare your graphs with the ones we have provided for these data in Figures 13.15 through 13.17.

Summary

Data collection is an essential part of conducting interventions for challenging be-haviors. Without objective measures of behaviors, you probably will not be able to

Instructions: For each data collection period, cross off the number in a column (starting with 1) that corresponds with the number of minutes that the target behavior occurred. If the target behavior did not occur during the data collection period, cross off "zero" in the column. (Each column represents one data collection period.) To chart the duration data, collect the last numbers crossed off in each column.

STUDENT: _Emmy_

TARGET BEHAVIOR: _Self-Stim (rocking back and forth)_

DATA COLLECTION PERIOD: _play time on carpet (1:20–1:35)_

25	25	25	25	25	25	25	25	25	25	25	25
24	24	24	24	24	24	24	24	24	24	24	24
23	23	23	23	23	23	23	23	23	23	23	23
22	22	22	22	22	22	22	22	22	22	22	22
21	21	21	21	21	21	21	21	21	21	21	21
20	20	20	20	20	20	20	20	20	20	20	20
19	19	19	19	19	19	19	19	19	19	19	19
18	18	18	18	18	18	18	18	18	18	18	18
17	17	17	17	17	17	17	17	17	17	17	17
16	16	16	16	16	16	16	16	16	16	16	16
15	15	15	15	15	15	15	15	15	15	15	15
~~14~~	14	14	14	14	14	14	14	14	14	14	14
~~13~~	13	13	13	13	13	13	13	13	13	13	13
~~12~~	12	~~12~~	~~12~~	12	12	12	12	12	12	12	12
~~11~~	11	~~11~~	~~11~~	11	11	11	11	11	11	11	11
~~10~~	~~10~~	~~10~~	~~10~~	~~10~~	10	10	10	10	10	10	10
~~9~~	~~9~~	~~9~~	~~9~~	~~9~~	9	9	9	9	9	9	9
~~8~~	~~8~~	~~8~~	~~8~~	~~8~~	~~8~~	8	8	8	8	8	8
~~7~~	~~7~~	~~7~~	~~7~~	~~7~~	~~7~~	~~7~~	7	7	7	7	7
~~6~~	~~6~~	~~6~~	~~6~~	~~6~~	~~6~~	~~6~~	~~6~~	6	6	6	6
~~5~~	~~5~~	~~5~~	~~5~~	~~5~~	~~5~~	~~5~~	~~5~~	5	5	5	5
~~4~~	~~4~~	~~4~~	~~4~~	~~4~~	~~4~~	~~4~~	~~4~~	4	4	4	4
~~3~~	~~3~~	~~3~~	~~3~~	~~3~~	~~3~~	~~3~~	~~3~~	3	3	3	3
~~2~~	~~2~~	~~2~~	~~2~~	~~2~~	~~2~~	~~2~~	~~2~~	2	2	2	2
~~1~~	~~1~~	~~1~~	~~1~~	~~1~~	~~1~~	~~1~~	~~1~~	1	1	1	1
0	0	0	0	0	0	0	0	0	0	0	0

Date:	1/19	1/20	1/21	1/24	1/25	1/26	1/27	1/28				
	Baseline			Intervention								

Note. Seconds are rounded to nearest minute.

Figure 13.9. Self-graphing data collection form for duration recording.

determine if target behaviors are improving and, thus, whether your interventions are working. In this chapter, we provided many examples of forms that would be appropriate for observational recording, including forms for both restricted event data (in which both the stimulus and the response must be counted) and unrestricted

---

Instruction: Note the date of each data collection session. In the "Total Time" column, record the total number of minutes and/or seconds that the target behavior occurred on each date.

STUDENT: _Michael_

TARGET BEHAVIOR: _Rocking body back and forth while sitting or standing_

OBSERVATION PERIOD: _Morning language session (10:15–10:35)_

Date	Total Time
9/01	11 min., 42 sec.
9/02	9 min., 15 sec.
9/03	18 min.
9/04	14 min., 53 sec.
9/05	12 min., 33 sec.

Figure 13.10. Sample form for recording total time accumulated when monitoring duration of behavior.

---

event data (in which only the student's target behavior is counted). Duration recording forms that we provided consisted of a form to note the length of each occurrence of the target behavior and a form to note cumulative time engaged in the target behavior during an observation period. Finally, we provided several examples of forms for monitoring multiple behaviors in a single student or a target behavior or behaviors across several students.

We encourage you to practice data collection until it is second nature to you. This may mean practicing outside of the classroom. The following are a few examples of sample data collection practice activities that might help you sharpen your skills:

- Pets—How many times does your cat meow during an evening (unrestricted event)? How long does your dog sleep in one position before moving (duration)?

- Family—How many questions does your child ask during a certain period of time (unrestricted event)? How many directions does your child follow without further reminders (restricted event)?

- Television—How long does each commercial last (duration)? How many times does the audience laugh during a comedy (unrestricted event)?

We are more likely to engage in tasks such as data collection when we are fluent in them, and such fluency is attained through practice. We encourage you, and other adults in your classroom, to practice the important skill of data collection until you can easily and effortlessly collect data while engaging in the many other required tasks. Data collection will thus more likely be an integral part of your daily teaching activities, increasing your effectiveness in planning and monitoring interventions to reduce challenging behaviors. You will also be better prepared to discuss the effectiveness of interventions during IEP meetings and parent conferences.

Instructions: First, note codes and descriptions for up to three target behaviors. Next, record those codes in the three boxes under "Behavior." During each observation period, use a check mark or tally mark to record each occurrence of a target behavior in the column corresponding with that target behavior. At the end of the observation period, count the number of occurrences of each target behavior and record it in the "Total" columns for each behavior. Finally, note the total number of occurrences of all target behaviors in the last column on the right.

STUDENT: Benjamin   **OBSERVER:** Mr. Jacobs

OBSERVATION PERIOD: Lunch

BEHAVIOR CODES:

_E_ = _eye gouging: poking finger or knuckle into any part of own eye_

_N_ = _self-stimulatory noises: making a high-pitched sound while cupping hand between mouth and ear_

_S_ = _sniffing objects: holding any item under nose_

Date	Behavior			Total "E"	Total "N"	Total "S"	Total for All Behaviors
	E	N	S				
10-21	✓ ✓	✓ ✓ ✓	✓ ✓ ✓ ✓ ✓	2	3	6	11
10-22	✓	✓ ✓ ✓ ✓ ✓	✓ ✓ ✓ ✓ ✓ ✓ ✓ ✓ ✓	1	5	9	15
10-23		✓ ✓ ✓ ✓ ✓ ✓	✓ ✓ ✓ ✓ ✓ ✓ ✓	0	6	7	13

Figure 13.11. Sample form for monitoring multiple target behaviors (unrestricted events).

Instructions: First, note codes and descriptions for up to four target behaviors. Next, record one code on each line in the four boxes under "Behavior" in the second column. During the observation period, each time a target behavior occurs, place a check mark or tally mark under the consecutively numbered columns on the row corresponding to that target behavior. At the end of the observation period, count the number of occurrences of each target behavior and record it in the "Total" column.

STUDENT: Mark   **OBSERVER:** Ms. Preston

OBSERVATION PERIOD: Vocational work time on job-training site

BEHAVIOR CODES:

   M   = attempting to chew on or mouth objects by placing any object or part of body in mouth

   H   = hitting self with fist or open hand on any part of body

   R   = rocking back and forth while sitting or standing

   L   = tilting head to side, looking upwards into space, and laughing (not in response to any external stimuli)

Date	Behavior	1	2	3	4	5	6	7	8	9	10	11	12	13	14	15	16	17	18	19	20	Totals
1/19	M	✓	✓	✓	✓	✓	✓	✓	✓	✓	✓	✓										11
	H	✓																				1
	R	✓	✓	✓	✓	✓																5
	L	✓	✓	✓	✓	✓	✓	✓	✓	✓												9
1/20	M	✓	✓	✓	✓	✓	✓	✓	✓	✓	✓	✓	✓	✓	✓							14
	H																					0
	R	✓	✓	✓																		3
	L	✓	✓	✓	✓	✓	✓															6
1/21	M																					
	H																					
	R																					
	L																					
1/22	M																					
	H																					
	R																					
	L																					

Figure 13.12. Sample form for monitoring multiple target behaviors (unrestricted events).

Instructions: On the line next to the check mark, write the operational definition for the behavior that should occur in response to the stimulus. On the line next to the "X," describe the stimulus and behavior to be reduced. In the data-recording section, list students whose behaviors are being monitored. During the observation session, record appropriate codes to reflect occurrences or nonoccurrences of the behaviors being measured. After the observation session ends, calculate the percentage of problem behaviors by dividing the number of incorrect responses by the total number of behaviors (correct plus incorrect responses) and multiplying by 100.

DATE: 10-17

OBSERVATION PERIOD: Morning Group Academics

TARGET BEHAVIOR: Noncompliance

✓ = _Command given, student complies_

X = _Command given, student does not comply_

Students	Target Behavior	Percentage of Responses Targeted for Reduction
Erica	X X ✓ ✓ ✓ X X X X ✓ ✓ ✓ X	$\frac{7}{13} = 54\%$
Hodari	X X X X X ✓ ✓ ✓ X X X X	$\frac{9}{12} = 75\%$
Toni	X ✓ X X ✓ ✓ ✓ ✓ ✓	$\frac{3}{10} = 30\%$
Michael	X X X X X ✓ X X X ✓	$\frac{8}{10} = 80\%$
Kip	✓ ✓ ✓ ✓ ✓ X X X ✓ ✓ ✓	$\frac{3}{11} = 27\%$

Figure 13.13. Sample form for simultaneously monitoring one restricted event behavior for more than one student.

Instructions: Under "Target Behaviors," list the target behavior being monitored for each student. In the data collection section, list each student to be monitored in the column on the left. Place a check mark or tally mark for each occurrence of the target behavior in the row corresponding with the student's name. Note the total for each student in the column on the right.

DATE: 2/13

OBSERVATION PERIOD: Group Language (1:40–2:00)

TARGET BEHAVIORS: Self-stimulatory behavior (see notes for each student, below)

Jake = rocking or flapping hands in front of face

Ignacio = posturing (holding any part of body in unusual, posed position by stiffening muscles)

Colin = flicking or waving fingers between eyes and light source

Kaitlyn = making clicking noises with tongue

Student	Occurrences	Total
Jake	✓ ✓ ✓ ✓ ✓ ✓	7
Ignacio	✓ ✓ ✓	3
Colin	✓ ✓ ✓ ✓ ✓	6
Kaitlyn	✓ ✓ ✓ ✓ ✓ ✓ ✓ ✓ ✓	10

Figure 13.14. Sample form for simultaneously monitoring different target unrestricted behaviors for multiple students.

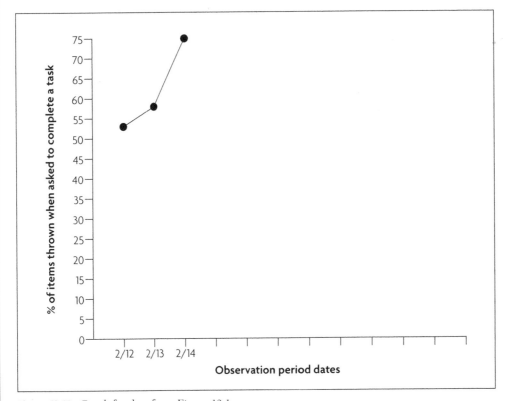

Figure 13.15. Graph for data from Figure 13.1.

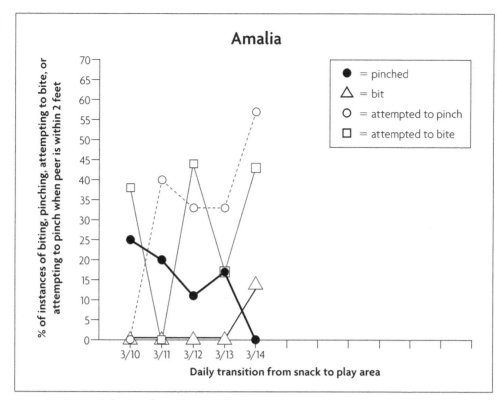

Figure 13.16. Graph for data from Figure 13.3.

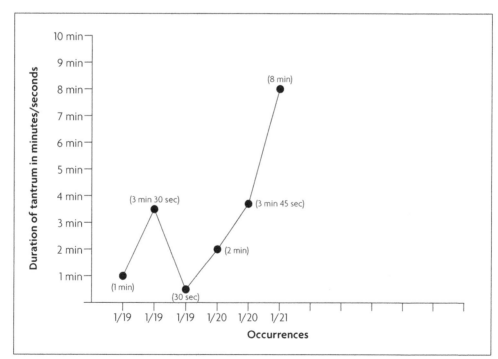

Figure 13.17. Graph for data from Figure 13.8.

Appendix:
Data Collection Forms for Behaviors Targeted for Reduction

Restricted Event Recording Form (With Calculations)

Restricted Event Recording Form (Without Calculations)

Multiple Restricted Event Recording Form

Unrestricted Event Recording Form (Rate of Occurrences)

Unrestricted Event Recording Form (Total Occurrences)

Self-Graphing Data Collection Chart for Unrestricted Event Recording

Form for Recording Multiple Unrestricted Event Behaviors Over Multiple Activities

Duration Recording Form

Self-Graphing Data Collection Form for Duration Recording

Form for Recording Total Time Accumulated When Monitoring Duration of Behavior

Form for Monitoring Multiple Target Behaviors

Form for Monitoring Multiple Target Behaviors (Self-Graphing)

Form for Simultaneously Monitoring One Restricted Event Behavior for More Than One Student

Form for Simultaneously Monitoring Different Target Behaviors for Multiple Students

Restricted Event Recording Form (With Calculations)

Instructions: Note each occurrence of the specified stimulus and each occurrence of the target behavior. Calculate the percentage of occurrences (number of occurrences of the target behavior divided by the total occurrences of the stimulus × 100).

STUDENT: _____

TARGET BEHAVIOR: _____

_____

OBSERVATION PERIOD: _____

Date	Stimulus	Target Behavior	Calculation	Percentage

Restricted Event Recording Form (Without Calculations)

Instructions: Place a check mark for each occurrence of the stimulus and a boxed check mark for each occurrence of the behavior.

STUDENT: _____

TARGET BEHAVIOR: _____

_____

OBSERVATION PERIOD: _____

✓ = _____

☑ = _____

Date	Behaviors	Percentage

Multiple Restricted Event Recording Form

Instructions: Determine a code for each target behavior being monitored (up to four behaviors). Record these codes in the shaded boxes. Begin recording on the next line. Note the date, then place a check each time the stimulus occurs. Place a check mark or tally mark in the column corresponding with the target behavior. After the observation period ends, calculate the percentage for each behavior (number of occurrences of the behavior divided by the total number of stimuli × 100) and record the percentage in columns.

STUDENT: _____

TARGET BEHAVIOR: _____

_____

OBSERVATION PERIOD: _____

292

Date	Stimulus: ✓ =	Student responses:				Percentage of occurrences for each response			
Codes for Student Responses:		(1)	(2)	(3)	(4)	(1)	(2)	(3)	(4)

Unrestricted Event Recording Form (Rate of Occurrences)

Instructions: Note each activity occurring during the data collection periods and the time in minutes/seconds of the data collection period. Place a check mark in the "Occurrences" column each time the target behavior occurs. Calculate the rate by dividing the total number of occurrences by the total number of minutes and/or seconds of the data collection period.

STUDENT: _____

TARGET BEHAVIOR: _____

_____

DATA-COLLECTION PERIOD: _____

✓ = Target Behavior			
Activity	Time	Occurrences	Rate (occurrences/units of time)

Unrestricted Event Recording Form (Total Occurrences)

Instructions: Note the date and the time of each data collection session. In the "Notations of Occurrences" column, place a check mark or tally mark each time the target behavior occurs. Enter the total number of occurrences in the "Total Occurrences" column.

STUDENT: _____

TARGET BEHAVIOR: _____

Date	Time	Notations of Occurrences	Total Occurrences

Self-Graphing Data Collection Chart For Unrestricted Event Recording

Instructions: Use a new column for each data collection period (each column represents one data collection period). Each time the target behavior occurs, cross out the next number in the column (beginning with 1). If the target behavior does not occur during the data collection period, cross off "zero" in the column. Chart the data by connecting the last number crossed out in each column.

STUDENT: _____

TARGET BEHAVIOR: _____

_____

DATA COLLECTION PERIOD: _____

25	25	25	25	25	25	25	25	25	25	25	25
24	24	24	24	24	24	24	24	24	24	24	24
23	23	23	23	23	23	23	23	23	23	23	23
22	22	22	22	22	22	22	22	22	22	22	22
21	21	21	21	21	21	21	21	21	21	21	21
20	20	20	20	20	20	20	20	20	20	20	20
19	19	19	19	19	19	19	19	19	19	19	19
18	18	18	18	18	18	18	18	18	18	18	18
17	17	17	17	17	17	17	17	17	17	17	17
16	16	16	16	16	16	16	16	16	16	16	16
15	15	15	15	15	15	15	15	15	15	15	15
14	14	14	14	14	14	14	14	14	14	14	14
13	13	13	13	13	13	13	13	13	13	13	13
12	12	12	12	12	12	12	12	12	12	12	12
11	11	11	11	11	11	11	11	11	11	11	11
10	10	10	10	10	10	10	10	10	10	10	10
9	9	9	9	9	9	9	9	9	9	9	9
8	8	8	8	8	8	8	8	8	8	8	8
7	7	7	7	7	7	7	7	7	7	7	7
6	6	6	6	6	6	6	6	6	6	6	6
5	5	5	5	5	5	5	5	5	5	5	5
4	4	4	4	4	4	4	4	4	4	4	4
3	3	3	3	3	3	3	3	3	3	3	3
2	2	2	2	2	2	2	2	2	2	2	2
1	1	1	1	1	1	1	1	1	1	1	1
0	0	0	0	0	0	0	0	0	0	0	0

Date:

Baseline | Intervention

Form for Recording Multiple Unrestricted Event Behaviors Over Multiple Activities

Instructions: List each target behavior to be monitored in the column on the left. List up to four activities during which data will be collected in the four boxes under "Activities." During each activity, record a check mark or tally mark in the appropriate row each time one of the target behaviors occurs. At the end of the day, record the daily total for each target behavior in the column at the right.

DATE: _____

STUDENT: _____

OBSERVER: _____

Target Behavior	Activities				Total Daily Occurrences per Behavior
Total Occurrences per Activity					

Duration Recording Form

Instructions: Each time the target behavior occurs, record the start time and end time and then note the total duration of each instance.

STUDENT: _____

TARGET BEHAVIOR: _____

_____

OBSERVATION PERIOD: _____

DATE	START	STOP	DURATION

Self-Graphing Data Collection Form for Duration Recording

Instructions: For each data collection period, cross off the number in a column (starting with 1) that corresponds with the number of minutes that the target behavior occurred. If the target behavior did not occur during the data collection period, cross off "zero" in the column. (Each column represents one data collection period.) To chart the duration data, collect the last numbers crossed off in each column.

STUDENT: _____

TARGET BEHAVIOR: _____

_____

DATA COLLECTION PERIOD: _____

25	25	25	25	25	25	25	25	25	25	25	25
24	24	24	24	24	24	24	24	24	24	24	24
23	23	23	23	23	23	23	23	23	23	23	23
22	22	22	22	22	22	22	22	22	22	22	22
21	21	21	21	21	21	21	21	21	21	21	21
20	20	20	20	20	20	20	20	20	20	20	20
19	19	19	19	19	19	19	19	19	19	19	19
18	18	18	18	18	18	18	18	18	18	18	18
17	17	17	17	17	17	17	17	17	17	17	17
16	16	16	16	16	16	16	16	16	16	16	16
15	15	15	15	15	15	15	15	15	15	15	15
14	14	14	14	14	14	14	14	14	14	14	14
13	13	13	13	13	13	13	13	13	13	13	13
12	12	12	12	12	12	12	12	12	12	12	12
11	11	11	11	11	11	11	11	11	11	11	11
10	10	10	10	10	10	10	10	10	10	10	10
9	9	9	9	9	9	9	9	9	9	9	9
8	8	8	8	8	8	8	8	8	8	8	8
7	7	7	7	7	7	7	7	7	7	7	7
6	6	6	6	6	6	6	6	6	6	6	6
5	5	5	5	5	5	5	5	5	5	5	5
4	4	4	4	4	4	4	4	4	4	4	4
3	3	3	3	3	3	3	3	3	3	3	3
2	2	2	2	2	2	2	2	2	2	2	2
1	1	1	1	1	1	1	1	1	1	1	1
0	0	0	0	0	0	0	0	0	0	0	0

Date:

| Baseline | Intervention |

Note. Seconds are rounded to nearest minute.

Form for Recording Total Time Accumulated
When Monitoring Duration of Behavior

Instructions: Note the date of each data collection session. In the "Total Time" column, record the total number of minutes and/or seconds that the target behavior occurred on each date.

STUDENT: _____

TARGET BEHAVIOR: _____

_____

OBSERVATION PERIOD: _____

Date	Total Time

Form for Monitoring Multiple Target Behaviors

Instructions: First, note codes and descriptions for up to three target behaviors. Next, record those codes in the three boxes under "Behavior." During each observation period, use a check mark or tally mark to record each occurrence of a target behavior in the column corresponding with that target behavior. At the end of the observation period, count the number of occurrences of each target behavior and record it in the "Total" columns for each behavior. Finally, note the total number of occurrences of all target behaviors in the last column on the right.

STUDENT: _____   OBSERVER: _____

OBSERVATION PERIOD: _____

BEHAVIOR CODES:

_____ = _____

_____ = _____

_____ = _____

Date	Behavior			Total "_____"	Total "_____"	Total "_____"	Total for All Behaviors

Form for Monitoring Multiple Target Behaviors (Self-Graphing)

Instructions: First, note codes and descriptions for up to four target behaviors. Next, record one code on each line in the four boxes under "Behavior" in the second column. During the observation period, each time a target behavior occurs, place a check mark or tally mark under the consecutively numbered columns on the row corresponding to that target behavior. At the end of the observation period, count the number of occurrences of each target behavior and record it in the "Total" column.

STUDENT: _____ OBSERVER: _____

OBSERVATION PERIOD: _____

BEHAVIOR CODES:

_____ = _____

_____ = _____

_____ = _____

_____ = _____

Date	Behavior	1	2	3	4	5	6	7	8	9	10	11	12	13	14	15	16	17	18	19	20	Totals

Form for Simultaneously Monitoring One Restricted Event Behavior for More Than One Student

Instructions: On the line next to the check mark, write the operational definition for the behavior that should occur in response to the stimulus. On the line next to the "X," describe the stimulus and behavior to be reduced. In the data-recording section, list students whose behaviors are being monitored. During the observation session, record appropriate codes to reflect occurrences or nonoccurrences of the behaviors being measured. After the observation session ends, calculate the percentage of problem behaviors by dividing the number of incorrect responses by the total number of behaviors (correct plus incorrect responses) and multiplying by 100.

DATE: _____

OBSERVATION PERIOD: _____

TARGET BEHAVIOR: _____

✓ = _____

X = _____

Students	Target Behavior	Percentage of Responses Targeted for Reduction

Form for Simultaneously Monitoring Different
Target Behaviors for Multiple Students

Instructions: Under "Target Behaviors," list the target behavior being monitored for each student. In the data collection section, list each student to be monitored in the column on the left. Place a check mark or tally mark for each occurrence of the target behavior in the row corresponding with the student's name. Note the total for each student in the column on the right.

DATE: _____

OBSERVATION PERIOD: _____

TARGET BEHAVIORS: _____

_____

_____

_____

_____

Student	Occurrences	Total

CHAPTER 14

Interventions for Specific Challenging Behaviors

Children with autism characteristically exhibit the following types of challenging behaviors: self-stimulatory (e.g., rocking, twirling, flicking fingers), self-injurious (e.g., biting hands and arms, banging the head, gouging the eyes), and aggression (e.g., hitting, biting, pinching, pulling hair). Such behaviors pose serious problems for these students, their teachers, and families, and they interfere with learning and socialization (Horner, Carr, Strain, Todd, & Reed, 2000; Lee, Odom, & Loftin, 2007; National Research Council, 2001). For example, among other problems, students who exhibit high levels of these types of challenging behaviors may require more restrictive instructional arrangements (e.g., special education classrooms with one-on-one instruction; Conroy, Asmus, Sellers, & Ladwig, 2005). Furthermore, because of the potential risks associated with their behaviors, they will be less able to participate in community-based instructional activities, such as trips to the grocery store to practice shopping skills or bus transportation skills (Dunlap, Ferro, & Deperczel, 1994). Finally, this type of student with autism may be more likely to require placement outside the home, particularly as he or she gets older and stronger. Parents may eventually be unable to ensure the safety of the child or of other children in the family (Buschbacher, Fox, & Clarke, 1993).

As you've learned so far in this book, the best approach to managing such behaviors is to provide an effective, comprehensive educational program that: (a) teaches students functional communication skills (see Chapter 9); (b) uses effective instructional interventions to teach important skills in all areas of functioning (see Chapters 3, 4, 7, 8, and 10); (c) provides consistent reinforcement for desired behaviors (see Chapter 2); and (d) provides high levels of structure and predictability (see Chapter 5). In addition, when challenging behaviors occur, the first step must be to conduct a comprehensive functional behavioral assessment (see Chapter 11).

In this chapter, we describe common functions of challenging behaviors exhibited by students with autism and interventions based on those functions. It may be tempting to apply these interventions in a "cookbook"-type fashion: You determine a student is noncompliant for escape, so you select one of the strategies we describe for that situation. This is not our intent. We are simply offering ideas about relating interventions to hypothesized functions to facilitate your own creativity in developing function-related strategies. In addition, any intervention should be part of an overall A–B–A process: Assess the behavior, design and implement the intervention, collect data to monitor the behavior, and adjust the intervention as needed.

In Chapter 11, we presented common functions served by various challenging behaviors and possible indicators for each. Be sure that you conduct a thorough functional assessment for any challenging behavior, including assessing the behavior under all conditions in which it occurs. Be careful to explore all potential functions of each behavior. Research has shown that one challenging behavior may actually serve multiple functions (Dunlap et al., 1994). For example, Jasper may scream and scratch himself when he is presented with a disliked task, when he wants something, or when the toys on the shelf have been rearranged. Also, several behaviors may serve the same function; for example, Jasper may also try to bite the teacher when asked to do disliked tasks.

As we noted in Chapter 12, interventions for challenging behavior should be part of a comprehensive behavior intervention plan (BIP). The BIP should describe replacement behaviors for each challenging behavior and then should address antecedent interventions and functionally determined reinforcers for replacement behaviors, as well as consequences for challenging behaviors.

The following sections are devoted to challenging behaviors commonly exhibited by children with autism. Within each section, we have listed potential functions for the challenging behavior and possible interventions. Our goals are (a) to illustrate how interventions must be matched to hypothesized functions and (b) to assist IEP teams in developing function-based interventions.

Noncompliance

Noncompliance can range from a passive form (e.g., the student simply ignores the teacher's direction) to aggression or intense tantrums. Regardless of the form, you need to determine the function of the noncompliant behavior and then apply interventions that reflect that function. At-a-Glance 14.1 lists common functions of noncompliance and sample interventions for each function. In addition to the function-based interventions described in At-a-Glance 14.1, certain antecedent interventions may improve compliance. Two effective antecedent interventions are teaching compliance and behavioral momentum. *Teaching compliance,* sometimes referred to as *compliance training* (Colvin & Englemann, 1983; Scheuermann & Webber, 2002), involves teaching compliance as a new skill. The student is taught to comply by first using discrete trial teaching to teach simple, easily prompted behaviors (e.g., "touch head," "arms up," "clap hands"). When the student consistently complies to these commands, more difficult commands are introduced (e.g., "put the block on the shelf," "get your backpack," "close the door").

When the student is consistent in complying with simple requests during DTT, the teacher should begin teaching compliance in other settings using naturalistic/ milieu techniques. For example, teaching adults may use the mand-model procedure for common daily tasks (e.g., retrieving daily schedule, following hand washing procedure, going through lunchline). Throughout this teaching time, compliance is strongly reinforced and behavior reductive techniques may be used as a consequence for noncompliance, particularly if the noncompliance is in the form of severe challenging behaviors (e.g., aggression, self-injury).

A second antecedent intervention for noncompliance is behavioral momentum. *Behavioral momentum* involves presenting one or more *high-probability requests* (i.e., instructions that the student is likely to follow) before giving a *low-probability request* (i.e., a mand to which the student is likely to be noncompliant). The high-probability requests can be mands to do a desirable activity, questions about a topic that is of interest to the student, or requests to do an easy task (Banda & Kubina, 2006). This technique has been shown to be an effective way of increasing compliance for students with autism and developmental disabilities (Banda & Kubina, 2006; Ducharme, Harris, Milligan, & Pontes, 2003). To use behavioral momentum, teachers must first determine those requests that are highly likely to result in compliance (high-probability requests) and those that are highly unlikely to result in compliance (low-probability requests). Next, all teaching adults must be instructed to give two or three high-probability requests before delivering a low-probability request. For example, James is highly noncompliant, especially when given instructions for

At-a-Glance 14.1 Noncompliance: Functions and Interventions

Potential Functions	Interventions
Escape or avoidance	• Teach student to communicate "No," ask for a break, or ask to leave situation • Change how tasks are done • Increase reinforcement during disliked tasks • Provide shorter tasks • Make tasks more functional (e.g., teach tasks that are immediately usable and/or relevant, teach tasks in naturalistic/milieu settings)
Communication	• Identify communicative intent and teach appropriate communicative expressions and methods (e.g., teach student to point to picture card that communicates "I want to take a break") • Differentially reinforce appropriate communication (DRC)
Skill deficit	• Teach compliance using discrete trial training, beginning by teaching simple one-step commands that are easily prompted (e.g., touch head, stand up) and gradually increasing complexity of commands • Differentially reinforce compliance (DRI)
Confusion or uncertainty about expected behavior	• Provide concise and clear instructions, using as few words as possible • Use picture communication cues, visual schedules, and other methods to enhance clarity and expectations (see Chapter 5) • Present one task or instruction at a time; for complex tasks, give instructions or prompts for one step at a time

transitions (e.g., put away your materials, get your schedule, line up). James loves Legos, music, raisins or other chewy dried fruit, and puzzles. Before giving James a direction for a transition behavior, the teaching adult first asks him one or two questions (e.g., "James, did you listen to your music on the bus?" or "James, what did you build with your Legos?") and gives him one simple, desired task to complete (e.g., "James, put this piece in your puzzle to finish it" or "James, get two raisins to eat"). Of course, compliance to low-probability requests is reinforced. In addition, any compliance intervention should be monitored using one of the measuring systems described in Chapter 2 and one of the data forms presented in Chapters 8 and/or 13.

Aggression

Aggression, especially that directed toward adults, is not necessarily any more difficult to manage than any other challenging behavior. However, the emotional responses that teacher-directed aggression produces in the teacher may act as obstacles to effective intervention. Getting hit, kicked, bitten, or spat upon may engender a response from the teacher that is based on anger or fear, making it difficult to objectively implement the intervention specified in the BIP. For this reason, it is important for teachers and paraprofessionals to be working as a well-coordinated team when dealing with aggressive students. For example, if a student hurts one of the adults, another adult might carry out the consequence. Interventions for aggression should not be exclusively consequence-based, however, as we indicate in At-a-Glance 14.2. In fact, if the function(s) for the aggression are correctly addressed, punishment-based consequences should play a small role in managing this behavior. In addition to the function-based interventions presented in At-a-Glance 14.2, two other interventions may be effective in reducing aggressive behaviors: video self-modeling and social stories. Video modeling was discussed in Chapter 5. Video self-modeling uses the same principle: the student observes a videotaped model for information on how to perform a task. However, in video self-modeling, the model is the student himself, videotaped while engaging in an appropriate performance of a target behavior—a desired replacement behavior for the aggression. Video self-modeling has been shown to reduce aggressive behaviors in children with autism (Buggey, 2005). The self-model exemplar may be staged (i.e., the student role-plays the target behavior, perhaps by following a script), or the student may be videotaped during natural activities, and then the video is edited to show desired behaviors only (Buggey, 2005). While video self-modeling is potentially an effective intervention, it may be a bit cumbersome to prepare and implement, so it might not be the first intervention selected for managing aggressive behaviors.

Another potentially effective intervention for aggression is the use of social stories. Social stories, as discussed in Chapter 10, are brief text and/or picture stories that communicate to a student information about an approaching social situation and appropriate responses to that situation. Researchers have shown that social stories can reduce aggression (Swaggart et al., 1995). As an intervention for aggression, the social story would describe the desired alternative target behavior to the aggressive behavior. Given that social stories are relatively easy to use, this may be an appropriate first intervention, or a component of a combined intervention approach, for managing aggression.

Stereotypic Behaviors

Stereotypic behavior in the form of self-stimulatory behavior may interfere with learning, play, socialization, and even neurological development (Koegel, Valdez-Menchaca, & Koegel, 1994). Increasingly over the last 10 years, researchers have demonstrated that stereotypic behaviors, and self-injurious behaviors in particular, may have organic bases, including genetic and neurochemical explanations (National Research Council, 2001). Such knowledge enhances our understanding of these difficult behaviors and facilitates identification of medications for treatment purposes. Even if organic causes explain some stereotypic behaviors, however, teachers and other adults who are responsible for intervention planning must still identify and implement effective behavioral interventions to teach new, functional, replacement behaviors and must differentially reinforce the child for engaging in those alternative behaviors.

Most explanations of stereotypic and self-injurious behavior have focused on how such behaviors are influenced by environmental conditions. Kennedy and his colleagues (2000) offered several explanations for self-stimulatory behavior. Drawing on research on this topic, they speculated that self-stimulatory behaviors may increase in the absence of preferred alternative activities, may be for the purpose of gaining social attention, may function to avoid or escape social or instructional demands, or may serve as positive sensory reinforcement. To further complicate matters, Kennedy and his colleagues demonstrated that the same or similar forms of self-stimulatory behavior might serve multiple functions. They emphasized that

At-a-Glance 14.2 Aggression: Functions and Interventions

Potential Functions	Interventions
Communication	• Identify communicative intent and teach more appropriate form of communication • Use differential reinforcement of communication (DRC) to reinforce communicative attempts
Avoidance or escape	• Teach student to communicate "No," ask for break, or ask to leave situation • Assess environmental conditions for factors that may exacerbate aggression (e.g., proximity of other students, other students' using student's favorite materials); modify those conditions if possible • Modify task to increase reinforcement or functional value • Present shorter tasks; gradually increase duration of task as student's ability allows • Ensure that student is not allowed to avoid or escape tasks as a result of aggression • Intersperse disliked tasks with preferred activities; use picture schedules to remind student of availability of desired task
Result of interruption of routine or ritual	• Differentially reinforce student for using communication to express distress (DRC) • Differentially reinforce student for gradually longer periods of time when no aggression occurs after disruption (DRO) • Differentially reinforce student for nonritualistic alternatives (e.g., eating lunch items in different order than usual, scattering puzzle pieces instead of lining them up) (DRI) • Provide cues to warn student of impending changes in routine or schedule (e.g., through the use of social stories or during calendar activities) • Teach student to better tolerate change by exposing student to planned minor changes or interruptions and providing strong reinforcement for an appropriate response

we cannot assume that sensory stimulation is the sole, or even the main, purpose for self-stimulatory behaviors.

For these reasons, we again emphasize the importance of conducting a functional behavioral assessment of self-stimulatory behaviors prior to designing interventions. The FBA should include indirect and direct data collection that covers all situations in which self-stimulatory behaviors occur. When analyzing data, care should be taken to look for patterns than indicate multiple functions. Interventions should then target all hypothesized functions, perhaps using different interventions under different circumstances. For example, Isabella's self-stimulatory behavior on the playground may serve both a self-entertainment function and a social avoidance function. During work sessions, the same self-stimulatory behaviors may serve a task avoidance function. Interventions may consist of using peer confederates to initiate, prompt, and reinforce social behaviors on the playground, and a communication intervention to teach her to ask for a break during work times. In addition, during all of these situations, she is differentially reinforced for engaging in appropriate alternatives to the self-stimulatory behaviors (e.g., playing with peers, asking for a break).

At-a-Glance 14.3 provides possible interventions for self-stimulatory behavior based on various common functions. One intervention that we wish to emphasize is the use of peer confederates to help provide high levels of social engagement. Researchers have shown that peer-mediated social interventions can produce lower rates of stereotypic behaviors (Lee, Odom, & Loftin, 2007; Lee & Odom, 1996; Lord & Hopkins, 1986). The peer-mediated interventions described in Chapter 10 may not only increase social interactions in students with autism, but may produce collateral reductions in undesired behaviors as well.

When developing interventions for self-stimulatory behavior, remember the most common explanations for this behavior: social avoidance, task avoidance, sensory reinforcement, and social attention. You should also remember that self-stimulatory behavior may serve multiple functions, and so multiple interventions may be needed. Typically, three general types of interventions will be needed: differential reinforcement of functional alternative behaviors, peer-mediated social interventions, and functional communication training.

At-a-Glance 14.3 Self-Stimulatory Behavior: Functions and Intervention

Potential Functions	Interventions
Sensory stimulation	• Teach socially acceptable forms of self-stim:
	—visual (flicking fingers, gouging eyes): kaleidoscope; ViewMaster; pinwheel; sparkler toy; lava lamp; perpetual motion balls; or any toy or object with spinning or moving parts, blinking or flickering lights, shiny or sparkly surfaces
	—auditory: listen to music or other sounds through headphones; hold seashells to ears; use noisemakers
	—tactile: carry pieces of textured cloth; play with Slime; hold stress balls; hold smooth stones or marbles
	—proprioceptive (positioning, flapping hands, bouncing): small trampoline; isometric exercises; weight-lifting exercises
	—olfactory (sniffing): provide favorite scents (e.g., lemon, cologne, pine, vanilla, cinnamon) on cards or swatches of cloth the student can carry
	—gustatory (licking, mouthing objects): provide gum, hard candy, suckers
	—vestibular (spinning, bouncing, rocking): tire swing; Sit-and-Spin toy (for young children); hammock; somersaults; rocking chair; rocking horse
	• Use differential reinforcement of incompatible behaviors (DRI) to reinforce use of desired alternative stimulatory behaviors
	• Allow contingent access to self-stim activities after compliance, task completion, communicative attempts, or other target behaviors
	• Use sensory extinction (see At-a-Glance 12.3)
Escape	• Teach student to communicate "No," ask for a break, or ask to leave situation
Social avoidance	• Use peer confederates to initiate, prompt, and reinforce social behaviors

Self-Injurious Behavior

Self-injurious behavior (SIB) in children and youth with autism is extremely troubling for educators, parents, and other caregivers. High levels of SIB may interfere with learning, and may result in a child being unable to participate in mainstream educational, social, and community environments (National Research Council, 2001). SIB appears to be more prevalent in individuals who have autism accompanied by mental retardation (Dominick et al., 2007).

A growing body of research points to several possible biological and social explanations for SIB in children with autism. Evidence suggests that some self-injurious behaviors have a neurobiological basis related to neurotransmitters in the brain (King, 2000; National Research Council, 2001). It also appears that some SIB may be genetically based (Edelson, 2004; National Research Council, 2001). Of particular concern for educators are social explanations for SIB. SIB has been shown to be related to low language abilities, particularly expressive language deficits (Dominick et al., 2007). Also, research has shown that SIB may be functional for a child, producing attention, access to desired items, or facilitating escape from or avoidance of disliked or difficult tasks (Crosland et al., 2003; Edelson, 2004).

Given the biological underpinnings of at least some forms of SIB, it is no surprise that many children, youth, and adults with autism are prescribed medications to help control challenging behaviors such as SIB, aggression, and sterotypy. While a comprehensive discussion of medication for behavioral control is beyond the scope of this manual, one of the most commonly prescribed medications for treatment of aggression and SIB in individuals with autism is risperidone (also known by the brand name Risperdal). Teachers should be aware of the medications their students take and should have a basic understanding of why the medication was prescribed. The school nurse will be an important resource for teachers; he or she can help teachers find information about medications, and may be involved in administering and monitoring the effects of medications. In addition, teachers should be aware of potential side effects of students' medications. Medications commonly used for behavioral purposes may have multiple physical side effects (e.g., weight gain, increased appetite, unusual movements, fatigue) (Crosland et al., 2003; National Research Council, 2001; Troost et al, 2005). They may also result in external stimuli being more aversive or more reinforcing for the child than before the medication treatment began (Crosland, 2003). Finally, teachers should maintain close communication with parents about any changes in medication and behavioral or other changes that students exhibit in proximity to adjustments in medication.

Medication should not be considered the sole treatment for challenging behaviors. Even when students take medication for behavioral control, educators must continue to use functional assessment to formulate hypotheses about possible environmental factors related to challenging behaviors. Also, medication does not replace the need for comprehensive language, curricular, and behavioral interventions that reflect functional assessment hypotheses.

Summary

Challenging behaviors pose significant obstacles to the child's overall success, limiting the likelihood that he or she will be able to participate in inclusive environments, learn desired skills, and attain any level of independence. Challenging behaviors are also difficult for teachers to deal with because the behavior itself is often

At-a-Glance 14.4 Self-Injurious Behavior: Functions and Interventions

Potential Functions	Interventions
Escape or avoidance	• Teach student to communicate "No," ask for a break, or ask to leave situation • Modify tasks or presentation to increase functionality or interest • Assess environmental conditions (e.g., noise levels, amount of confusing activity, number of people present) and either modify those that may be contributing to the behavior or provide the student with accommodations to buffer the impact of those stimuli (e.g., headphones to wear in the noisy cafeteria) • Ensure that student is not allowed to avoid or escape tasks or situations as a result of the behavior
Communication	• Identify communicative intent and teach appropriate communicative expressions and methods • Differentially reinforce appropriate communication (DRC)
Sensory stimulation	• Mask reinforcing effects of the behavior (e.g., helmet for banging the head, gloves or mittens for biting or scratching the hand, goggles for gouging eyes) (see At-a-Glance 12.3 for ideas) • Differentially reinforce for gradually longer periods of no self-injurious behavior (DRO) • Teach and differentially reinforce other, safer forms of sensory stimulation (see At-a-Glance 2.4)
Positive reinforcement	• Differentially reinforce target behaviors; use a behavior reductive strategy for self-injurious behavior

intimidating or scary. When faced with a behavior that is frightening to observe (e.g., a behavior that causes injury to the child or others), it is easy to forget to follow systematic steps for assessing and managing the behavior.

It is insufficient to ask, "What do I do when the child does _____?" The correct questions should be as follows:

1. "Why does the child do this behavior?"
2. Under what conditions is the child likely to do this behavior?"

The answers will dictate the interventions to use.

Noncompliance, aggression, stereotypic behaviors, and self-injurious behaviors all present major potential obstacles to learning and successful functioning. Such behaviors are also highly challenging for teachers, especially when those individuals have not been trained in comprehensive functional behavioral assessment techniques, interventions to increase communication skills, and applied behavior analysis. In this chapter, we attempted to demystify these challenging behaviors by explaining how they may be related to environmental conditions, and how to use functional assessment data (and resulting hypotheses) to develop effective interventions. Some forms of challenging behaviors may have biophysical bases. Despite this fact, the behavioral interventions described in this chapter (and throughout this manual) will help reduce the frequency and/or intensity of challenging behavior while teaching new, more adaptive replacement behaviors.

References

Banda, D. R., & Kubina, R. M. (2006). The effects of a high probability request sequencing technique in enhancing transition behaviors. *Education and Treatment of Children, 29*, 507–516.

Buggey, T. (2005). Video self-modeling applications with students with autism spectrum disorder in a small private school setting. *Focus on Autism and Other Developmental Disabilities, 20*, 52–63.

Buschbacher, P., Fow, L., & Clarke, S. (2004). Recapturing desired family routines: A parent–professional behavioral collaboration. *Research and Practice for Persons with Severe Disabilities, 29*(1), 25–39.

Colvin, G., & Engelmann, S. (1983). *Generalized compliance training.* Austin, TX: PRO-ED.

Conroy, M. A., Asmus, J. M., Sellers, J. A., & Ladwig, C. N. (2005). The use of an antecedent-based intervention to decrease stereotypic behavior in a general education classroom. *Focus on Autism and Other Developmental Disabilities, 20*, 223–230.

Crosland, K. A., Zarcone, J. R., Lindauer, S. E., Valdovinos, M. G., Zarcone, T. J., Hellings, J. A., & Schroeder, S. R. (2003). Use of functional analysis methodology in the evaluation of medication effects. *Journal of Autism and Developmental Disorders, 33*, 271–279.

Dominick, K. C., Davis, N. O., Lainhart, J., Tager-Flusberg, H., & Folstein, S. (2007). Atypical behaviors in children with autism and children with a history of language impairment. *Research in Developmental Disabilities, 28*, 145–162.

Ducharme, J. M., Harris, K., Milligan, K., & Pontes, E. (2003). Sequential evaluation of reinforced compliance and graduated request delivery for the treatment of noncompliance in children with developmental disabilities. *Journal of Autism and Developmental Disabilities, 33*, 519–526.

Dunlap, G., Ferro, J., & Deperczel, M. (1994). Nonaversive behavioral intervention in the community. In E. C. Cipani & F. Spooner (Eds.), *Curricular and instructional approaches for persons with severe disabilities* (pp. 117–146). Needham Heights, MA: Allyn & Bacon.

Edelson, S. M. (2004). *Understanding and treating self-injurious behavior.* Retrieved September 9, 2007 from http://www.autism.org/sibpaper.html

Horner, R. H., Carr, E. G., Strain, P. S., Todd, A. W., & Reid, H. K. (2000). *Problem behavior interventions for young children with autism: A research synthesis.* Paper presented at the Second Workshop of the Committee on Educational Interventions for Children with Autism, National Research Council, April 12, 2000. Department of Special Education, University of Oregon.

Kennedy, C. H., Meyer, K. A., Knowles, K. A., & Shukila, S. (2000). Analyzing the multiple functions of stereotypic behavior for students with autism: Implications for assessment and treatment. *Journal of Applied Behavior Analysis, 33*, 559–571.

King, B. H. (2000). Pharmacological treatment of mood disturbances, aggression, and self-injury in persons with Pervasive Developmental Disorders. *Journal of Autism and Developmental Disorders, 30*, 439 – 445.

Koegel, L. K., Valdez-Menchaca, M. C., & Koegel, R. L. (1994). Autism: Social communication difficulties and related behaviors. In V. B. Van Hasselt & M. Hersen (Eds.), *Advanced abnormal psychology* (pp. 165–187). New York: Plenum Press.

Lee, S. H., & Odom, S. L. (1996). The relationship between stereotypic behavior and peer social interaction for children with severe disabilities. *The Journal of the Association for Persons with Severe Handicaps, 21*, 88–95.

Lee, S., Odom, S. L., & Loftin, R. (2007). Social engagement with peers and stereotypic behaviors of children with autism. *Journal of Positive Behavior Interventions, 9*, 67–79.

Lord, C., & Hopkins, L. M. (1986). The social behavior of autistic children with younger and same-age nonhandicapped peers. *Journal of Autism and Developmental Disorders, 16*, 249–262.

National Research Council, Division of Behavioral and Social Sciences and Education, Committee on Educational Intervention for Children with Autism. (2001). *Educating children with autism.* (C. Lord & J. P. McGee, Eds.). Washington, DC: National Academy Press.

Scheuermann, B., & Webber, J. (2002). *Autism: Teaching DOES Make a Difference.* Belmont, CA: Wadsworth.

Swaggart, B. L., Gagnon, E., Bock, S. J., Earles, T. L., Quinn, C., Myles, B. S., et al. (1995). Using social stories to teach social and behavioral skills to children with autism. *Focus on Autism and Other Developmental Disabilities, 10,* 1–16.

Troost, P. W., Lahuis, B. E., Steenhuis, M-P., Ketelaars, C. J., Buitelaar, J. K., Van Engeland, H., et al. (2005). Long-term effects of risperidone in children with autism spectrum disorders: A placebo discontinuation study. *Journal of the American Academy of Child and Adolescent Psychiatry, 44,* 1137–1144.

Understanding and Working With Families

Given what you have learned about autism so far, it should come as no surprise that parenting these children is a difficult task—one for which most parents are ill-prepared (Moes, 1995). The stresses of parenting these children have been well documented (Bristol & Schopler, 1983, 1984; Moes, Koegel, Schreibman, & Loos, 1992; Schopler & Mesibov, 1984). Parenting any child who has a disability is known to be difficult and stressful for parents, but evidence has indicated that parents of children with autism may experience even greater stressors than parents of children with other disabilities (Abbeduto et al., 2004; Schieve, Blumburg, Rice, Visser, & Boyle, 2007). Understanding the stressors faced by parents will better prepare educators to establish collaborative relationships with them and other family members and to provide the necessary support (Webber, Simpson, & Bentley, 2000). It will also, we hope, reduce "finger-pointing," that is, the tendency of some educators to blame parents for their child's disability, for not doing enough to help their child, for not accepting "reality" when it comes to their child's needs, for not choosing the best treatments, and so forth. As the saying goes, "walking a mile in their shoes" will build empathy and should make for a better parent–teacher relationship. Our experiences have been that parents are invaluable sources of information; in fact, they are sometimes significantly more informed about current research, legislation, and issues than teachers. We urge you to welcome this expertise and not be intimidated by it.

In this chapter we will describe some of the problems and challenges faced by parents of children with autism, and the implications these have for teachers. In addition, we will describe essential elements of a collaborative relationship with parents and the type of information and support parents may need from educators.

Our advice throughout this chapter is for teachers to view parents with respect, as equals in the education of their child with autism. This is sometimes difficult for teachers, especially individuals who are new to dealing with autism. Teachers must understand that the challenges of raising a child with autism often motivate parents to seek training and education. This should not be threatening for the teacher; on the contrary, such expertise should be welcomed and viewed as a resource to make the teacher's job easier.

Challenges for Families of Children With Autism

The Struggle to Figure Out What Is Wrong

Teachers should understand how a child with autism may affect the family. In doing so, it is helpful to think about how any family prepares for the birth of a child. Usually, this is one of happiest of life events for a family. Parents and family members spend months getting ready for the birth of their baby: choosing a name, preparing their home, and fantasizing about their child's future. They envision the perfect child: exceptionally bright, talented, and high achieving. Parents also worry about their unborn child's health, often making comments such as, "We don't care if we have a boy or a girl, as long as the child is healthy." Seldom do parents specifically anticipate that their child will be born with a disability; therefore, they usually are not prepared for the emotional and logistical impacts that discovery of their child's disability brings.

Unlike disabilities that are readily apparent at birth (e.g., physical disabilities, Down syndrome, spina bifida), infants with autism look like a typical baby and are usually physically healthy. Discovery of the disability is usually a long, slow process of realizing that something is wrong, followed by the trauma of trying to pinpoint the problem. Many parents of children with autism have reported spending years visiting different professionals while trying to find an accurate diagnosis for their child (Simpson & Zionts, 1992; Turner-Oberg, 1997). When mentioning their concerns to pediatricians (e.g., "He cries when I hold him and is only content when he's laying in his crib," "She stiffens every time I try to cuddle her"), parents are often reassured that their child is fine, that this unusual behavior is just a "phase," or that the child is simply on the slow end of a normal developmental window and will eventually "catch up" (Koegel & LaZebnik, 2004; Simpson & Zionts, 1992; Turner-Oberg, 1997; Ziskin, 1995).

This struggle to identify what is wrong with their child—and what they need to do to fix the problem—undoubtedly shapes parents' interactions with caregivers from that point on. Teachers should be sensitive to the frustrations that parents have encountered over the years and understanding if parents are wary of school district personnel or policies, demanding of better services, and seemingly over-involved in educational planning for their child. These parents probably watched helplessly as their child failed to exhibit typical developmental milestones. Now that the problem has been identified, they may be impatient to make up for lost time and opportunities.

Parents may also still be searching for answers to their many questions and reassurance for their concerns (Webber et al., 2000). Teachers should listen carefully and respond honestly and appropriately to parents' questions and concerns, provide parents with information about autism (e.g., definitions, prevalence, etiology) and available services, and never use falsehoods or misinformation to reassure parents. For example, a parent of a 3-year-old may express concern that her son is not yet talking. It would be inappropriate for the teacher to respond nonchalantly, "Oh, don't worry about that! Sure, he's a little late in talking, but we'll get him talking in no time. Pretty soon he'll be talking nonstop!" Of course, teaching speech will probably be a goal, but the reality is that the child may never learn to talk or may learn only limited speech. Don't offer false hope while at the same time communicating documented positive effects of intensive early instruction.

Learning to Live With Autism

Once a definitive diagnosis has been obtained, parents begin the process of learning to accept the fact that their child has a lifelong disability. Many parents of children with autism recount experiencing progressive emotional stages similar to the stages of mourning that are associated with death (Koegel & LaZebnik, 2004; Siegel, 1996; Wing, 1974). The stages most commonly reported by parents of children with autism (Ackerley, 1995; Koegel & LaZebnik, 2004; Turner-Oberg, 1997; Ziskin, 1995) are listed in Focus Here 15.1. Individuals may experience these stages at different times, with different levels of intensity, in varying order, and multiple times.

Focus Here 15.1 Family Emotional Responses

Stage	Characteristics	Implications for Teachers
Discovery—the first unique experience for parents of children with autism is learning their child's diagnosis	Searching for a diagnosis to explain their child's difficulties; visiting many different types of health-care professionals in search of someone who can help	Understand the frustrations of knowing something is wrong with your child but being unable to pinpoint the problem; remember that the diagnosis of autism may still be new for the parents, and they may need information, guidance, and resources; be prepared to answer questions, provide information about resources, and inform yourself about best practices for teaching children with autism
Denial—parents convince themselves there is no problem or the problem stems from something that can be fixed (e.g., by spending more time with the child or insisting that the school not treat the child differently)	Refusal to seek help or accept services; comments such as, "Our first child was a late talker, so we're not worried!"	Develop a trusting relationship with parents; provide factual information about the child's performance; provide positive, realistic developmental expectations; maintain open and nonthreatening communication
Guilt or bargaining—parents believe the child's problems are due to their own behavior (e.g., the child's mother had a glass of wine during pregnancy; placed the infant in day care while parents worked), and/or if they work hard enough, they can fix the problem	Shopping for treatments; trying unproven, even highly bizarre treatments (unusual diets, swimming with dolphins)	Maintain a high-level awareness about nontraditional treatments and the claims made by their backers; be prepared to give knowledgeable and accurate information about these treatments
Anger—parents want to blame someone for their child's condition; anger may be directed at family members (spouse in particular), doctors, or teachers	Continual complaints or dissatisfaction with the child's educational program; nonspecific complaints; inability to come to agreement on components of the Individualized Education Program	Make information available about local family counselors or autism support groups; use effective, active listening techniques to expressions of anger, offering support and concern, not just advice; if anger is directed toward you, examine your behavior and instructional practices to assess whether any of the parent's complaints are justified
Depression—parents realize their child is not going to be cured; may become pessimistic about future	Lack of involvement with school processes; failure to follow through on agreed-upon activities or interventions	Invite participation, share information, and ask for suggestions and input; maintain diligence in communicating with parents on a regular basis; develop manageable systems for informing parents of children's progress; highlight improvements in skill performance

Stage	Characteristics	Implications for Teachers
Acceptance or coping—the point where parents are able to talk openly and honestly about their child's disability, strengths, needs, and future	Involved in child's educational program; has realistic goals for child	Welcome parents' involvement in their child's educational program; view parents as the true expert on their child and as excellent sources for both direct and indirect support for educational programs

Of course, it is possible that some parents will not experience any of the stages. Focus Here 15.1 also lists implications for teachers when working with parents who exhibit the behavioral characteristics of the various stages.

A word of caution: it is not our job as educators to "diagnose" a stage that parents might be in, nor should we label parents (e.g., "Mrs. Ogden is simply in denial about her child") or use perceived stages as reasons to avoid communication with parents (e.g., "I can't talk to him—he's so angry about his child's autism"). Also, be careful not to interpret a difference of opinion as characteristics of a stage. For example, if a parent doesn't agree with your choice of intervention for a challenging behavior, it doesn't necessarily mean the parent is in denial about the child's behavior. If you do notice that parents are exhibiting behaviors that are characteristic of one or more of the stages, our recommendations should help you in your relationship with the parents.

A Child With Autism May Affect All Aspects of Family Life

Parenting any child is stressful at times. Parents are forced to deal with situations they don't know how to handle; they must balance the demands of children and family, careers, and their own individual needs; money may be in short supply, and parents thus aren't able to provide their children with the material goods and activities they would like; and every family has times of emotional, physical, or other types of crises. Parenting a child with autism adds to the stresses normally associated with parenting, bringing types of stresses most parents never face (Ackerley, 1995; Brown, MacAdam-Crisp, Wang, & Iarocci, 2006; National Research Council, 2001; Turnbull & Turnbull, 1997; Ziskin, 1995). Focus Here 15.2 describes a few of the areas that may be affected by the presence of a child with autism in a family and how educators might be able to help. Of course, in all these areas, the most important thing that teachers can do is to maintain close communication with parents, for example, ask appropriate questions and listen carefully to the parents' responses to identify skills the child needs to learn to help the family with daily living activities. School personnel must work closely with parents to identify those skills the student needs not only for school functioning but also for home and community functioning.

Essential Practices in Effective Home–School Collaboration

Developing a robust, productive relationship with family members doesn't happen automatically. To accomplish this, educators must engage in certain behaviors that

Focus Here 15.2 Life Areas That May Be Affected by the Presence of a Child With Autism

Life Area Affected	Explanation	How Educators Might Help
Family Relationships—marital relationship, parent–child relationship, sibling relationships	The time required to meet the needs of the child with autism may interfere with time spouses have to spend with each other or to spend with their other children; children may have to assume more responsibilities (e.g., caring for siblings, cooking, cleaning); extended family members may have difficulty learning how to interact with the child with autism; one of the most difficult aspects of parenting a child with autism must be the lack of affection or even recognition given to the parent by the child with autism	• Provide parents with local resources, such as parent and/or sibling support groups or agencies that provide respite care • Provide parents with literature for family members • Teach students with autism to express affection and to accept expressions of affection from others (e.g., hugs, pats)
Family Finances—how a family earns money, the costs of caring for the family	A child with autism may create additional financial burdens: intensive in-home training, medical care, specially trained babysitters, home modifications (e.g., placing locks on cabinet doors, removing electrical outlets in the child's room); even simple dental or medical procedures may be more expensive (e.g., general anesthesia may be needed for routine dental procedures because the child will not stay in the chair or keep his or her mouth open); parents' jobs may also be affected by a child with autism (e.g., a parent may not be able to change jobs for fear of losing insurance coverage for the child; because of the difficulty finding appropriate child care, a parent may need to stay home with a preschooler with autism; parents may decide where to live based on the quality of services available for their child with autism rather than other variables [e.g., quality of job, climate, etc.]); parents of children with autism must plan for lifelong financial support for their child; parents must make provisions for the child's financial welfare when they die, which may affect current finances	• Understand the financial impact of raising a child with autism • Provide parents with information about local service providers (e.g., doctors, dentists, hairstylists) who provide accommodative services for children with disabilities and about agency support services in your community, county, and state
Daily Living Tasks—chores required by everyday living: cooking, cleaning, laundry, errands,	Because children with autism typically do not do well when unattended, the myriad of jobs families do every day may require careful planning (e.g., cooking dinner may mean first arranging for	• Teach students with autism to help with daily living tasks (e.g., fold laundry, load the dishwasher, operate the

(continues)

Life Area Affected	Explanation	How Educators Might Help
lawn care, and so forth	supervision for the child with autism or a special activity the child can do in the kitchen close to the parent; grocery shopping, laundry, housecleaning, and other chores may be planned around the availability of a family member to supervise the child with autism)	vacuum cleaner, clean bathtubs and sinks) • Teach students to engage in appropriate independent activities (e.g., playing with a toy, looking at a book, drawing or writing, using a computer) • Be sure to address inappropriate behaviors that may interfere with a family's ability to carry out daily chores (e.g., taking a child who runs to any public place or taking a child who does not remain seated during meals to a restaurant)
Family Activities— those activities a family does together for social, recreational, or leisure purposes	For the same reasons as we described in Daily Living Tasks, typical family activities may require careful planning or even changing when a child with autism is involved (e.g., a family trip by airplane to see grandparents may not be feasible because the child with autism cannot tolerate ear discomfort caused by air pressure changes; family outings to a movie may mean that one family member spends most of the time walking around the lobby or playing videogames with the child with autism because he or she has little interest in sitting for the movie; choosing restaurants, hotels, vacation destinations, and other activities may be based on the extent to which they accommodate the child with autism)	• Work with parents to develop skills that will help the family include the child with autism in their leisure activities (e.g., family members who enjoy camping might wish their child to learn to tolerate eating outside and leisure skills such as fishing, hiking, inflating an air mattress) • Teach students quiet activities for riding in cars, airplanes, or trains
Lifelong Responsibilities	While most children become increasingly less dependent upon parents through the years, children with autism may always require some level of care, supervision, and financial support; retirement for parents may be very different than they dreamed, given the responsibilities of either caring for or finding appropriate living arrangements for their child with autism; siblings may be called upon to continue care or supervision after parents die; securing appropriate living arrangements for an adult with severe disabilities is often difficult—cost is always a factor, as is	• Careful, thorough transition planning will be of great assistance to the family; this planning, which the Individuals with Disabilities Education Act requires to begin by age 14 for most students, should consider long-term goals for the child in independent living, leisure skills, vocational options, and other areas of adult functioning; long-term goals are then addressed by more immediate objectives

(continues)

| | availability; residential placements have criteria concerning the types of individuals they will accept (e.g., some group homes require that clients be able to take their medications with little or no assistance or will not accept clients who have behavior problems); if appropriate living arrangements are unavailable, the family must decide where the child with autism will live after the parents die (options may include living with siblings or living with a roommate who can provide full- or part-time supervision); parents must secure these arrangements and arrange for lifelong support for the adult child with autism if he or she is unable to live independently | for skills that will eventually lead to attainment of those goals |

have been shown to have a greater likelihood of improving collaborative relationships. In this section, we provide descriptions of essential practices for effective home–school relationships.

Know Yourself

Be cognizant of your attitudes concerning families of children with autism. For example, do you believe that autism and pervasive developmental disorders (PDDs) may be caused by some controllable prenatal event? Do you think that parents who do not spend time working with their child at home or who seldom attend teacher or IEP meetings are less caring or interested than parents who do? Do you find yourself thinking a student would fare much better "if only the parents would _____"? Do you think that you, as a trained educator, know what is best for the child, particularly when the parents disagree with you? Do you believe it is your job to do most of the talking in parent conferences because you are the expert on the child's school experiences?

A positive response to any of these questions may suggest attitudes that will potentially interfere with an equal, collaborative relationship with parents. Teachers may find it difficult to change their attitudes; therefore, they must be diligent about monitoring their interactions with parents to ensure an open environment that welcomes parents' input.

Know Your Families

This may mean anything from ensuring that you use the parents' native language in communications to understanding the implications of a child with autism for families from various cultures (National Research Council, 2001). It also means trying to understand the obstacles encountered by the families of your students. For example, is finding a babysitter difficult? Do families stay home because their child has tantrums in crowded public places? Are parents kept awake at night by a child who doesn't sleep? Knowing your families also means being aware of their life circumstances; for example, has a parent recently lost a job, creating financial stress? Is the family also responsible for caring for an ailing parent? Do parents feel pulled trying to meet the needs of nondisabled siblings as well as the child with autism?

Maintain Regular and Frequent Communication

Ongoing communication between home and school is important for several reasons. First, research has shown that parent involvement enhances student outcomes (Sussell, Carr, & Hartman, 1996). Second, regular communication can strengthen home–school relationships (Williams & Cartledge, 1997). Finally, regular home–school communication can facilitate several goals, including sharing information about how school- or home-based skills generalize to other environments, sharing data and evaluation of progress, posing questions, or describing new strategies being implemented. Types of school and home communication strategies include those described in the following subsections.

Home Notes

Each day, send home a note in which you have written one positive thing about the child's day. Perhaps the student him- or herself can contribute to this note. During the last 15 minutes or so of the day, seat students in a circle and ask each in turn to describe something he or she did well that day. If the student is unable to offer anything, you can provide a prompt (e.g., "Think about PE. What did you do that was special today?"). When this is established as a routine, you can remind students throughout the day when they do something well that "this is something you can talk about in group," and perhaps place a visual reminder of the activity or behavior (e.g., a picture card or item) in the student's cubby where he or she stores items to go home. At the end of the day, each student could retrieve their objects and bring them to group. If having the students contribute information for the home note is not feasible, the teacher should explain to each student what he or she is writing on the note.

To save time, teachers might develop an individualized checklist of skills or behaviors on which each student is working. At the end of the day, the teacher can simply check the particular skill(s) that the student did well that day. See Figure 15.1 for an example of this type of form.

Home–School Journals

Home–school journals are notebooks that are sent daily between home and school. Teachers write a brief summary of the child's day or other information, date the entry, and send the journal home with the student. At home, parents can read the teacher's notes and respond or write down information about the child's evening or morning. One advantage to this system is that a running record of communication is maintained over time. Also, both teachers and parents are kept abreast of current events in the child's life, which may facilitate understanding of the child's behavior or instructional needs.

Teachers can use simple narrative entries, and parents can respond with notes about home performance, questions, or other information. The home–school journal can be more structured, if desired, with current goals listed and space provided for comments from both teachers and parents. Figure 15.2 offers an example of this format. Finally, a simpler version involves using a graph on which teachers and parents chart progress on specific goals, such as the example shown in Figure 15.3.

Name: _____ Date: _____

Your child did a good job today on:

_____ initiating greetings or other social initiations

_____ asking for desired objects

_____ completing tasks

_____ academic

_____ leisure

_____ vocational

_____ following directions

_____ using communication system

_____ doing self-help tasks independently

_____ brushing teeth

_____ combing hair

_____ washing face

_____ tying shoes

_____ eating

Figure 15.1 School–home communication form.

Electronic Home–School Notebooks

This is simply an electronic version of the home–school journal, using either e-mail or e-mail with an attachment. We should raise a caution here about using e-mail: It can easily be abused (e.g., overuse, messages sent in anger or frustration). Be careful that your e-mail messages are as professional as other types of correspondence with families. Using a structured format should help avoid problems.

Telephone Calls

Teachers should identify preferred times to make telephone calls to students' homes. Some parents can be contacted at work, whereas others prefer to be contacted only at home. This may mean that calls will need to be made in the evening or on weekends. While we strongly urge teachers to keep their personal life separate from work to help avoid burnout, sometimes calls must be made during nonschool hours. If you choose not to use your own time for these activities, you must develop another equally effective method for communicating with parents.

Teachers should maintain a call log to document calls made to students' families. This log might include the following information:

- date and time
- student's name
- family member you spoke to, and where (i.e., home, work)
- purpose for call
- brief summary of call
- outcome: notes about anything you or the parent promised to do

Entry Date: Monday, October 10

Behavior/Goals	School	Home
Hitting head	**Comments:** Jason did a good job using his "stop" card during language sessions. He needed only verbal prompts. **Questions:** Have you begun using the "stop" card at home? **Data:** 2 head hits during lunch *(Data: Day total = 5 hits)*	**Comments:** Jason's cold is almost gone, so I think he is feeling much better. We just started using his "stop" card yesterday. We're using it mostly during our homework times. **Questions:** Should we use the card all the time or only during work times? That's when his head-hitting is worst, but he also hits himself at other times (when asked to brush his teeth and bathe to get ready for bed, for example) **Data:** 7 hits during two 20-minute work times
Participating in public places without crying or self-injuring	**Comments:** Jason did well with this today. He stayed in the cafeteria for his entire lunch! **Questions:** None **Data:** 2 head hits during lunch	**Comments:** Yea!! We took Jason to mall last night. He had one minor incident (cried, hit), but otherwise did well. **Questions:** None **Data:** 2 hits

Entry Date: Tuesday, October 11

Behavior/Goals	School	Home
Hitting head	**Comments:** I suggest using the "stop" card all the time, especially during activities he doesn't like. This will help with consistency. Today was a little more difficult. Jason needed physical prompts to use his cards instead of hitting. **Questions:** None **Data:** Day total = 17 hits	**Comments:** **Questions:** **Data:**
Participating in public places without crying or self-injuring	**Comments:** Jason asked to go back to the classroom before we even got to the cafeteria. He would not wear his headphones today. **Questions:** None **Data:** 4 hits in hallway	**Comments:** **Questions:** **Data:**

(continues)

Figure 15.2. Structured format for home–school notebooks. *Note.* Adapted from "The Home-to-School Notebook," by T. E. Hall, P. S. Wolfe, and A. A. Bollig, 2003, *Teaching Exceptional Children, 36*(2), pp. 70–71. Copyright 2003 by the Council for Exceptional Children. Adapted with permission.

Entry Date: Monday, October 10

Behavior/Goals	School	Home
Self-stim	**Comments:** This was a little harder today. He wanted to stim more than usual. **Questions:** None **Data:** 15 attempts during morning	**Comments:** Yes, we've seen this, too. **Questions:** Do you think we should meet and talk about his self-stimming? **Data:** did not count
Using cards to initiate communication	**Comments:** He did a good job during language sessions but needed prompts the rest of the day. **Questions:** What pictures does Jason use most at home? **Data:** 4 initiations	**Comments:** Jason uses his food cards mostly. We haven't been very consistent about prompting him to use his activity cards. We'll work on that. **Questions:** None **Data:** None

Special Attention

School	Home
We are planning a field trip to the Pioneer Farm next month (November 15). Would you like to come with us?	I would be happy to go. We'll start working with Jason on animal and farm words!

Entry Date: Tuesday, October 11

Behavior/Goals	School	Home
Self-stim	**Comments:** I think we should give our interventions a few more days. If we're not seeing any changes, we should meet. Jason asked for his stim toys 3 separate times today! **Questions: Data:**	**Comments: Questions: Data:**
	Comments: Jason used his activity cards (the stim toy cards) more today. I think it will really help him when you use these regularly at home. **Questions:** What activity cards will you be using at home? Are there any that I should use at school, too? **Data:** 7 initiations	**Comments: Questions: Data:**

Special Attention

School	Home
Jason fell on the playground today and skinned his knee slightly. The nurse cleaned it and put a bandage on it. It doesn't seem to bother Jason. He whimpered when it happened but seemed to forget about it soon after.	

Figure 15.2. *Continued.*

Working With Families

325

Number of communicative initiations with picture cards during meal and leisure times

	10/3	10/4	10/5	10/6	10/7	10/10	10/11	10/12	10/13	10/14
10										
9		✓		✓						
8		✓		✓						
7		✓		✓						
6	✓	X		X						
5	✓	X	✓	X						
4	X	X	✓	X						
3	X	X	X	X						
2	X	X	X	X						
1	X	X	X	X						

Key:
X = School
✓ = Home

Figure 15.3. Sample graph for a home–school notebook. *Note.* Adapted from "The Home-to-School Notebook," by T. E. Hall, P. S. Wolfe, and A. A. Bollig, 2003, *Teaching Exceptional Children, 36*(2), p. 72. Copyright 2003 by The Council for Exceptional Children. Adapted with permission.

Messages

Some schools have voice mail systems that parents can access to listen to messages left by their child's teacher concerning information about their child's class activities, homework, and so forth. The advantages to this system are that parents can access the information any time of day or night. The major disadvantages are that this often provides only one-way communication because parents may not be able to leave messages for the teacher. Also, the information available to parents is not individualized for each child.

Class Newsletters

Class newsletters are a potential way to keep parents informed of class activities and news on a monthly, bimonthly, or quarterly basis. Of course, this method does not allow for frequent, two-way communication. One advantage of newsletters, however, is that students may assist with their production. Students can produce artwork for the newsletter, use desktop publishing software to write some of it, and help with duplication and assembly. The other advantage to newsletters is that the completed newsletter might serve as a communication stimulus for parents to use to discuss class activities with their child.

Home Visits

Every teacher must decide whether he or she will make visits to students' homes. While we encourage this because of the wealth of information you can glean from such visits, we understand that home visits may not always be feasible for numerous reasons, including time, location, safety, or school policy.

Types of Support Needed by Families

While support needs vary from family to family, three particular areas appear to be widespread among families of children with autism. According to Scheuermann and Webber (2002) and Webber et al. (2000), these families typically need information, knowledge and skills for dealing with their child, and support services to help with the ongoing challenges of parenting a child with autism. The following sections describe how teachers can help in each of these areas.

Information

Teachers should maintain a file or library of literature relevant to autism that can be shared with parents. Included should be a list of organizations and other sources to which parents can turn for more information and support, such as those listed in Appendix A of this book.

Teachers and other professionals may also want to share on an ongoing basis new information about autism with parents and family members. For example, teachers may want to share knowledge gained from conferences or workshops or from reading professional journals on such topics as causes, diagnosis, treatment, and services. Speech–language pathologists might share information on new assistive communication technologies or descriptions of new techniques for eliciting language. This information could be summarized in 1-page briefs and sent home with students. Teachers could also add these to their library of autism literature. Such a library might also be helpful for other professionals, such as school administrators, general education teachers, and paraprofessionals.

Finally, teachers may wish to inform parents about workshops, conferences, new books, journal articles, Web sites, or other sources of information or training. Teachers will usually have access to a lot of information about events relating to autism, especially training workshops and conferences that may be of interest to parents and other family members. Many teachers have their own Web sites that can be accessed through a link on the school's Web site. Upcoming trainings and other events could be posted on the teacher's Web site.

Knowledge and Skills

While most public school programs do not routinely provide formal training for parents, some schools or individual teachers address this need in different ways. One possibility is for the school district to provide in-home training for parents. This option may be suggested by school personnel, or families may request such training. If all parties agree that this is necessary, the school may pay for a set number of sessions with a qualified in-home trainer. Such training would be specified in the student's IEP as a related service.

Another possibility is for the teacher to teach parents certain skills to help them work more effectively with their child. This could be done at school as part of a parent–teacher conference or regularly scheduled parent groups or in the child's home. For example, the teacher may show the parents how to use a particular time-out technique or may demonstrate strategies for eliciting verbalizations from the child.

One teacher we know held group parent meetings, with each meeting having a particular topic or focus (e.g., language–communication, functional skills, leisure–play skills). Interested parents brought their children with autism to the meeting. During the meeting, the teacher demonstrated specific techniques with the children present. For example, the teacher might demonstrate how to prompt a student to use a picture communication card to request a favorite toy or how to structure a functional skills task (such as loading the dishwasher or setting the table) to ensure completion. If they wished to do so, parents would then practice the technique as the teacher gave feedback. These meetings offered multiple benefits. First, the teacher was able to demonstrate effective techniques to parents. Second, encouraging parents to use these same techniques may facilitate children's generalization of skills from school to home. Finally, the teacher was able to observe parent–child interactions and make suggestions that might benefit both parties (e.g., provide higher levels of reinforcement, use simpler instructions that involve fewer words). Although these meetings were held on the teacher's time, school administrators might agree to give teachers time off or other benefits for providing this service.

Related to this, but probably not as effective, is written information provided by the teacher. For example, the teacher may send home "how to" information flyers that describe strategies for dealing with specific problems, such as "How to Deal With Perseveration" or "How to Help Your Child Be More Independent in Doing Household Jobs."

Still another option is for parents to obtain skills training through local agencies or organizations. State and local agencies that deal with disabilities and disability issues frequently offer training that parents can access, as do regional educational service centers and conferences sponsored by disability organizations. As we noted in the previous section, teachers should inform parents about these opportunities.

Support Services

This area goes hand-in-hand with information. Teachers should be informed about available support services that would benefit families of students with autism. The types of support services vary widely but may include the areas of respite care, case management, state and federal waiver programs, transportation, specialized health care (e.g., a physician who is knowledgeable about autism), financial support, specialized baby-sitting, and parent and/or sibling support groups. Schools seldom provide these types of services directly, but school personnel should be aware of agencies that do provide such services and pass this information along to parents.

Summary

This chapter has provided a glimpse into the complex world of families of children with autism. Parenting a child with autism comes with unique challenges that probably cannot be fully understood by anyone who has never been in that position. However, we believe that effective teachers will make every effort to understand the general demands of parenting children with autism and also get to know individual families as rich and valuable sources of information. The teacher in turn must be a source for parents, who often need information about autism in general, local services, training in how to better address their child's needs, behavior, language, socialization, and so forth. Some teachers are fortunate to have students whose parents have specialized skills in areas relevant to autism. Should you find yourself in this position, rather than being intimidated by these parents, invite them to share their expertise with you and other parents. In any case, a strong working relationship with families will benefit teachers, parents, and—most of all—students.

References

Abbeduto, L., Seltzer, M. M., Shattuck, P., Krauss, M. W., Orsmond, G., & Murphy, M. M. (2004). Psychological well-being and coping in mothers of youths with autism, Down syndrome, or fragile X syndrome. *American Journal on Mental Retardation, 109*(3), 237–254.

Ackerley, M. S. (1995). False gods and angry prophets. In H. R. Turnbull & A. P. Turnbull (Eds.), *Parents speak out* (2nd ed., pp. 22–31). New York: Macmillan.

Bristol, M. M., & Schopler, E. (1983). Stress and coping in families of autistic adolescents. In E. Schopler & G. B. Mesibov (Eds.), *Autism in adolescents and adults* (pp. 251–278). New York: Plenum Press.

Bristol, M. M., & Schopler, E. (1984). A developmental perspective on stress and coping in families of autistic children. In J. Blacher (Ed.), *Severely handicapped young children and their families* (pp. 91–141). Orlando, FL: Academic Press.

Brown, R. I., MacAdam-Crisp, J., Wang, M., & Iarocci, G. (2006). Family quality of life when there is a child with a developmental disability. *Journal of Policy and Practice in Intellectual Disabilities, 3*(4), 238–245.

Koegel, L. K., & LaZebnik, C. (2004). *Overcoming autism.* New York: Penguin Group USA.

Moes, D. (1995). Parent education and parenting stress. In R. L. Koegel & L. K. Koegel (Eds.), *Teaching children with autism* (pp. 79–93). Baltimore: Brookes.

Moes, D., Koegel, R. L., Schreibman, L., & Loos, L. M. (1992). Stress profiles for mothers and fathers of children with autism. *Psychological Reports, 71,* 1272–1274.

National Research Council, Committee on Educational Interventions for Children with Autism, Division of Behavioral and Social Sciences and Education. (2001). *Educating children with autism* (C. Lord & J. P. McGee, Eds.). Washington, DC: National Academy Press.

Scheuermann, B., & Webber, J. (2002). *Autism: Teaching DOES make a difference.* Belmont, CA: Wadsworth.

Schieve, L. A., Blumberg, S. J., Rice, C., Visser, S. N., & Boyle, C. (February, 2007). The relationship between autism and parenting stress. *Pediatrics, 119*(Suppl.), S114–S121.

Schopler, E., & Mesibov, G. B. (Eds.). (1984). *The effects of autism on the family.* New York: Plenum Press.

Siegel, B. (1996). *The world of the autistic child.* New York: Oxford University Press.

Simpson, R. L., & Zionts, P. (1992). *Autism.* Austin, TX: PRO-ED.

Sussell, A., Carr, S., & Hartman, A. (1996). Families R us: Building a parent/school partnership. *Teaching Exceptional Children, 28*(4), 53–57.

Turnbull, A. P., & Turnbull, H. R. (1997). *Families, professionals, and exceptionalities: A special partnership.* Upper Saddle River, NJ: Merrill/Prentice Hall.

Turner-Oberg, T. (1997, November–December). Dealing with guilt [Letter to the editor]. *Advocate,* p. 6.

Webber, J., Simpson, R. L., & Bentley, J. K. C. (2000). Parents and families of children with autism. In M. J. Fine & R. L. Simpson (Eds.), *Collaboration with parents and families with children and youth with exceptionalities* (2nd ed., pp. 303–324). Austin, TX: PRO-ED.

Williams, V. I., & Cartledge, G. (1997). Passing notes to parents. *Teaching Exceptional Children, 30*(1), 30–34.

Wing, L. (1974). *Autistic children.* Secaucus, NJ: Citadel.

Ziskin, L. (1995). The story of Jennie. In H. R. Turnbull & A. P. Turnbull (Eds.), *Parents speak out* (2nd ed., pp. 64–78). New York: Macmillan.

Epilogue

Throughout this guide to teaching students with autism, we have made the case that to produce desirable changes in learning and behavior, educators must use the most effective interventions available. Over the past decade, an ever-increasing amount of attention has been given to autism in television, books, magazines, professional journals, and the Internet. This proliferation of information has produced mixed outcomes. On the positive side, awareness of autism has never been greater, and a substantial research base that documents effective practices for individuals with autism now exists. On the other hand, the ease with which information is shared also means that practices based on "bad science" spread just as quickly, or more so, than knowledge of sound practices. Many of the practices that are based on weak evidence, or no evidence at all, promise dramatic results, even to the point of curing autism (Heflin & Simpson, 1998; Scheuermann & Webber, 2002). Unfortunately, these claims, while appealing to families and even educators, have little basis in the type of rigorous scientific study that supports use of the interventions described in this guide (e.g., systematic assessment of behavior; use of positive reinforcement, negative reinforcement, and punishment; systems to provide visual structure; an array of communication systems).

Determining what constitutes evidence or sufficient support for an intervention has been the subject of much debate. The importance of evidence-based practices gained attention with the passage of the No Child Left Behind (NCLB) Act of 2001. According to NCLB, scientifically based research is "research that involves the application of rigorous, systematic, and objective procedures to obtain reliable and valid knowledge relevant to education activities and programs." However, the NCLB criterion for scientifically based research has been criticized as inappropriate for certain populations, such as children with autism and developmental disabilities whose limited numbers preclude the types of research designs supported by the NCLB definition. For this reason, we support the definition of scientifically based practices provided by Simpson et al. (2005): practices that have "significant and convincing empirical efficacy and support" (p. 9).

The strategies described in this book have significant and convincing empirical support and efficacy. There are a multitude of interventions beyond those described in this text, however, that are widely promoted for children and youth with autism. Some of these interventions have strong research support, some have limited research support, and some are based on questionable or weak standards of effectiveness (e.g., case studies, testimonials, research conducted only by individuals who promote the strategy). Focus Here 16.1 describes essential features of many popular interventions, including the extent and nature of research support for each. The techniques presented in this table are organized according to prominent theoretical

(text continues on p. 338)

Focus Here 16.1 Summary of Interventions Categorized by Theoretical Model

Perceptual/Cognitive

Program	Purpose	Authors	Method	Research
Social Stories	Improve socialization and social competence in individuals functioning on the higher end of the autism continuum	Gray, 1995; Gray and Garand, 1993	Social situations and appropriate responses are described in clear, concrete, and personal terms using descriptive, directive, and perspective sentences and using no more than 1 directive sentence for every 5 of the other types; stories are read as often as needed	A promising practice with a growing body of research (Delano & Snell, 2006; Crozier & Ticani, 2005; Hagiwara & Myles, 1999; Kuttler, Myles, & Carlson, 1998; Rogers & Myles, 2001; Swaggart et al., 1995)
Visually Cued Instruction	Assists students to organize their world, predict scheduled events, understand expectations, anticipate changes in routine, make choices and function more independently	Dalrymple, 1995; Earles, Carlson, and Bock, 1998; Hodgdon, 1995; MacDuff, Krantz, and McClannahan, 1993; Quill, 1997	Visual cues are selected, based on the abilities of the student, on a continuum from objects to words; cues are then used to create schedules, label environments, give directions, allow for choices, communicate expectations, and so forth	The use of visual systems for persons with autism is well supported (Boucher & Lewis, 1989; Grandin, 1995; Hermelin & O'Conner, 1970; Layton & Watson, 1995; Mirenda & Santogrossi, 1985; Wolfberg & Schuler, 1993), although additional research is needed to determine who is most likely to benefit and which forms of representation are most beneficial

Developmental

Program	Purpose	Authors	Method	Research
Van Dijk Approach	Develop sensory perception, organizational skills, and communication	MacFarland, 1995; van Dijk, 1967, 1986	Originally developed for students who are deaf-blind, the program consists of a curriculum and 14 basic instructional strategies	Limited research conducted several years ago demonstrates some effectiveness (Siegel-Causey & Guess, 1989; Stillman & Battle, 1984); lack of recent research raises questions regarding validity

(continues)

Behavioral

Program	Purpose	Authors	Method	Research
Discrete Trial Training	Train specific skills as identified through analysis of deficits in child's functioning	Many researchers have used applied behavior analysis and discrete trial training to teach skills; Lovaas (1987) suggested that his particular version of discrete trial training could lead to a recovery from autism; Maurice (1993, 1996) perpetuates the myth	Discrete trial training consists of giving a command, waiting for a response, consequating the response, and recording data during an inter-trial interval; variations in the procedures are advocated by different authors, who modify prompts used, consequences applied, trial presentation (massed vs. distributed), and individual versus collective implementation, among other things	There is copious empirical evidence supporting the use of applied behavioral analysis and discrete trial training for developing skills; use of the Lovaas version of discrete trial training has not been replicated as valid for promoting autistic recovery (Gresham & MacMillan, 1997)
Picture Exchange Communication System (PECS)	Functional nonverbal communication system based on initiation of communicative interactions	Bondy and Frost, 1994; Frost and Bondy, 1994	Behaviorally based techniques of shaping, physical prompts, backward chaining, reinforcement, and fading are used to move through six phases of the program, from simple initiation to complex comments	Replicated in numerous environments by different practitioners; support by Earles et al., 1998
Applied Behavior Analysis (ABA)	ABA includes a variety of techniques to strengthen current adaptive behaviors, teach new behaviors, and reduce or eliminate problem behaviors through antecedent- and consequence-based interventions	Countless authors have researched the techniques that fall under the umbrella of ABA	ABA is not a single program, although many parents and professionals erroneously refer to it as such; instead, it is an array of techniques based on the principles described in Chapter 2 of this text	ABA is supported by a substantial base of methodologically sound research conducted across environments, with children of all ages and abilities (National Research Council, 2001; Steege, Mace, Perry, & Longenecker, 2007)

(continues)

Behavioral *(continued)*

Program	Purpose	Authors	Method	Research
Pivotal Response Training	Teach a set of general skills that are usable in multiple settings and for multiple purposes	Koegel, Koegel, Harrower, and Carter, 1999; Koegel, Koegel, Shoshan, and McNerney, 1999	Behavioral techniques are used in one-on-one teaching and in natural environments to teach pivotal skills in socialization, communication, motivation, behavior, recreation, self-help, and academics (pivotal skills [e.g., self-management skills] are widely usable in multiple contexts and for multiple purposes)	An ever-increasing body of research supports the use of pivotal response training as an efficacious approach for children and youth with autism (Humphries, 2003; Koegel, Koegel, Shosan, and McNerney, 1999; National Research Council, 2001; Simpson, 2005)

Relationship

Program	Purpose	Authors	Method	Research
Gentle Teaching	Establish relationship through unconditional acceptance and positive experiences	McGee and Gonzales, 1990; McGee, Menolascino, Hobbs, and Menousek, 1987	Adults engage with children in preferred activities; other activities modified for errorless learning so child will be successful; high levels of noncontingent positive and negative reinforcement are used; inappropriate behavior is ignored and redirected	One study conducted with 73 adults, most of whom were self-injurious; none were cured, but reduction of behavior was maintained during follow-up period; critics suggest the approach is ineffective (Mudford, 1995), and even harmful (Smith, 1996)
Options	Establish relationship through unconditional acceptance and promote child's unique interests and abilities; unconditional acceptance is the ultimate goal, and a cure is neither sought nor promised	Kaufman, 1976, 1994; Options Institute, 1999	Spend all waking hours with the child, emulate his or her actions and build on interests as possible; approach is taught through training programs available from the Options Institute in Sheffield, Massachusetts	No empirical research has been conducted; approach was popularized through the publication of *Son-Rise* and the subsequent TV movie titled *Son-Rise: A Miracle of Love;* validation is in the form of testimonials published by Kaufman

(continues)

Relationship (continued)

Program	Purpose	Authors	Method	Research
Floor Time	Establish affective contact with primary caregivers and then foster warmth, intimacy, and pleasure in interactive relationships	Greenspan, 1992a, 1992b; Greenspan and Wieder, 1997, 1998; Wieder, 1996	Adult follows child's lead in activities, "plays dumb," and uses "creative obstructions" to entice the child to interact; emphasis is on building and lengthening "circles of communication" and on promoting growth on the *Functional Assessment Scale*	Support is in the form of testimonials, case studies, and research conducted by the authors; Greenspan and Wieder (1997) conducted a retrospective review of charts of 200 children and reported that 58% had "very good outcomes," a term that was loosely defined; DeGangi and Greenspan (1997) conducted a study on children who did not have autism
Holding Therapy	Repair broken symbiotic bond with caregiver so that relationships can be formed	Allan, 1977; Tinbergen and Tinbergen, 1983; Welch, 1988; Zaslow and Breger, 1969	Caregiver holds child closely and returns gaze and affection when child makes eye contact; even when not holding the child, caregiver must remain in close proximity, with breaks of no longer than 2 hours; not commonly used in the United States because it is so invasive	Little research has been conducted to validate the approach; Stades-Veth (1988) reported on a study conducted in Germany in which 13 of 104 participants were purportedly cured of autism

(continues)

Physiologically Based Interventions

Program	Purpose	Authors	Method	Research
Sensory Integration	Reduces autism symptomology by changing individual's ability to perceive, process, and modulate sensory information	Ayers, 1972, 1979; Fisher and Murray, 1991; Wilbarger and Wilbarger, 1991	Evaluate sensory needs and develop programming to increase or decrease stimulation as appropriate; sensory exercise (e.g., weight bearing, deep pressure, brushing) are used to adjust individual's sensory integration system	Neuroscientific basis provides inherent plausibility, but validation consists of testimonials with little independent empirical research to date; results of one study indicated improvement in play behaviors, limited improvement in interactions with adults, and no improvements in peer interactions (Case-Smith & Bryan, 1999)
Auditory Integration Training (AIT)	Reduces sound sensitivity to improve behavioral, social, and cognitive functioning	Berard, 1993, 1995; Rimland and Edelson, 1994	Individuals use headphones to listen to sounds that have been modulated to eliminate certain frequencies; slowly, frequencies are reintroduced; a typical treatment consists of five 2-hour sessions	Popularized by Stehli (1991), who published a book chronicling her daughter's cure from autism through AIT; there is little research to support its effectiveness; Rimland and Edelson (1994), as well as Edelson et al. (1999), support its effectiveness, but theirs is clearly a minority view; most other researchers consider the treatment ineffective (Bettison, 1996; Gillberg, Johansson, Steffenburg, & Berlin, 1997)

(continues)

Physiologically Based Interventions (*continued*)

Program	Purpose	Authors	Method	Research
Facilitated Communication	Overcomes individual's global apraxia to allow emergence of communication	Biklen, 1990, 1992, 1993; Crossley, 1988, 1992	A trained facilitator supports the individual's arm/hand so that she or he can operate an augmentative communication device; over time, the facilitator fades the full physical support until only a light touch on the shoulder or mere proximity are required for the individual to operate the augmentative device	No empirical evidence supports this approach; validity has been discredited by numerous authors (Autism Society of America, 1992–1993; Calculator, 1992; Mulick, Jacobson, & Kobe, 1993; Prior & Cummins, 1992; Rimland, 1992; Schopler, 1992; Simpson & Myles, 1995; Szempruch & Jacobson, 1993; Wheeler, Jacobson, Paglieri, & Schwartz, 1993)

explanations for autism (many of which we described in Chapter 1; see also Scheuermann & Webber, 2002):

- *Perceptual–cognitive theory*—children with autism have deficits in thinking and perception due to brain malfunctions (Schuler, 1995; Tager-Flusberg & Cohen, 1993). Withdrawal from the external world may be due to overstimulation by auditory, visual, and tactile stimuli. Interventions should be designed to provide high levels of structure, clarity, and simplicity.
- *Developmental theory*—children with autism fail to meet typical developmental milestones because of neurological impairments. Interventions are intended to facilitate progress through typical developmental sequences (Scheuermann & Webber, 2002).
- *Behavioral theory*—neurological impairments result in behavioral excesses and deficits due to failure to learn more appropriate, typical behaviors. Interventions are based on applied behavioral analysis and are designed to correct behavioral errors through direct skill instruction, antecedent manipulation, positive reinforcement, and behavior reduction strategies.
- *Relationship-based theory* (Heflin, 2002)—the atypical language, cognitive, and behavioral characteristics of children with autism are due to relationship and emotional deficits (Ricks & Wing, 1976), an inability to experience empathy (Gillberg, 1992), and problems with perspective-taking (Wimmer & Perner, 1983). Interventions focus on developing attachment and bonding and on helping the child feel safe in relationships.
- *Physiologically based theory* (Heflin, 2002)—also based on the assumption that autism is the result of neurological processing deficits. The goal of interventions is to correct these neurological functions by modifying input, processing, and output of external stimuli.

We understand the appeal of many of the unproven interventions described in Focus Here 16.1. However, educators must rely on those interventions that have the highest probability of producing desired outcomes in terms of (a) increases in language and socialization skills and (b) improvements in behavior. In our opinion, research evidence has overwhelmingly supported the behavioral and perceptual–cognitive approaches and associated interventions. Educators are responsible for ensuring effective programming for students with autism, which means choosing approaches and techniques based on evidence. When parents insist on interventions that are not well supported by acceptable scientific evidence, educators have three options:

1. attempt to persuade parents that other approaches may be more effective, using data-based articles from professional journals as support (see Appendix A of this book for resources);
2. try to find a mutually agreeable compromise in which approaches supported by parents are used in conjunction with other interventions; or
3. agree to the approaches preferred by parents, with the caveat that student progress will be closely monitored using objective measures (see Chapters 8 and 13). If sufficient progress does not result, new interventions must be implemented.

References

Allan, J. A. B. (1977). Some uses of "holding" with autistic children. *Special Education in Canada, 51,* 11–15.

Autism Society of America. (1992–1993, Winter). Facilitated communication under the microscope. *Advocate*, pp. 19–20.

Ayers, J. (1972). *Sensory integration and learning disorders.* Los Angeles: Western Psychological.

Ayers, J. (1979). *Sensory integration and the child.* Los Angeles: Western Psychological.

Berard, G. (1993). *Hearing equals behavior.* New Canaan, CT: Keats. (Original published 1982)

Berard, G. (1995). Concerning length, frequency, number, and follow-up AIT sessions. *The Sound Connection Newsletter, 2*(3), 5–6.

Bettison, S. (1996). The long-term effects of auditory training on children with autism. *Journal of Autism and Developmental Disorders, 26,* 179–197.

Biklen, D. (1990). Communication unbound: Autism and praxis. *Harvard Educational Review, 60,* 291–314.

Biklen, D. (1992). Typing to talk: Facilitated communication. *American Journal of Speech and Language Pathology, 1*(2), 15–17.

Biklen, D. (1993). *Communication unbound: How facilitated communication is challenging traditional views of autism and ability/disability.* New York: Teachers College Press.

Bondy, A., & Frost, L. (1994). The picture exchange communication system. *Focus on Autistic Behavior, 9*(3), 1–19.

Boucher, J., & Lewis, V. (1989). Memory impairments and communication in relatively able autistic children. *Journal of Child Psychology and Psychiatry, 30,* 90–122.

Calculator, S. N. (1992). Perhaps the emperor has clothes after all: A response to Biklen. *American Journal of Speech and Language Pathology, 1*(2), 18–20.

Case-Smith, J., & Bryan, T. (1999). The effects of occupational therapy with sensory integration emphasis on preschool-age children with autism. *American Journal of Occupational Therapy, 53*(5), 489–497.

Crossley, R. (1988, October). *Unexpected communication attainments by persons diagnosed as autistic and intellectually impaired.* Paper presented at the annual meeting of the International Society of Augmentative and Alternative Communication, Los Angeles, CA.

Crossley, R. (1992). Who said that? In DEAL Communication Centre (Eds.), *Facilitated communication training* (pp. 42–54). Melbourne, Australia: DEAL Communication Centre.

Crozier, S., & Tincani, M. J. (2005). Using a modified social story to decrease disruptive behavior of children with autism. *Focus on Autism and Other Developmental Disabilities, 20,* 150–157.

Dalrymple, N. (1995). Environmental supports to develop flexibility and independence. In K. A. Quill (Ed.), *Teaching children with autism: Strategies to enhance socialization and communication* (pp. 243–264). Albany, NY: Delmar.

DeGangi, G. A., & Greenspan, S. I. (1997). The effectiveness of short-term interventions in treatment of inattention and irritability in toddlers. *Journal of Developmental and Learning Disorders, 1,* 277–298.

Delano, M., & Snell, M. E. (2006). The effects of social stories on the social engagement of children with autism. *Journal of Positive Behavior Interventions, 8,* 29–42.

Earles, T., Carlson, J., & Bock, S. (1998). Instructional strategies to facilitate successful learning outcomes for students with autism. In R. Simpson & B. Myles (Eds.), *Educating children and youth with autism: Strategies for effective practices* (pp. 55–111). Austin, TX: PRO-ED.

Edelson, S. M., Arin, D., Bauman, M., Lukas, S. E., Rudy, J. H., Sholar, M., & Rimland, B. (1999). Auditory integration training: A double-blind study of behavioral and electrophysiological effects in people with autism. *Focus on Autism and Other Developmental Disabilities, 14*(2), 73–81.

Fisher, A., & Murray, E. (1991). Introduction to sensory integration theory. In A. Fisher, E. Murray, & A. Bondy (Eds.), *Sensory integration theory and practice* (pp. 3–27). Philadelphia: Davis.

Frost, L. A., & Bondy, A. (1994). *The picture exchange communication system training manual.* Wilmington, DE: Pyramid Educational Consultants.

Gillberg, C. (1992). Autism and autistic-like conditions: Subclasses among disorders of empathy (Emmanuel Miller Memorial Lecture 1991). *Journal of Child Psychology and Psychiatry, 33,* 813–842.

Gillberg, C., Johansson, M., Steffenburg, S., & Berlin, O. (1997). Auditory integration training in children with autism. *Autism: The International Journal of Research and Practice, 1,* 97–100.

Grandin, T. (1995). *Thinking in pictures.* New York: Doubleday.

Gray, C. (1995). Teaching children with autism to "read" social situations. In K. A. Quill (Ed.), *Teaching children with autism: Strategies to enhance socialization and communication* (pp. 219–241). Albany, NY: Delmar.

Gray, C., & Garand, J. (1993). Social stories: Improving responses of students with autism with accurate social information. *Focus on Autistic Behavior, 8*(1), 1–10.

Greenspan, S. I. (1992a). *Infancy and early childhood: The practice of clinical assessment and intervention with emotional and developmental challenges.* Madison, CT: International Universities Press.

Greenspan, S. I. (1992b). Reconsidering the diagnosis and treatment of very young children with autistic spectrum or pervasive developmental disorder. *Zero to Three, 13*(2), 1–9.

Greenspan, S. I., & Wieder, S. (1997). Developmental patterns and outcomes in infants and children with disorders in relating and communicating: A chart review of 200 cases of children with autistic spectrum diagnoses. *Journal of Developmental and Learning Disorders, 1,* 87–141.

Greenspan, S. I., & Wieder, S. (1998). *The child with special needs: Encouraging intellectual and emotional growth.* Reading, MA: Addison-Wesley.

Gresham, F. M., & MacMillan, D. L. (1997). Autistic recovery? An analysis and critique of the empirical evidence on the Early Intervention Project. *Behavioral Disorders, 22,* 185–201.

Hagiwara, T., & Myles, B. S. (1999). A multimedia social story intervention: Teaching skills to children with autism. *Focus on Autism and Other Developmental Disabilities, 14*(2), 82–95.

Heflin, J., & Simpson, R. (1998). Interventions for children and youth with autism: Prudent choices in a world of exaggerated claims and empty promises: Part I. Intervention and treatment option review. *Focus on Autism and Other Developmental Disabilities, 13*(4), 194–211.

Heflin, J., & Simpson, R. (2002). Understanding intervention controversies. In B. Scheuermann & J. Webber (Eds.), *Autism: Teaching does make a difference* (pp. 248–277). Belmont, CA: Wadsworth.

Hermelin, B., & O'Conner, N. (1970). *Psychological experiments with autistic children.* London: Pergamon Press.

Hodgdon, L. (1995). *Visual strategies for improving communication.* Troy, MI: QuirkRoberts.

Humphries, T. L. (2003). Effectiveness of pivotal response training as a behavioral intervention for young children with autism spectrum disorders. *Bridges, 2*(4), 1–7.

Kaufman, B. N. (1976). *Son-rise.* New York: Harper & Row.

Kaufman, B. (1994). *Son-rise: The miracle continues.* Tiburon, CA: H. J. Kramer.

Koegel, L. K., Koegel, R. L., Harrower, J. K., & Carter, C. M. (1999). Pivotal response intervention I: Overview of the approach. *Journal of the Association for the Severely Handicapped, 24,* 174–185.

Koegel, L. K., Koegel, R. L., Shoshan, Y., & McNerney, E. (1999). Preliminary long-term outcome data. *Journal of the Association for Persons with Severe Handicaps, 24,* 186–198.

Kuttler, S., Myles, B. S., & Carlson, J. K. (1998). The use of social stories to reduce precursors to tantrum behavior in a student with autism. *Focus on Autism and Other Developmental Disabilities, 13*(3), 176–182.

Layton, T. L., & Watson, L. R. (1995). Enhancing communication in nonverbal children with autism. In K. A. Quill (Ed.), *Teaching children with autism: Strategies to enhance communication and socialization* (pp. 73–101). Albany, NY: Delmar.

Lovaas, O. I. (1987). Behavioral treatment and normal educational and intellectual functioning in young autistic children. *Journal of Consulting and Clinical Psychology, 55,* 3–9.

MacDuff, G., Krantz, P., & McClannahan, L. (1993). Teaching children with autism to use pictographic activity schedules: Maintenance and generalization of complex response chains. *Journal of Applied Behavior Analysis, 26,* 89–97.

MacFarland, S. Z. C. (1995). Teaching strategies of the van Dijk curricular approach. *Journal of Visual Impairment and Blindness, 89,* 222–228.

Maurice, C. (1993). *Let me hear your voice: A family's triumph over autism.* New York: Ballantine.

Maurice, C. (Ed.). (1996). *Behavioral interventions for young children with autism: A manual for parents and professionals.* Austin, TX: PRO-ED.

McGee, J. J., & Gonzalez, L. (1990). Gentle teaching and the practice of human interdependence: A preliminary group study of 15 persons with severe behavioral disorders and their caregivers. In A. C. Repp & N. N. Singh (Eds.), *Perspectives on the use of nonaversive and aversive interventions for persons with developmental disabilities* (pp. 237–254). Sycamore, IL: Sycamore.

McGee, J. J., Menolascino, F. J., Hobbs, D. C., & Menousek, P. E. (1987). *Gentle teaching: A nonaversive approach to helping persons with mental retardation.* New York: Human Sciences Press.

Mirenda, P., & Santogrossi, J. (1985). A prompt-free strategy to teach pictorial communication system use. *Augmentative and Alternative Communication, 1,* 143–150.

Mudford, O. C. (1995). Review of the gentle teaching data. *American Journal on Mental Retardation, 99,* 345–355.

Mulick, J. A., Jacobson, J. W., & Kobe, F. H. (1993). Anguished silence and helping hands: Autism and facilitated communication. *Skeptical Inquirer, 17*(3), 270–280.

National Research Council, Division of Behavioral and Social Sciences and Education, Committee on Educational Interventions for Children with Autism. (2001). *Educating children with autism* (C. Lord & J. P. McGee, Eds.). Washington, DC: National Academy Press.

No Child Left Behind Act of 2001, 20 U.S.C. 70 § 6301 *et seq.* (2002)

Options Institute. (1999). *Autism Treatment Center of America: Son-Rise program.* Retrieved September 6, 2007, from http://www.autismtreatmentcenter.org

Prior, M., & Cummins, R. (1992). Questions about facilitated communication. *Journal of Autism and Developmental Disorders, 22,* 331–338.

Quill, K. (1997). Instructional considerations for young children with autism: The rationale for visually cued instruction. *Journal of Autism and Developmental Disorders, 27,* 697–714.

Ricks, D. M., & Wing, L. (1976). Language, communication, and the use of symbols in normal and autistic children. In J. K. Wing (Ed.), *Early childhood autism: Clinical, social, and educational aspects* (pp. 93–134). Oxford, England: Pergamon Press.

Rimland, B. (1992). A facilitated communication "horror story." *Autism Research Review, 6*(1), 1, 7.

Rimland, B., & Edelson, S. (1994). The effects of auditory integration training on autism. *American Journal of Speech-Language Pathology, 3*(2), 16–24.

Rogers, M. F., & Myles, S. B. (2001). Using social stories and comic strip conversations to interpret social situations for an adolescent with Asperger syndrome. *Intervention in School and Clinic, 36,* 310–313.

Scheuermann, B., & Webber, J. (2002). *Autism: Teaching DOES make a difference.* Belmont, CA: Wadsworth.

Scheuermann, B., & Hall, J. (2008). *Positive behavioral supports for the classroom.* Columbus, OH: Merrill/Pearson Educational.

Schuler, A. L. (1995). Thinking in autism: Differences in learning and development. In K. A. Quill (Ed.), *Teaching children with autism: Strategies to enhance communication and socialization* (pp. 11–32). New York: Delmar.

Schopler, E. (1992). Facilitated communication—hope or hype? *Autism Society of North Carolina, 8*(3), 6.

Siegel-Causey, E., & Guess, D. (1989). *Enhancing nonsymbolic communication interactions among learners with severe disabilities.* Baltimore: Brookes.

Simpson, R. L. (2005). Evidence-based practices and students with autism spectrum disorders. *Focus on Autism and Other Developmental Disabilities, 20*(3), 140–149.

Simpson, R., de Boer-Ott, S., Griswold, D., Myles, B., Byrd, S., Ganz, J. B., et al. (2005). *Autism spectrum disorders: Interventions and treatments for children and youth.* Thousand Oaks, CA: Corwin Press.

Simpson, R. L., & Myles, B. S. (1995). Effectiveness of facilitated communication with children and youth with autism. *The Journal of Special Education, 28,* 424–439.

Smith, T. (1996). Are other treatments effective? In C. Maurice (Ed.), *Behavioral intervention for young children with autism: A manual for parents and professionals* (pp. 45–59). Austin, TX: PRO-ED.

Stades-Veth, J. (1988). *Autism broken symbiosis: Persistent avoidance of eye contact with the mother. Causes, consequences, prevention and cure of autism form behavior in babies through "mother–child holding"* (Descriptive report). (ERIC Document Reproduction Service No. ED 294 344)

Steege, M. W., Mace, C., Perry, L., & Longenecker, L. (2007). Applied behavior analysis: Beyond discrete trial teaching. *Psychology in the Schools, 44*(1), 91–99.

Stehli, A. (1991). *The sound of a miracle: A child's triumph over autism.* New York: Doubleday.

Stillman, R. D., & Battle, C. W. (1984). Developing prelanguage communication in the severely handicapped: An interpretation of the van Dijk method. *Seminars in Speech and Language, 5,* 159–170.

Swaggart, B., Gagnon, E., Bock, S. J., Earles, T., Quinn, C., Myles, B. S., & Simpson, R. (1995). Using social stories to teach social and behavioral skills to children with autism. *Focus on Autistic Behavior, 10*(1), 1–14.

Szempruch, J., & Jacobson, J. W. (1993). Evaluating facilitated communication of people with developmental disabilities. *Research in Developmental Disabilities, 14,* 253–264.

Tager-Flusberg, H., & Cohen, D. (1993). An introduction to the debate. In S. Baron-Cohen, H. Tager-Flusberg, & D. J. Cohen (Eds.), *Understanding other minds: Perspectives from autism* (pp. 3–9). New York: Oxford University Press.

Tinbergen, N., & Tinbergen, E. A. (1983). *"Autistic" children: New hope for a cure.* London: Allen and Unwin.

van Dijk, J. (1967). The non-verbal deaf-blind child and his world: His outgrowth toward the world of symbols. In *Proceedings of the Jaarverslag Instituut voor Doven, 1964–1967* (pp. 73–110). Sint Michielsgestgel, The Netherlands: Instituut voor Doven.

van Dijk, J. (1986). An educational curriculum for deaf-blind multihandicapped persons. In D. Ellis (Ed.), *Sensory impairments in mentally handicapped people* (pp. 374–382). London: Croom-Helm.

Welch, M. G. (1988). Mother–child holding therapy and autism. *Pennsylvania Medicine, 91*(10), 33–38.

Wheeler, D., Jacobson, J., Paglieri, R., & Schwartz, A. (1993). An experimental assessment of facilitated communication. *Mental Retardation, 31,* 49–60.

Wieder, S. (1996). Integrated treatment approaches for young children with multisystem developmental disorder. *Infants and Young Children, 8*(3), 24–34.

Wilbarger, P., & Wilbarger, J. (1991). *Sensory defensiveness in children ages 2–12: An intervention guide for parents and other caretakers.* Denver: Avanti Educational Programs.

Wimmer, H., & Perner, J. (1983). Beliefs about beliefs: Representation and constraining function of wrong beliefs in young children's understanding of deception. *Cognition, 13,* 103–128.

Wolfberg, P., & Schuler, A. (1993). Integrated play groups: A model for promoting the social and cognitive dimensions of play. *Journal of Autism and Developmental Disorders, 23,* 1–23.

Zaslow, R. W., & Breger, L. (1969). A theory and treatment for autism. In L. Breger (Ed.), *Clinical cognitive psychology* (pp. 246–289). Englewood Cliffs, NJ: Prentice Hall.

Appendix A:
Resources Pertaining to Autism

Journals and Periodicals

The Analysis of Verbal Behavior and *The Behavior Analyst* and *Behavior Analysis in Practice*
> Available from Association for Behavior Analysis International; http://www.abainternational.org/journals.asp

Autism Advocate
> Available from the Autism Society of America, 7910 Woodmont Ave., Suite 650, Bethesda, MD 20814-3015; phone: 301-657-0881/800-3AU-TISM; fax: 301-657-0869; http://www.autism-society.org/

Autism—The International Journal of Research and Practice
> Available from Sage Publications, in association with The National Autistic Society, 393 City Rd., London, EC1V 1NE, United Kingdom; phone: +44 (0)171 833 2299; fax: +44 (0) 171 833 9666; http://www.sagepub.co.uk/journalsProdDesc.nav?prodid=journal200822

Autism Research Review International
> Available from Autism Research Institute, Bernard Rimland, PhD, Director, 4182 Adams Ave., San Diego, CA 92116; phone: 619-281-7165; http://www.autismwebsite.com/ari/arri/arriindex.htm

e-Speaks Newsletter
> On-line newsletter from Autism Speaks, 2 Park Ave., 11th Floor, New York, NY 10016; phone: 212-252-8676; fax: 212-252-8676; http://www.autismspeaks.org

Exceptional Parent Magazine
> 65 East Route 4, River Edge, NJ 07661; phone: 800-489-0074; http://www.eparent.com

Focus on Autism and Other Developmental Disabilities
> Available from PRO-ED, Inc., 8700 Shoal Creek Blvd., Austin, TX 78757; phone: 512-451-3246/800-897-3202; fax: 512-451-8542; http://www.proedinc.com/Scripts/prodView.asp?idProduct=1649

inSight
> Available from the The ARC of the United States, 1010 Wayne Ave., Suite 650, Silver Spring, MD 20910; phone: 301-565-3842; fax: 301-565-3843

Journal of Autism and Developmental Disorders
> Available from Springer, 233 Spring St., New York, NY 10013-1578; phone: 212-460-1501; fax: 212-460-1595; http://www.springer.com/east/home/psychology?SGWID=5-10126-70-3554341

MAAP Services, Inc., P.O. Box 524, Crown Point, IN 46308; phone: 219-662-1311; fax: 219-662-0638; http://www.maapservices.org/index.html

Books

Introduction/General Reference

Autism: Facts and Strategies for Parents, by Jan Janzen (Therapy Skill Builders, 1999)

Autism, Understanding the Disorder, by Gary B. Mesibov, Lynn Adams, and Laura Klinger (Plenum Press, 1997)

Targeting Autism: What We Know, Don't Know and Can Do to Help Young Children With Autism and Related Disorders, by Shirley Cohen (University of California Press, 1998)

World of the Autistic Child: Understanding and Treating Autistic Spectrum Disorders, by Bryna Siegel (Oxford University Press, 1996)

Asperger Syndrome

Asperger Syndrome: A Guide for Educators and Parents (2nd ed.), by Brenda Smith Myles and Richard Simpson (PRO-ED, 2003)

Asperger Syndrome: A Practical Guide for Teachers by Val Cumine, Julia Leach, and Gill Stevenson (David Fulton Publishers, 1998)

Asperger's Syndrome: A Guide for Parents and Professionals, by Tony Attwood (Jessica Kingsley, Inc., 1998)

Asperger Syndrome in the Inclusive Classroom by Stacy Betts, Dion Betts, and Lisa Gerber-Eckard (Jessica Kingsley, 2007)

Children and Youth with Asperger Syndrome by Brenda Smith Myles (Cowin Press, 2005)

The Complete Guide to Asperger's Syndrome by Tony Attwood (Jessica Kingsley, 2007)

Treatment Methods

The ABA Program Companion: Organizing Quality Programs for Children with Autism and PDD by J. Tyler Fovel (DRL Books, Inc., 2002)

Autism Spectrum Disorders: Interventions and Treatments for Children and Youth, by Richard L. Simpson, Sonja R. deBoer-Ott, Deborah E. Griswold, Brenda S. Myles, Sandra E. Byrd, Jennifer B. Ganz, Katherine T. Cook, Kaye L. Otten, Josefa Ben-Arieh, Sue Ann Kline, and Lisa G. Adams (Corwin Press, 2005)

Autism Treatment Guide (2nd ed.), by Elizabeth K. Gerlach (Four Leaf Press, 1996)

Behavioral Intervention for Young Children With Autism: A Manual for Parents and Professionals, by Catherine Maurice, Gina Greene, and Stephen Luce (PRO-ED, 1996)

Biological Treatments for Autism and PDD, by William Shaw (Sunflower Press, 1997)

Educating Children with Autism, by the National Research Council (National Academy Press, 2001)

Making a Difference: Behavioral Intervention for Autism by Catherine Maurice, Gina Green, and Richard Foxx (PRO-ED, 2001)

Right From the Start: Behavioral Intervention for Young Children with Autism, by Sandra Harris and May Jane Weiss (Woodbine House, 1998)

Social and Communication Development in Autism Spectrum Disorders: Early Identification, Diagnosis, and Intervention edited by Tony Charman and Wendy Stone (The Guilford Press, 2006)

Taking the Mystery Out of Medications in Autism/Asperger's Syndromes by Luke Tsai (Future Horizons, 2001)

Teaching Developmentally Disabled Children: The ME Book, by O. Ivar Lovaas (PRO-ED, 1981, reprinted 1992)

A Work in Progress: Behavioral Management Strategies and a Curriculum for Intensive Behavioral Treatment of Autism, by Ron Leaf and John McEachin (Different Roads to Learning, 1999)

Personal/Family Accounts

Emergence: Labeled Autistic, by Temple Grandin (Warner Books, 1986)

Let Me Hear Your Voice: A Family's Triumph Over Autism, by Catherine Maurice (Fawcett Columbine, 1993)

Thinking in Pictures and Other Reports of My Life With Autism, by Temple Grandin (Vintage Books, 1995)

Education

Autism: Teaching DOES Make a Difference, by Brenda Scheuermann and Jo Webber (Wadsworth, 2002)

Creating a Win–Win IEP for Students With Autism, by Beth Fouse (Future Horizons, 1997)

Educating Children and Youth With Autism, by Brenda Smith Myles and Richard Simpson (PRO-ED, 1998)

One-on-One: Working With Lower-Functioning Children With Autism and Other Developmental Disabilities, by Marilyn Chassman (IEP Resources, 1999)

Parent Survival Manual, edited by Eric Schopler (Plenum Press, 1995)

The Picture Exchange Communication System Training Manual, by Lori A. Frost and Andy Bondy (Pyramid Educational Consultants, 1994)

Solving Behavior Problems in Autism: Improving Communication With Visual Strategies, by Linda Hodgdon (Quirk Roberts, 1999)

Steps to Independence (3rd ed.), by Bruce Baker and Alan Brightman (Paul H. Brookes Publishing, 1997)

Students with Autism: Characteristics and Instruction Programming by Jack Scott, Claudia Clark, and Michael Brady (Singular, 2000)

Teaching Children With Autism: Strategies to Enhance Communication and Socialization, by Kathleen Ann Quill (Delmar/ITP, 1995)

Teaching Students with Autism by Teresa Robinson (DayOne publishing, 2005)

Toilet Training Individuals With Autism and Related Disorders, by Maria Wheeler (Future Horizons, 1999)

Visual Strategies for Improving Communication, by Linda Hodgdon (Quirk Roberts, 1995)

Visual Structured Tasks: Independent Activities for Students With Autism and Other Visual Learners, by Division TEACCH (Autism Society of North Carolina, 1998)

Other

Autism How-To Handbook, by Beverly Braman and Susan Catlett (Autism Consultation and Education, 2006) Available at http://autism-how-to.com

Autism: Identification, Education, and Treatment (2nd ed.), edited by Dianne Berkell Zager (Lawrence Erlbaum Associates, 1999)

Autism Through the Lifespan: The Eden Model, by David L. Holmes (Woodbine House, 1998)

The Complete IEP Guide: How to Advocate for Your Special Ed Child, by Lawrence M. Siegel (Nolo Press, 1999)

Helpful Responses to Some of the Behaviors of Individuals With Autism, by Nancy Dalrymple (Indiana Resource Center for Autism, 1992)

Pervasive Developmental Disorders: Finding a Diagnosis and Getting Help, by Mitzi Waltz (O'Reilly & Associates, 1999)

Appendix B:

Handouts for Professional Team Training

Characteristics of Autism

Individuals with severe forms of the disorder exhibit characteristics in all of the following categories:

Communication and Language Deficits

- Deficits in language, including mutism, perseveration, and echolalia
- Lack of communicative intent
- Lack of communicative reciprocity
- Idiosyncratic speech
- Literal, rigid use of speech, usually with immature grammar
- Lack of appropriate use of prosody and nonverbal communication
- Problems with language comprehension

Cognitive Deficits

- Here-and-now thinking (literal, restricted, and rigid patterns)
- Lack of curiosity and motivation to explore the environment
- Tendency to overselect irrelevant environmental stimuli and not attend to important phenomena (e.g., social cues)
- Lack of appropriate play, especially imaginary play
- Obsessive desire for sameness and repetition
- Good rote memory in some instances
- Occasionally, extraordinary skills (memory, math, art)
- Often, mental retardation

Social Deficits

- Resistance to being touched, cuddled, held
- Lack of joint attention
- May not respond to name
- Seems oblivious to parental presence
- Inability to relate to others in an ordinary manner
- Little or no interest in peers or their activities
- Isolation from the outside world: Autistic aloneness
- Little or no eye contact or social smiling
- Prefers objects to people and often treats people as objects
- No friendships or only a few
- Does not display social reciprocity or empathy
- Social skill and social competency deficits

- Lack of typical play behaviors
- Lack of responsiveness to stimuli that typically produce emotional responses

Sensory Processing Deficits

- Extreme fear reactions to loud noises, strangers, new situations, changes, surprises
- Low-level responses to physical pain and interaction from others
- May appear as deaf and blind
- Distinct food and clothing preferences often related to texture
- Tactile defensiveness

Stereotypic Behavior

- Stereotyped (habitual and repetitive) movements, such as rocking or spinning objects
- Stereotyped activities and interests
- Compulsive adherence to a few routines and/or activities
- Preoccupation with a few objects
- Self-injurious behaviors
- Sometimes aggressive and tantrum behaviors

The Antecedents–Behavior–Consequences (A–B–C) Model

All of the instructional and behavior management principles of applied behavior analysis can be categorized in an easy-to-understand format, called the A–B–C model. We illustrate this model as:

Antecedents ——————➤ Behavior ◄—————— Consequences

Antecedents

- Occur prior to the behavior
- Identify antecedents to challenging behaviors
- Plan antecedents for desired behaviors
- To increase the controlling power of an antecedent for desired behavior, establish stimulus control by teaching that antecedent as a discriminative stimulus

Behaviors

- Target behaviors should be operationalized (described specifically and precisely)
- Measure behaviors using event recording (restricted or unrestricted) or duration recording

Consequences

- Positive reinforcement—a consequence following a behavior that increases the probability that the behavior will be repeated
  - Primary reinforcers
  - Secondary reinforcers
  - Idiosyncratic reinforcers
- Reinforcement schedules—planned timing of reinforcement: frequency with which reinforcement is given
  - Continuous schedule of reinforcement—every correct response is reinforced
  - Intermittent schedules of reinforcement—only some correct responses are reinforced
    - ratio schedules—used to increase discrete behaviors; reinforcement is given after a predetermined number of behaviors
    - response duration schedules—used to increase ongoing behaviors; reinforcement is given following a predetermined duration of the target behavior

- ◆ interval schedules—reinforcement is given for the first correct response following a predetermined period of time
- Negative reinforcement—removing or ending a negative stimulus following a behavior, which increases the probability that the behavior will be repeated when the individual encounters that same aversive stimulus
- Punishment—a consequence following a behavior that decreases the probability the behavior will be repeated
  - —Response cost
  - —Time-out
  - —Administration of an aversive stimulus

Data Collection Systems

For students with autism, we use data collection for two general purposes: to monitor progress in learning new skills and to monitor behaviors targeted for reduction.

Data Collection Systems Are Either

- **Permanent product recording**—data are collected from tangible results of behavior (e.g., number of menus wiped off, percentage of items correctly sorted)
- **Observational recording**—data are collected by directly observing the student

Observational Recording Systems Include

- **Event recording**—for counting discrete behaviors
  - —Unrestricted event—for behaviors that occur any time and not in response to identifiable antecedents
  - —Restricted events—for behaviors that occur only in the presence of an antecedent; you must count both the antecedent and the response
- **Duration recording**—for measuring how long behaviors occur
- **Latency recording**—for measuring how long it takes a behavior to begin once a cue for the behavior is given

Baseline Data

A few days of baseline data should be collected before beginning intervention, except for behaviors that are dangerous or highly disruptive.

Data May Need to Be Converted Before Graphing

- Unrestricted event data—do not need to be converted OR you may wish to convert to rate:

$$\text{Rate of behavior per minute, hour, day} = \frac{\text{Number of responses}}{\text{Total time observed}}$$

- Restricted event data—convert to a percentage:

$$\text{Percentage of responses that are correct} = \frac{\text{Number of correct responses}}{\text{Number of opportunities to respond}} \times 100$$

- Duration data may be reported simply as number of minutes and/or seconds, or they may be converted to the total percentage of time that the target behavior occurs:

$$\text{Percentage of time that student responds} = \frac{\text{Total response time}}{\text{Total observed or allotted time}} \times 100$$

- Duration may also be reported as the average amount of time that the behavior occurs:

$$\text{Average duration} = \frac{\text{Total response time for all sessions}}{\text{Number of sessions, opportunities,}\atop\text{or observation times}}$$

- For latency data, simply report number of minutes and/or seconds

To Set Up a Graph for Graphing Data

- Determine whether you need a raw number graph, a percentage graph, a rate graph, or a minutes/seconds graph
- Label the vertical axis to reflect the amount of behavior to be graphed
- Label the horizontal axis to reflect the observation sessions
- Indicate mastery criterion by drawing a horizontal line from the appropriate level on the vertical axis across the graph
- Record baseline data
- Divide baseline data from intervention data with a vertical dotted line
- Connect data points (but do not connect data points across the vertical intervention line)

How to Conduct
Discrete Trial Teaching (DTT)

DTT is an intensive method for bringing discrete behaviors or responses under stimulus control. It is best used for new learning or when a student needs drill-and-practice to master behaviors or skills.

Step 1. Discriminative Stimulus (S^D)

- Get attention first
- Make it clear and simple
- Make it prominent
- Make it relevant
- Give S^{D}s consistently at first
- Give only one S^D per trial

Step 2. Prompt

- Administer as part of the S^D
- Select an effective prompt that is the least intrusive
- Plan to fade the prompt systematically
- Probe occasionally to see if prompts have become unnecessary

Step 3. Response

- Ensure it is something the student needs to learn
- Define it operationally
- Ensure you are able to observe it and measure it

Step 4. Consequence

- Reinforce correct responses; DO NOT reinforce incorrect responses
- Ensure that the reinforcers are effective
- Manipulate the power of the reinforcers
- Use frequent reinforcement for new learning and then fade to intermittent reinforcement
- Reinforce prompted trials in most cases
- Provide consequences immediately and consistently
- Make consequences contingent on specified student behavior
- Make sure the student can discriminate punishing from reinforcing consequences
- Use only a mild punisher, "No," for incorrect responding, or give no response at all

Step 5. Intertrial Interval

- Provide enough time to distinguish each trial
- Use this time to record data and make instructional decisions
- Reinforce other behaviors but keep student on task
- Manipulate nature of intertrial interval according to individual reactions

Naturalistic/Milieu Teaching Procedures

Naturalistic/milieu teaching procedures consist of a set of teaching strategies, based on ABA principles, primarily for the purpose of teaching communication and language (Westling & Fox, 2004). The word *milieu,* which is French for *environment* or *setting,* implies that instruction directly relates to the natural context.

Model

- Note student interest in objects or situations
- Establish joint attention with the student
- Give appropriate model for the student to achieve the desired effect
- If response is correct, praise and allow the desired effect
- If response is incorrect, present the correct model again
- If response is correct, praise and allow the desired effect
- If response is incorrect, present the correct model a last time and allow the desired effect

Mand–Model

- Set up situations to stimulate student interest
- Note when student becomes interested
- Establish joint attention with the student
- Present a verbal mand related to the situation of interest
- If response is correct, praise and allow desired effect
- If response is incorrect, repeat mand and model, if necessary
- If response is correct, praise and allow desired effect
- If response is incorrect, repeat mand and model and allow the desired effect

Time Delay

- Identify situations in which the student might require assistance or want something
- In these situations, establish joint attention
- Wait 5 to 15 seconds for a correct behavior
- If response is correct, praise and allow desired effect
- If response is incorrect, implement either a mand–model or model procedure

Constructing and Using
Individual Schedules

1. **Teach matching and sequencing.** Students will need to be able to match the schedule symbol to the designated activity.

2. **Begin with concrete objects to represent scheduled tasks and activities.** If students do not understand symbols (pictures, line drawings, or the printed word), begin by using concrete objects. For example, a spoon signifies lunch, an audiotape signifies music time, a small ball signifies physical education, a bolt signifies vocational time, a small chair or a piece of leather signifies the bean-bag chair (leisure time). Concrete objects can be placed in cubbies, put in boxes, or Velcroed onto some type of backing.

3. **Work toward printed schedules.** Printed schedules are certainly the most versatile and efficient; however, students who never learn to read can probably be taught to interpret line drawings (pictures) as symbols for activities and tasks.

4. **Make the symbols salient.** The schedule symbols should stand out from background material.

5. **Provide finished indicators.** Finishing a task or activity can be indicated in several ways: The student can place a symbol in a different spot that signifies "finished," such as a designated pocket or a "finished" box. The student may be taught to cover up each completed activity symbol with a black card (these would also need Velcro) or with a card that says "finished," or to turn the activity symbol around so only the back is visible once the activity is completed. For students who can read, you might try teaching them to cross through the activity description or check it off.

6. **Develop schedules that are flexible.** Schedules will inevitably change as school-wide activities change and as the student progresses through the curriculum.

7. **Use Velcro to affix objects or pictures to the schedule card.** Velcro will have many uses in instructional materials for students with low-functioning autism.

8. **Match the type of schedule to individual student characteristics.** Consider each student's preferences and cognitive abilities when developing a schedule.

9. **Work toward portable schedules.** Portable schedules will allow students to use schedules in a wider variety of situations.

10. **Teach a routine of checking schedules as each activity is completed.** Teach students the routine of checking their schedules after each task or activity is completed or in response to other cues (e.g., entering the class in the morning, hearing the timer, hearing a bell).

Common Classroom Procedures
and Routines

Entering the Classroom

1. Open door
2. WALK straight into classroom QUIETLY
3. If carrying items, go to cubby, closet, desk (pick one)
4. Place items in proper place
5. Check schedule

Leaving the Classroom

1. Put away materials
2. Go to cubby, closet, desk (pick one)
3. Obtain items to take (e.g., items to go home, lunch money, kickball)
4. Line up at door
5. WALK out of the classroom after teacher gives cue

Obtaining Materials

1. Walk to the cubby, closet, desk
2. Open door or drawer
3. Remove necessary materials (e.g., pens, pencils, paper, markers, pots, pans)
4. Ask teacher if you need help
5. Close closet, drawer, and so forth
6. Take materials to proper place

Following the Daily Schedule

1. Go to schedule
2. Look at picture or word card at top or left
3. Pull picture and/or word from schedule (or take schedule with you)
4. Complete designated activity
5. Remove that picture, word, and so forth
6. Look at the next item to the left or on top
7. Repeat steps

Choosing Activities

1. Walk to the choice board
2. Choose a picture, description, and so forth
3. Take the picture, description, item, etc., with you

4. Go to the activity of choice
5. Replace the picture, description, etc., after completing the activity

Completing Activities

This will require cues to indicate when something is finished, such as finished boxes, bells, timers, jigs.

1. Keep working until one of the following occurs:
   - Finished box is full
   - Card is filled with tokens
   - Timer is sounded
   - Bell sounds
   - Music stops
   - Teacher stands up
2. Put materials away
3. Go to schedule and check it

Making Transitions

1. Listen/watch for cue
2. Stop working, eating, playing when cue is given
3. Stand up
4. Check schedule
5. WALK to wait chair or area if
   - Others are not ready
   - The bell has not sounded
   - Teacher says to wait
6. Line up if leaving room in a group
7. WALK to next activity or place

Waiting

1. Listen/watch for cue to wait (teacher command, hand signal, red light)
2. Go to wait place (bench, chair) and sit
3. Choose a wait activity (e.g., comic book, hand-held computer, listening to tape on Walkman) and QUIETLY perform activity
4. Stop activity when there is a cue to move to next activity
5. Put material away and move to next place

Toileting

1. Ask to use toilet (signs, pictures, speech)
2. Wait for teacher to open bathroom door
3. Go into bathroom and close door

4. Go to toilet

5. Pull down pants (or unzip pants)

6. Sit on toilet (or stand facing toilet)

7. Eliminate

8. Pull up pants (zipper)

9. Flush toilet

10. Go to sink and wash hands

11. Dry hands

12. Walk out of door

Eating

1. Wash hands before sitting at table

2. Sit with feet on floor facing front; scoot chair close to table

3. Put napkin on lap (or in shirt collar)

4. Shake milk and open carton

5. Cut meat, if necessary

6. Using fork or spoon, take a bite

7. Keep second hand on lap

8. Chew quietly, with mouth closed

Teaming: Effective Communication Skills

The main ingredient for building a team, motivating performance, and ensuring consistency across teaching adults is effective communication. This includes giving information in a way that others can hear it, listening to others, and knowing how to use negotiation.

- **Listen well.** When other individuals are speaking, attend to them by making eye contact and appropriate facial expressions. Communicate interest with your body by leaning forward, nodding, and asking questions. Try to reflect the speaker's feelings and paraphrase the speaker to clarify the message. For example, say things such as, "You seem pretty upset about that," or "Are you saying you want me to help you with this task?" Pay attention to the speaker's body language and behavior. Many times people say one thing (e.g., how happy they are) but communicate another (e.g., anger). After the conversation, summarize what was discussed and/or decided.

- **Speak in a lively way, fluently, and with confidence.**

- **Use the language of feelings and positive one-liners.** For example, respond to comments with "I feel . . ." statements or ask, "How does that make you feel?" Give quick feedback with phrases such as, "Great smile," "Dynamite technique," or "Super job."

- **Use self-disclosure to help build relationships and keep communication lines open.** The more open you are with information, the safer others will feel about sharing personal information.

- **Interpret behavior and use body language to enhance your message.** Crossed arms, a tight face, and glaring eyes communicate anger and/or defensiveness. Open arms, a relaxed face, and smiling eyes communicate happiness, relaxation, and contentment. Be sure that your body language is communicating interest and respect.

- **Express open-mindedness.** Remain open to alternate ideas and suggestions. For example, refrain from becoming defensive and protective of a particular method. Ask often for other adults' opinions and encourage discussion.

- **Give constructive feedback.** Just as with students, adults will benefit from feedback about their performance. Feedback is necessary for people to know whether they should continue to behave in certain ways or should change their behavior. Feedback is best given after someone has been instructed to behave a certain way and has tried it. Ask questions in a conversational tone and listen to the answers. Avoid telling someone they "should" and/or "must" do something and using other judgmental phrases. Instead, tell them they "might try" a different technique or "would do well" to do something different. Justify your feedback and use "I" language. Offer assistance if it seems to be needed. Model the behavior you want. Adults also learn well through visual cues.

- **Genuinely reinforce people when they do what you asked.** Adults like praise, if it is genuine and they earned it. Notes of gratitude, positive facial expressions or body language, and bragging to others about someone's work will all probably work as reinforcement for the team members.

- **Avoid communication roadblocks.**

  1. **Being overly punitive.** Most people will avoid persons who punish them severely and regularly. Avoid scolding, harsh criticism, and threats. Also avoid passive–aggressive behaviors, such as withholding necessary information or giving incorrect information, talking negatively about individuals behind their back, "forgetting" to invite someone to a meeting or a gathering, or allowing a person to fail when it could have been prevented.

  2. **Displays of impatience.** Body language that communicates that you do not want to have the conversation or that you are uninterested in what is being said is a real "turn-off." Remember to communicate interest and attention.

  3. **Expressions of overconcern.** Communication can be blocked by someone who is too serious or who blows things out of proportion. Take what people are willing to tell you and probe sparingly.

  4. **Arguing.** Arguing about who or what is right is a way to halt communication. Discussions can be useful, but if the goal is to be right and have everyone agree that you are right, arguments may follow. The goal of a discussion is to acquire and digest information. We recommend avoiding topics that might cause arguments, such as religion or politics.

  5. **Ridiculing or belittling.** Making fun of someone's actions or beliefs may impair a relationship forever. Everyone is to be treated with respect. People need to feel psychologically safe.

  6. **Making false promises.** It will not take long for team members to develop mistrust and miscommunication if false promises are made. Say what you mean and mean what you say. Follow through on commitments in a timely manner, and other adults will probably do the same.

  7. **Rejecting the individual.** Be careful to not criticize or reject a person. It is acceptable to correct, change, or request behavior. Thus, comments such as, "I prefer that graphs be done every Friday," are very different from "You're a procrastinator, and you need to change!"

Teaming: Planning Steps

1. Decide where you want to go.
2. Decide where you are now.
3. Delineate steps, activities, or objectives for reaching the goal from the starting point.
4. Assign responsibility for each step, activity, or objective.
5. Assign a time line for accomplishing each step, activity, or objective.

Teaming: Problem-Solving Steps

1. Identify the problem.
2. Brainstorm solutions to the problem.
3. Analyze the solutions in terms of costs and benefits.
4. Pick a solution and plan a course of action (assign responsibilities and time lines).
5. Implement the solution.
6. Evaluate the results.

Considerations for Developing Curricula

- Develop the curricula as a team that includes family members and other individuals who are invested in long-term goals.
- Choose a curriculum that will facilitate a student's ability to live a productive, fulfilling life.
- The chosen curricula should result in functional skills.
- The chosen curricula should be longitudinal.
- The chosen curricula should be horizontally integrated.
- The chosen curricula should be chronologically age appropriate.
- The chosen curricula should be community referenced.
- The chosen curricula should include communication and social skills.

Curriculum Development Process

1. Set long-term goals
2. Develop an individualized curricular inventory (Ecological inventory)
3. Refine the curricula (Task analysis and levels of learning)
4. Determine what to teach this year
5. Determine current functioning level within a curriculum (Assessment)
6. Develop units of instruction
7. Write annual goals and objectives
8. Teach to generalization

Progress Data Recording

Types of Progress Data Recording

- Permanent product recording: You can count this at a later time
- Observational recording: You record when you observe the behavior occurring

Types of Observational Recording

- Event recording: Count the number of times a behavior occurs
- Duration recording: Count how long a behavior occurs
- Latency recording: Count how long it takes for the behavior to begin after a cue is given
- Rate data: Count how many behaviors occur relative to a given time period

Types of Recording Forms

- General event recording forms for single or multiple behaviors
- Task analytic forms depicting prompts
- General duration and latency forms
- Trial-by-trial forms depicting controlled presentations and prompts
- Naturalistic/milieu teaching forms depicting natural S^Ds and prompts

Skinner's Verbal Behavior Categories (Verbal Operants)

Expressive Behavior Categories

1. **Echoic.** An *echoic* is simply vocal imitation. Someone says something, and the learner imitates what was said. For example, the teacher points to another child and says, "Sam." The learner repeats "Sam." Sam and the teacher smile.

2. **Motor imitation.** The learner imitates motor movement made by someone else. For example, a speech therapist sticks her tongue out, and the learner produces the same behavior.

3. **Mand.** *Mand* is short for the word *command* or *demand*. It means to make a request. The antecedent in this case has to be something the learner wants (e.g., yogurt). The child says, "Yogurt, please" (mand) and usually receives what he or she wanted (*reinforcement*).

4. **Tact.** *Tact* could be short for *contact* or *tactile*. *Tact* means to label or name objects, events, relations, properties, and so forth (perhaps as a result of sensual stimulation, such as smell or sight). Adjectives and prepositions are also tacts. For example, a teacher holds up a pair of glasses, and the learner says, "Glasses."

5. **Intraverbal.** An *intraverbal* is responding to someone else's verbal behavior with a response that does not directly match (echoic) what the other person said. An intraverbal is conversational and includes answering "Wh–" questions. For example, the teacher says, "What did you watch on TV last night?" and the student says, "I watched cartoons."

Receptive Categories

1. **Receptive language.** The learner follows directions (nonverbal behavior) or complies with another person's mands. For example, a teacher tells the learner to line up at the door, the learner complies, and the teacher nods in approval.

2. **Receptive by feature, function, and class (RFFC).** The learner can identify items in the environment when provided with a description of them. For example, a teacher says, "Show me your backpack," and the student points to his or her backpack. Another example would be the teacher says, "Get the big red ball," and the student retrieves it.

Strategies for Improving Social Skills

Teacher-Mediated Interventions

- Direct instruction
- Pivotal response training
- Social scripts
- Antecedent prompting
- Social stories

Peer-Mediated Interventions

- Peer confederates
- Partners-at-lunch (PAL)

Facilitating Generalization of Social Skills

- Teach pivotal behaviors
- Use naturalistic/milieu teaching
- Use peer confederates in natural social contexts
- Teach students to attend to social models
- Teach other individuals (a) to expect social behavior from students with autism and (b) how to prompt those behaviors
- Teach other individuals to recognize social attempts
- Teach other individuals to reinforce social behavior
- Teach students with autism to recognize reinforcement

Steps in Functional Assessment and Intervention Planning

1. Identify challenging behavior(s)
2. Collect data for challenging behaviors
   a. Indirect data
      i. Brief Functional Assessment Interview Form
         1. Completed by teachers, paraprofessionals, and other adults who know the student well
         2. May be completed during an interview, or individuals may fill out the form independently
      ii. Functional Behavioral Assessment Inventory
         1. Completed by teacher
      iii. Functional Analysis Screening Tool
         1. Completed by teacher and other adults who work closely with the student
         2. Indicates possible functions for challenging behaviors
   b. Direct data
      i. A–B–C Report Form
         1. Observe during time when challenging behaviors are likely to occur
         2. Record only facts relating to challenging behaviors: immediate antecedents and consequences
         3. Complete summary questions following each observation
      ii. Structured A–B–C Analysis Form
         1. Complete as instances of target behaviors occur
         2. Produces scores that indicate possible functions for challenging behaviors
3. Analyze data
   a. Examine data for patterns of antecedents and consequences
   b. Examine data for indications of functions
4. Formulate hypotheses for challenging behaviors
   a. Hypotheses should address each of the following:
      i. Antecedent hypotheses (when and where behavior is likely to occur; conditions under which behavior is likely to occur)
      ii. Skill-deficit hypotheses (new skills the student needs to learn)
      iii. Function hypotheses (functions that the challenging behavior serves for the student)
   b. More than one hypothesis for each challenging behavior may be needed
   c. Ensure that each hypothesis is supported by the data (suggested in either the indirect or direct data); the more data support for a hypothesis, the stronger the hypothesis

    d. Use Hypothesis Development Form to record hypotheses

5. Develop interventions

    a. Use Behavior Management Analysis Chart for planning interventions

    b. Each hypothesis should be addressed in one or more interventions

6. Monitor interventions

    a. Use data-monitoring systems described in Chapters 2, 8, or 13 to measure target behaviors

    b. If target behaviors are not changing in the desired direction:

        i.   Adjust the intervention (e.g., increase reinforcement, change reinforcers)

        ii. Design a new intervention based on existing hypotheses

        iii. Collect additional data and develop new hypotheses

Consequence Strategies for Reducing Challenging Behaviors

Differential Reinforcement

- Differential reinforcement of incompatible behavior (DRI)—reinforce behaviors that are incompatible with the challenging behavior(s)

- Differential reinforcement of communicative behavior (DRC)—a variation of DRI; reinforce communicative behaviors designed to address the communicative function of the challenging behavior(s)

- Differential reinforcement of other behavior (DRO)—reinforce increasingly long periods of time during which the target challenging behavior(s) does not occur

- Differential reinforcement of lower levels of behavior (DRL)—reinforce the student when the number or duration of the challenging behavior(s) is less than a predetermined level; gradually lower the amount of behavior allowed for reinforcement until the behavior reaches the desired criterion

Extinction

- Withhold all forms of reinforcement for the target behavior(s); as soon as the target challenging behavior ceases, reinforce student for appropriate behavior; will only be effective if you are able to control all sources of reinforcement for the inappropriate behavior

- May be ineffective for youngsters with autism whose behaviors are seldom maintained by the attention of others

Response Cost

Remove previously earned reinforcers contingent upon inappropriate behavior: examples include minutes of free time and tokens. Response–cost is somewhat abstract and therefore may not be the best behavior-reduction strategy for many children.

Time-Out

Time-out can take a variety of forms; use the least exclusionary form that will control the target behavior. Ensure that time-out is not reinforcing for student; students with autism may actually like time-out if, for example, it provides a time for uninterrupted self-stimulation.

Aversives

Reprimands are a common aversive and the only type of aversive that we recommend. *Caution:* aversives should be used sparingly, if at all; traditional aversives may be ineffective for some children with autism. Aversives should only be used *after* less intrusive and positive support strategies have been tried and should only be used *in conjunction with* more positive strategies (reinforcement of desired behaviors, teaching replacement behaviors).

Overcorrection

- Positive practice overcorrection—student practices the appropriate behavior multiple times each time the inappropriate behavior is exhibited
- Restitutional overcorrection—student is required to correct any damage resulting from an inappropriate behavior
- Use overcorrection procedures sparingly: Only after other, more positive strategies have proven ineffective and only in conjunction with reinforcement of desired behaviors

Possible Functions and Interventions for Specific Challenging Behaviors

Potential Functions	Interventions
Noncompliance	
Escape or avoidance	• Teach student to communicate "No," ask for a break, or ask to leave situation • Change how tasks are done • Increase reinforcement during disliked tasks • Provide shorter tasks • Make tasks more functional (e.g., teach tasks that are immediately useable and/or relevant, teach tasks in naturalistic/milieu settings)
Communication	• Identify communicative intent and teach appropriate communicative expressions and methods (e.g., teach student to point to picture card that communicates "I want to take a break") • Differentially reinforce appropriate communication (DRC)
Skill deficit	• Teach compliance using discrete trial format; begin by teaching simple one-step commands that are easily prompted (e.g., touch head, stand up); gradually increase complexity of commands • Differentially reinforce compliance (DRI)
Confusion or uncertainty about expected behavior	• Provide concise and clear instructions, using as few words as possible • Use picture communication cues, visual schedules, and other methods to enhance clarity and expectations (see Chapter 5) • Present one task or instruction at a time; for complex tasks, give instructions or prompts for one step at a time
Aggression	
Communication	• Identify communicative intent and teach more appropriate form of communication • Use DRC to differentially reinforce communicative attempts
Avoidance or escape	• Teach student to communicate "No," ask for break, or ask to leave situation • Assess environmental conditions for factors that may exacerbate aggression (e.g., proximity of other students, other students using student's favorite materials); modify those conditions if possible • Modify task to increase reinforcement or functional value • Present shorter tasks; gradually increase duration of task as student's ability allows

(continues)

Potential Functions	Interventions
	Aggression (*continued*)
	• Ensure that student is not allowed to avoid or escape tasks as a result of aggression • Intersperse disliked tasks with preferred activities; use picture schedules to remind student of availability of desired task
Result of interruption of routine or ritual	• Differentially reinforce student for using communication to express distress (DRC) • Differentially reinforce student for gradually longer periods of time when no aggression occurs after disruption (DRO) • Differentially reinforce student for nonritualistic alternatives (e.g., eating lunch items in different order than usual, scattering puzzle pieces instead of lining them up) (DRI) • Provide cues to warn student of impending changes in routine or schedule (e.g., through the use of social stories, during calendar activities) • Teach student to better tolerate change by exposing student to planned minor changes or interruptions and providing strong reinforcement for an appropriate response
	Self-Stimulatory Behavior

Sensory stimulation	• Teach socially acceptable forms of self-stimulation:
	  — visual (flicking fingers, gouging eyes): kaleidoscope, ViewMaster, pinwheel, sparkler toy, lava lamp, perpetual motion balls, or any toy or object with spinning or moving parts, blinking or flickering lights, shiny or sparkly surfaces
	  — auditory: listen to music or other sounds through headphones, hold seashells to ear, use noisemakers
	  — tactile: carry pieces of textured cloth, play with Slime, hold stress balls, hold smooth stones or marbles
	  — proprioceptive (positioning, flapping hands, bouncing): small trampoline, teach isometric exercises, weight-lifting exercises
	  — olfactory (sniffing): provide favorite scents (e.g., lemon, cologne, pine, vanilla, cinnamon) on cards or swatches of cloth the student can carry
	  — gustatory (licking, mouthing objects): provide gum, hard candy, suckers
	  — vestibular (spinning, bouncing, rocking): tire swing, Sit-and-Spin toy (for young children), hammock, somersaults, rocking chair, rocking horse
	• Use DRI to reinforce use of desired alternative stimulatory behaviors
	• Allow contingent access to self-stim activities after compliance, task completion, communicative attempts, or other target behaviors
	• Use sensory extinction (see At-a-Glance 11.3)

Escape	• Teach student to communicate "No," ask for break, or ask to leave situation

(continues)

Potential Functions	Interventions

Self-Stimulatory Behavior (*continued*)

Social avoidance	• Use peer confederates to initiate, prompt, and reinforce social behaviors

Self-Injurious Behavior (SIB)

Escape or avoidance	• Teach student to communicate "No," ask for a break, or ask to leave situation • Modify tasks or presentation to increase functionality or interest • Assess environmental conditions (e.g., noise levels, amount of confusing activity, number of people present) and either modify those that may be contributing to the SIB or provide the student with accommodations to buffer the impact of those stimuli (e.g., headphones to wear in the noisy cafeteria) • Ensure that student is not allowed to avoid or escape tasks or situations as a result of SIB
Communication	• Identify communicative intent and teach appropriate communicative expressions and methods • Differentially reinforce appropriate communication (DRC)
Sensory stimulation	• Mask reinforcing effects of the behavior (e.g., helmet for banging the head, gloves or mittens for biting or scratching the hand, goggles for gouging the eyes) (see At-a-Glance 12.3 for ideas) • Differentially reinforce for gradually longer periods of no SIB (DRO) • Teach and differentially reinforce other, safer forms of sensory stimulation (see At-a-Glance 12.4)
Positive reinforcement	• Differentially reinforce target behaviors, use a behavior reductive strategy for SIB

Understanding and Working With Families

Challenges Facing Families

- Finding the correct diagnosis for their child
- Learning to live with the sometimes overwhelming needs of a child with autism: finding appropriate services, managing the demands of daily living, ensuring that other children get the attention they need, juggling work and other responsibilities while trying to find the time to provide the interventions needed by the child with autism

Types of Support Needed by Families

- Information about autism, effective interventions, resources
- Knowledge and skills for dealing with their child
- Support services to help with the on-going challenges of parenting a child with autism: support groups, books, journals, parent organizations

Essential Practices in Effective Home–School Collaboration

- **Know yourself**—know your attitudes about families of children with autism
- **Know your families**—their culture, the challenges they face, the effects of the child with autism on the families' day-to-day lives
- **Maintain regular and frequent communication with families**—use home notes, home–school journals, electronic methods, telephone calls, school voice-mail systems, class newsletters, and home visits

Interventions Categorized
by Theoretical Model

Perceptual/Cognitive

- Social Stories™
- Visually Cued Instruction

Developmental

- Van Dijk Approach

Behavioral

- Discrete Trial Training (DTT)
- Picture Exchange Communication System (PECS)
- Applied Behavior Analysis (ABA)
- Pivotal Response Training

Relationship

- Gentle Teaching
- Options
- Floor Time
- Holding Therapy

Physiologically Based Interventions

- Sensory Integration
- Auditory Integration Training (AIT)
- Facilitated Communication

Appendix C:
Commercially Available Curricula

Published Functional Skills Curricula and Activity Guides, With Descriptions

The Activities Catalog: An Alternative Curriculum for Youth and Adults with Severe Disabilities (activities-based curriculum in areas of leisure, personal management, and work that lists activities as units of instruction), Wilcox & Bellamy, 1987. Baltimore: Brookes (www.brookespublishing.com).

The Assessment of Basic Language and Learning Skills [ABLLS] (assessment, curriculum guide, and skills-tracking system for language, self-help, and social skills training), Partington & Sundberg, 1998. Pleasant Hill, CA: Behavior Analysts, Inc. (www.behavioranalysts.com; 925/210-9378).

Choosing Outcomes and Accommodations for Children–2nd Ed. [COACH] (guide to educational planning for students with disabilities; futures planning process for determining individualized functional curriculum), Giangreco, Cloninger, & Iverson, 1998. Baltimore: Brookes (www.brookespublishing.com).

Community Living Skills (list of functional community goals leading toward independent living for school-age individuals and adults: personal maintenance, homemaking, community life, vocational, leisure, and travel), Dever, 1988. Washington, DC: American Association on Mental Retardation (www.aamr.org).

The Consultant's Companion [CD-ROM] (Includes assessment and lesson plan forms), Fovel, 2002. New York: DRL Books (www.drlbooks.com).

Functional Assessment and Curriculum for Teaching Everyday Routines (assessment and task analyses of functional living, academic, transition, leisure, community or career routines), Arick et al., 2004. Austin, TX: PRO-ED (www.proedinc.com).

A Functional Assessment & Curriculum for Teaching Students with Disabilities (4 volumes addressing 6 domains), Bender et al., 2007. Austin, TX: PRO-ED (www.proedinc.com).

Functional Curriculum for Elementary, Middle, and Secondary Age Students With Special Needs–2nd Ed. (framework for functional and longitudinal curriculum). Austin, TX: PRO-ED (www.proedinc.com).

Functional Independence Skills Handbook (assessment, lesson plans, 421 tasks), Killion. Austin, TX: PRO-ED (www.proedinc.com).

Impact: A Functional Curriculum Handbook for Students with Moderate to Severe Disabilities (curriculum planning process), Neel & Billingsley, 1989. Baltimore: Brookes (www.brookespublishing.com).

Individualized Assessment and Treatment for Children with Autism and Developmental Disabilities. Austin, TX: PRO-ED (www.proedinc.com).

Individualized Goal Selection Curriculum (19 curricular areas, 2000 tasks), Romanczyk, Lockshin, & Matey, 1997. Apalachin, NY: Clinical Behavior Therapy Associates (607/625-4438).

Life Centered Career Education: A Competency-Based Approach (assessment, sample IEP forms, 21 priority life skills with objectives and activities), Brolin, 1997. Arlington, VA: Council for Exceptional Children (www.cec.sped.org).

The STAR Program. Strategies for Teaching Based on Autism Research (3 kits: assessment forms; curriculum; lesson plans; teaching materials for language, social skills, functional routines, readiness, and academic skills), Arick et al., 2004. Austin, TX: PRO-ED (www.proedinc.com).

The Syracuse Community-Referenced Curriculum Guide for Students with Moderate and Severe Disabilities (provides scope and sequence charts for functional living skills in self-management, home living, vocational, recreation and leisure, and general community functioning; additional sections on functional academic skills, social, communication, and motor skills), Ford et al. (Eds.), 1989. Baltimore: Brookes (www.brookespublishing.com).

Teacher Organized Training for Acquisition of Language [TOTAL] (comprehensive, easy-to-use language developmental curriculum, lesson plans, and materials), Witt & Morgan. Austin, TX: PRO-ED (www.proedinc.com).

A Work in Progress (birth–kindergarten, 50 curricular areas, 500 skills; Spanish translation version also available), Leaf & McEachin (Eds., 1999). New York: DRL Books (www.drlbooks.com).

Communication, Social Skills, and Basic Academic Curricula (listing only)

Communication Curricula

The AAC Communication Training Kit. Austin, TX: PRO-ED.

Beginning ASL (video course). Salem, OR: Sign Enhancers.

Building Communication Competence With Individuals Who Use ACC. Baltimore: Brookes.

Communication-Based Intervention for Problem Behavior: A User's Guide for Producing Positive Change. Baltimore: Brookes.

DISTAR Oral Language Kit. Chicago: Science Research Corporation.

First Steps (early language learning). Educational Productions (800/950-4949).

Focus on Function (objectives, techniques, materials to improve functional communication skills in home and community). Austin, TX: PRO-ED.

Fokes Sentence Builder. Boston: NYT Teaching Resource Corp.

Functional AAC Intervention. Austin, TX: PRO-ED.

Implementing Augmentative and Alternative Communication: Strategies for Learners With Severe Disabilities. Baltimore: Brookes.

Karnes Early Language Activities. Champaign, IL: Generators of Educational Materials.

Language Time: Autism and PDD. East Moline, IL: LinguiSystems.

Peabody Language Kit. Circle Pines, MN: American Guidance Service.

Picture Exchange Communication System (PECS). Newark, DE: Pyramid Educational Consultants.

The SCERTS^{TM} Model. Baltimore, MD: Brookes.

Teaching Developmentally Disabled Children: The ME Book. Austin, TX: PRO-ED.

Teaching Individuals with Developmental Delays: Basic Intervention Techniques. Austin, TX: PRO-ED.

Teach Me Language: A Language Manual for Children With Autism, A.S., and Related Developmental Disorders. Langley, B.C. Canada: SKF Books.

WH Question and WH Programs. Austin, TX: PRO-ED.

Social Skills Curricula

ACCEPTS (elementary) and ACCESS (secondary). Austin, TX: PRO-ED Publishing (www.proedinc.com)

ASSET: A Social Skills Program for Adolescents. Champaign, IL: Research Press (www.researchpress.com)

Comic Strip Conversations. Arlington, TX: Future Horizons (www.futurehorizons-autism.com)

Getting Along with Others: Teaching Social Effectiveness to Children. Champaign, IL: Research Press (www.researchpress.com)

The Hidden Curriculum: Practical Solutions for Understanding Unstated Rules in Social Situations. Shawnee Mission, KS: Autism Asperger Publishing Co. (www.asperger.net)

My Social Stories. Book, PA: Jessica Kingsley

The New Social Story Book. Arlington, TX: Future Horizons (www.futurehorizons-autism.com)

The Original Social Story Book. Arlington, TX: Future Horizons (www.futurehorizons-autism.com)

Scripting: Social Communication for Adolescents. Eau Claire, Wisconsin: Thinking Publications (www.thinkingpublications.com)

Skillstreaming in Early Childhood, Skillstreaming the Elementary School Child, and *Skillstreaming the Adolescent.* Champaign, IL: Research Press (www.research press.com)

Social Skills Intervention Guide. Circle Pines, MN: American Guidance Service (www.agsnet.com)

The Social Skills Picture Book: Teaching Play, Emotion, and Communication to Children with Autism. Arlington, TX: Future Horizons (www.futurehorizons-autism.com)

Social Skills Stories: Functional Picture Stories for Readers and Nonreaders K–12. Solana Beach, CA: Mayer-Johnson

Social Skills Strategies. Eau Claire, WI: Thinking Publications (www.thinking publications.com)

Social Star: Peer Interaction Skills. Greenville, SC: Thinking Publications (www.thinkingpublications.com)

The Tough Kid Social Skills Book. Longmont, CO: Sopris West (www.sopriswest.com)

Academic Curricula

Developmental 1 Reading Laboratory. Chicago: Science Research Associates.

Edmark Reading Program. Austin, TX: PRO-ED.

Functional Reading Series. Bellevue, WA: Edmark.

Hopping Good Cents: A New Method for Teaching Counting of Money. Austin, TX: PRO-ED.

I Can + and − Arithmetic Program. Portland, OR: ASIEP Education.

I Can Write. Austin, TX: PRO-ED.

Programmed Reading: A Sullivan Association Program. New York: McGraw-Hill.

Pyramid and Phonics Pathways. Austin, TX: PRO-ED.

The Reading and Writing Program: An Alternative Form of Communication. Austin, TX: PRO-ED.

Reading for Independence. Chicago: Science Research Associates.

Reading Mastery (phonics, fluency, comprehension); Direct Instruction; Corrective Reading; Corrective Mathematics. New York: SRA, Macmillan/McGraw-Hill.

Reading Milestones. Austin, TX: PRO-ED.

Real-Life Math. Austin, TX: PRO-ED.

SRA Skills Series. Chicago: Science Research Associates.

Appendix D:

A Typical School Day at Valdez Intermediate School for Jamie and His Classmates

Jamie attends Valdez Intermediate School, a large fifth- and sixth-grade campus in a small city. Jamie has moderate to severe autism, and he spends the majority of his time in a self-contained classroom with three other students with autism: two boys—Carlos and Caleb—and one girl—Leah. Ms. Harris teaches this class, assisted by one paraprofessional, Ms. Preston. Jamie requires a structured, closely supervised setting virtually all of the time, and the low adult-to-student ratio makes this possible. Because Jamie is nonverbal, a great deal of his time is spent working on communication skills. Receptive language is a relative strength for Jamie, but finding ways for him to express himself is a real challenge. He is extremely hyperactive and distractible, so everything must be done rapidly to keep up with his activity level and his need for constant sensory input. Ms. Harris and his speech–language pathologist, Ms. Carter, have drawn from several different approaches based on applied behavior analysis (ABA). All of the students in Jamie's class exhibit characteristics of classic autism, such as various stereotypic behaviors and low levels of communication and socialization. In addition, Caleb and Leah exhibit several forms of challenging behaviors. Caleb is highly noncompliant; communication and compliance are two major goals for him. Leah is extremely withdrawn, preferring rocking, hand-flapping, and posturing over any other activities. Carlos exhibits self-injurious behavior (SIB), and he is aggressive toward teachers.

A typical school day for Jamie begins before 7:00 A.M. with an hour-long bus ride. He usually enjoys the motion and vibration of the bus, and his bus driver and monitor have known him for several years. He often sleeps during the ride to school. Ms. Preston meets him and his classmates at the bus and walks them to the classroom, where each student finds his or her name on a cubby and puts away his or her backpack. After a trip to the rest room (Jamie still needs to be reminded to use the bathroom and needs verbal prompts for hand-washing), each student checks his or her schedule.

On each student's schedule, the day's activities are represented in a vertical list of words, photographic pictures, picture communication symbols (Mayer-Johnson, 1994), or representational objects attached with Velcro. At the end of each activity, the student removes the word, symbol, or object for that activity and places it in the "Finished" pocket on his or her chart. Jamie uses written words, Carlos and Caleb use pictures or symbols, and Leah uses objects with a voice-output device to represent the day's activities. This device contains six partitions. When Leah removes an object attached by Velcro to a partition, a recorded voice announces the next activity. For example, when she picks up the spoon, the device says, "Time for breakfast," and when she picks up the toothbrush, it says, "Brush your teeth." The teacher may record any word or short phrase that Leah needs to represent a given activity.

The students then choose the foods they want for breakfast by using their individual communication methods. Leah can make her choices by pointing to the actual objects (e.g., cereal, toast). Jamie signs what he wants. The students must also request help opening their milk or yogurt, request a spoon with which to eat, and request more of a specific food when they want it. The students have their breakfast in the classroom because their arrival times may vary, but they have lunch with typically developing peers in the cafeteria. Breakfast is followed by a sequenced grooming routine. Their toothbrushes, toothpaste, cups, washcloths, and hairbrushes are arranged in plastic silverware trays in order from left to right. Next, the class participates in calendar activities. They use a very large wipe-off calendar (approximately 5 feet tall and 7 feet wide), with pictures representing weather, foods on the lunch menu, and the special events of the day. Using picture communication symbols, objects, and verbal cues, the students point to and name the correct day on the calendar, name the month, identify the day's weather, and identify any special event for that day or upcoming days.

Students spend 20 to 40 minutes working individually with the teacher or assistant, who use discrete trial training to work on IEP goals. These goals are divided into the following categories: Language/Communication Skills from the ABLLS curriculum (Partington & Sundberg, 1998), Lifelong Learner (academic skills, such as counting, money, time, signs and symbols), Recreation and Leisure, Work Skills (prevocational), and Self-Help. During DTT, Ms. Harris and Ms. Preston record data for each student using various progress monitoring forms. Approximately every 10 minutes, the students have a break. These work times will be lengthened gradually. During their break, the students participate in sensory input or movement activities, or they rest, as needed. The goal is for work times to be associated with positive experiences for the students. Each child learns to request the reinforcers he or she wants during work time, using his or her most effective communication method for quick answers. Leah is presented with pairs of choices for reinforcers on two One-Step voice-output devices (AbleNet, Inc.). Jamie uses sign language, and Carlos and Caleb use a combination of signs and pictures.

Work time is followed by music or computer lab on alternating days, in which the students are included with their typically developing peers. Earlier, during calendar time, they have seen and heard which special class they will be attending. Each adult accompanies two students during inclusion. The amount of time spent in the class is increased or decreased according to the students' tolerance and interest. The goal of inclusion here is for the students to practice their social and communication skills. Five minutes might be the limit for a student's tolerance of the general education class on some days, but on other days, he or she might stay for 20 minutes or more. Jamie, for example, might find listening to band music engaging, but his classmates dislike loud noises. On the other hand, Jamie is not usually able to sit at the computer long enough to become engaged, but one of the other students typically enjoys computer time.

After the inclusion class, the four students with autism return to the classroom for a schedule check and then begin another one-to-one discrete trial work time, which varies in length from 20 to 40 minutes. During breaks from working on their IEP goals, the students might go for walks around the school building or on the sidewalks around the campus. One of Jamie's classmates, who has motor deficits, might ride his adapted bicycle. All of the students like bouncing on the big occupational therapy ball between work sessions or jumping on the small therapy trampoline. During any break time, Ms. Harris and Ms. Preston use naturalistic/milieu teaching to elicit communication (particularly mands) from the students. For example, the teacher might put her hand on the therapy ball and have the student sign or say, "More," or "Ball," to be able to resume bouncing.

After their work time, the students again check their schedules, removing the "work time" indicators and placing them in the "Finished" pocket of their charts.

Next on the schedule is lunch. Four general education peers stop by the classroom to pick up Jamie and his classmates for lunch. These peers are part of a group of approximately 10 students who have volunteered to assist special needs students in the school. The peers have been taught how to interact with Jamie and his classmates with autism, including how to initiate social interactions and how to prompt appropriate social and communication responses. They all walk together to the cafeteria, and the peers assist Jamie and the other students in choosing their lunch items as they move through the cafeteria line. Jamie, Carlos, Caleb, Leah, and their general education peers move to one of the many round lunch tables. They split up into two pairs at two different tables. Most days, the students are joined by two or three other friends. During lunch, the peers initiate conversations with each other and with Jamie and his classmates, using the techniques they learned from Ms. Harris. If Jamie, Carlos, Caleb, or Leah begins to engage in an inappropriate behavior (e.g., stereotypic, self-injurious), the peers provide a brief reminder and gestural prompt for an alternate appropriate behavior. Ms. Harris eats her lunch during this same period, monitoring the lunch activities from a slight distance. She does not intervene unless she sees that one of her students is becoming agitated and needs assistance. After the students clear their lunch trays, the general education peers walk with their friends back to the special education classroom and then move on to their own classes.

After lunch, the students have a 15-minute break, during which they can choose an individual activity such as listening to music with headphones; using the Kaleidoscope or ViewMaster; or playing with Slime, doing a puzzle, or even resting. Once again, the students must practice manding for the activity of choice and for help in using their choices (e.g., turning on the music). After this time, several other students from another special education class join Jamie, Carlos, Caleb, and Leah for a socialization period. Each student with autism is paired with one of the students from the other class, and each pair chooses an activity. Choices include playing music on a CD player, playing a video game, using art materials, shooting baskets or tossing the football, putting together a model, and playing with class pets. Language and communication are primary goals of this activity, so peers are taught to elicit communication and language at every opportunity. For example, when listening to music, the peer might turn off the music and prompt Jamie to mand with the sign, "I want music," or the peer might elicit an intraverbal by asking, "Which CD do you want to play?" Jamie's responses control the situation (e.g., the music is turned back on when Jamie requests it, or he gets to play the CD that he identifies in response to the peer's query). These exchanges occur multiple times during this period so Jamie can practice various types of communicative responses.

The next afternoon activity is prevocational work. Jamie, Carlos, Caleb, and Leah each have several prevocational goals, including ones for work-related behaviors (e.g., attention to task, following directions), as well as several areas of work skills (e.g., helping in the library or office, helping coaches with materials, gardening tasks). The students alternate two jobs during each grading period. For example, they may work on gardening tasks on Monday and Friday and help with mail, shredding, duplicating, and other office tasks on Tuesday, Wednesday, and Thursday. The next grading period, those jobs might change slightly. For example, one or both days of gardening may be replaced with assisting the coaches with laundry, arranging materials, and setting out materials for after-school practice.

The last period of the day is for adapted physical education or related services (speech and occupational therapies). Ms. Harris has her planning period during this time. During her planning period, she and Ms. Preston review the day's data and plan the next day's activities. When Jamie and his classmates return, they put needed items in their backpacks as they remove the picture or symbol for each item from their charts. During the day, Ms. Harris puts items that need to go home in the "Home" basket in each student's cubby, and she places the picture, representational object, or symbol for the item on the student's Velcro chart. For example, Jamie may have his home–school journal, a "Good News" note from the coach, a class newsletter, and an announcement for the Parent–Teachers Association meeting. Once backpacks are ready, the students walk to their buses, accompanied by Ms. Harris and Ms. Preston.

Throughout the day, Ms. Harris and Ms. Preston use multiple behavioral interventions to increase specific appropriate behaviors and reduce targeted challenging behaviors. In addition, they monitor these behaviors (using many of the data-collection forms presented in Chapters 8 and 13).

Caleb's IEP includes the goal of increasing compliance. Because he exhibits such high levels of noncompliance, Ms. Harris is using multiple interventions to improve this behavior. One intervention she uses is teaching compliance through discrete trial training sessions. She began by presenting S^Ds for simple, easily prompted behaviors (e.g., touch your head, clap, put your arms up). Once Caleb reached criterion for independent responding (90% unprompted responses for 3 consecutive days) on these behaviors, Ms. Harris targeted compliance in naturalistic settings as part of daily routines. At first, she focused on presenting S^Ds for high-probability behaviors (e.g., get your milk, pick up your spoon, get the sparkle toy) using intrusive prompts (e.g., visual prompts, models, physical prompts) as needed to ensure correct responding. As soon as Caleb met criterion for these behaviors, Ms. Harris began fading the prompts. Because Caleb now responds independently to high-probability requests, Ms. Harris has begun focusing on teaching Caleb to respond to low-probability S^Ds (e.g., get your toothbrush, wash your hands, finished—put sparkle toy on shelf).

Without structure and powerful interventions, Leah's stereotypic self-stimulatory behaviors would interfere with socialization attempts by other children, instruction, and communication. Ms. Harris and Leah's mother agreed that these self-stimulatory behaviors were the most powerful reinforcer available for Leah, so Ms. Harris implemented a DRO intervention in which Leah is allowed brief periods of time to engage in her self-stim behavior contingent upon designated periods during which no self-stim behavior occurs. At first, the "no stim" periods were short (approximately 10 minutes). As Leah has learned to control her self-stim behaviors, the length of the periods has been increased. She is now able to participate in class activities for 30 minutes before earning a "stim break." To clearly differentiate "stim break" time from "no stim" periods, Ms. Harris uses two different timers: The timer that marks the "no stim" periods is a combination auditory and visual timer that is placed close to Leah throughout the day. The "stim break" timer is an auditory timer on which a picture of Leah sitting on her stim rug (a small rug used only for this purpose) has been placed.

In addition to this DRO intervention, Ms. Harris uses a DRI intervention to reinforce Leah for engaging in appropriate play/leisure activities during work breaks. For these breaks, Ms. Harris uses a large, laminated copy of the picture of Leah on her stim rug, with 10 marked spaces around the edge. During the breaks, as Ms. Harris or Ms. Preston observes Leah using a toy or engaging in an activity appropriately, they praise Leah and place a colorful clothespin on the picture. When all 10 spaces are covered with clothespins, Leah earns a stim break. As a result of these two interventions, Leah's self-stimulatory behaviors during work and leisure times have decreased by more than 80%.

Earlier in the year, Ms. Harris conducted a functional behavioral assessment to assess Carlos' aggressive behaviors. The data indicated that the function of these behaviors was escape/avoidance and possibly frustration. Based on this information, the IEP team developed two interventions to address the problem. First, Ms. Harris is teaching Carlos to point to his "No" picture card to indicate when he wants to stop an activity. Because the aggressive and self-injurious behaviors both occur at high rates, Ms. Harris uses a continuous reinforcement schedule to reinforce his use of the "No" card: Each time he points to it, she stops the activity for a time, and he is allowed to engage in an alternate, desired activity. As Carlos' use of the "No" card becomes more consistent, Ms. Harris will begin requiring him to work for a very brief time after he points to the card. Gradually, she will increase the length of time he must work before earning his break.

Ms. Harris also evaluated all of the tasks Carlos is asked to do during the day. Whenever possible, she modified those tasks to ensure that they had high functional or reinforcement value. For example, Carlos may now use an MP3 player and headphones to listen to his favorite music and sounds (he likes animal sounds) during vocational tasks. Carlos also loads the dishwasher each day, but Ms. Harris changed the time of this task (he previously did it at the end of the day, just before he went home) to allow him to complete it just before his afternoon snack. As soon as he finishes the job, he may have his snack.

Ms. Harris and Ms. Preston each carry a clipboard containing different data sheets for the students. Some of the data sheets allow them to monitor the same behavior in each student simultaneously (e.g., they use one data form to monitor compliance during calendar time). Other data forms are for individual students (e.g., one form is used to monitor Jamie's signing during music or computer lab; another data form is used to monitor Leah's self-stim behaviors during work and leisure times). During their daily data review sessions, Ms. Harris and Ms. Preston transfer the day's data (converting the data as needed) to graphs kept in each student's notebook. These graphs are used to monitor the students' progress toward their IEP goals and to communicate with parents about their progress.

Ms. Harris understands the importance of creating a clear, highly structured environment for her students. She also understands the critical role of data in guiding decision making about interventions. Providing such intensive programming is demanding but also very rewarding. Ms. Harris experiences reinforcement when Jamie spontaneously initiates communication, when Leah engages in a leisure activity without self-stimming, when Carlos points to his "No" card instead of biting his arm, or when Caleb follows an instruction without a tantrum. Those successes are reminders about why she chose this profession.

References

Mayer-Johnson Company. (1994). *The picture communication symbols combination book*. Solana Beach, CA: Author.

Partington, J. W., & Sundberg, M. L. (1998). *The assessment of basic language and learning skills (ABLLS)*. Pleasant Hill, CA: Behavior Analysts.

Glossary

Compiled by Andrea Scott

A

Acquisition level—the initial stage of learning in which a skill is first learned. Skills at the acquisition stage are not yet performed quickly or, possibly, easily.

Adaptive physical education teacher—a certified physical education teacher who has received training in skills for adapting typical physical education activities for students with disabilities.

Aided augmentative and alternative communication devices—supplementary materials or equipment (e.g., electronic voice-output aids, communication boards, pictures, concrete objects) used for communication.

Antecedent (or antecedent stimulus)—an event or environmental condition that occurs immediately before a behavior and is functionally related to the behavior.

Antecedent prompting—a socialization intervention in which students are prompted to exhibit contextually appropriate behaviors during social exchanges.

Applied behavior analysis—the application of behavioral principles to change socially significant behavior; scientific procedures are used to demonstrate a functional relationship between interventions and resulting behavior change.

Asperger syndrome (AS)—a condition characterized by social deficits and restricted patterns of activities and interest. Individuals with AS show few or no cognitive or language delays but they may exhibit motor clumsiness in early childhood.

Assistive technology—any device intended to increase an individual's independence. Many forms of assistive technology are for communication.

Augmentative and alternative communication device (AAC)—an aided or unaided communication device that replaces or supplements speech.

Autism spectrum disorder—any one of a number of disorders in which symptoms across the disorders are similar but individuals differ in the number of symptoms, the severity of symptoms, or age of onset.

Autistic disorder—autism, as defined by the fourth edition of the *Diagnostic and Statistical Manual of Mental Disorders*.

Aversive—any consequence that the individual dislikes.

B

Baseline data—data collected before an intervention is implemented. Allows for evaluation of effectiveness of the intervention by observing changes in data in comparison to baseline.

Behavior—an observable, measurable response exhibited by an individual.

Behavioral (or operational) goals—specific statements of desired learning outcomes; components of a behavioral goal are (a) student; (b) behavior, described in operational terms; (c) condition under which the behavior is to be exhibited; and (d) criteria.

Behavioral momentum—a technique to increase compliance by delivering several high-probability requests before a low-probability request.

Behavioral theory or behavioral explanation—theoretical model that explains behavioral differences; normal social learning fails to occur, which results in behavior deficits and/or behavior excesses.

Behavior specialist—teachers, usually in special education, who have demonstrated effective skills in the area of behavior management or who have received specialized training in applied behavior analysis and its applications in the school setting. A behavior specialist's role is to provide assistance to teachers regarding challenging student behavior.

Biological explanation—theoretical model that explains challenging behaviors as a genetic predisposition to atypical behavior, or abnormal brain structure and chemistry.

C

Communication book—book containing pictures of activities, people, and things that the student enjoys and may wish to talk about; used for communicative interactions.

Complex chained skills—several related behaviors chained together to complete a complicated task.

Compliance training—teaching compliance through the use of discrete trial teaching and/or naturalistic/milieu teaching.

Concurrent group instruction—instructional format in which the teacher instructs the entire group interspersed with individual responding.

Consequence—any stimulus following a behavior that influences the future occurrence of the behavior.

Contingent—making a consequence dependent upon a specific behavior.

Continuous ongoing behaviors—behaviors that appropriately occur over extended periods of time.

Continuous reinforcement—reinforcement of every correct response.

Criterion of the immediate environment—short-term goals that focus on the skills necessary to function in the current environment.

Criterion of the next environment—intermediate goals that are based upon the student's placement within the next 3 to 5 years.

Criterion of ultimate functioning—establishing long-term goals to guide current curriculum decisions.

Critical effect—the naturally occurring result or consequence of performing a set of behaviors.

Curriculum-based assessment—using an established curricular sequence (from either an ecological inventory or a commercial guide) to determine a student's current level of functioning.

D

Differential reinforcement—set of unique procedures that rely on positive approaches to reduce behaviors.

Differential reinforcement of communicative behavior (DRC)—behavior-reduction technique involving reinforcement of an appropriate form of communication in place of an inappropriate behavior.

Differential reinforcement of incompatible behavior (DRI)—behavior-reduction technique involving reinforcement of one or more behaviors that are incompatible to the target inappropriate behavior; the incompatible behaviors increase while the inappropriate behavior diminishes.

Differential reinforcement of lower levels of behavior (DRL)—behavior-reduction technique involving reinforcement when the number or duration of target inappropriate behaviors is less than a predetermined criterion.

Differential reinforcement of other behavior (DRO)—behavior-reduction technique in which reinforcement is provided at the end of a period of time during which the target inappropriate behavior was not exhibited.

Discrepancy analysis—planning process for creating a curricular plan that involves analyzing the discrepancy between the long-term goal for a student and the student's present level of performance.

Discrete trial teaching—also known as discrete trial format or trial-by-trial teaching; a highly structured teaching format consisting of cue, response, consequence, and intertrial interval.

Discrimination training—learning to match a behavior to a certain stimulus rather than behaving randomly.

Discriminative stimulus (S^D)—a specific antecedent stimulus or group of stimuli that predictably cue a particular response or class of responses.

Distributed trials—teaching technique in which a single trial is presented every once in a while to check for skill retention.

Duration recording—technique to measure how long a behavior occurs; graphed in minutes and/or seconds.

E

Echolalia—the behavior of repeating or echoing words or phrases said by others with no regard for the meaning.

Ecological inventory—process in which an individualized curriculum is developed by determining skills needed in specific environments in which the student must function, task-analyzing those skills, and assessing the student's current functioning against that task analysis. Any steps in the task analyses that have not been mastered by the student become targets for instruction.

Error correction—responding to student response errors in a precise, predetermined manner.

Errorless learning—an instructional procedure in which the instructional task is designed to facilitate correct responding through the nature of the task or prompts used by the teacher and in which the student receives frequent reinforcement; based on the philosophy that students learn more effectively and efficiently when they do not make errors.

Establishing operations—environmental conditions that evoke attention and motivation to act.

Event recording—counting the number of times a particular behavior occurs. Used for discrete behaviors that have a clearly observable beginning and end and that do not occur over long periods of time.

Expansion—repeating a child's utterance or gesture and adding one or more words or signs for more complex grammar.

Expressive language—using language that other people can understand.

Extinction—a behavior-reduction technique in which reinforcement (usually attention) is withheld for a behavior that previously was reinforced.

F

Fading—gradual removal of prompts.

First–then procedure—procedure used to provide structure in which students are taught to engage in activities in a specific order.

Fluency—the rate of performance of a behavior and the next stage of learning after acquisition. Fluency is achieved when behaviors can be produced quickly and effortlessly.

Functional routines—procedure of embedding mands, tacts, and intraverbals into regular routines. Helps students learn self-help and social skills along with language skills in a meaningful context.

Futures planning—allowing future goals to dictate what will be taught as opposed to simply following a curriculum or choosing immediate goals with no clear, systematic sequence.

G

Generalization level—the final level of learning in which students can perform a behavior under different conditions (varying stimuli, with different people, in different settings), and adapt or change the behavior regardless of the conditions.

Gestural prompts—gestures such as touching, tapping, or pointing to the correct response that are designed to help the student respond correctly.

H

Here-and-now thinking—thinking patterns common in individuals with autism; characterized by extremely literal, egocentric thinking with little reliance on logic.

High-functioning autism (HFA)—a form of autism in which the individual may have an average or above-average IQ and highly developed verbal skills but displays odd interpersonal interaction skills.

High-probability request—a direction that a student is likely to follow.

Home–school journals—notebooks that travel daily with each student between home and school.

I

Idiosyncratic reinforcer—activities, behaviors, materials, or other stimuli that would be either neutral or undesirable to other children but are reinforcing to a particular child with autism. Idiosyncratic reinforcers may include self-stimulatory behaviors; rituals; and unusual tastes, odors, or materials.

Incidental teaching—used only in requesting situations. Teacher arranges items such that the individual wants them; teacher then uses other naturalistic/milieu teaching techniques to elicit a request, more complex language, or conversation.

Individual schedules—individualized plan for each student that lists each activity the student will do in order throughout the day.

Infantile autism—a term formerly used to describe classical autism; now described as *autistic disorder* and included under the umbrella term of *pervasive developmental disorders*.

Instructional scripts (social scripts)—scripts that specify words for students to use during social interactions.

Intermittent reinforcement—reinforcement schedule in which some, but not all, correct responses are reinforced. Intermittent reinforcement can occur after several separate behaviors or after a single behavior has been exhibited for a certain period of time.

Intertrial interval—a 3- to 5-second period during which no instructions are given; occurs between the end of one trial (after the consequence) and before the initiation of another trial (before the cue).

Interval schedule of reinforcement—reinforcement for the first instance of a target behavior following a predetermined interval.

Intraverbal—responding to someone else's verbal behavior with a response that does not directly match (echoic) what the other person said.

Islands of precocity—also known as *splinter skills*; unusually advanced, isolated skills or skill areas; they are typically nonfunctional for the individual (i.e., serve no purpose for daily living needs).

J

Job coach—a school employee, sometimes known as an employment specialist, whose responsibility it is to train job skills and place and monitor youth with disabilities in community-based employment.

Joint attention—shared, mutual attention to an external event.

L

Lack of communicative intent—not motivated to communicate; a cardinal characteristic of individuals with autism.

Language form—the type of communicative response, such as speech, sign, tantrums, or pointing.

Language function—communicative purpose or intent.

Latency recording—a data collection system used to measure the time between the discriminative stimulus and the beginning of a response.

Learning levels—refers to the depth of knowledge or level of skill mastery; includes acquisition, fluency, maintenance, and generalization.

Least restrictive environment (LRE)—the setting most like the general education classroom in which the educational needs of a student with disabilities can be successfully met.

Least-to-most prompting—a prompt system in which the first prompts given in a learning session are the lowest level prompts (prompts that give the least amount of information) and more complete prompts are only used if needed to cue correct responding.

Left–right and top–down orientation—procedure used to teach students to approach tasks sequentially by placing the task (or components of the task) in either a left-to-right or top-to-bottom orientation.

Low-functioning autism (LFA)—form of autism in which the individual typically has mental retardation, often has no language, and seldom initiates social interactions.

Low-probability request—a direction the student is not likely to follow.

M

Maintenance level—a stage of learning that occurs after fluency; students can perform the response at an acceptable rate over an extended period of time without having to be retaught it.

Mand—also known as an instruction model; a verbal instruction about how to respond or request; also refers to a verbal request initiated by a student.

Massed trials—occur when the same series of steps with the same antecedent is presented several times in a row.

Mental retardation—low cognitive functioning accompanied by deficits in adaptive behavior.

Milieu teaching—taking advantage of a naturally occurring teaching opportunity in actual contexts where skills need to be used; also called *naturalistic teaching*.

Model—a form of visual prompt in which the desired response is displayed for the student to imitate.

Most-to-least prompting—a prompt system in which the first prompts used are the most intrusive or are ones that leave little or no allowance for an incorrect response; once the correct response occurs consistently, the prompts are faded.

Mute—possessing few or no verbal skills.

N

Natural environment training (NET)—a set of teaching strategies based on principles of applied behavior analysis in which language and communication skills are taught in environments where those skills are needed; also known as *milieu teaching*.

Negative reinforcement—a process in which an aversive condition is avoided or ended contingent upon a particular behavior. For negative reinforcement to take place, an undesired stimulus must be in place prior to a behavior; that stimulus is then avoided or ended as a result of the behavior.

O

Observational learning—an approach to learning in which students learn skills, including language, by watching and listening to others.

Observational recording—observing student responses and making some notation about the actual response. Two types of observational recording are *event recording* and *duration recording.*

Occupational therapist (OT)—related service provider who is primarily interested in improving, restoring, or developing independent functioning skills, specifically, the abilities needed to participate in daily living, recreational, and employment activities.

Operant behavior—a voluntary behavior.

Operant conditioning—systematically manipulating environmental variables (antecedents and consequences) to influence a voluntary behavior.

Operational definition—behavior that is described in observable, measurable terms. A behavior is said to be operationally defined if two people can consistently agree on the occurrence or nonoccurrence of the behavior.

Overcorrection—a behavior-reduction procedure in which the student is required to engage in an appropriate alternative behavior multiple times, contingent upon inappropriate behavior.

P

Pairing—the process of associating a primary reinforcer with a secondary reinforcer for the purpose of establishing reinforcement value for the secondary reinforcer.

Peer confederates—typical peers, usually close in age, who are taught strategies for initiating, prompting, and reinforcing social interventions for students with autism.

Peer-mediated intervention—socialization interventions involving the use of peer confederates to initiate, prompt, and reinforce social behaviors in students with autism.

Permanent product recording—a data-collection tool that uses some permanent change in the environment caused by a behavior as an indicator that the behavior occurred; specific data is then recorded from the permanent product.

Perseveration—repeating the same words or phrases over and over.

Pervasive developmental disorder (PDD)—a condition in which a child demonstrates patterns of the autistic syndrome but the child's age of onset is later than 3 years and/or the child has only some of the symptoms or less severe symptoms.

Physical prompts—also called manual prompts; physically assisting or guiding the student through the desired response.

Physical therapist—related service provider who is primarily interested in the development and maintenance of motor skills, movement, and posture.

Pivotal behaviors—behaviors that are used in a wide range of situations and that have multiple uses.

Positional prompts—the correct response is placed in close proximity to the student, making it more likely to be chosen.

Positive behavioral supports (PBS)—the evolution and expansion of applied behavior analysis into broader, more systemic, and more preventive applications that also address quality-of-life issues.

Positive practice overcorrection—a behavior-reduction technique in which the individual is required to engage in extensive practice in a behavior that is an appropriate alternative to the nondesired behavior.

Positive reinforcement—the contingent presentation of a consequence stimulus following a behavior that increases the likelihood that the behavior will be repeated.

Pragmatics—situational context of language, including speaker–listener interaction and determining who says what to whom, how they say it, and why and when they say it.

Primary reinforcer—an unlearned stimulus that is needed for survival (food, liquid, warmth, shelter, sexual stimulation).

Prompt dependence—a condition in which the student relies on the prompt to respond correctly.

Prompts—extra assistance given to individuals for them to perform the correct response.

Prosody—use of cadence, rhythm, and pitch in spoken language.

Psychogenic pathology—a widely discarded theory of autism in which children with the disorder were thought to withdraw from the world because of cold, unresponsive, punitive parents, particularly mothers.

R

Rate—a data-reporting format in which the total number of responses are divided by the amount of time observed to obtain a measure of fluency of performance.

Ratio schedule of reinforcement—providing reinforcement after a predetermined number of behaviors.

Receptive by feature, function, and class (RFFC)—a receptive language verbal operant in which an individual can identify stimuli by feature (e.g., "Show me the round blue one"), function (e.g., "Pick up the one that you cook with"), and class (e.g., "Where is the animal?").

Receptive language—understanding what other individuals are communicating.

Reflexive behavior—behavior that is not under voluntary control.

Reinforcer—any consequence stimulus that functions to increase the future occurrence of behavior.

Reinforcer sampling—Determining specific stimuli that may serve as reinforcers by presenting an array of potential reinforcers to a student and observing the student's preferred choices.

Response cost—a behavior-reduction procedure in which reinforcers are removed as a consequence for inappropriate behavior.

Response duration schedule of reinforcement—providing reinforcement after a predetermined number of minutes during which the target behavior has been continuously exhibited.

Restitutional overcorrection—a behavior-reduction technique in which the student makes up for the inappropriate behavior by extensively rectifying anything in the environment that was damaged as a result of the misbehavior.

Restricted event—a behavior that appropriately occurs only in response to a particular antecedent.

S

Satiation—a condition that occurs when an individual tires of a reinforcer and the stimulus thus no longer functions as a reinforcer.

Secondary reinforcer—a learned reinforcer that has acquired reinforcing value through association with primary reinforcers.

Self-injurious behavior (SIB)—behaviors that are hurtful or dangerous to one's self.

Self-stimulatory behavior—any repetitive, stereotypic behavior that is performed for self-gratification or self-entertainment. Common self-stimulatory behaviors in individuals with autism include flapping the hands, rocking, spinning, humming, and twirling objects.

Sensory integration—an unproven technique that involves stimulating one or more sensory systems (i.e., visual, tactile, auditory) to facilitate their simultaneous or integrated functioning.

Setting events—conditions distant in time and/or place that may affect a behavior.

Sequential group instruction—instructional format in which the teacher briefly teaches each student individually while sitting in a group, with other students either watching or engaging in their own independent tasks.

Shadow—Individual hired to provide a one-to-one ratio of support for a particular student with autism for part or all of the school day.

Simple discrete behaviors—behaviors that have a clearly observable beginning and end and that do not occur over long periods of time; also called *discrete behaviors*.

Social competence—other people's perceptions of the social performance of an individual.

Social skills deficits—lack of knowledge about how to perform specific social skills.

Social stories—brief, individualized stories that describe expected behaviors for specific social situations.

Speech–language pathologist (SLP)—related service provider who is primarily responsible for diagnosing and appraising speech and language functioning, developing goals and objectives to enhance communication, and monitoring progress toward those goals.

Splinter skills—also known as *islands of precocity*; unusually advanced, isolated skills or skill areas; they are typically nonfunctional for the individual (i.e., serve no purpose for daily living needs).

Stereotypic behavior—any repetitive, perseverative behavior that is performed for self-gratification or self-entertainment. Common self-stimulatory behaviors in individuals with autism include flapping the hands, rocking, spinning, humming, and twirling objects.

Stimulus control—the process in which a particular antecedent stimulus (called a *discriminative stimulus* [S^D]) or class of stimuli predictably cue a particular behavior or class of behaviors. The association between the discriminative stimulus and response is established through reinforcement of a target response when it occurs following a certain S^D, but not in response to other stimuli.

Stimulus overselectivity—the tendency of children with autism to focus on small, irrelevant aspects of stimuli to the exclusion of other more salient components.

T

Tact—to label (noun, verb, adjective, or adverb) objects, people, places, events, or relationships.

Tactile defensiveness—condition in which an individual dislikes physical touch or contact.

Tandem group instruction—instructional format in which the teacher starts with one-to-one instruction and systematically expands to include more students.

Task analysis—breaking skills down into subskills or breaking content down into components so that the steps of learning are more accessible to the learner.

TEACCH (Treatment and Education of Autistic and Communication Handicapped Children)—an instructional approach for students with autism that emphasizes structured classrooms.

Teacher assistant—individuals hired to assist teachers in their educational duties.

Thinning—the process of moving from a continuous schedule of reinforcement to an intermittent schedule.

Time delay—after a stimulus has occurred, the teacher waits 5 to 10 seconds for the student's response before prompting.

Time-out—a behavior-reduction procedure in which an individual is denied access to reinforcement for a specific period of time.

Token reinforcer—any object that has no intrinsic value but can be exchanged for primary or secondary reinforcers.

Tool subjects—basic subjects or skills that are used to learn academic content; examples include reading, writing, and computer skills.

Total communication—simultaneous use of speech and sign language.

Trials—a series of learning opportunities, each with a clear onset and end and consisting of four clear steps: cue, response, consequence, and intertrial interval.

U

Unaided augmentative and alternative communication devices—communication systems that do not require supplementary equipment or materials (e.g., sign language).

Units of instruction—incorporating skill training into units based on specific activities, routines, themes, work tasks, social skills lessons, or some other type of organization.

Unrestricted event—a discrete behavior that may be exhibited at any time rather than in response to a particular stimulus.

V

Variable schedule of reinforcement—reinforcement that is delivered at varying points; reinforcement is contingent upon an average number of behaviors or an average length of time.

Verbal behavior—Skinner's reference to a specific subset of operant behaviors that are language based.

Verbal operants—any of Skinner's six categories of verbal behaviors.

Verbal prompts—verbal instructions or cues about how to perform a desired response.

Visual prompts—use of pictures, objects, words, symbols, or other visual means to provide a cue about how to perform a desired response.

Visual–spatial symbols—objects, pictures, symbols, or printed words that are arranged on the activation display of an assistive technology device.

Visual supports—physical stimuli, such as body language, objects, physical structures, pictures, photographs, labels, printed materials, and organizational tools, that visually cue an individual to take action, not to take action, to communicate, or to cognitively process information.

Voice output communication aids (VOCAs)—portable devices that can produce computerized speech at the touch of a button or with the use of other types of switches.

W

Within-stimulus prompts—altering a stimulus in some way to make it more likely that the student will respond correctly.

Whole-class schedules—a list of all the activities in the day, organized in terms of what activity occurs at what time of day, what each student is to do during each period of the day, and what each teaching adult is to do during each period of the day.

Subject Index

A–B–C model
  antecedents in, 17–21, 350
  assumption underlying, 18–19
  behavior reduction procedures in, 30–31
  behaviors in, 18–19, 21–22, 350
  consequences in, 18, 19, 22–33, 350–351
  data collection in, 31–41
  graphing and graph construction in, 36–41
  handout on, 350–351
  negative reinforcement in, 29–30, 351
  positive reinforcement in, 22–29, 350–351
  punishment in, 22, 351
  stimulus control in, 19–21, 44
A–B–C Report Form, 223, 227–229, 246–247
AAC (augmentative and alternative communication) system, 117, 186, 189–191
AAIDD (American Association on Intellectual and Developmental Disabilities), 13
AAMR Adaptive Behavior Scales (ABS), 141
ABA. *See* Applied behavior analysis (ABA)
ABA (Association for Behavior Analysis International), 13
ABAS-II (*Adaptive Behavioral Assessment System–Second Edition*), 141
ABLLS-R (*Assessment of Basic Language and Learning Skills–Revised*), 182–184, 188
ABS (*AAMR Adaptive Behavior Scales*), 141
Academic assessment instruments, 141. *See also* Assessment
Academic curricula, 381–382. *See also* Curriculum development
Acquisition level of learning, 143
Activity or task sequences, 109
Activity reinforcers, 23, 24. *See also* Reinforcement and reinforcers
Adaptive Behavioral Assessment System–Second Edition (ABAS-II), 141
Adaptive physical education (PE) teachers, 118
ADI-R (*Autism Diagnostic Interview–Revised*), 11, 12
ADOS (*Autism Diagnostic Observation Schedule*), 11, 12
Aggression, 8, 305, 307–308, 309, 373–374

AIMS: Pre-reading Kit, 141
AIT (auditory integration training), 336
American Association on Intellectual and Developmental Disabilities (AAIDD), 13
American Sign Language (ASL), 190
American Speech-Language-Hearing Association (ASHA), 13
Antecedent prompting, 207–208
Antecedent strategies for preventing challenging behaviors, 254, 256–258
Antecedents
  in A–B–C model, 18–21, 350
  definition of, 19
Applied behavior analysis (ABA). *See also* Discrete trial teaching (DTT); Naturalistic/milieu teaching
  A–B–C model of, 17–41
  antecedents in, 18–21
  assumptions of, 18–19
  behaviors in, 18, 21–22
  consequences in, 18, 19, 22–33
  data collection, 31–41
  definition of, 17
  research on, 333
  as underlying theory, 1
APSE (Association for Persons in Supported Employment), 13
ARC (Association for Retarded Citizens), 13
Arrival routine, 137, 138
AS. *See* Asperger Syndrome (AS)
ASA (Autism Society of America), 13
ASHA (American Speech-Language-Hearing Association), 13
ASL (American Sign Language), 190
Asperger Syndrome (AS), 2, 3, 344
Assessment
  academic assessment instruments, 141
  adaptive behavior scales, 141
  commercially available language assessments, 188–189
  curriculum-based assessment (CBA), 140
  functional behavioral assessment, 215–251
  of language and communication, 182–185, 187–189, 200
  task analytic assessment, 135, 136
Assessment of Basic Language and Learning Skills–Revised (ABLLS-R), 182–184, 188

Assistive technology, 190
Association for Behavior Analysis
    International (ABA), 13
Association for Persons in Supported
    Employment (APSE), 13
Association for Retarded Citizens (ARC),
    13
Auditory integration training (AIT), 336
Augmentative and alternative communica-
    tion (AAC) system, 117, 186, 189–191
Autism. *See also* Assessment; Challenging
    behaviors; Classroom structure;
    Curriculum development; Discrete trial
    teaching (DTT); Families; Grouping;
    Naturalistic/milieu teaching
    behavioral explanation of, 10
    biological explanation of, 10
    characteristics of, 3–9, 348–349
    cognitive deficits, 4–6, 8, 348
    communication and language character-
        istics of, 3–4, 8, 179–180, 348
    definition of, 1–3
    diagnosis of, 11, 12
    glossary on, 389–399
    interventions summarized, 331–338, 377
    mental retardation and, 5–6
    psychogenic pathology explanation of, 10
    resources, 11–15
    sensory processing deficits, 7, 9, 349
    social deficits, 6–7, 9, 348–349
    statistics on, 3
    stereotypic behavior, 7–8, 9
    theories about, 9–10, 338, 377
Autism Diagnostic Interview–Revised
    (ADI-R), 11, 12
Autism Diagnostic Observation Schedule
    (ADOS), 11, 12
Autism Reinforcer Checklist, 23, 24
Autism Research Institute, 13
*Autism Screening Instrument for
    Educational Planning*, 12
Autism Society of America (ASA), 13
Autism Speaks, 13
Autism spectrum disorders (ASD), 2–9. *See
    also* Autism
Autistic disorder, 2, 3. *See also* Autism
Aversives, 264, 266–267, 371–372

Baseline data. *See also* Data collection
    collection of, 35–36
    definition of, 35, 53
    graphing and, 39
    for prompts, 53
Behavior intervention plans (BIPs),
    253–256, 272, 306
Behavior management, 102–103, 109, 112.
    See also Challenging behaviors

Behavior Management Analysis Chart, 234,
    235, 251
Behavior reduction procedures, 30–31
Behavior specialists, 119
Behavioral momentum, 306–307
Behavioral theory, 10, 333–334, 338, 377
Behaviors. *See also* Challenging behaviors
    in A–B–C model, 18–19, 21–22, 350
    continuous ongoing behaviors, 135
    definition of, 19, 21
    operant behavior, 180
    operational definitions of, 21–22
    reflexive behaviors, 180
    simple discrete behaviors, 135
    verbal behavior, 180–182
BFAI (*Brief Functional Assessment
    Interview*), 217, 218, 238
Biological explanation
    of autism, 10
    of self-injurious behavior, 311
    of self-stimulatory behaviors, 216
Biological makeup, 18
BIPs (behavior intervention plans),
    253–256, 272, 306
Brainstorming, 126
Brief Functional Assessment Interview
    (BFAI), 217, 218, 238
Brigance Diagnostic Inventories, 141

Calendars, monthly, 108–109
Cambridge Center for Behavioral Studies,
    14
CAN (Cure Autism Now Foundation), 14
CARD (Center for Autism and Related
    Disorders), 14
CARS (*Childhood Autism Rating Scale*), 12
CBA (curriculum-based assessment), 140
CBVI (computer-based video instruction),
    108
CCBD (Council for Children with
    Behavioral Disorders), 14
CEC (Council for Exceptional Children),
    14
CELF-4 (*Clinical Evaluation of Language
    Fundamentals*), 188
Center for Autism and Related Disorders
    (CARD), 14
Challenging behaviors. *See also* Functional
    behavioral assessment (FBA)
    aggression, 8, 305, 307–308, 309,
        373–374
    antecedent strategies for preventing,
        254, 256–258
    aversives for reducing, 264, 266–267,
        371–372
    behavior intervention plans (BIPs),
        253–256, 272, 306

consequence strategies for reducing, 258–268, 371–372

data collection for monitoring, 273–303

differential reinforcement for reducing, 258–262, 371

extinction for reducing, 262, 263, 371

functions and indicators of, 231, 305–306, 307, 310, 312, 373–375

handouts, 371–375

medications and, 268, 269, 311

noncompliance, 306–307, 373

overcorrection for reducing, 267–268, 372

positive behavioral supports for reducing, 253

reinforcers for replacement behaviors for, 233

response cost for reducing, 262–264, 371

risks of, 305

self-injurious behavior (SIB), 8, 305, 311, 312, 375

self-stimulatory behaviors, 8, 25, 26, 203, 216, 308–310, 374–375

stereotypic behavior, 308–310, 374–375

time-out and, 264, 266–267, 371

Childhood Autism Rating Scale (CARS), 12

Childhood disintegrative disorder, 2

Choice boards, 109

Class newsletters, 326

Classroom aides, 116

Classroom structure

    for behavior management, 102–103, 109, 112

    cafeteria example of, 89

    choice boards, 109

    choosing activities, 91, 358–359

    clutter to be avoided, 103

    color for, 102, 105

    communicating *no*, 109

    completing activities, 92, 94, 359

    curricular expectations communicated through visual supports, 102

    daily schedule, 91, 358

    distractions to be eliminated, 102

    dividers for, 105

    eating, 93, 106, 360

    entering the classroom, 91, 358

    first–then procedure, 93

    furniture for, 105

    handout on, 358–360

    importance of, 89

    individual schedules, 97–101, 357

    jigs for, 107

    leaving the classroom, 91, 358

    left–right orientation, 93

    making transitions, 92

    materials for visual support, 103, 105–108

    monthly calendars, 108–109

    obtaining materials, 91, 358

    people/place locators, 110

    physical organization for visual support, 102–105

    procedures and routines for, 90–94

    refraining from changing routines and procedures, 94

    resources on, 113

    rules and behavior guidelines, 112

    sample classroom arrangement, 104

    tape for, 105

    task or activity sequences, 109

    TEACCH (Treatment and Education of Autistic and Communication Handicapped Children), 110–111

    toileting, 92–93, 106–107, 359–360

    top–down orientation, 93

    for transitions, 92, 103, 359

    video and computers for visual support, 108

    visual schedules for, 94–101

    visual supports for, 101–110

    waiting, 92, 93–94, 359

    whole-class schedules for, 94–97

    work systems for, 107

Clinical Evaluation of Language Fundamentals (CELF-4), 188

Cognitive deficits, 4–6, 8, 348

Color in classroom, 102, 105

Commercially available materials. *See* Resources

Communication and Symbolic Behavior Scales (CSBS), 188

Communication book, 195

Communication skills. *See* Language and communication skills

Communication with families, 322–327

Communication with teaching adults

    roadblocks in, 122, 123, 362

    strategies for, 121–123, 361–362

Completion of classroom activities, 92, 94, 359

Complex chained skills, 134

Compliance training, 306

Computer-based video instruction (CBVI), 108

Concurrent group instruction, 86–87

Consequences. *See also* Reinforcement and reinforcers

    in A–B–C model, 18, 19, 22–33, 350–351

    definition of, 19, 22, 55

    in discrete trial teaching (DTT), 45, 55–58, 354

intervention strategies for challenging behaviors based on, 258–268, 371–372

tips on effective reinforcement during discrete trial teaching (DTT), 56–58

Consistency in educational practices, 120–121

Consultation with team members, 124–125

Contingent reinforcement, 27, 28

Continuous ongoing behaviors, 135

Continuous schedule of reinforcement (CRF), 27, 28, 57

Coordination of team members, 122–124

Council for Children with Behavioral Disorders (CCBD), 14

Council for Exceptional Children (CEC), 14

CRF (continuous schedule of reinforcement), 27, 28, 57

Criterion of the immediate environment, 133

Criterion of ultimate functioning, 133

CSBS (*Communication and Symbolic Behavior Scales*), 188

Cure Autism Now Foundation (CAN), 14

Curriculum-based assessment (CBA), 140

Curriculum development
  choosing academic goals, 139–140
  commercially available curricula, 379–382
  commercially available language assessments, 188–189
  commercially available social skills curricula, 206
  considerations for, 131–132, 365
  current functioning level determined within curriculum, 140
  definition of curriculum, 129
  determining what to teach first, 139
  ecological inventory in, 133–138
  functional skills and, 131
  handout on, 365
  IDEA and, 129–131, 142
  IEP team and, 129–131
  long-term goals in, 133
  process of, 133–140, 365
  public school curricular areas, 130
  refining the curriculum, 135, 139
  standardized curriculum, 129
  task analysis and, 135, 136
  units of instruction, 140–142
  writing goals and objectives for, 142–144

Daily narrative of school day, 383–387

Daily schedule in classroom, 91, 358

Data collection
  in A–B–C model, 31–41
  baseline data, 35–36, 39
  blank forms, 167–177, 289–303
  duration recording, 32, 33, 37, 38, 275–276, 280–282, 298, 299
  event recording, 32–33, 148–152, 168–169, 273–279
  graphing and graph construction, 31, 36–41, 278, 280, 281, 286–287
  handouts on, 352–353, 366
  latency recording, 32, 33, 37, 38
  for monitoring challenging behaviors, 273–303
  for multiple behaviors or monitoring behaviors in multiple students, 276, 278–279, 283–286, 292, 296, 300–303
  notebook files for, 163, 164
  observational recording, 32, 148, 352
  permanent product recording, 32, 352
  practice activities for, 282
  progress data collection techniques, 147–152, 366
  purposes of, 31
  rate data, 33, 38
  restricted event recording, 33, 37–38, 148, 273–276, 290–292
  sample forms, 36, 148–161, 274–287
  of samples of student performance, 35
  self-graphing data collection form, 278, 280, 281, 295, 298
  for specific target behaviors, 34
  steps in measurement of target behaviors, 32
  steps of, 31
  timing of collection of progress data, 160–163
  unrestricted event recording, 33, 37, 274–275, 277–279, 293–297

DDD (Division on Developmental Disabilities), 14

Developmental theory, 332, 338, 377

Diagnostic and Statistical Manual of Mental Disorders (DSM), 2, 11, 202

Differential reinforcement, 258–262, 371

Differential reinforcement of communicative behavior (DRC), 258–261

Differential reinforcement of incompatible behavior (DRI), 258, 259

Differential reinforcement of lower levels of behavior (DRL), 260, 261–262

Differential reinforcement of other behaviors (DRO), 259–260, 261

Differential reinforcement of zero rates of behavior, 261

Direct instruction of socialization skills, 205–207

Discrete trial format (DTF). *See* Discrete

trial teaching (DTT)
Discrete trial teaching (DTT)
  advantages and disadvantages of, 64–68
  consequence in, 45, 55–58, 354
  definition of trials, 44
  discrimination training and, 44
  discriminative stimulus in, 45–47, 354
  error correction during, 59–63
  errors to be avoided in, 64, 66
  handout on, 354–355
  interaction of naturalistic/milieu teach-
    ing and, 82–83, 85
  intertrial interval in, 45, 58–59, 355
  for language and communication skills,
    191–194
  method summarized, 333
  motivation of students and, 63–64
  overview of, 43–44
  planning for, 63–64, 65
  prompt in, 45, 47–53, 354
  punishers and, 55–56
  reinforcement during, 55–58
  research on, 333
  resources on, 69
  response in, 45, 54–55, 354
  sample lesson plan, 65
  for socialization skills, 204
  steps/components of, 44–59, 354–355
  stimulus control and, 44, 47
  teacher's checklist for, 68
Discrimination training, 44
Discriminative stimulus
  definition of, 19, 46
  in discrete trial teaching (DTT), 45–47,
    354
  recommendations for choosing and de-
    livering, 46–47
  stimulus control and, 19, 47
Division TEACCH, University of North
  Carolina, 14
Distributed trials, 44
Dividers in classroom, 105
Division on Developmental Disabilities
  (DDD), 14
DRC (differential reinforcement of com-
  municative behavior), 258–261
DRI (differential reinforcement of incom-
  patible behavior), 258, 259
DRL (differential reinforcement of lower
  levels of behavior), 260, 261–262
DRO (differential reinforcement of other
  behaviors), 259–260, 261
Drugs. See Medications
DSM (Diagnostic and Statistical Manual of
  Mental Disorders), 2, 11, 202
DTF (discrete trial format). See Discrete
  trial teaching (DTT)

Duration recording. See also Data collection
  blank forms, 170, 298, 299
  definition of, 33
  graphing of, 33, 37, 38
  sample forms, 152, 153, 280–282
  for specific target behaviors, 34

Early Learning Accomplishments Profile, 141
Eating, 93, 106, 136, 360
Echoic, 181, 367
Echolalia, 4, 179
Ecological inventory
  for curriculum development, 133–138
  for language and communication skills,
    184–185
  for socialization skills, 205
Edible reinforcers, 23, 24. See also
  Reinforcement and reinforcers
Education Resources Information Center
  (ERIC), 14
EEG (electroencephalography), 11
Electroencephalography (EEG), 11
Electronic home–school notebooks, 323
Empathy, 202
Employment specialists, 119
Environmental Language Inventory, 188
Environmental manipulation, in naturalis-
  tic/milieu teaching, 78, 79
EOs (establishing operations), 192
ERIC (Education Resources Information
  Center), 14
Error correction
  definition of, 52
  in discrete trial teaching (DTT), 59–63
  prompts and, 52
  scenarios on, 59–63
  tips for, 60
Errorless learning, 50
Establishing operations (EOs), 192
Event recording. See also Data collection
  blank forms, 168–169
  definition of, 32–33
  for monitoring challenging behaviors,
    273–279
  sample forms, 148–152, 274–279
Expansion, 194–195
Expressive language, 179, 181–182, 367. See
  also Language and communication skills
Extinction, 262, 263, 371

Facilitated communication, 337
Families
  academic goals for students and, 140
  challenges for, 315–318, 376
  class newsletters for, 326
  communication between teachers and,
    322–327

curriculum development and, 131
daily living tasks and, 319–320
emotional responses of, 317–318
family activities of, 320
finances of, 319
handout on, 376
home notes to, 322, 323
home–school collaboration and, 318,
    321–329, 376
home–school journals/notebooks and,
    322–326
home visits to, 326–327
interventions and, 338
and learning to live with autism, 316,
    318
life areas affected by child with autism,
    318–321
lifelong responsibilities of, 320–321
relationships within, 319
and struggle to figure out what is wrong,
    315–316
support needed by, 327–328, 376
teacher's attitudes and, 321
teacher's knowledge of, 321–322
telephone calls and messages to, 323,
    326
Families for Early Autism Treatment
    (FEAT), 14
FAST (*Functional Analysis Screening Tool*),
    219, 224–226, 243–245
FBA. *See* Functional behavioral assessment
    (FBA)
FEAT (Families for Early Autism
    Treatment), 14
Federation for Children with Special
    Needs, 14
Finishing classroom activities, 92, 94
First–then procedure, 93
Floor time, 335
Fluency level of learning, 143
*Fluharty Preschool Speech and Language
    Screening Test*, 188
Functional Analysis Screening Tool (FAST),
    219, 224–226, 243–245
Functional behavioral assessment (FBA).
    See also Challenging behavior
    A–B–C Report Form, 223, 227–229,
    246–247
    assumptions underlying, 216–217
    Behavior Management Analysis Chart,
    234, 235, 251
    Brief Functional Assessment Interview
    (BFAI), 217, 218, 238
    conducting observations in contexts as-
    sociated with challenging behaviors,
    219, 223, 226, 369
    data analysis, 226, 229, 369

forms for, 238–251
    Functional Analysis Screening Tool
    (FAST), 219, 224–226, 243–245
    *Functional Behavioral Assessment
    Inventory*, 219, 220–223, 239–242
    functions and indicators of challenging
    behavior, 231
    gathering indirect data about behavior
    and contexts of behavior, 217–219,
    369
    handout on, 369–370
    hypotheses development, 229, 231–232,
    369–370
    Hypothesis Development Form, 232,
    250
    IDEA and, 215
    intervention plan development,
    232–234, 370
    monitoring interventions, 234, 370
    sample interventions, 233
    steps in, 217–235, 369–370
    Structured A–B–C Analysis Form, 223,
    226, 230, 248–249
Functional Behavioral Assessment Inventory,
    219, 220–223, 239–242
Functional communication skills, 208
Functional Communication Training, 233
Functional routines, 134, 195
Functional skills, 131, 379–380
Furniture in classroom, 105

GARS-2 (*Gilliam Autism Rating Scale*), 12
Generalization
    reinforcement and, 144
    response generalization, 143
    of social skills, 211–212, 368
    stimulus generalization, 143
    strategies for teaching to, 144
Generalization level of learning, 143
Gentle teaching, 334
Gestural prompts, 48, 49
Gilliam Autism Rating Scale (GARS-2), 12
Glossary, 389–399
Goals
    academic goals, 139–140
    learning levels in, 143
    long-term goals in curriculum develop-
    ment, 133
    operational goals, 142
    writing goals for curriculum develop-
    ment, 142–144
Goldman-Fristoe Test of Articulation, 188
Graphing and graph construction. *See also*
    Data collection
    in A–B–C model, 31, 36–41
    baseline data, 39
    construction of graph, 38–39

converting data for graphs, 36–38
handout on, 352–353
importance of, 280
progress data collection and, 161–163
rate data, 33, 38
on recording forms, 150, 152–153, 155, 168, 169, 172
rules for converting data for, 37
sample line graphs, 39–41, 278, 281, 286–287
self-graphing data collection form, 278, 280, 281, 295, 298, 301
Grouping
advantages of, 83–84, 86
concurrent group instruction, 86–87
sequential group instruction, 86
tandem group instruction, 87

HFA. *See* High-functioning autism (HFA)
High-functioning autism (HFA), 3, 8. *See also* Autism
High-probability requests, 306
Holding therapy, 335
Home notes, 322, 323
Home–school collaboration. *See* Families
Home–school journals/notebooks, 322–326
Home visits, 326–327
Hypothesis Development Form, 232, 250

IDEA (Individuals with Disabilities Education Act), 117, 129, 142, 190, 201, 215, 253
IEPs (Individualized Education Programs), 122–124, 129–131
Immature grammar, 4, 179
Incidental teaching. *See* Naturalistic/milieu teaching
Inclusion, 201, 203–204
Individual schedules, 97–101, 357. *See also* Schedules, classroom
Individualized Education Programs (IEPs), 122–124, 129–131
Individuals with Disabilities Education Act (IDEA), 117, 129, 142, 190, 201, 215, 253
Instructional scripts, 207
Instructional strategies. *See* Classroom structure; Curriculum development; Discrete trial teaching (DTT); Grouping; Naturalistic/milieu teaching
Intermittent schedule of reinforcement, 27, 28, 29
Intertrial interval, 45, 58–59, 355
Interval schedules of reinforcement, 27, 29
Interventions. *See* Challenging behaviors; and specific interventions
Intraverbals, 182, 194, 367

Islands or precocity (splinter skills), 5–6
Itard, Jean-Marc-Gaspard, 1, 9–10

Jigs, 107
Job coaches, 119
Joint attention
definition of, 6, 73
lack of, 6, 202
in naturalistic/milieu teaching, 73
teaching strategies for, 208
Journals and periodicals, 343–344

Kanner, Leo, 1–2, 6, 10
Khan-Lewis Phonological Analysis, 188

Language and communication skills
assessment of, 182–185, 187–189, 200
augmentative and alternative communication (AAC) system, 117, 186, 189–191
best form of communication, 185–186
characteristic of, 3–4, 8, 179–180, 202, 348
commercially available language assessments, 188–189
components of language, 180–182
curricula for, 380–381
in curriculum generally, 132
facilitated communication, 337
form of language, 180, 185–186, 200
function of language, 180, 200
functional communication skills, 208
Functional Communication Training, 233
handout on, 367
lesson plans, 185, 186
no communication, 109
schedules for students for improvement of, 101
and Skinner's theory of operant conditioning, 180–182, 367
speech–language pathologists (SLP) and, 117
teaching strategies for, 191–195
Latency recording. *See also* Data collection
definition of, 33, 152
form for, 152, 154
graphing of, 37, 38
for specific target behaviors, 34
Learning Accomplishments Profile, 141
Learning levels, 143
Least restrictive environment (LRE), 201
Left–right orientation, 93
Lesson plans. *See* Planning
"Let's Talk" Inventory for Adolescents, 188
LFA. *See* Low-functioning autism (LFA)
Low-functioning autism (LFA), 3, 5–6, 8. *See also* Autism

Low-probability requests, 306
LRE (least restrictive environment), 201

MAAP Services for Autism and Asperger
    Spectrum, 14
Magnetic resonance imaging (MRI), 11
Mainstreaming, 201, 203
Mand and manding, 182, 192, 367
Mand–model, 75–76, 356
Manual prompts, 48, 50
Massed trials, 44
Mastery criterion statement in objectives,
    142
Material reinforcers, 23, 24. *See also*
    Reinforcement and reinforcers
Materials
    obtaining classroom materials, 91, 358
    visual support through, 103, 105–108
Medications
    administration of, 118
    challenging behaviors and, 268, 269, 311
    resources on, 269
    side effects of, 216–217
Mental retardation, 5–6
Milieu teaching. *See* Naturalistic/milieu
    teaching
Model
    aggression reduction, 308
    in naturalistic/milieu teaching, 72–75,
        356
    video modeling, 108, 308
Model prompts, 48, 49
Monthly calendars, 108–109
Motivation
    deficits in, 179, 202
    discrete trial teaching (DTT) and,
        63–64
    teaching strategies for, 208
Motor imitation, 181–182, 193, 367
MRI (magnetic resonance imaging), 11

National Dissemination Center for
    Children with Disabilities (NICHCY),
    15
National Institute of Child Health and
    Human Development, 15
National Institutes of Health (NIH) Autism
    Research Network, 15
Natural environment training (NET). *See*
    Naturalistic/milieu teaching
Natural language paradigm. *See*
    Naturalistic/milieu teaching
Natural reinforcers, 28, 144. *See also*
    Reinforcement and reinforcers
Naturalistic/milieu teaching
    advantages and disadvantages of, 80, 82
    assumption underlying, 71–72

definition/overview of, 71–72
environmental manipulation in, 78, 79
errors to be avoided in, 80
features of, 72
grouping and, 83–84, 86–87
handout on, 356
interaction of discrete trial teaching
    (DTT) and, 82–83, 85
joint attention in, 73
for language and communication skills,
    191–194
mand–model in, 75–76, 356
model in, 72–75, 356
planning and, 78–80, 81
procedures of, 72–78
progress data collection for, 159–161,
    176–177
resources on, 83
sample lesson plan and, 81
for socialization skills, 204, 211
teacher's checklist for, 84
time delay in, 76–78, 356
NCLB (No Child Left Behind Act), 129,
    147, 331
Negative reinforcement, 29–30, 351. *See
    also* Reinforcement and reinforcers
NET (natural environment training). *See*
    Naturalistic/milieu teaching
NICHCY (National Dissemination Center
    for Children with Disabilities), 15
NIH (National Institutes of Health) Autism
    Research Network, 15
No Child Left Behind Act (NCLB), 129,
    147, 331
No communication, 109
Noncompliance, 306–307, 373
Nonrestricted event recording and graph-
    ing, 33, 37, 274–275, 277–279, 293–297
Notebook files, 163, 164
Nurses, 118

Objectives
    behavioral or operational objectives,
        142–144
    and condition under which learner per-
        forms behavior, 142
    curriculum development and, 142–144
    identification of learner in, 142
    learning levels in, 143
    mastery criterion statement in, 142
    target behavior in, 142
Observational learning, 194
Observational recording, 32, 148, 352. *See
    also* Data collection
Occupational therapists (OTs), 117–118
Operant behavior, 180
Operant conditioning, 180–182

Operational definitions, 21–22, 54
Operational goals, 142
Options, 334
Organization for Autism Research, 15
OTs (occupational therapists), 117–118
Overcorrection, 267–268, 372

Pairing, and secondary reinforcers, 26
PAL (Partners at Lunch) Club, 210–211
Paraeducators, 116
Paraprofessionals, 116
Parents. *See* Families
Partners at Lunch (PAL) Club, 210–211
PBIS (Positive behavioral interventions and supports), 215
PBS (positive behavioral supports), 253
PDD (Pervasive Developmental Disorder), 2
PDD-NOS (Pervasive Developmental Disorder–Not Otherwise Specified), 2
PE (physical education) teachers, 118
Peabody Individual Achievement Test, 141
Peabody Picture Vocabulary Test (PPVT-4), 188
PECS (*Picture Exchange Communication System*), 189, 333
Peer confederates, 209–210, 211
Peer-mediated interventions for socialization skills, 209–211
People/place locators, 110
PEP (*Psychoeducational Profile*), 12, 188
Perceptual impairments. *See* Cognitive deficits
Perceptual–cognitive theory, 332, 338, 377
Periodicals and journals, 343–344
Permanent product recording, 32, 352. *See also* Data collection
Perseveration, 3–4
Perspective-taking, 202
Pervasive Developmental Disorder (PDD), 2–3
Pervasive Developmental Disorder–Not Otherwise Specified (PDD-NOS), 2
Physical education (PE) teachers, 118
Physical organization of classroom, 102–105
Physical prompts, 48, 50, 51
Physical therapists (PTs), 118
Physiologically based theory, 336–337, 338, 377
Picture Communication Symbols, 189
Picture Exchange Communication System (PECS), 189, 333
Pivotal behaviors for socialization, 205, 207, 208, 211
Pivotal response training (PRT), 207, 334
Place/people locators, 110

Planning
    discrete trial teaching (DTT) and, 63–64, 65
    naturalistic/milieu teaching and, 78–80, 81
    by team members, 363
Play behaviors, 209
PLS-4 (*Preschool Language Scale*), 188
Positional prompts, 49
Positive behavioral interventions and supports (PBIS), 215
Positive behavioral supports (PBS), 253
Positive reinforcement, 22–29, 56–58, 350. *See also* Reinforcement and reinforcers
PPVT-4 (*Peabody Picture Vocabulary Test*), 188
Pragmatics, 180
Preschool Language Scale (PLS-4), 188
Prescription medications. *See* Medications
Primary reinforcers, 23, 24, 28. *See also* Reinforcement and reinforcers
Probes, 160–161
Problem solving by team members, 125–126, 364
Procedures and routines for classroom structure, 90–94
Professionals working with students with autism. *See* Supervision of teaching adults
Progress data collection
    blank forms for, 167–177
    for controlled presentation, 158, 175
    duration recording form, 152, 153, 170
    event recording forms, 148–152
    graphing, 161–163, 168, 169, 172
    handout on, 366
    for naturalistic/milieu teaching, 159–161, 176–177
    notebook files, 163, 164
    probes and, 160–161
    recording forms for, 148–160
    restricted event recording form, 148
    task analytic forms, 150, 151, 155, 168, 172
    techniques for, 147–152
    timing of, 160–163
    trial-by-trial forms, 153, 155–159, 173–174
Prompt dependence, 51, 52
Prompts
    baseline for, 53
    definition of, 47
    in discrete trial teaching (DTT), 45, 47–53, 354
    error correction and, 52
    errorless learning and, 50
    fading prompts, 51, 52–53

gestural prompts, 48, 49
manual prompts, 48, 50
model prompts, 48, 49
physical prompts, 48, 50, 51
positional prompts, 49
and power of reinforcers, 51–52
techniques for, 50–53
time delay and, 53
types of, 48–50
verbal prompts, 48
visual prompts, 48, 49
within-stimulus prompts, 48–49, 50
Prompts. dependence on, 51, 52
Prosody, 4
PRT (pivotal response training), 207, 334
Psychoeducational Profile (PEP), 12, 188
Psychogenic pathology explanation of autism, 10
Psychologists, 119
PTs (physical therapists), 118
Punishment and punishers
in A–B–C model, 22, 351
definition of, 22, 55
in discrete trial teaching (DTT), 55
Pyramid Scales, 141

Queries, 195

Rate data
definition of, 33
form for, 154
graphing of, 38
Ratio schedules of reinforcement, 27, 29
Receptive by feature, function, and class
(RFFC), 182, 367
Receptive language, 179, 182, 193, 367. *See
also* Language and communication skills
*Receptive–Expressive Emergent Language
Scale* (REEL-3), 189
Recording forms. *See also* Data collection;
Progress data collection
blank forms, 167–177, 289–303
for controlled presentations, 158, 175
for data collection, 36, 148–160,
274–287
developing and using data collection
forms, 279–280
duration recording form, 152, 153,
280–282, 298, 299
event recording forms, 148–152
graphing included on, 150, 152–153,
155, 168, 169, 172, 278, 281
latency recording forms, 152, 154
for monitoring challenging behavior,
274–287
for multiple behaviors or monitoring behaviors in multiple students, 276,

278–279, 283–286, 292, 296,
300–303
for naturalistic/milieu teaching,
159–161, 176–177
rate data form, 154
restricted event recording form, 148,
274–276, 290–292
self-graphing data collection form, 278,
280, 281, 295, 298, 301
task analytic forms, 150, 151, 155, 168,
172
trial-by-trial forms, 153, 155–159,
173–174
unrestricted event recording form,
277–279, 293–297
REEL-3 (*Receptive–Expressive Emergent
Language Scale*), 189
Reflexive behaviors, 180
Reinforcement and reinforcers
activity reinforcers, 23, 24
as contingent on desired target behaviors, 27, 28
continuous schedule of reinforcement
(CRF), 27, 28, 57
correct use of, 2527
definition of, 22
differential reinforcement for reducing
challenging behaviors, 258–262, 371
in discrete trial teaching (DTT), 55–58
edible reinforcers, 23, 24
generalization and, 144
idiosyncratic reinforcers, 23, 25
intermittent schedule of reinforcement,
27, 28, 29
interval schedules, 27, 29
material reinforcers, 23, 24
most and least preferred reinforcers, 23
natural reinforcers, 28, 144
negative reinforcement, 29–30, 350, 351
pairing, 26
positive reinforcement, 22–29, 56–58,
350
power of, and discrete trial teaching
(DTT), 56–57
power of, and prompts, 51–52
primary reinforcers, 23, 24, 28
punishment and punishers, 22, 55, 351
ratio schedules, 27, 29
reinforcer sampling, 25
for replacement behaviors based on
function of challenging behavior, 233
response duration schedules, 27, 29
rules for using positive reinforcement, 28
satiation and, 56
schedules, 27–29, 57, 350–351
secondary reinforcers, 23, 24
selection of, 25

self-stimulatory behaviors and, 25, 26
social reinforcers, 23, 24, 58
thinning and, 27
types of reinforcers, 23, 25
variable schedule of reinforcement, 57
Reinforcement schedules, 27–29, 57,
    350–351
Reinforcer sampling, 25
Relationship-based theory, 334–335, 338,
    377
RESNA Technical Assistance Partnership,
    15
Resources
    academic assessment instruments, 141
    adaptive behavior scales, 141
    autism, 11–15, 343–346
    classroom structure, 113
    commercially available curricula,
        379–382
    discrete trial teaching (DTT), 69
    journals and periodicals, 343–344
    language assessments, 188–189
    medications, 269
    naturalistic/milieu teaching, 83
    social skills curricula, 206
Response cost, 262–264, 371
Response duration schedules of reinforce-
    ment, 27, 29
Response generalization, 143
Responses
    definition of, 54
    in discrete trial teaching (DTT), 45,
        54–55, 354
    operational definition of, 54
    sample observable and measurable stu-
        dent responses, 55
Restricted event recording and graphing,
    33, 37–38, 148, 273–276, 290–292. See
    also Data collection
Rett's Disorder, definition of, 2
RFFC (receptive by feature, function, and
    class), 182, 367
Routines and procedures for classroom
    structure, 90–94

Samples, data collection of, 35
Satiation, 56
Scales of Independent Behavior–Revised
    (SIB-R), 141
Schafer Autism Report, 15
Schedules, classroom
    handout on, 357
    individual schedules, 97–101, 357
    sample schedules, 95, 96, 99, 100
    uses of, for communication and social-
        ization, 101
    whole-class schedules, 94–97

Schedules of reinforcement, 27–29, 57,
    350–351
School nurses, 118
School psychologists, 119
Scientifically based practices, 331
Secondary reinforcers, 23, 24, 26. See also
    Reinforcement and reinforcers
Self-injurious behavior (SIB), 8, 305, 311,
    312, 375. See also Challenging behaviors
Self-management behaviors, 208
Self-stimulatory behaviors. See also
    Challenging behaviors
    biological basis of, 216
    definition of, 8
    functions of, 310, 374–375
    inclusion and, 203
    interventions for, 308–310, 374–375
    reinforcement and, 25, 26
    sensory system stimulated by, 26
    types of, 305
Sensory extinction, 262, 263
Sensory integration techniques, 117–118,
    336
Sensory systems
    self-stimulatory behaviors and, 26
    sensory extinction and, 262, 263
    sensory processing deficits, 7, 9, 349
Sequential group instruction, 86
Shadows, 116
SIB (self-injurious behavior), 8, 305, 311,
    312
SIB-R (Scales of Independent Behavior–
    Revised), 141
Sign language, 189, 190–191
Simple discrete behaviors, 135
Skinner, B. F., 180–182, 367
SLPs (speech–language pathologists),
    116–117
Social competence, 6
Social cues, 6
Social reinforcers, 23, 24, 58. See also
    Reinforcement and reinforcers
Social stories, 208–209, 308, 332
Socialization and social skills
    antecedent prompting, 207–208
    characteristics of, 6–7, 9, 201, 202,
        348–349
    commercially available social skills cur-
        ricula, 206
    curricula for, 381
    curriculum development for, 132
    direct instruction for, 205–207
    generalization of social skills, 211–212,
        368
    handout on, 368
    and inclusion, 201, 203–204
    instructional scripts, 207

joint attention, 6, 73, 202
peer confederates, 209–210, 211
peer-mediated interventions, 209–211,
    368
pivotal behaviors for, 205, 207, 208, 211
pivotal response training (PRT), 207,
    334
schedules for, 101
social stories, 208–209, 308, 332
teacher-mediated interventions,
    205–209, 368
teaching strategies for, 204–211
Speech difficulties. See Language and com-
    munication skills
Speech–language pathologists (SLPs),
    116–117
Splinter skills (islands or precocity), 5–6
Stereotypic behavior
    aggressive behavior, 8, 305, 307–308,
        309, 373–374
    as characteristic of autism, 7–8, 9, 349
    intervention for, 308–310
    self-injurious behavior (SIB), 8, 305, 311,
        312, 375
    self-stimulatory behaviors, 8, 25, 26,
        203, 216, 308–310, 374–375
Stimulus control
    in A–B–C model, 19–21, 44
    definition of, 19, 44
    discrete trial teaching (DTT) and, 44, 47
    discriminative stimulus, 19, 47
    establishment of, 21
    examples of, 20
    generalization and, 144
Stimulus generalization, 143
Stimulus overselectivity, 208
Structure in classroom. See Classroom
    structure
Structured A–B–C Analysis Form, 223, 226,
    230, 248–249
Supervision of teaching adults
    adaptive physical education (PE) teach-
        ers, 118
    behavior specialists, 119
    communication for, 121–122, 361–362
    consistency and, 120–121
    consultation and training of team mem-
        bers, 124–125
    coordination of team members, 122–124
    creating educational team, 120–122
    factors hampering team functioning, 127
    handouts for professional team training,
        347–377
    job coaches, 119
    occupational therapists (OTs), 117–118
    overview of, 115

paraprofessionals, 116
physical therapists (PTs), 118
planning steps and, 363
problem solving by team members,
    125–126, 364
roles and responsibilities of teaching
    adults, 115–119
school nurses, 118
school psychologists, 119
shadows, 116
speech–language pathologists (SLPs),
    116–117
team building and, 120

Tact and tacting, 182, 193–194, 367
Tactilely defensive, 7
Tally counters, 274–275
Tape for classroom structure, 105
TASH, 15
Task analysis
    blank forms, 168, 172
    curriculum development and, 135, 136
    sample forms, 150, 151, 155
Task analytic assessment, 135, 136
Task or activity sequences, 109
TEACCH (Treatment and Education of
    Autistic and Communication
    Handicapped Children), 110–111
Teacher–parent relationship. See Families
Teaching adults. See Supervision of teach-
    ing adults
Teaching assistants, 116
Teaching compliance, 306
Team building, 120. See also Supervision of
    teaching adults
TELD-3 (Test of Early Language
    Development), 189
Telephone calls and messages to families,
    323
TERA-3 (Test of Early Reading Ability), 141
Test of Adolescent and Adult Language
    (TOAL-2), 189
Test of Early Language Development
    (TELD-3), 189
Test of Early Reading Ability (TERA-3), 141
Test of Early Written Language (TEWL-2),
    141
Test of Language Development–Primary
    (TOLD-P:3), 189
TEWL-2 (Test of Early Written Language),
    141
Thinning, 27
Time delay
    in naturalistic/milieu teaching, 76–78,
        356
    prompts and, 53

Time-out, 264, 266–267, 371
TOAL-2 (*Test of Adolescent and Adult Language*), 189
Toileting, 92–93, 106–107, 137, 359–360
Token Test for Children (TTFC-2), 189
TOLD-P:3 (*Test of Language Development– Primary*), 189
Top–down orientation, 93
Training of team members
    discussion of, 124–125
    handouts for, 347–377
Transitions in classroom, 92, 103, 359
Treatment and Education of Autistic and Communication Handicapped Children (TEACCH), 110–111
Trial-by-trial recording forms, 153, 155–159, 173–174
Trial-by-trial training. *See* Discrete trial teaching (DTT)
Trials, 44. *See also* Discrete trial teaching (DTT)
TTFC-2 (*Token Test for Children*), 189

Units of instruction, 140–142
University of North Carolina, Division TEACCH, 14
Unrestricted event recording and graphing, 33, 37, 274–275, 277–279, 293–297. *See also* Data collection

Van Dijk approach, 332
Variable schedule of reinforcement, 57
Verbal behavior, 180–182, 367. *See also* Language and communication skills
Verbal imitation, 193
Verbal operants, 181–182
Verbal prompts, 48
Video for training teaching adults, 124–125
Video modeling, 108, 308
Vineland Adaptive Behavior Scales, 141
Visual prompts, 48, 49
Visual schedules. *See* Schedules, classroom

Visual–spatial symbols, 189
Visual supports
    avoidance of clutter through, 103
    for behavior management, 102–103, 109, 112
    cafeteria example of, 101–102
    choice boards, 109
    communicating *no*, 109
    for curricular expectations, 102
    definition of, 101
    for elimination of distracters, 102
    individual schedules, 97–101
    materials for, 103, 105–108
    monthly calendars, 108–109
    people/place locators, 110
    physical organization for, 102–105
    sample classroom arrangement, 104
    sample visual supports and cues, 111–112
    task or activity sequences, 109
    for transitions, 103
    video and computers for, 108
    visually cued instruction, 332
    whole-class schedules, 94–97
Visually cued instruction, 332
VOCAs (voice output communication aids), 190, 191
Voice output communication aids (VOCAs), 190, 191

Waiting in classroom, 92, 93–94, 359
Weekly schedule, 95, 96
Whole-class schedules, 94–97. *See also* Schedules, classroom
Within-stimulus prompts, 48–49, 50
Woodcock-Johnson Tests of Achievement, 141
Woodcock Reading Mastery Test, 141
Work systems, 107
Wright's Law, 15

Yale University Child Study Center, 15

About the Authors

Jo Webber

Jo Webber, PhD, is a professor of special education at Texas State University–San Marcos and associate dean for academic affairs for the College of Education. She began teaching students with autism in 1976 and has been active as a consultant, in-service and preservice trainer, author, and statewide leader in this area for 30 years.

Dr. Webber received her doctoral degree in special education from The University of Texas at Austin and served as the executive director of the Austin–Travis County Mental Health and Mental Retardation Autism Center, executive director of the Communities in Schools Dropout Prevention Program, and assistant special education director for the Austin Independent School District. Dr. Webber has also consulted with various school districts across the country regarding the management of challenging behavior, programming for students with emotional and behavioral disorders, and school applications of applied behavioral analysis and positive behavioral supports.

Dr. Webber is past president of the Council for Children with Behavior Disorders and currently serves as chair of the Austin Regional Autism Task Force and as an Advisory Committee member to the Texas Council for Autism and Pervasive Developmental Disorders. Dr. Webber has published widely in the areas of autism, behavior management, and educational strategies for students with emotional and behavioral disorders. She co-authored, with Brenda Scheuermann, the textbook *Autism: Teaching DOES Make a Difference* (Wadsworth, 2002) and, with Cindy Plotts, the textbook *Emotional and Behavioral Disorders: Theory to Practice* (Allyn & Bacon, 2002).

Brenda Scheuermann

Brenda Scheuermann, PhD, has been a professor of special education at Texas State University in San Marcos for 18 years. She received her doctoral degree in emotional disturbance/autism from The University of Texas at Austin. Prior to that time, she was a special education teacher for students with autism, behavioral disorders, and cognitive disabilities in Illinois and Texas, a behavior specialist in Texas, and a lecturer at The University of Texas at Austin and Laredo State University. Dr. Scheuermann frequently consults with school districts around the country on issues related to student behavior, programs for students with emotional and behavioral disorders, and schoolwide positive behavioral supports. She also provides professional development for teachers and administrators at the local, state, and national levels in the areas of teaching students with emotional and behavioral disorders, best practices in instruction, and positive behavioral supports. She has served in leadership roles in various professional organizations, including chair of the Advocacy and Governmental Relations Committee of The Council for Children with Behavioral Disorders.

Dr. Scheuermann is the author of numerous publications in the areas of autism, behavior management and instruction, and advocacy. In addition, she is co-author, with Jo Webber, of the textbook *Autism: Teaching DOES Make a Difference* (Wadsworth, 2002) and, with Judy A. Hall, of the textbook *Positive Behavioral Supports for the Classroom* (Merrill/Pearson Educational, 2008).